GOLDEN TRIANGLE
Odisha
BHUBANESWAR, PURI AND KONARK

A BOOK ON ODISHA TOURISM AND CULTURE

GOLDEN TRIANGLE Odisha

BHUBANESWAR, PURI AND KONARK

BISHNU MOHAN PANDA

AUTHORSPRESS

Worldwide Circulation through Authorspress Global Network
First Published in 2022
by
Authorspress
Q-2A Hauz Khas Enclave, New Delhi-110 016 (India)
Phone: (0) 9818049852
E-mail: authorspressgroup@gmail.com
Website: www.authorspressbooks.com

Golden Triangle – Odisha
(Bhubaneswar, Puri and Konark)
(A Book on Odisha Tourism and Culture)
ISBN 978-93-5529-339-8

Printed in India at Kensington Press

This Book is Dedicated
In Memory of my Parents

BANSHIDHAR PANDA

ROHINI PANDA

My Source of Inspiration
For Whom
Service To Humanity Is Service To God

Preface

Odisha is a paradise for visitors. Numerous Temples, Buddhist monasteries, Jain shrines, Sikh Gurdwaras, Mosques, Churches, Caves, Pillars, ancient and medieval forts, heritage palaces, art and culture, beaches, wildlife, hills, forests, springs, tribal and village life etc. glorify the state of Odisha.

Apart from the major temples, there are large number of small temples which speaks a lot about religiosity and spiritualism of this state.

Some of these places have left an imprint in the lives and minds of the people.

These ancient wonders still stand there awaiting those, who are yet to reach them.

Centuries old traditional, cultural practices, festivals, arts and crafts are still alive and can be experienced in every part of the state.

Author, who had spent most part of his life outside Odisha, was disappointed when tried to know / explore/ visit various scenic, religious and historical places of the state, in the absence of any informative material in a consolidated form.

Although, most of these places are having abundant serenity and tranquillity, the beauty of these places, it's people, legends and history associated with them are less known to the people in and outside the state.

The actual writing of this book started on 27th July, 2017 AD on a rainy day, (when river Mahanadi was flowing full and while visiting Lord Nilamadhav of Kantilo (ie. in Nayagarh district on the bank of mighty Mahanadi, where the river is around 7-kms wide and which looks like a sea in the rainy season).

The name "Lord Nilamadhav" connotes, – "Nila" as Lord Jagannath, "Ma" as Goddess Subhadra and "Dhav" as Balabhadra (ie. the inseparable bonding of three deities). Here, Lord Shiv of the temple changes side with the movement of earth between Tropic of

Cancer and Tropic of Capricorn, a phenomenon rare in India as told by the priests.

At the outset, I thought the task is extremely simple, because I am a son of the soil and lived early part of my growing up in this part of the Golden Triangle. I thought that at the present era, where there is no dearth of information, things will move faster and smoothly. However, with every passing day I felt the height of the Himalayas is getting increased day by day.

I started covering each and every district of the State of Odisha (30-districts) in my attempt to link various dotted lines.

I have also touched the neighbouring state of Chhattisgarh (27-districts) and in the process covered more than 1-lakh kms, talked to thousands of persons, tried to collect the available information on various aspects from each and available sources including various publications, Odisha Gazetteer, hearsay, words of mouth and legends. Participated in the planation drive and cleaning of some areas to visualise the feeling of folklores.

The feeling of local people in these two states to save the heritage structures from the encroachers and especially the Panchayat representatives of Jaugada (Ganjam) to save the ancient Ashokan rock edicts / structures from extinction really touched me.

During this span of four and half years, I have written the following books:

Chhattisgarh (27 Districts)

1. *Beautiful Bastar*
2. *Uncharted Surguja*
3. *Captivating Bilaspur Division*
4. *Unique Raipur and Durg Divisions*

Odisha (30 Districts)

1. *Unexplored North Odisha* (covering 4-districts, ie. Mayurbhanj, Kendujhar, Bhadrakh and Balasore)
2. *151-Weekend Gateways near Bhubaneshwar, Odisha*

3. *Amazing KBK Region* and *Lord Ram's Trail* (covering 8-districts, i.e., Koraput, Malkangiri, Navararangpur, Rayagada, Kalahandi, Nuapada, Balangir, Subarnapur)
4. *Incredible South and Central Odisha* (covering 4 districts of Ganjam, Gajapati, Bouda and Kandhamal)
5. *Alluring West Odisha* (covering 5 districts of Baragada, Deogarh, Jharsuguda, Sambalpur and Sundargarh)
6. *Exciting Central and Coastal Odisha* (covering 6 districts of Cuttack, Jajpur, Jagatsinghpur, Kendrapara, Dhenkanal and Angul)
7. *Charming South-East Odisha* (covering 3 districts of Khordha, Nayagarh and Puri)
8. *Exploring Odisha: Forts and Palaces*
9. *Along the Footprints of Lord Ram* (ie. which covers epic journey of Lord Ram inter-alia in the state of Odisha and Chattisgarh and His influence on culture of these two states).
10. *Enchanting Odisha – Caves, Rock Shelters, Rock Arts , Forests and Trekking Routes*
11. *Golden Triangle – Odisha* (Bhubaneshwar, Puri and Konark)

Other 5 books of the author, ie. Tribes of Chhattisgarh, Tribes of Odisha, Lord Jagannath, Mesmerising Nepal and Ethical Banking are in various stages.

But on reaching Puri, I got the blessing of Lord Jagannath. The completion of all these books including the present book (*Golden Triangle – Odisha*) would not have been possible without the blessings of Lord Lingaraj, Lord Jagannath and heavenly blessings of my parents.

The author also got the unstinted support from wife – Snigdha, son-Debdarshan, daughter-in-law – Samikshya during this endeavour.

Support of other family members and friends from PNB like – Sadananda Sahoo, Ashok Kumar Pattanyak, Hemanta Mahapatra, Sarat Mishra and Mukund Kumar from REC are invaluable.

While writing all these books, some forgotten places of these districts have been covered to raise awareness of their past glory and to bring these places to lime light. The nearby important places are also indicated to reach them.

The photos and materials are collected through field visits and from locals.

Any resemblance with any material is coincidence and unintentional, as the beauty of these places are eternal and no one can replicate them without visit and seeing the places in one's own eyes.

Any further correction and suggestions for improvement of these books are welcome.

Although, infrastructure is lacking in some places, the author requests one and all to visit these places covered in all the above books, at least once. The visit will definitely help for the development of these places/ areas and will take one to a new level of experience.

The present book, *Golden Triangle – Odisha* covers the tourist circuit of Bhubaneshwar, Puri and Konark. The three major temples of this circuit, ie. Lord Jagannath, Lord Lingaraj and world heritage Konark Sun temple, are having extreme monumental, architectural resplendence and values.

Some of the other finest temples of Odisha, ie. Mukteswara, Rajarani, Vaitali Temple, Yogini Temple, Parasurameswara Temple, Sri gundicha Temple, Maa Bimala Temple, Lokanatha Temple, Batamangala etc. and many more old Temples built by the different kings / dynasties as old as of 6th century AD are in existence. This circuit is dotted with numerous temples which reflect the architectural and sculptural skills of the ancient time.

Dhauli, famous for the Kalinga War and Emperor Ashok, due to which Buddhism became the world religion, is also famous for Ashokan edicts and The Shanti Stupa Peace Pagoda – ie. emblem of the Buddhist art and sculpture, attracts millions of tourists including Buddhists to the state.

The rock-cut caves of Udaygiri and Khandagiri are a major center of Jainism. These sites along with Dhauli show physical evidences of presence of a rich civilisation in the region during 3rd century B.C.onwards.

Here, one will find harmonious blending of Hinduism, Buddhism and Jainism and other religions and their co-existence.

Rivers, beaches, hills, forts, forests and wild life of the area are other attractions. The pristine beauty of Puri beach and Chandrabhaga beach (ie. where there is the confluence of river and sea and the panoramic scenery) is seen to be believed.

Celebration of various religious festivals like – Maha Shivratri, the annual car festival (Rath Yatra), other festivals and light and sound music at Konark Sun temple attract millions of devotees and tourists from all across the globe.

Similarly some of the major cultural shows annually celebrated in the temples, like – Konark dance festival, Rajarani Festival and Mukteswar festival etc. create huge platform for music and dance from throughout the country, where celebrated classical dancers / singers from the state and various parts of the country participate.

Excepting some major temples, beaches and important festivals, other heritage structures of this area are neglected and some of them are buried in oblivion. Many religious places, numerous ancient temples, ponds and Mathas etc. of the area are in precarious conditions, although they carry the legacies of the past and large number of people travel to these holy places even now. There is mindless encroachment in such places.

Preservation and restoration of these places and structures are essential for the future generations, as these Houses of Gods are driven by religious beliefs, faith and spiritualism.

This would enrich the knowledge of any visitor by going through their history, heritage, cultural and ritualistic practices associated with them.

These can be developed further through restructuring and reengineering as pillar of growth in the area of socio-economic and cultural arena. It would provide not only employment opportunities and revenue generation but also would help in eradicating poverty.

Temple Tourism can be developed where the visitors will learn and experience the history, heritage, philosophy and cultural rituals of particular temples. Destination marketing is required and spiritualism can be revived through temple Tourism.

As per experts, Tourism Department should promote temple tourism by chalking out a well-planned marketing strategy blending it with the various cultural fairs and festivals to attract more visitors.

The book *Golden Triangle – Odisha* is written in the above background covering the details of the area so that everyone can play an active part in the process of their development and can contribute to the society.

To find out the true essence of life and to feel God and divinity, one may visit this area. Getting away from the materialistic life, visitors can have a glimpse of the nature and beauty of the places along with the majestic art and architecture of the temples which would be a life time experience. The area provides a beautiful linkage between the past and present.

Any further corrections and suggestions for improvement and incorporation in the book is welcome.

Contents

Overview

Bhubaneshwar-Puri-Konark form the three vertices of "Golden Triangle" of Odisha. Jagannath Temple of Puri, Konark Temple – a UNESCO world heritage site, EKAMRA KSHETRA – Bhubaneshwar and the attractive beaches attract numerous visitors and pilgrims from all over the country and the world. Every nook and corner of the area is dotted with monuments, temples, shrines / holy places and other archaeological sites. This area consists of coastal stretches, beaches, forests, wild life sanctuary, beautiful monuments and temples which are also major pilgrimage destinations of the country. All the places have their own importance. The enchanting golden triangle circuit starts from the capital city Bhubaneswar, which is best known as the – city of temples and EKAMRA KSHETRA. The city boasts of ancient temples and monuments spreading over a period of more than 2-thousand years. One can take a Journey to Dhauli near Bhubaneshwar, the site of historic Kalinga war of 3rd century BC, where emperor Ashok was transformed and embraced Buddhism, which became a world religion because of Kalinga. The 1st century rock – cut caves of Khandagiri and UDAYAGIRI show the jain influence and records the life chronicle of illustrious Kharavela, the mighty emperor of Kalinga. The sacred place Puri resembles the shape of a conch shell and it's beach is one of the best in the country. Puri, apart from the holy abode of lord Jagannatha, is one of the 4-shrines/ Peethas where Adiguru Shankaracharya had established the Govardhan Matha. In various Sahis, Jagagharas and Akhadas, traditional cultural practices are still alive even after many centuries. Similarly the distinguished world heritage monument of Sun Temple, Konark is the glory of Kalinga architecture, where the language of stone surpasses the language of man (ie. As said by Vishwa Kavi Rabindranath). Firmly rooted in the past, the Golden Triangle reflects the spirit of Odisha and it's glorious past. It is a treasure trove of sculptures and ancient temples. As per Mehek Ahuja – Conservation architect, the golden

Triangle can be used to understand the evolution of Kalinga architecture. It is a great tourist destination for explorers, pilgrims, students, historians and scholars.

The 35-kms marine drive from Puri to Konark in the midst of coastal jungles and beach is one of the best drives. There are large number of beach resorts on both sides of the road. The confluence of the Kushabhadra river stream with sea and accompanying sea beach on this road would mesmerise any traveler. Chilika lake, the queen of natural beauty is included in the book as it is nearby to Puri. Similarly, in the heritage villages of Raghurajpur and Pipili which are on the Bhubaneswar-Puri road, one will find congregation of artists who produce different types of handicraft items like appliqué and Patta Paintings etc. which are unique art and crafts of the state. Many religious festivals and cultural events associated with the major temples of Bhubaneshwar and Puri including Rath Yatra are vibrant cultural traditions of the state. Present day tourists / visitors in the midst of busy life seeking solace and in-depth meaning of life would get a life time learning experience by glancing over the history, heritage, art, architecture and cultural essence by visiting these temples and craft villages. These destinations would definitely captivate any tourist from any part of the world. The rich cultural heritage, temple culture and the vibrant markets of Puri and Bhubaneshwar would also spellbind them. As per experts, the temple tourism of this area can be developed as special interest tourism (SIT) and this can be promoted as emblems of spiritualism and for sustainable development. Author is of the view that, one should visit all these place, at least once in a lifetime, which would take one on a journey down the memory lane.

CHAPTER 1

Bhubaneswar

BHUBANESHWAR – THE HERITAGE CITY

Bhubaneshwar is the present capital city of State of Odisha and the second planned city of independent India after Chandigarh. It's foundation stone was laid on 13th April – 1948 AD by the first Prime Minister of India, Jawaharlal Nehru. German architect Otto Koenigsberger planned the city in 1948 AD, on small neighbourhood unit concept which would preserve the sense of community.

It is designed in a linear pattern for the city, i.e. main administrative bodies in the main artery and neighbourhood units are attached to it. With the growth in population, the plan of the city was revised by Julius Vaz to accommodate additional neighbourhood units. Starting from a linear form, the city has developed in to a rectangular form.

It's total area is around 422-square kms (163-square miles) including old town area of around 25-square kms, which is more than 1-thousand years old. As per experts, if the suburbs and surrounding villages are included, the area may 250 square miles. As per Odisha Gazetteer, the Bhubaneshwar Urban Development Area is spread over 393.57 square kms.

It is bounded by river Daya in the south and river Kuakhai to the east. Chandaka wild life sanctuary and Nandankanan sanctuary lie in the western and northern part of the city.

This was made the new capital of the state because of good communication, high altitude, vast plateau like high uplands (ie. average altitude of 148-feet above sea level) sloping to the sides and deep rooted historical significance of the town. Capital was shifted from Cuttack to Bhubaneshwar in 1948 AD.

The iconic sandstone warrior horse replica sculpture of Sun Temple, Konark which is the stone work of late sculpture Padma Vibhushan Raghunath Mohapatra (ie. a part of the emblem of the state) and one of the landmark of the city along with the Selfi-Zone (ie. I love Bhubaneshwar greet the visitor, at Master canteen square, near Bhubaneshwar Railway station.

Broad avenues, planned habitations, institutional, commercial and industrial areas are the hallmarks of this modern and well planned city.

It is known as temple city of India, sports capital of India, IT HUB and START UP Hub of East India. This is also a cyber city.

It is famous for hosting various sports events Internationally and promoting startups. It has hosted the Men's Hockey World Cup 2018 AD, which was a proud moment for the country.

It is coined as new Bangalore and the city was declared as the smartest city in the year 2016-AD. It was selected as one of the first 20- Indian cities being developed under PM's Smart Cities Mission.

This is the only Tier-2 city of India, where India's top 5 (five) companies (ie. TCS, INFOSYS, WIPRO, TECH MAHINDRA AND MIND TREE) have bases.

It was ranked as the third best place to do business in India by the World Bank, one of the planned four IT investment regions in India and winner of American planning Association's Pierre l Enfant International Planning Excellence Award of 2017 AD.

This is the only city in the country where one will find wilderness in the close proximity, (ie. the exquisite natural beauty in the forests of Chandaka – Dampara sanctuary and Nandankanan sanctuary would charm any visitor).

The city is part of Golden Triangle, one of the eastern India's most visited destinations.

The name Bhubaneshwar came from Lord Shiv's Sanskrit name Tribhuvaneswar, means lord/master of three worlds. Some also opine that, as the presiding deity of the city is Swayambhu, who came from PATAL to BHOOLOKA (ie. Bhoo se Eshwar), it was known as Bhubaneshwar.

This was known as Ekamra Vana, a forest of single mango tree, as per mythological texts.

The antiquity of the town can be traced back to 3rd / 4th century BC to Sishupalgarh. The next episode of importance was Kalinga war at Dhauli (ie. DHAULI is around 10-kms from Bhubaneswar) around 261-BC. The Dhauli war of Ashok clearly indicated the presence of Mahajanapada with enough knowledge and prosperity in this area. This was the place where Ashok defeated the king of Kalinga. But the bloody battle filled the heart of Ashok with remorse and he renounced war and violence and embraced Buddhism from this land and Buddhism became a world religion. After Ashok's death, under mighty king Kharavela, Odisha (ie. the then Kalinga) attained new heights in art, culture, trade and commerce. Jainism had it's sway under him which is reflected in the caves of UDAYAGIRI and Khandagiri. Although UDAYAGIRI witnessed decline after 11th century, but Khandagiri has kept it's status as jain pilgrimage centre till today. The area / city was ruled by the Sailodvabas, Bhaumakars, Somavamshis Gangavamshi and Gajapati kings from time to time. After fall of Gajapatis, although Bhubaneswar continued to enjoy the religious importance, the centre of activities shifted to Khordha and Puri.

The city has evolved through the centuries (ie. more than 2500-years old).

A conducive environment for development of Hinduism, Buddhism and Jainism was provided by the rulers of the city and it became the confluence of Hindu, jain and Buddhist heritage.

It is the repository of some of the finest temples of the country around which the religious and spiritual life of the city revolves.Its cluster of temples provides a complete record of Odisha Temple Architecture from its early beginning to its culmination.

Bhubaneshwar is an important Buddhist, Jain and Hindu pilgrimage centre. This is a city which has been able to balance it's rich ancient culture with stunning modern industrial development. The beauty of the city will make one awe-inspired. Visit to this city would enrich any traveller to capture the cultural heritage of India and it's excellent artistic motifs.

EKAMRAVANA/EKAMRA KSHETRA

EKAMRA KSHETRA is the ancient Hindu Temple city in Bhubaneshwar.

Ekamra Kshetra signifies – an area (kshetra) adorned with mango trees (ekamra) ie. EKAMRA means – mango tree and KSHETRA means – area.

It has been described in various texts/ Puranas / by some researchers as under: As per Ekamra Purana (ie. a 13th-century Sanskrit treatise), the presiding state deity of Lingaraj was originally under a mango tree, hence the name Ekamra Kshetra.

As per noted architectural historians James Ferugsson, "EKAMRA KSHETRA is an outstanding example of Hindu city planning based on the application of the Mandal concept, which is an unique system of planning unparalleled in the world".

As per the Anantavasudeva Inscription of Paramarddi, Ekamra was a sacred area "...adorned with hundreds of mango-groves, wherein exists a single Devakula [temple] surrounded by numerous temples."

The Brahmeswar inscription of Udyotkeshari Mahabhavagupta IV describes EKAMRA as Siddhakshetra.

As per Ekamra Purana, this sacred kshetra was Panchakrosa (10 miles) in circumference bordered by Khandagiri hills in the west, Kundalesvara temple in the village named Tankapani in the east, Balhadevi / Varahi Temple on the north and Bahirangesvara temple near Dhauli on the south, with Lingaraj Temple as its centre.

In 1568 AD, there were around 8000 temples however most of the temples were destroyed during the period of Afghan and Mogul occupation.

EKAMRA CHANDRIKA describe that, the inner circle of this holy Kshetra was bounded by Meghesvara temple in the east and Sundaresvara temple in the south.

Ekamra KSHETRA comprised of 45 villages and was divided into asta-ayatan or eight sacred precincts, each with its water body, temples, small shrines, tirthas and prescribed pilgrim/ritual procession routes that were ritualistically and symbolically connected with the Lingaraj Temple.

Although Lingaraj Temple was the centre of Ekamra Kshetra, the old town of Bhubaneswar itself was focused towards the Bindusagar Tank in the near vicinity of Lingaraj Temple. A geomantic approach was adopted in town planning with specific directions vis-à-vis topography, location and orientation of water bodies, land – use zoning etc. The town structure was a not-so-geometric but organic derivative of the Mandala concept.

The tanks such as Bindusagar, Devipadahara Tank, Papanashini and Kapilesvara Tank etc. were attached with religious symbolisms and considered holy.

As per historians and researchers, EKAMRA KSHETRA is mainly the old town area of Bhubaneshwar which contains hundreds of temples. It is unique in the sense that, its temples/ monuments are not restricted to one large temple complex. Rather these are spread in large areas and there are people/ priests living around them.

As per official documents there are: A) Total Historic Structures in Ekamra Kshetra are – 199 B) Centrally protected monuments are – 23 and C) State protected monuments are – 11.

EKAMRA KSHETRA /BHUBANESHWAR – AS "UNESCO WORLD HERITAGE CITY"

The Temple city of Bhubaneshwar is a part of the tentative site in India for inclusion in the UNESCO WORLD HERITAGE list.

To qualify for inclusion as a world heritage city, this ancient Temple City has the following unique features:

- Criteria (i): The presence of such a large number of temples at one location with the culminating architectural marvel of Lingaraj Temple is a sheer case of human creative genius.
- Criteria (ii): Ekamra Kshetra exhibits an important interchange of human values throughout ancient and medieval periods at Bhubaneswar that is manifest in the development of Kalinga architecture so much so that the entire range of this style is evident within Ekamra Kshetra.

- Criteria (iii): Ekamra Kshetra bears an exceptional testimony to the multi-religious, multi-sectoral holy city and associated traditions that are still living. The design and development of Ekamra Kshetra as a Hindu sacred city based upon the principles of Mandala are still evident.

The city has a continuous history of the development of art and architecture from the 4th / 3rd century BC to the 15th / 16th century AD, a period of about two thousand years, which covers almost the whole dated history of Odisha from its very dawn to the last Hindu dynasty.

As per legend, this ancient city is linked to Chedi king Sishupal of Mahabharat period. The ruins of Sishupalgarh near Bhubaneshwar were excavated, which appears to be predated to the Mayuran empire and before Kalinga war. Bhubaneshwar was the capital during the time of Ashok's Kalinga war in 261-BC and also during Kharavela, the mighty king of Kalinga who was ruling over Kalinga during 1st century BC.

It's history is more than 2500-years (ie. 4th /3rd century BC to till date) old and in the past the area was named as Tri-Bhubaneshwar (ie. Lord of 3-worlds).

It is a confluence of Hindu, Buddhist and jain heritage. It is one of the earliest Jain rock cut shelters at UDAYAGIRI and Khandagiri which command a unique place. The Buddhist heritage of Dhauligiri would enthrall any visitor.

It is home to largest concentration of Hindu temples in the world and some of the finest Kalinga architecture in the form of temples are found here.

According to the chronology so far established, the temples of Laxmanesvara, Satrugnesvara, Parsuramesvar and Swarna Jaleswar were the earliest one (ie. 6th century AD). Vaital and Sisireswar group of temples (700-to 900-AD), Brahmeswar group of temples (960 to 1065 AD), Mukteswar Group of temples (950-975 AD), Rajarani (950-975 AD), Lingaraj (11th century), kedareswar group of temples (12th century) and the latest one, that of Ananta-vasudeva, dates back to 13th century AD (ie. around 1278 AD) etc. record the remarkable continuity of culture in the old temple city. These temples span the entire spectrum of Kalinga architecture from 6th century to 13th century.

As per historians and researchers, the Kalingan temple architecture of Bhubaneswar represents the Nagara style temple architecture with regional ramification to be suitably called with the nomenclature Kalingan temple architecture depicting the grace, the joy and the rhythm of life in all its wonders varieties. The temples of Ekamarakshetra have been built by the creative impulse of the builders within evolved canonical texts or Silpa Sastras like Bhubanapradipa, Silpa Prakash and Silpa Ratnakosha etc. Many terms used in these, if not all, are even now used by the traditional Odia architect.

The temples are mostly built up sand stone and the Khandagiri and Udayagiri hills were providing the nearest quarry. The masonry is ashlar with the surface stones finely dressed and fitted together.

This proud sculptural and architectural wealth, coupled with its sanctity as Ekamra Kshetra, one of the five great religious centres in Odisha (ie. other four being – Jagannath Kshetra, Arka Kshetra, Biraja Kshetra and Ganapati Kshetra) since early medieval days, attracts thousands of visitors to Bhubaneswar from all corners of the world throughout the year. Even the most casual spectator is thrilled at the sight of the majestic and sublime grandeur of its soaring temples, the perfect symphony between their sculpture and architecture, the superb workmanship of their carvings and the grand repertoire of their sculptural and architectural motifs. To the connoisseur of fine arts, Bhubaneswar is one the most delightful resorts in India.

TOURIST PLACES OF BHUBANESHWAR

Bhubaneshwar is a modern happening place with top class infrastructure, that may be liked by the travellers belonging to all age groups. Further, the tourist places in the city and in it's surroundings are amazing which belong to a land with ancient history. The city is also having required infrastructural facilities to cater to every type of tourist. Some of the sought after tourist destinations of the city are as under:

Temples

The city is famous for it's architectural grandeur with innumerable temples in various sizes and designs. One will have a wonderful time visiting these magnificent sculptures and majestic architectural heritage.

TEMPLES OF EKAMRA KSHETRA /BHUBANESHWAR

The ancient and historic monumental temples are cultural heritage of Bhubaneshwar. The temple architecture of the city is diverse, as each and every aspect of it's various forms are present here.

Presence of almost every variation of temple is a testimony of age-long developments in many forms of art, culture and religious beliefs of the city.

Thousands of temples were present in the past (ie. more than 8-thousand temples during 11th century) and more than 700-temples still remain. The architecture, structure, sculptures, beautiful carvings and large variety of motifs make these temples unique.

It is known as the "City of Temples" due to these incredible ancient temples of the city.

Majority of these temples are dedicated to Lord Shiv. As per historian Rajendralal Mitra, "Every temple, every sacred pool, every rivulet, every ceremonial, every observance and every legend of Varanashi were reproduced at Bhubaneshwar. Nothing was omitted in the way of detail to make Bhubaneswar the exact counterpart of it's prototype – Varanashi."

As per Brahma Purana, EKAMRA KSHETRA is dedicated to Lord Krittivasa (Shiv) and equals varanashi in merits.

Lingaraj temple and Bindu Sagar are the centres of all religious institutions.

Old system of Sevayats (servitors) who are associated with day to day rituals of the temple are still present and their settlements are existing around the temples.

Brahma Purana further describes, crore Shivlings are enshrined in Ekamra KSHETRA. It was also known as "Gupta Kashi", as Lord Shiv had meditated here in a jungle under a large mango tree, without telling Goddess Parvati.

Most of the ancient temples are concentrated in the old city which was based on "Asta Ayatana" concept, ie. 8-sacred places, (ie. described in separate pages of this chapter) each with it's temples. The temples and pilgrim-routes were symbolically connected to Lingaraj temple, in the past.

Describing all the temples in this book is a mammoth task. The following are some of the prominent and unique temples of Bhubaneshwar which are described in an attempt to cover some of the representative and the best of the temples and which are a must – visit for every traveler seeking divine blessings.

1. LINGARAJ TEMPLE

This is the largest temple which is the most important landmark and attraction of the city. The term Lingaraj signifies "The king of lingas" / "Ruler of the Lingas" (ie. the iconic form or Shiv).

As per some researchers, the name of this Shivling was Krutibasa before 6th century AD, by 8th century AD it's name was Harihara Ekmreswar, by 9th century it's name was Tribhuvaneswar (ie. the name of the city is originated from this name) and around 11th century it was known as Lingaraj.

The temple is having Kalinga style architecture and represents medieval stages of the architectural traditions of Bhubaneswar.

History

This temple finds mention in Brahma Purana. It is believed that some part of the temple was built in 6th century. It was renovated and built by Somavamshi king Yayati Keshari – 1 in 10th century and was completed by king Lalatendu Keshari in 11th century. Some are of the view that the temple was constructed between 1025 AD to 1065 AD with later addition by Gangavamshi kings.

The Nata Mandir was constructed by the wife of Salini between 1099AD to 1104 AD.

The amicability of Shivaism and Vaishnavite culture are found in this temple.

Some opine that, by the time Lingaraj temple was completely built, there was growth of Vaishnavite culture/ Jagannath cult in the region. The co-existence of Shiv and Vishnu worship was to reduce the differences between the two sects.

Inscriptions

There were gift of gold coins to the temple by Rajaraja – ll as per an inscription of 1172AD. Inscription of Narasingha-l of 11th century indicates offer of betel leaves as Tambula to the presiding deity.

The stone inscriptions of the temple indicate royal grants from Chodaganga Dev to the nearby villages.

Temple

It is a Rekha DEULA constructed in the Pancharatha style without any platform.

It is divided in to 4-sections, ie. Viman (containing the inner sanctum/ Garbha Griha), Yagna Shala / Jagmohan (ie. hall of prayers/ assembly hall), Bhogamandap (ie. hall of offering) and Natya Shala (ie. hall of dance). Each is having increasing height to it's predecessor. The height of the main temple is around 180-feet.

This east facing temple is constructed with sand stone and laterite stones. This is surrounded by a compound wall which measures 520-feet by 465-feet. The wall is constructed with laterite stones and the thickness of the wall is 7.5 feet. It is capped with a simple slant coping and a terrace runs alongside the inner face of the boundary wall which protects the wall from outside attack.

The area of the complex is around 2.50 lac square feet. It is built in red stone.

The main entrance is on the east and there are two smaller entrances towards north and south, which are closed. The gate of the entrance porch is constructed with sandalwood.

Nata Mandir (Hall Of Dance)

This is 38-feet by 38-feet on the inside and 50-feet by 50-feet on the outside. There is one main entrance and 2-side entrances. It is having flat roof that slopes in stages. The hall is lined with substantial pylons/ thick arches. The side walls are adorned with decorative sculptures of women and couples. It is believed that there was Devdashi tradition in this temple.

BHOGAMANDAP (HALL OF OFFERING)

It is 42-feet by 42-feet inside and 56.25-feet by 56.25 feet on the outside. There are four doors. It is having pyramidal roofs with multiple horizontal layers arranged in pairs with an intervening platform. The exterior walls of the hall are adorned with sculptures of men and animals. An inverted bell and a Kalasha is on the top.

The Nata Mandap and Bhogamandap are both open air temples and these are of later period.

Jagmohan (Assembly Hall)

It is 35-feet by 30-feet on the inside and 55-feet by 50-feet on the outside. It is having south and north entrances. The entrance façades are adorned with perforated windows depicting a lion on hind legs.

The hall has a pyramidal roof having several horizontal layers arranged in pairs with an intervening platform. The height of the roof is around 98-feet.

There is an inverted bell which is adorned with lions and Kalash. The façade to the entrance is decorated with perforated windows with lion sitting on hind legs.

The Jagmohan is adorned with numerous sculptures.

Main Temple

It is a Rekha DEULA. From the inside the sanctum is square in shape. The height of this pyramidal tower is around 180-feet.

It is 22-feet by 22-feet on the inside and 52-feet by 52-feet on the outside. It is embellished with decorative elements and features a seated lion protruding from the walls.

The female figures in various poses are also found in the tower walls. Every inch of this tall tower is sculpted. The temple has large number of patio having many places of worship.

The Deity/Shivling

The presiding deity is known as Tribhubaneswar (ie. Lord of three worlds) and is known as Hari – Hara (ie. Combination of Shiv and Vishnu). He is known as "krutibasa", ie. naturally born.

The Swayambhu Shivling (ie. self-manifested) is of granite, natural and unshaped which rests on a shakti. It is in the inner sanctum and is worshipped everyday with milk, water and Bhang (cannibis). It rises to a height of 8- inches above the floor level and it's diameter is 8-feet. There are also Saligramas (ie. Representing Lord Vishnu).

There is existence of a natural line in the deity, which is generally believed as the line demarcating Lord Shiv and Vishnu, who is invoked as Hari-Hara. As per some visitors, it feels like "Lord Shiv has kept Lord Vishnu in his heart".

Similarly, the main doors of the temple have Lord Shiv's Trident on one side and Lord Vishnu's Chakra (wheel) on the other. It signifies co-existence of Shivaism and Vaishnavisim.

Curzon Mandap

This is located on the northern side of Lingaraj temple. Lord CURZON Governer General of India had wanted to visit this temple. As only Hindus were allowed inside the temple as per tradition, this platform was specifically erected for Lord CURZON to see the temples from the outside.

From this viewing platform one can view the entire complex.There is a marble plaque outside this Mandap.

Temple Complex

This magnificent religious structure with expansive courtyard contains around 125 shrines (ie. as understood from the priests and many of them identified by IGNCA) of different sizes and dedicated to different gods / goddesses and mostly to Lord Shiv .

The images of Parvati, Ganesha and Kartikeya are found in the northern, southern and western niches.

The side Gods / Goddess are made up of Chlorite stones. All the statues are beautifully decorated with draperies and ornaments.

The Ganga kings had introduced certain Vaishnavite elements in the temple, like – images of Vaishnava dwarpalas namely Jaya and Vijaya, Jagannath, laxmi narayan and Garuda etc.

Two other important temples of the complex are –

a) Goddess Bhubaneshwari

She is the presiding deity of EKAMRA peetha. Her worship is same with Lingaraj. She is also the most popular Tantric Goddess of Bhubaneswar. This is on the north of Jagmohan and she is the consort of Lord Lingaraj.

As per some views the "Anamika" (ring finger) of Goddess Sati fell here. It is also believed by many that, city of Bhubaneshwar is named after her name.

b) Goddess Savitri

This temple is on the south of Jagmohan.

The side Gods/Goddesses in these temples are distinctive type of "Parvati". i.e, minor shrines in the compound contain the images of Parvati, Kartikeya, Ganesh, Surya, Balaram, Krishna, Subhadra and Trivikram.

The early picture of Goddess Parvati is housed in a minor place of worship towards upper east of Lingaraj temple.

There are also many other temples/ places of worship within Lingaraj temple complex – like – Ananteswar temple, Baidyanath temple, Bhairabeswar temple, Candeswar temple, Chitreswar temple, Dakshin Kali temple, Ekadashi Mahadev temple, Ekamreswar temple, Gouri -Shankar temple, Gupteswar temple, Isaneswar Temple, Kapileswar temple, Kartikeya temple, Kashi Viswanatha temple, Ladukeswar temple, Lavaneswar temple, Laxmi Nrushingh temple, Mahavir temple, Mangala Devi temple, Prasana Durga temple, Pataleswar temple, Pejakhia Shiv temple, Ramlingeswar Shiv temple, Ram -Sita temple, Sakshi -Sankar temple, Sasthi temple, Satya narayan temple, Siddheswar temple, Shiv Kali temple, Tarakeswar Shiv temple, Ugreswar Shiv temple, Vishnu temple of Malayagiri area, Vishwakarma temple, Goddess Tarini , Nandi / Vrishveswar temple and many unidentified and ruined Shiv temples etc., which are of interest for many devotees and historians.

Tantra Peetha

Although Lingaraj is a Shaiva peetha, it is also a great Tantra peetha of Odisha.

The Shivling is situated to western and western faced Linga is linked to Tantra. As per Dr. Balaram Panda, "The worship of Lord Lingaraj is absolutely doing with Tantric method. It's mantra is also Tantric, ie. Om Hrim Hroom Sankar Narayana Namah Haroom Hrim Om".

Sculptures

From the architectural viewpoint, it is an outstanding specimen of Kalinga architecture and the whole architecture of stone carvings and interiors are extremely riveting.

One will be astonished to see how large pieces of rock could be lifted to such a great height in an era when modern technology was absent.

Marriage scene of Lord Shiv is depicted on the southern door of the Jagmohan where Lord Shiv wears the crown of the bridegroom but appears completely naked. It is associated with Bhrikuti, Brahma and Parvati.

The scene depicting Yashoda churning curd and Lord Krishna disturbing her as a child, is found on the southern side. It is also associated with image of Nanda.

On the western side of the Viman, there is depiction of Lord Shiv's marriage in a simplified manner.

The veranda of the temple features ten intricately carved mouldings. The janghas are intricately carved, particularly the lower janghas which are adorned with khakaramundis. The Mastaka, khapuri and Kalash are beautifully arranged.

These are magnificently decorated with sculptures of Gods, Goddesses, kings, queens, dancing girls, hunters and musicians.

One has to enter the temple through the lion's gate. There are lions on both the sides of the gate and lions crushing the elephants are showcased.

An optical effect is produced with the deep cut warped lines that run perpendicularly on the spire. Due to this optical influence, the temple looks much larger than actually what it is.

The spire of the temple has diminutive replicas of itself in the steeples, that are incorporated perfectly in the entire structure of the temple.

On the main entrance one can see a trident, representing Lord Shiv and chakra, representing Lord Vishnu on the either side of the door.

Uniqueness Of Lingaraj Temple

Compared to other Shiv temples, Lingaraj temple is unique, as Vaishnavite elements are seen as under (ie. these are not found in any other Shiv temples). It is believed that the synthesis has taken place during Gangavamshi kings.

- He is known as "Lingaraj", as he is the king of all 12-jyotirlingas.
- The images of Vaishnava dwarpalas, ie. Jaya and Vijay are seen instead of Chanda and Prachanda in the southern door jamb of Nata mandir.
- The Ayudha consists of half a disc and a trident.
- There is Aruna Stambha (Sun pole) like Jagannath temple, Puri.
- The images of Jagannath and Laxmi – Narayan are seen on the northern side of Bhoga Mandap and western side of main temple. Hence, devotees making Parikrama around main temple has to meet the Vaishnava deities.
- Garuda is at Garuda pillar to the left side of Nandi, carrier of Lord Shiva.
- Tulsi (ie. Basil) leaves are used to worship Lord Lingaraj along with Bela (ie. wood Apple) leaves.

- The flag on the Lingaraj temple is fixed to a pinak bow instead of trident usually found in Shiv temples.

The sacred sandalwood paste mark in the forehead of the priests is a big "U" with the dot in the middle on the horizontal lines (ie. sacred Mark which is combination of both Shiv and Vishnu).

- DOLA Purnima and Surya puja which are Vaishnavite fairs are performed here.
- Like Rath Yatra in Jagannath temple, a mock quarrel is staged between two parties of priests representing Lingaraj and Parvati, after return of the Rath during ASHOKASTAMI, as Lord Lingaraj has taken RUKUNA with him instead of Parvati. This is like Laxmi – Jagannath quarrel after return of the Rath at Jagannath temple, Puri.
- Like Jagannath temple, puri, ABHADA (cooked rice) is offered to Lingaraj and all caste Hindus take it as prasad.
- Like Daitapatis of Jagannath temple, puri, there are priests known as *Badus,* who are descendants of a Savar mother by a Shaiv Saint known as Siddhabuti.
- in place of Linga in the middle, it is vishnu's Shaligram Shila in the pindi of Lord Shiv.
- In every Shiv temple, Nandi is seen right in front of Shivling. Here, after making circumambulation of the temple, in the last Nandi is found.

TEMPLE DARSHAN / DARSHAN OF LORD LINGARAJ

As understood from the temple priests and from many experts, there are specific ways to visit LORD LINGARAJ (ie. known as Harihara Darshan). One has to take bath at Bindusagar tank and has to visit the Ananta Vasudev temple, as Lord of this temple is considered as guardian of Lingaraj. Thereafter, one has to enter the Lingaraj temple complex and have darshan of Lord Ganesh, Goddess Gouri /Parvati / Bhubaneshwari and Nandi. At last one has to visit Lord Lingaraj.

However, any devotee can visit the Lord without following any specific procedure, as the Lord is omnipresent and omnipotent.

Further, as per tradition, one should visit Lingaraj temple first, before visiting the temple of Lord Jagannath, Puri.

Rath Yatra on ASHOKASTAMI, Sitalasasthi and Maha Shivratri are the major festivals of the temple. Various festival observed in the temple and in EKAMRA KSHETRA are described below.

Lingaraj temple is unique and one of it's own kind of temple in the state and the country whose architectural grandeur would mesmerise any traveler. One should visit Lord Lingaraj and the magnificent temple which is one of the most ancient and largest temple of the country.

2. Ananta Vasudev Temple

This temple is dedicated to Lord Vishnu and was constructed by Chandrika Devi, the daughter of Anangabhima Dev lll, during the reign of Bhanu Dev, around 13th century AD (ie. 1278 AD). This is known as per the inscription, which is now lying in Asiatic Society, London.

As per some other legend, Queen of Chodaganga Dev built it in honour of her husband, who died in the battle (ie. However, it is without any authenticity).

As per hearsay, earlier Lord Vishnu was worshiped at this place and queen was inspired to build a new temple for all the devotees. The temple was renovated by the Marathas towards end of 17th century.

This temple signifies the assimilation of Vaishnavite culture, in the otherwise dominantly Shaiva culture of the city.

The temple comprising Jagmohan, Bhog Mandap and Nata Mandir stands on a uniform platform. It's architecture is of Rekha DEULA and it's lay out and structure is similar to Lingaraj temple. It is in a walled compound.

Lord Krishna, Balaram and Subhadra adorn the place and the idols are of black granite stone. As soon as one enters the temple, one will see the idols.

The idol of Lord Balaram stands under a seven hooded serpent while Lord Krishna holds mace, chakra, lotus and conch. Subhadra is holding a pot of jewels and lotus in her two hands.

There are large number of Vaishnavite sculptures in it's walls and there is a sculpture of Varaha (boar) incarnation of Lord Vishnu.

The sides Gods (ie. parswadevatas) are – Varaha on the south and Trivikram on the north. Many parts of the images are broken. The dikpalas and their shaktis are seated in Lalitasana.

It has various wall carvings that describes mythological stories related to Vishnu and the female sculptures of the temple are decorated with majestic ornaments. Garuda Stambha which was once facing the Jagamohan is now enclosed by the Nata Mandira.

Due to this temple, Bhubaneshwar is also known as "Chakra KSHETRA".

The temple kitchen is one of the largest in Bhubaneswar and large amount of food is prepared everyday for thousands of devotees, like Jagannath temple, Puri. It is cooked in fresh earthen pots on firewood. After being used, the pots are broken and discarded.

The Bhoga is also sold at the Ananda bazar, located within temple premises. It is the most sought after holy meal after Lord Jagannath's "Abhada Bhoga".

Janmashtami is the most important festival of the temple. Kartik Purnima, Tulshi Vivah and Diwali are some of other major festivals celebrated here. The morning and evening Aarati are attended by large number of devotees.

There is no restriction of entry to this temple.

The temple is in eastern bank of the Bindu Sagar lake and is behind the Lingaraj temple at Talabazar (ie. Gouri Nagar Area of old town).

The temple should be visited along with Brahma temple and Lingaraj temple (ie. Trinity of Hindu religion).

3. Brahma Temple

This temple was built in 15th century by the Gajapati kings and is surrounded by Bindusagar Tank. It is having south facing square Viman and east facing rectangular Jagmohan. The temple is of Kalinga type architecture.

The image of 4-handed Brahma made out of black Chlorite is holding water vessel and Veda in upper two hands while the lower hand has a rosary and another lower hand is in Abhay mudra. It is standing on a lotus pedestal. The lower left and right hands are resting over two female figures. At the base of the lotus pedestal there is a swan flanked by two female worshippers. The image is crowned with kirtimukha.

Legend

It marks the historic visit of Lord Brahma to the sacred place for coronation of Lord Lingaraj. The devotees and Gods requested him to stay at this place for ever. However, he refused to stay with the assurance that he would come every year in the month of Chaitra to celebrate the festival of ASHOKASTAMI. He also promised to become the Charioteer of the RUKUNA Rath of Lord Lingaraj. This temple was established to honour Lord Brahma, near Bindusagar. The locals refer to it as "Jagati" temple.

ASHOKASTAMI, Kartik Purnima, Guru Purnima and Diwali are major festivals of this temple.

It is situated on the eastern bank of Bindu Sagar, old town. This temple should be visited along with Lingaraj temple and Ananta Basudev temple, the trinity of Hindu religion.

4. Rajarani Temple

This ancient temple which stands on a raised platform was constructed around 11th century AD and has no idols to worship. It was earlier known as Indreswar temple. The height of the temple is around 59-feet.

The name "Raja-Rani" is believed to have it's origin to a particular variety of sandstone, locally known as Rajarani, (ie. dull red and yellow sandstone) of which temple is made. The use of sandstones gives a distinct appeal to the temple.

It has only two structures (ie. Viman and Jagmohan) instead of four as it was constructed several decades earlier, compared to other temples of the town.

Viman

The Viman is Pancharatha in plan and is surrounded by a cluster of miniature towers with double crowning elements and appears round, like Khajuraho temple. The temple plinth has 3-mouldings and the Bada consists of 5-divisions. The inner sanctum is square, ie. 10.25 feet by 10.25 feet from inside and 31-feet by 29-feet from outside. The spire is decorated with cluster of turrets (ie. replication of the spire itself) and emerging from the rib of the spire. The superstructure has a number of miniature turrets and is crowned with amlaka and a vase (Kalash) surmounts it.

Jagmohan

The Jagmohan is of pyramidal structure. It is provided with 2-balustrade windows. There are successive tier of projections rising to form the main tower. In the past, it was collapsed in to ruins and was repaired in 1903 AD. It is square in plan, ie. 17.83 feet by 17.83 feet from inside and 36-feet by 36-feet from the outside.

The stone carvings and beautiful artworks both inside and outside the temple are the specialty of the temple. It's exquisite carvings are considered as an unparallel example in the history of plastic art in Odisha.

The temple has strong Shaivaite association/ origin. There are figures of Lord Shiv and Parvati on the platform, Chanda and Prachanda and Shaiva dwarpalas with Jatamukha, on the entrance doorjambs.

The sculptures depict marriage of Lord Shiv with Parvati and also women in their daily chores.

The temple is having ornate carvings with numerous erotic sculptures. It is locally known as the "love temple" due to some sensuous carvings of women and couples.

The elegant Digapalakas and slender sophisticated nayikas, figures such as fondling her child, looking in to mirror, taking off her anklet, caressing the bird, playing instrument, holding branches of tree etc. would attract the tourists.

The figure of Varun with body ornamentation is intact.

The image of Lakulisha in a seated posture with yoga mudra along with his disciples is found in the lintel of the Jagmohan. The images of 8- bearded ascetics are arranged on both the sides of the image of Lakulisha.

There is presence of Naga and Naguni at the entrance and scroll motifs of foliage, creepers and vines etc.

As per Odisha Gazetteer, the images in the outer walls have inspired many foreigners to compose ballads which have gone viral in European countries.

The temple does not belong to any specific sect and is open to all.

The temple grounds are spacious and there is a well maintained garden in front of it.

It is a peaceful place to relax, if one wants a break from the sight seeing.

It is managed by ASI.

The Rajarani Music festival is held in the temple ground during January, each year. This festival focuses on classical musics / dances – Odissi, Carnatic and Hindustani etc.

This is a must visit for any traveler, which is renowned as the "symbol of love", "Khajuraho of the East" and one of the architectural wonders of Odisha.

The Temple is situated in Tankapani road, Raja Rani colony.

5. Mukteswar Temple

This 10th century sacred temple is dedicated to Lord Shiv and is one of the smallest and compact temple in Bhubaneswar. This 34-feet Rekha DEULA having a Pidha Jagmohan faces west. The beauty of the temple is described by M M Ganguly, "as a dream realised in sandstone".

As per K C Panigrahi, the temple was built during 966-aD by Somavamshi king Yayati-1.

Mukteswar signifies "God of freedom" (ie. Lord who gives freedom form the cycle of births and deaths). One will find ascetics in various teaching / meditations poses, figures of Hindu mythology and folk tales from Panchatantra as well as jain monks. The faces of Budhist and jain monks are carved with minute details.

This is the only temple of coastal Odisha, where five scenes of Monkey-Crocodile story of Panchatantra written by Bishnu Sharma are engraved in stone and found in the temple walls.

The temple has two structures, ie. Viman (structure above the sanctum) and a Mukhashala. Both of them are built in a raised platform. The doorway of the temple is ornate.

Viman

It is on a raised platform and is square in plan. The Shikara of the Viman is small compared to other temples and it has 4- Natarajas and 4-kirtimukhas on the four faces. The top portion of Shikar has the Kalash. Every inch of the Viman is having sculpted figures and decorative architectural patterns. The inner sanctum is cubical from inside with offset walls on the outside. There are sculptures of beautiful women entwined with Nagas and Nagins.

The doorway of inner sanctum houses the image of ketu with 3-hooded snakes.

Bho-decoration

This is a new form of decoration, which was developed in this temple. It is a highly Chaitya window crowned by masked demon head and dwarf figures. It has became an important feature in the later temples of Odisha.

Jagmohan

The pyramidal roof of the Jagmohan was the first of it's kind over the conventional two tier structure.

The ceiling of the Jagmohan is delicately carved in the form of full blown lotus and contains the representations of Virabhadra and Saptamatrukas with babies in their laps.

There are diamond shaped latticed windows on the north and south walls of Jagmohan. The outermost frame of the window depicts humorous scenes from monkey's life, as stated above.

The figure of Lakulisha, seated in bhumisparsa mudra and holding a lakuta is present in the lintel of Jagmohan. There are images of Gajalakshmi, Rahu and Ketu.

Both the Viman and the Jagmohan have incredible carvings which reflects the blending of architecture itself resulting from a blending of cultures.

The 8-petaled lotus in the ceiling of the porch and the carved images including lion head motif appear for the first time in the temple architecture. It is one of the most refined temple of odisha owing to it's elegant proportions, delicate carvings and beautiful sculptures in red sandstones.

Marichi Kunda

There is an attractive small water Kunda in the temple compound, known as Marichi Kunda which is situated just behind the temple. On the door frame of Marichi Kunda, there is a seated figure of Lakulisha (ie. a prominent shaivaite revivalist, reformist and preceptor of the Pashupata sect of Tantric Shaivism)

The water of the Kunda is famous for it's medicinal properties. As per hearsay, those women who have no children use the water of this tank with religious rituals / take a dip in the Kunda in the night before ASHOKASTAMI for the birth of a child. It was being filled by an underground stream in the past. There is also a well in the south-east corner of the temple.

Mukteswar Gate

The temple gate is well designed and lavishly decorated. This arched gateway known as Torana (ie. acts as a gateway to the compound), is a unique feature of Odishan temple art and is not part of any other temple in the area. It is having influence of Buddhist architectural element and the sculptures of deities on it's top are having Buddhist influence.

The archway is decorated with ornate carvings of reclining women, animals, flowers and combinations of Buddhist, Hindu and jain motifs.

There are delicate carvings of scroll bands, beads, and ornaments on the twin pillars of the archway. It provides perfect blend between architecture and sculpting.

The porch is a walled chamber with a low, massive roof and internal pillars.

Mukteswar Temple is the gem of Kalinga architecture and is one of the most refined and beautiful temples of Odisha.

Ornate stone carvings of lion over an elephant symbolises the dominance of Hinduism over Buddhism. Some of the carvings are defaced, may be by the Muslim invaders.

As per researchers, the temple is the successor to Parshurameswar temple and built earlier to Brahmeswar temple.

In the stylistic development of temple architecture, the Mukteswara Temple plays a pivotal role. It marks the end of early phase and initiates a period of experiment which continues for an entire century, as seen in such temples as the Rajarani Temple and Lingaraj temple etc (ie. It anticipates the next phase of experimentation of temple architecture with related plastic and iconography.).

Here, mouse is used as the mount of Ganesh, a cock associated with Kartikeya, babies carried in the arm of Saptamatrukas and Ketu among the planets.

There are also other shrines in the complex.

There is a beautiful garden in the temple premises to stroll. The compound walls are octagonal with elaborate carvings on it.

The outer face of the compound wall has deities like – Saraswati, Ganesh and Lakulisha in the niches. There are numerous images of Lakulisha in Chaitya arches in various mudras like – Bhumisparsha and Vyakyana etc. with yogapatta tied to the knees and are accompanied by the images of disciples.

Some researchers link this temple with Tantra.

Solar Clock

There was a solar clock in this temple complex. Depending upon the position of Sun and it's shadow, the time was known by measuring the length and angle of the shadow. During night time, the time was known by observing the Dhruba Star (North Star) and planet Venus etc.

The Mukteswar festival on the temple grounds during mid-January is nice to watch. It celebrates Odissi, the classical dance form of Odisha and the Odishi music. Mukteswar Temple is situated in kedar Gauri lane, old town, Bhubaneshwar.

6. Sidheswar Temple

It is a 10th century temple and is located in the premises of Mukteswar temple.

This is an east facing sandstone temple. As per some other opinion, it was constructed around 15th century AD.

It is taller than Mukteswar temple. It's outer walls have less carvings. It is not as ornate as Mukteswar temple. But the construction pattern has it's own charm.

The temple tower is built in Pancharatha type. Lord Shiv is worshipped in the inner sanctum. The beautiful standing Ganesh in a lotus pedestal and covered with thick layer of red vermillion is installed in the eastern side, which is another attraction. The four armed Kartikeya is in southern niche. All the four sides of the tower are surmounted by 4-lions.

One has to walk through a beautiful garden to reach the temple.

7. Parshurameswar Temple

Parshurameswar Temple is believed as the oldest surviving temple of Bhubaneshwar which was built around 650-AD during the rein of Sailodvab dynasty, who were worshippers of Lord Shiv. The temple derives it's name from the deep penance of Lord Parshuram and resultant grace of Lord Shiv.

However, as per famous historian and archeologist Prof. K C Panigrahi, the Parshurameswar temple built in 7th century was earlier named as Parasawara after the Pashupata teacher Parasara.

The structure of the temple is simple and small. Its exterior is covered with intricate carvings.

It has all the elements of pre 10th century style of kalinga architecture, like-pine spire and pyramid covered hall.

This is the first shrine in the region to have an additional structure of assembly hall (ie. Jagmohan / entrance hall) other than the Viman-topped sanctum.

Parshurameswar temple comprises of a Viman, the worshipping hall, an inner sanctuary and a spire, elevating at a height of 12.27 meters (ie. around 40. 25 feet). Large part of Jagmohan is bereft of decorative elements.

It's low assembly hall has latticed windows, through which light enters the sanctum and people can see inside.

There are some specific features which indicates it's antiquity. The panel above the sanctum door has eight planetary deities, although later temples have nine.

Lord Shiv is the main deity. The other deities present in the temple are – Ganesh, Kartikeya, Virabhadra, Ardhanareeswarar, Ganga, Yamuna, Vishnu, Indra, Surya, Yama and different Nagas.

The sculptures of Nataraja in various tandava positions are in the temple.

Lord Shiv can be seen on three sides, ie. 1) front facing Lord Shiv subduing the demon king Ravana who is seen trying to uproot mount kailash, the abode of Lord Shiv 2) Annapurna offering alms to Shiv 3) Marriage of Lord Shiv.

Though the temple is dedicated to Lord Shiv, it contains sculpted image of Shakti deities. It contains the earliest representation of 6-armed Mahishamardini Durga image. The Goddess is seen holding a sword in upper left hand, while in the upper right hand she is seen piercing the trident on the neck of demon. She is holding different weapons in her different hands.

This is one of the first temples to have Stone carvings of seven forms of Durga (Saptamatruka s) which are seen in the complex (ie. Chamunda, Varahi, Indrani, Vaishnavi, Kaumari, Shivani and Brahmi). The Saptamatruka images are located between the image of Ganesh and Virabhadra.

This is one of the best preserved ancient Hindu Shiv Temple in India which is beautifully carved and whose carvings include – horse and elephant processions, birds and animals, floral and human figures. These are depicted in scenes and part of designs.

The temple was repaired in 1903 AD with some changes in the roof of the inner sanctum while retaining most of the original structure.

Parshuramstami is the major festival celebrated in the temple on the 8th day of Ashadha (June-July) when the moving image of Lord Lingaraj is taken to the temple and a community feast is organised.

As per some researchers the temples like Parshurameswar, Vaital and Rajarani might have Devadasi system/ existence of Natyasastra tradition during the then period.As per legend Marirambha, an Apsara (ie. dancer in the heaven) had learnt the dance from Lord Shiv and Ganesh and this was passed on to later generations. This temple, which is the oldest structurally, is situated near Bindu Sagar pond, old town.

One can also visit the nearby Shiv temples like – Pabaneswar temple, Subarneswar temple, Champakeswar temple, DISHESWAR temple, GANGESWAR temple, Astasambhu temple and KAPILESWAR temple etc.

8. Baitala Temple (Deula) / VAITALI TEMPLE

Baitala Temple which was established around 8th century is built in Khakhara style and is known as Tini-Mundia DEULA among the locals. It appears, the name has been derived from "Vetal" which denotes "Spirit".

As per Odisha Gazetteer, the origin of the name can be traced to the type of cult practiced by the Kapatikas / Kapalikas, who used to invoke the aid of Vetals (spirits) for their Siddhis.

It was constructed during Bhaumakar kings who were originally Mahayana Buddhists and later converted to Shaivism.

During their period, Shaktism and Tantric cult had also made it's appearance in Odisha. It is believed that the temple was built by Bhaumakar queen Tribhuvana Mahadevi who was also known as Katyayini.

Eight armed Chamunda, locally known as Kapalini, is the main deity of the temple. She is the terrifying form of Goddes Durga (Mahisasura Mardini) / Tantric incarnation of Goddess Durga.

The presiding deity sits on a corpse flanked by a Jackal and an owl. It is adorned with garland of skulls. She holds a snake, bow, shield, trident, sword, thunderbolt and an arrow which is piercing the neck of the demon.

Her body is literally skeleton with sunken belly, sunken eyes and open mouth.

The appearance of Goddess in the lamp light can trigger the emotions of fear.

The seated position of Lord Shiv and Goddess Parvati are in the backside of the Chamunda and a small carving of Laxmi is found above the Chamunda.

Smaller sized deities are carved in lower part of the wall surrounding the Chamunda. This temple is related to Tantric cult and hardly any windows to bring in daylight.

The east facing temple has a rectangular Viman with semi cylindrical roof and Jagmohan. The Jagmohan which is flat roofed houses four smaller temples in it's four vertices and these are complete with their vimanas.

It's temple tower is slightly pyramidal rather than cylindrical. This and the three spires in the top, take it closer to a South Indian temple like those in Tamilnadu / slightly resembles the Dravidian Gopuram style.

As per M M GANGULY, the shape of the temple has been derived from the Rathas of Mahabalipuram.

As per Percy Brown, the Vaital temple is of Buddhist tradition and connects it with Chaitya hall of Buddhists.

The spires of the temple denotes three powers of the Goddess, ie. Mahalaxmi, Maha Saraswati and Maha Kali.

There are stunning stone sculptures of Hindu Gods and Goddesses, like – Ganesh, Veerbhadra, Saptamatrukas, Bhairav, Mahakala and Kuber etc. in sitting position along with their respective mounts.

Shivaduti is a rare deity found in this temple along with Saptamatrukas. Chamunda is in the central niche and other Matrukas in the side walls.

Here, Bhairav is in skeletal figure with sunken belly and is looking ferocious.

Mahakala (ie. form of Shiv) is sitting in corpse and Abhalakapeswara (ie form of Shiv) is found under a serpent.

The outer walls contained the sculptures mostly related to Shiv and Shakti in different forms, haunting scenes, erotic couples, and Nayikas in different postures.

Other important sculptures are 8-armed Mahishamardini Durga mounted on a lion and another sculpture of 4-armed Durga holding Japamala, trident, khadga and vase in her arms and flying Vidyadharas above her head.

The important carvings on the Jagmohan are the extremely fine image of Surya with Usha and Pratyusha, shooting arrows on his either side and Arun in front is driving the chariot of 7-horses. This is found on the eastern face of the temple.

There are other intricate decorative carvings on the walls of Jagmohan and the main shrine, like – elephants, lions, Ardhanareeswarar, Lakulisha, Vidyadharas and Mithun figures.

The temple base is below the ground level. There is a stand post in front of Jagmohan, where sacrificial offerings were made in the past.

There are also two pillars with some carvings and one of the important carving is the EKA PADA BHAIRAV.

This ancient temple (ie. more than 12-hundred years old) and the sanctuary tower which features a unique shape would be liked by any art loving traveler or devotee.

It's compound is common with another temple in the name of Sisireswar. The 8th century Sisireswar temple also contains Mahishamardini image in the northern central niche of the Viman. As per archeologists, the temple is of the same period of architecture as that of Vaital temple.

The Vaitali Temple is within walking distance from Lingaraj temple.

9. Brahmeswar Temple

Brahmeswar temple was built around 11th century according to Panchayatan plan (ie. four smaller shrines flanking the primary temple on each cardinal directions). It was built by Kolavati Devi during the rein of her son Udyota Keshari in 1058-60 AD, in honour of Lord Brahmeswar (ie. form of Lord Shiv). It is situated further out and to the east of other temples of EKAMRA KSHETRA.

The height of the temple is around 60-feet. It is a Rekha DEULA with Pidha Jagmohan. The Bada of the temple is of Panchanga type and the Gandi is Pancharatha. The temple is divided in to major two parts, ie. Viman and Jagmohan.

The iron beams were used in the construction of temple for the first time from this temple. Another first in temple iconography were the musicians and dancers that appear prolifically on the temple walls.

The main shrine is dedicated to Lord Shiv. The sculptures of Lord Shiv and Goddess Parvati are found along side the main deity.

The temple is famous for carvings and reflects the brilliance of Kalinga architecture in it's sand stone walls.

The carvings over the doorframe contain beautiful flower designs as well as flying figures.

The temple has borrowed designs like – a porch having carved ceiling with lotus, plentiful of lion head motifs on it's walls etc., from Mukteswar temple.

There are several carvings of erotic couples and voluptuous damsels similar to Rajarani temple. The exterior is decorated with several Gods / Goddesses, religious scenes, animals and birds etc. On the western façade there are some Tantric related images.

A carving of Chamunda holding trident and human head standing on a corpse appears on the western façade. Shiv and other deities are depicted in their frightening forms.

The exterior is lavishly sculpted with different forms of Shiv such as Nataraja, Bhairav, Ardhanareeswarar, Ajaikapada etc. and there are erotic couples, Nayika and Gaja – Vidalas.

This is the second temple in Bhubaneswar with internal embellishments in the Jagamohan after Mukteswar temple.

Like Rajarani temple, there are images of Dikpals or guardians of 8-directions in Brahmeswar temple besides number of Tantric related sculptures.

A pyramid stone is used to carve out the structure, making it a medieval master piece.

One of the lost inscriptions of the temple stated that kolavati Devi presented many beautiful women to the temple. It is believed that it is an evidence of the "Devadasi tradition" which assumed great importance in later Odishan temple architecture and temple life.

It is at Brahmeswar patna,Siba Nagar,near Tankapani road, Bhubaneshwar.

The temples of Lord BHASKARESWAR and Lord Megheswar are also situated nearby.

10. KEADAR GAURI TEMPLE

Two temples, ie. Kedareswar Shiv and Gouri (Maa Parvati) temple are both in the complex and is one of the eight Astasambhu temples. It is very popular and people pray in this temple to make their love/ family life successful.

There are 10-monuments in the premises.

Kedar Temple

It is believed that this temple was built by Ganga kings around 12th century AD. The temple is architecturally akin to Siddheswar temple located in Mukteswar temple complex. The structure of the temple is Rekha type Viman and Pidha type Jagmohan. It is Pancharatha in plan and panchanga Bada on elevation. The Jagmohan (rectangular hall) has a three divisional wall with crowning ornamentation.This south facing temple is having the Shivling known as Kedareswar. The linga at the centre is missing and enshrined deity is a circular Yoni pitha made of sand stone. The sanctum is 2.5 square meters and is around 0.8 meters below the ground. As per hearsay, the lingam located inside the temple is Dakshina Murti installed at this place by Giriraj Himalaya. The images of Ganesh, Kartikeya and Parvati are found as side Gods / Goddess in the outer walls. There is an inscription on the right jamb of the door frame of the Jagmohan which records the donation of the perpetual land by, Paramardi Dev, the younger brother of Chodaganga Dev in 1142AD

Gauri Temple

The Gauri temple is said to have been erected during the period (8th-10th century AD) of Somavamshi kings by one Gauri Mahadevi. It is older than Kedar temple.This east facing temple is of Khakhara DEULA type Vimana and Pidha type Jagmohan. The outer walls are intricately carved with sculptures.

Legend – I

Lord Shiv along with Goddess Parvati had come to this place from Varanashi, as it was calm and quiet. Here, Lord Lingaraj got married to Goddess Parvati on sitalsasthi day.The annual procession is held to commemorate the marriage of Shiva and Parvati. The procession starts from Lingaraj and goes all the way till Kedar-Gauri temple.

Ponds/Kundas

There are three ponds / kundas in the temple complex, Ie. Kedara Kunda, Gauri Kunda, Khira Kunda (Dudha Kunda) which are fed by a perennial spring. They are having healing powers. It is believed that one would be relieved from the cycle of birth and death by taking a bath in Gauri Kunda. It's water was used for various ritual purposes.The water of Kedar Kunda is used for the rituals of Kedar – Gauri Temple and for preparing the prasad of the temple. In the past tourists from different parts of the state / country/ specially from West Bengal used to take water from the Khaira Kunda / tank of Kedar – Gouri to cure acidity. The water of khira Kunda was used for curing different diseases. In the past, the water of this Kunda was whitish. As per Dr Bijay kr Rath, the water in the tanks of Kedar – Gouri comes in contact with the roots of Kochila trees. So they imbibe medicinal properties from these plants. However, all these kundas require cleaning and maintenance. The 8-feet statue of Hanuman and Goddess Durga standing on a lion are also in the complex. Kedar-Gauri temple is surrounded by Dutiya Kedareswar on it's west.

Hearsay About Kedar-Gouri Temple

Some locals believe that the temple is dedicated to a couple with the name Kedar and Gauri.

As per hearsay, a couple named – Kedar and Gauri had decided to marry. As the society was against them they fled from the village.

During journey, Gauri felt hungry and Kedar went to search for food and he was killed by a tiger. When Gauri heard this sad incident, she jumped in to a pond. After hearing the tragic episode, king laletendu Keshari raised this Kedar-Gauri temple.

This incident is immortalised by great poet Kabibara Radhanath Ray in his famous work "Kedar Gouri".

However, as per historians both the temples were constructed in different periods of time.

One should visit this temple, which is also known as 'love temple' by some and where many couples pray who want their love to become successful.

The temple is aesthetically endearing with its graceful sculptures and covered with erotic carvings of women and couples.

It is situated near Bindu Sagar pond and behind Mukteswar temple.

11. Bhaskareswar Temple

BHASKARESWAR temple of Bhubaneswar is the only known free-Standing specimen of pidha DEULA style. It has only one structure which is raised on a plinth and a circular platform. This double storied west facing temple with a Pidha Viman was built by Gangavamshi kings around 12th century AD.

This type of Pidha DEULA is also known as "flat sheet temple", where the Shikhara is like a stepped but compressed pyramid.

It is marked by a series of flat platforms placed one over the other in diminishing order and each one representing a storey. It is 9-Storied and is topped by an Amalaka.

The height of the Shivling is around 3-meters and circumference is around 4-meters. One can access the Linga on the doorways lying on all the four sides.There is no ornamentation excepting the side Gods / parshwadevatas – Ganesh, Kartikeya and Parvati.

As per some historians, it was earlier a Buddhist Stupa, which might have been modified and converted in to a temple. The remains of Buddhist Stupa railing pillar and lion capitol was discovered nearby. Some believe there might be an Ashokan pillar nearby, which was broken and it's column was used as a Shivling. It may be the reason for unadorned, in terms of carvings.

As understood from the locals, the Shivling is growing over a period of time.

This Shivling finds mention in the sacred text as Vrihalingam / Vrihatlingam (ie. Biggest linga).

The movable image of Lord Lingaraj is taken to this temple on Magha Saptami, where the Lord is bathed, clothed, worshipped and a feast is arranged. It shows the antiquity of the temple.

Some researchers compare this temple with Madhukeswar and Bhimeswar temple of Mukhalingam.

Legend

As per EKAMRA Purana, Lord Brahma advised Sun God to visit beautiful EKAMRA Kanan. Surya visited this place and was charmed by it's beauty. As per his request, Vishwakarma erected the temple.

This temple which resembles a Buddhist Stupa and Pidha DEULA is the main super structure of the temple. It is situated in the eastern part of old city in the midst of a beautifully curated landscape.

This most unusual and debatable temple is next to Megheswar Dev temple on the left side of Tankapani Road.

12. Yameswar Temple

This is a west facing temple which consists of a DEULA, Jagmohan and a detached Nata Mandap opposite the Jagmohan, similar to Konark temple. Like Nandi Mandapas of South India, a small Nandi sits inside a small raised platform.

Viman is Rekha DEULA structure, Jagmohan is Pidha DEULA structure and it was constructed by Gangavamshi kings. The architecture of the temple is around 13th century. It is built in sand stone and outer portion/ walls are built by laterite.

Legend

Lord Yama (ie. God of death) had worshipped Lord Shiv at this place.

Some others opine that YAMESWAR is the brother-in-law of Lord Lingaraj.

As per some researchers the structure might be much older, as a small shrine emerging from below the present ground level was excavated and restored. Architecturally it has been estimated as 7th century (ie. during period of Bhaumakar kings) and contemporary to Parshurameswar temple. There are also many shrines in the complex, some of which are partially buried but unexacavated and others are later constructions.

The moving idol of Lord Lingaraj stops here on the date of Yama Dwitiya (ie. around October/ November) and begs forgiveness for his sin.

The Lord is worshipped in Yama Mantra.

This indicates that YAMESWAR temple is a much earlier temple, as showing respect and paying homage to important older icons was an old practice.

There are many standalone Shivlings in the complex. There is a Sahasra lingas whose surface is carved with hundreds of miniature Shivlings.

The exterior walls of the temple are intricately decorated with sculptures like – Nagas, elephants, processions, dancing females and large number of amorous couples. But many of the carvings are weathered. Damaged Ganesh and Kartik idols are found in the niches.

The interesting carving of a woman straddling a fire depicts the process of healing the vagina after childbirth. This carving is also found in the Konark Sun Temple. As understood, the Bonda tribes still perform this practice today.

The carvings of Navagraha and Laxmi carvings are found above the entrance.

There are number of images in the Jagmohan including Parvati and Shivling which are found above the doorway of the sanctum.

The Kalingan style lions with the first two legs raised and lions on top of elephant-heads are found in many places in the walls and Viman.

The main festivals of the temple are Paujiuntia/Jiuntia/ Dwitivahana OSHA which is performed in the month of Ashwin. Bharani Nakshatra Shivratri, Kartik Purnima and Dev Diwali are other major festivals of the temple.

It is believed that people who visit this temple during Bharani Nakshatra would be freed from all miseries.

As per hearsay, if Yama Dwitiya is performed during the second day of the bright fortnight of Kartik month all wishes would come true of a devotee.

It is located near Bharati Matha of Jameswar patna.

This temple is directly opposite the Bakreswar temple and is at the western extent of ancient temples of the city.

MEGHESWAR TEMPLE

Megheswar temple is the first Nava -Ratha plan temples in Odisha. As per the inscription, the temple along with the water tank near it was built towards end of 12th century, with the instructions of SWAPNESWAR who was the brother in law of Ganga king Rajaraja.

The temple is famous for it's beautiful architecture although many are damaged. The temple structure consists of Vimana, Jagmohan and Sapta-Ratha.

Megheswar Shivling is the presiding deity. The exterior temple walls are having carvings of graceful dancers, animals, birds, flowers and numerous postures of Lord Shiv.

Some of the best images are found around the entrance of the Jagmohan, like – Naga – Nagi pillar flanking the doorway, nine celestial bodies of the universe in separate niche, mini dwarpalas along with river Ganga and Yamuna in door jamb and the side Gods-ganesh, Kartikeya and Parvati etc. with attendants. A small sized Nandi is facing towards main shrine.

The presence of Hero Stones indicated the then maritime trade of Kalinga with different countries.

It is close to BHASKARESWAR and Brahmeswar temple at Badagada, Tankapani road.

14. SAMPOORNA JALESWAR TEMPLE

This east facing temple which is opposite of Subarnajaleswar temple, has only a Viman with an attached porch.

It is an abandoned Hindu temple and has no prime deity in the complex. As per wall inscriptions, the temple is believed to be dedicated to Lord Shiv.

It is built in sand stone. The temple walls are full of ornate sculptural carvings which are small and detailed.

The temple was an architectural marvel, but after renovation it has lost much of the beauty. It is of Kalinga style architecture and locals believe that the temple was built by Keshari kings around 9th - 10th century.

Some visitors describe this temple as the hidden secret of Bhubaneswar.

It is located at Kotiteertha lane on the left side of Lingaraj west canal.

15. Chitrakarini Temple

This is an east facing Panchayatan temple, where the main temple is in the middle and other four temples are situated in each corner. This is surrounded by a compound wall built with laterite stones.

It is believed that the temple was built around 13th century during the period of Ganga kings (ie. between 1238-AD to 1264 AD by Narasingha Dev – 1).

Some opine that the artisans of the Pathuria Sahi stayed in this area. They used to paint different sculptures on the stones (ie. known as – Chitrakarita) and the temple was known as Chitrakarini.

It is believed that the temple was dedicated to CHITRAKARINI, the Goddess of painting / Goddess of creative expressions/ female painter (ie. paintress), a form of Goddess Saraswati.

This is the only known temple in the world, which is dedicated to Goddess CHITRAKARINI (ie. who is the Devine sub-form of Goddess Saraswati).

It is a two chambered temple having the Rekha style main shrine and Pidha style Jagmohan.

However, it appears the image was stolen / broken by the invaders and a red coloured stone idol of Chamunda is enshrined in the inner sanctum.

As per historians, there were five idols in the main temple and 4-idols (ie. one idol each) in 4-sub-shrines (ie. total-9 idols of shakti in the temple). Presently, there are no idols in the sub-shrines.

The main temple, Jagmohan and sub-shrines are well decorated with sculptures like – elephants, lions, dancing girls, Digpals, amorous couples, marriage of Lord Shiv, Lord Krishna with Gopis, erotic figures, Nagas and many Gods / Goddesses. Although many of the carvings are weathered, however, whatever is left would attract any traveller for it's intricate work.

The depiction of Lord Krishna playing his flute in the midst of followers and cattle would draw the attention of any traveller.

This Vaishnavite temple is situated west of Lingaraj temple. It is under ASI.

16. Rameswar Temple (Mausi Maa Temple)

RAMESWAR Temple is known as the Maushi Maa temple (ie. Maternal Aunt's house of Lord Lingaraj). This east facing temple is built of sand stones having 16-pillars. It consists of a single hall and the Shikhara is of tiered structure.

The temple faces east so that the first rays of the Sun falls on the temple.

The Shivling within a circular yonipitha made of Chlorite is in the hall. An image of Durga is also worshipped within the sanctum.

The temple was built by Samavamshi kings around early part of 12th century AD. The Jagmohan was built much later. Some others opine that, it was built around 9th century AD.

There are some beautiful carvings of amorous couples, the images of Durga, Kartikeya and Ganesh in the sanctuary walls and Navagrahas over the temple doorway etc. The Ganesh idol of the complex is believed as of 7th century, by some.

There is a rectangular Mandap having two doorways which is standing before the temple independently.

Legend

When Lord Ram was returning from Lanka after victory over Ravana, Mata Sita asked to worship Lord Shiv at the site of the temple. Seeing her devotion, Lord Ram built the lingam at the site for the purpose of worship. As Lord Ram built the lingam, it was known as RAMESWAR temple (Details are covered under-festivals of Lingaraj / EKAMRA KSHETRA of this chapter).

Every year during RUKUNA Rath Yatra, the annual chariot festival of Lord Lingaraj, bronze image of 3-deities-chandrasekhar (representing Lord Lingaraj, Rukmini/ RUKUNA and Basudev are taken to RAMESWAR temple in a procession. It is also known as

ASHOKASTAMI, which falls one day before to Rama Navami in Chaitra Month.

The deities stay in the temple for 4-days before returning in chariot to Lingaraj temple. As the chariot does not take a turn for it's return journey it is known as "ANA LEUTA RATHA YATRA".

Towards east of the RAMESWAR temple, there are twin temples of Kuseswar and labeswar and small complex of three temples of Lakshmaneswar, Bharateswar and Satrugneswar.

This group of 6-temples in the name of all the sons of Dasaratha and both the sons Shri Ram are considered as some of the oldest temples of Bhubaneswar.

There is a lily pond which enhances it's beauty. An Ashokan bell was found in the pond (ie. now kept in Odisha state museum) and the temple tank is called Ashokjhar. Some researchers link this with Mauryan period.

However, the tank requires renovation and maintenance.

The temple stands in the midst of a beautiful park.

17. Markandeswar Temple

This is a very old and beautiful temple. As per archeologists, it is almost duplicate of the Sisireswar temple. The design is similar to Parshurameswar temple.

The temple is in ruined conditions, although most of the images in the niches still exist.

As per historians, the temple was built towards the end of 8th century. All the original Jagmohan has been lost and this is replaced by plain block of sandstones. The remains of the original temple has also been rebuilt at some point using original masonry where possible and further plain sandstone blocks where the pieces were missing.

The Mandap of this temple is new which is built over the low base of earlier one.

There are lot of carvings on the Shikhara. The Nataraja in the east facing central medallion is unique. The image of Navagraha is on the doorway and images of Brahma, Agni and Varuna etc are in the door jamb. It is situated in south-west corner of Bindu Sagar tank near Mohini temple. However, there are encroachments from the three sides. Urgent steps are required to save this monument from the encroachment.

If one moves south towards Bindu Sagar tank, the remains of Paschimeswar temple is found. The temple is having only plinth. The side Gods and Goddess are kept near the plinth of the former temple.

18. Astasambhu Temples

Astasambhu temples are situated in the precinct of Uttarereswar Shiv temple. There are 8-Shiv temples ranging in height from 14-feet to 20-feet. They are of identical structures and dimensions. 5-temples are arranged in one dimension and are known as Panchu PANDAV. The remaining 3-are situated closer to Godavari Kunda.

Legend

Goddess Parvati expressed her desire for "Rati Krida" with Lord Shiv at EKAMRA KSHETRA. Lord Shiv agreeing to this had transformed in to 8-forms, which are known as Asta Sambhu.

As per historians these east facing Shiv temples made up of grey sand stone were built around 10th century and are of Rekha style. It is surrounded by Godavari tank in the east, Uttareswar temple compound wall in west and Bindusagar tank in south.

The temple is square Viman of around 2.45 meters with a frontal porch of 0.53 meters.

A four armed Ganesh holding Parshu in lower left, a rosary with Varada Mudra pose in lower right and upper hands are broken, is found in the southern niche. Lord Ganesh is flanked by two flying Vidyadharas.

The doorjamb is decorated with three vertical bands. At the base of the doorjamb, there are Saivite dwarpalas holding the trident.

The image of Gajalakshmi holding a lotus in her left hand and right hand in Varada mudra is at the Lalat Bimba. The Navagrahas flanked by attendants are above the doorjamb.

The Shivlings are made up of precious stones. Some are white, some are red and some are black.

The Shivlings appear in different colours when looked at different directions. They are known as – Markandeswar, Yagneswar, NILAKANTHESWAR, Vilweswar, Kapalmochan, Baleshwar, Ishaneswar and pataleswar

19. Koti Tirtheswar Temple

This temple is famous for the Swayambhu Shivling. This Kalinga style temple is small and was constructed by Somavamshi kings around 11th century AD. The importance of this temple is found in the Skandha Purana. The Kotitirtha pond in front of the temple is also treated as holy.

It is believed that, if one worships the Shivling in this temple after a dip in the sacred tank, than it will be pilgrimage equivalent to visit of a crore Shivlingas.

The 14th day of the bright fortnight of Chaitra Month (ie. Vishnu Damanak Chaturdashi) is the most important festival of this temple, when Lord Lingaraj visit the temple (ie. representative of Lord Lingaraj is taken inside and is worshipped). It is celebrated with much funfair.

This is also known as Devi Padahara Kotitirtha temple.

20. Kapileswar Temple

This east facing temple is situated on the northern embankment of Manikarnika tank. It is one of the largest temple complex of the city.

KAPILESWAR temple complex is having around 34- big and small temples/ monuments and the main temple of the complex is the KAPILESWAR temple.

Like Lingaraj temple, this temple was also acting as a centre of social, political and educational activities of Bhubaneshwar.

Legend

Kapileswar village was the birth place of sage Kapila, who was one of the founders of Sankhya School. He was considered as an incarnation of Lord Vishnu. Hence, Kapileswar village and the temple are sacred places.

As per Prof K C Panigrahi Kapileswar temple is named after a Pashupata teacher Kapila, who was one of the successors of Kushika, a disciple of Lakulisha. This was reconstructed by the Gajapati ruler Kapilendra Dev in 14th century. From the architectural elements and fragments found in the complex, it is believed that the original temple complex may be earlier than 11th century AD.

The height of the temple is around 60-feet and consists of Viman, Jagmohan, Nata Mandap and Bhoga Mandap. The Nata

Mandap and Bhoga Mandap are flat roofed and later additions. The Viman is of Rekha style and Jagmohan is Pidha style. As per archeologists, the temple is Pancharatha in plan and Panchangavada in elevation.

Lord KAPILESWAR in the form of Shivling is the presiding deity and is placed at the centre of inner sanctum within a circular Yonipitha.

Uniqueness

A) As per the priest, the Shivling is having a hole in the middle known as "NASA" (ie. nose). It is believed that the Shivling breathes through this NASA. When a burning lamp is placed near the NASA, it is extinguished.

B) The Abhishek of the God is performed in a different style. The noodle point is tied up with a cloth / Dhoti. All the water exits are packed with wooden sheet and mud. The water is taken from the holy well and is poured over the Shivling till the water level rises above the Shivling.

The idols of Ganesh, Kartikeya and Parvati are found in the niches of the outer shrine walls.

The image of Gajalakshmi is in lalitasan and is seated over a lotus pedestal. She is having lotus in her both hands and two elephants are pouring water over the deity. Dwarpalas along with Ganga and Yamuna over their mount are found at the base of the doorjambs.

Exquisite carvings are found in different portions of the temple. The carvings of king and his aids obeying the orders of the king are artistic features of the temple.

The temple is having two entrances with sculptures of lions on both the sides. The outer entrance is pyramidal in shape.

The major shrines found in the complex are – Adi KAPILESWAR, Baidyanath temple, Ghanteswar temple, Gupteswar temple, Kalika Shiv temple, Laxmi Narayan temple, Siddheswar temple, Somavareswa temple, BHASKARESWAR temple, Chakreswari temple, Dula Devi temple, Jareswar temple, Dutiya KAPILESWAR temple, Dakshina Kali temple, Shaneswar temple, Baa-khia Mandap, Hazara Mandap, Sombara Mandap and Bada Kua etc.

There are many other sub-shrines / Shivlings with and without shrines in the temple complex.

The images of Durga, Surya with seven horses and Kali with Shiv on her feet and marble idols of Lord Ram and Sita, Laxman, Radha-Krishna and others adorn the complex

The interior walls of the Temple tank is decorated with beautiful carvings and deities.

During Shivratri, the devotees offer prayers at the holy Manikarnika pond and take dip in it. It is believed that taking a dip in the pool during Mahashivratri cleanness the soul.

Many inscription in praise of Gajapati king Kapilendra Dev are found in the temple complex.

Some researchers also link Kapileswar village with Kapilvastu, birth place of Lord Buddha. However, there is no authenticity and further research required in the matter.

The temple complex is at the end of Kapileswar Road at KAPILESWAR village.

LINGARAJ AND KAPILESWAR – HANDI BHANGA YATRA

This is a connecting ritual between Lingaraj temple and Kapileswar temple.

Handi Bhanga ritual of Lord Lingaraj is observed on the first Saturday after Shivratri. During this Yatra the portable image of Lord Lingaraj visits to Kapileswar temple in a procession to invite Lord Kapileswar. He is taken in a palanquin along with Goddess Parvati. This is an annual ritual.

Lord Lingaraj invites Kapileswar to attend his Chandan Yatra and Sital SASTHI. It is also believed that Lord Lingaraj visits Kapileswar to get rid of the effects of Shani planet (ie. Saturn).

The devotees arrange a feast with new earthen pots in the Kapileswar temple premises. Lord Lingaraj returns after being worshipped there and after the feast is over. Once the feast concludes and Lord Lingaraj leaves the premises, all the earthen pots are broken. On the way back, Lord Lingaraj visits Aisaneswar temple.

Similarly Lord Kapileswar visits Lingaraj temple during Chandan Yatra and Sital SASTHI. Lord Kapileswar has a bigger role in the Yatra.

A series of rituals are observed at the Lingaraj and Kapileswar temple on these occasions.

The khuntia sevayats are from the Lingaraj temple and Malia sevayats are from the Kapileswar temple. During this period, the khuntia sevayats of Lingaraj temple offer their services to Lord Lingaraj at Kapileswar Temple premises and the same services are offered by the Malia Sevayats at the Lingaraj temple. This is a centuries – old ritual.

PEETHAS / PITHAS IN BHUBANESWAR – OLD TOWN/ EKAMRA KSETRA AREA

Large number of peethas are found in Bhubaneswar, which are concentrated mostly in the old town area (ie. EKAMRA KSHETRA). They are as under:

1. *Astamurti:* They are – Ganesh, Devi, Kartikeya (Skanda), Brushava (bull) Ganachakra, Sabitri, Kalpabrukshya and God (Deva – mainly Lingaraj). They are present mostly in the Lingaraj temple complex.
2. *Asta Tirtha:* These are holy ponds and they are – Bindusagar, Papanashini, Ganga-Yamuna, Kotitirtha, Brahmeswar, Megheswar, Albukeswar and RAMESWAR.
3. *Asta Sambhu*: They are – Rudreswar, Ishaneswar, Vaidyanatha, Murteswar, Sukhameswar, Uttameswar, Uttareswar and Kadareswar.
4. Asta Chandi: These are the most popular Tantric Goddesses of Bhubaneswar. They are situated mostly around Bindusagar in different directions. They are – Sukapola (Kapali Devi), Ramayani (west), Mohini and Bindhyabasini (South), Uttarayani (north), Dwarbasini and Ambika (east). Siva Gauri is situated in Sidhasram.

These peetha s can be developed like Astavinayaka temples near Pune.

IMPORTANCE OF EKAMRA KSHETRA

Mythology

As per Astadasa Purana, Lord Brahma had described the importance of EKAMRA KSHETRA to Godess Parvati.

The Purusottama Khanda of Skanda Purana and Antya-Khanda of Chitanya Bhagabat describes that, it was the residence of Lord Shiv.

Sage Jaimini had described the glories of Bhubaneshwar as under: "Lord Shiv had built the beautiful city of Kashi on the bank of the Ganges to please Sati and to counteract king Daksha, who was thinking him (Lord Shiv) as pauper (ie. As Lord Shiv was aloof from the affairs of the material world). Lord Shiv and Goddess Sati had remained in Kashi for many years.

During Dwapar – era, Lord Krishna was challenged by king Pundraka and was killed. As king of Kashi was in the side of Pundraka, he was also killed and his head was thrown in to Kashi.

However, Sudakshina, son of Kashi king performed severe penance to please Lord Shiv to get the power to destroy Lord Krishna. As advised by Lord Shiv, Sudakshina performed black ritualistic ceremony and a fierce demon emerged from the fire. He ordered the demon and his companions to go to Dwarka and to kill Lord Krishna. Lord Shiv had followed them with his Pashupata weapon. Lord Krishna came to know that, the demon was the creation of Lord Shiv. He invoked and ordered Sudarshan to kill the demon and his supporters. Accordingly the demon, his companions and Sudakshina was killed. Sudarshan wheel had also devastated the city of Kashi. However, Lord Shiv was angry and he released the Pashupata Weapon to counter it. As the Lord Shiv's weapon was no match for Sudarshan Wheel, it retreated back. Lord Shiv had also fled the battle field and took shelter in the lotus feet of Lord Krishna and prayed for forgiveness. Lord Krishna forgave Lord Shiv and recalled the Sudarshan wheel.

Lord Shiv requested Lord Krishna to provide him shelter, as his residence at Kashi was destroyed.

Accordingly, Lord Krishna had offered EKAMRAVANA to Lord Shiv and had also described it's importance as under:

"This place is known as EKAMRA VANA". In this idyllic surrounding, he would appear and would be worshipped. This place was in every way as captivating as Varanashi and spiritually elevated. Few people knew about it's importance.

As per Lord Krishna, this EKAMRA VANA was dear to him which was near the Nilachala KSHETRA, which is the abode of Lord Jagannath. It had the most pleasing and peaceful atmosphere. The place was intact even during the cosmic annihilation. The place EKAMRA VANA was north of Jagannath, Puri. As per Lord Krishna, EKAMRA VANA was charming and peaceful and here, one can attain liberation and bliss. This place would be famous as Bhubaneshwar. Lord Krishna had advised Lord Shiv to stay here all the time and to protect his Dharma.

This is how Lord Shiv came to reside in Bhubaneshwar.

(Source – TIRTHA YATRA)

As per another hearsay, Lord Brahma ordered Vishwakarma to make 1.25 lakh temples for all Gods and Goddesses in one day and one night to make it Shree KSHETRA. He completed temples for all, but could not make one Lokanath temple, which is in Puri. Lord Jagannath stayed here for 3-days and went back angrily. Since this KSHETRA could not be kept empty, Lord Shiv came from inside the earth "ie. Bhoo se Eshwar" which was known as Bhubaneshwar.

Similarly, with the request of many saints, Maharishi Vyas (ie. the most knowledgeable and great Hindu Sage) had described in details about the importance of EKAMRA VANA/EKAMRA KSHETRA, the abode of Lord Krutibasa Shiva as under: "During ancient period, this was a dense forest area of a huge mango tree whose branches had spread across all the four sides, for around one kosha / krosha (ie. around 3-kms). Accordingly, this KSHETRA was popularly known as EKAMRA KSHETRA (ie. the word "EKAMRA" means "a mango tree").

After self-immolation and consequent death of Goddess Sati, Lord Shiv was inconsolable. He came to this forest area and commenced his tapasya / meditation under the huge mango tree. As Lord Shiv had meditated here and the deity of the temple was originally under the mango tree, the site was known as EKAMRA KSHETRA.

During the then period, this KSHETRA was spread over an area of one Yojana, i.e., four Koshas (ie.around 12-kms).

As per many other legends, "In this Shiva KSHETRA, a total number of one linga less than one crore lingas and 8 (eight) holy places (tirthas) are present. This place is as holy as Varanashi (ie. another important Shiva KSHETRA).

Here, the Sanatan Linga (ie. Lord Krutibasa Shiva) himself is present who is also known as Lord Tribhuvaneswar and Lord Lingaraj. This is a very powerful LInga and all the twelve famous and powerful lingas of Hindu religion are part of Lord Tribhuvaneswar.

Lord Lingaraj which is a Brahma-linga is one of the most ancient Brahma-lingas. The colour of Lord Lingaraj is white in the base, green in the middle and maroon in the top. He resides on the top of "Swarnakutagiri" which is towards north of Ananta – Basudev temple. Lord Krutibasa Shiv is the king and Ananta Basudev is the area commander.

Further, as per legend, Lord Shiv had revealed to Goddess Parvati that he favoured Bhubaneshwar more than Varanashi. Hearing this, Goddess Parvati embarked on a journey to know the details about Bhubaneshwar. She transformed herself in to a cowherd woman and roamed in different parts to explore the place. However, two demons (ie. Kritti and Vasa) came in to her way and wanted to marry her. Despite continuous refusal, they kept on following her. Goddess requested them to carry her upon their shoulders. When they carried her, they were crushed to death. The place where the demons were crushed is known as Devi Padahara pond. Lord Shiv created Bindu Sagar lake to quench her thirst. Lord Shiv took her abode at this place and was known as Krittivasa / Lingaraj.

As per Ekamra Purana (13th century Sanskrit treaties), Bhubaneshwar was famous as Ekamra KSHETRA. It was one of the favourite place of Lord Shiv, where he liked to spend time under a huge mango tree.

EKAMRA Purana also describes that, the deity which was under a mango tree was not seen as lingam in Satya and Treta era and it revealed itself as lingam in Dwapar era and Kali era (ie. era of darkness).

It is also said that Lord Krutibasa Shiva dug the Bindu Sarovar /Bindu Sagara himself, in the presence of all Gods(devatas) and Rishis /Sages.

He filled the entire huge pond/Sagar with water collected form all holy(pious) places, rivers, oceans etc. of the Universe.This huge pond/Sagar is known as Bindu Sarovar /Bindu Sagar, as water drops from all holy places(tirthas) are present in it.

A person gets all his desires fulfilled, if he/she takes bath in this pond on the fourteenth day of every month and performs puja at Lord Anantabasudeva and Godess Devipadahara before offering his obeisance to Lord Lingaraj.

B) Astayatans Of Ekamra Kshetra

EKAMRA KSHETRA is based on Astayatan concept of town planning. This is an ancient Hindu system, where the shrines are located at the four cardinal points and four intermediate points of cosmos. Eight sectoral regions (ASTAYATANS) which emerge out of such system is guarded by their respective Gods.

As per legend, the importance of "Astayatan" which is headed by "Astamurtis" was also described by Maharshi Vyasadev to many Rishis / sages. It is said that Lord Tribhubaneswar is Astamurtidhar and a person achieves immortality if he visits the entire area and pray/pay obeisance to all eight main Shivlings. The Astayatan of EKAMRA KSHETRA are as under:

First(Prathama) Ayatan:

Out of 8(eight) Astaayatans, Bindu Sarovar /Bindu Sagar is described as Pratahama Ayatan which is a very holy pond created by Lord Krutibasa Shiva himself. It is surrounded by important Gods/Goddesses like – Lord Ananta Basudeva, Godess Devipadahara, Lord Tirtheswara and Astamurti Mahadeva.

Second (Dwitiya) Ayatan:

In second/dwitiya Ayatan, Papanasini Kunda(Pond) is the main religious place. It fulfils all the desires of a person, if he/she takes bath and prays before both Lord Maitreswar and Lord Baruneswar. Further, a person who takes bath in the Papanasini pond becomes sin-free (Papamukta).

Towards the south side of the pond, a Shivling named Lord Isaneswar and on the south-west side of the Pond, a Shivling named Lord Jameswar are present. It is said that, if a person worships Lord Jameswar after taking bath in the Papanasini Pond, he would be freed from taking rebirth.

Third (Trutiya) Ayatan:

In Third(Trutiya) Ayatan, there are two pious holy places named Ganga-jamuna ponds.If a person, after taking bath in both the ponds, worships the nearby Lord Gangeswar shivlinga with devotion, he /she would get results of hundreds of Yagnas (sacrifices).

The Third Ayatan also includes another holy place/pond named Devipadahara which is an important religious pond. As per

Shaivatora Purana, it is the most religious pond in the entire Universe and is the abode of Godess Parvati.

Laxmiswar Shiv temple is in the south-east corner of this pond. The Shivling named as Lord Laxmiswar was placed/ worshipped by Lord Vishnu (Basudeva) with Kamallochana Goddess Laxmi. If a person worships Lord Laxmiswar after taking bath in Devipadahara pond, he /she would achieve good luck, strength and wealth.

Fourth (Chatrutha) Ayatan:

In the Fourth (Chaturtha) Ayatan, Lord Kotiswar of Kotitirtha temple is very affectionate, reliever of all sins of the worshipper and giver of beneficial results of Koti (ie. one crore) Yagnas (sacrifices). This is one of the holiest Ayatans among the Astaayatans.

If a person dips/takes bath in the Kotitirtha pond and worships Lord Kotiswar Mahadev, he/she would be relieved of all his/her sins committed in life.

Similarly, if a person after taking bath in the Bindu Sagar/Bindu Sarovar tank, worships Lord SwarnaTaleswar Shiv stationed at the north-west corner of Kotitirtha, he /she would also be relieved of all sins.

In the north-east direction of Lord Tribhubaneswar/Lord Lingaraj temple (ie. after about 250 meters), *Lord Sidheswar Shivling* is present in the *Sidheswar temple*. It is said that Lord Vishnu after worshipping Lord Sidheswar, requested Lord Tribhubaneswar/Lord Lingaraj to reside in this Sidheswar Linga only if he is satisfied with his worship. This was duly accepted by Lord Tribhubaneswar/Lord Lingaraja. Lord Sidheswar became famous in the Universe. This Sidha LInga is a unified linga of both Vishnu and Shiva.

Whoever prays at this Sidheswar Shivling with utmost devotion, he would get huge wealth and all his/her desires would be fulfilled by Lord Sidheswar (ie. another form of Lord Lingaraj). In the past the sages/rishis were engaged in meditation and prayers to Lord Sidheswara, in the nearby Siddhashram.

Lord Mukteswar, who is the reliever of all sins and giver of nirvana (salvation) is present here. A person, who after taking bath in the pond attached with the Mukteswar temple, worships Lord Mukteswar, he / she would be relieved of the human sufferings and would attain nirvana. Even barren woman may get children.

Further to the south of Lord Sidheswar temple, there is temple of Lord Kedareswar and Godess Gouridevi along with a pond named as "Gouri Kunda", which is famous for its mineral rich water all over the world.

Lord Kedareswar is a very powerful shiva linga and is also known as "Daskhina murti". It is a "Swayambhu" Shivling i.e. the Shivling is not created by anybody. It is believed that, the shiva linga of Lord Kedareswar/Daskhina murti was established by Himalaya, the mountain king.

Lord Kedareswar blesses all and fulfils all their desires, if one prays him with pure devotion (ie. Like Lord Tribhubaneswar/Lord Lingaraj).

Goddess Gouri is another image of Goddess Parvati and wife of Lord Tribhubaneswar/Lord Lingaraj. Their marriage celebration is held every year with festivities on the day of Shitalasasthi in Ekamra ksetra.

To the west of Sidheswar temple, there is a temple with a Shivling known as "Daityaswar temple". It is said that the Demon king Hiranyakashyup used to worship this Shivling regularly and accordingly this Shivling is known as Lord Daityaswar. One would get rid of all types of problems, if one worships Lord Daityaswar.

To the east of Sidheswar temple, there is a temple which was constructed by Viswakarma. The Shivalinga established in this temple was known as Indreswar, as this Shivling was worshipped by Lord Indra.

With passage of time, this Shivling is no more inside the temple and this temple is now known as "Rajarani Temple".

5. Fifth(Panchama) Ayatan

In this Pancham Ayatan, which is towards the north-east direction of Lord Tribhubaneswar/Lord Lingaraj temple (ie. after about 350 meters), there is presence of Brahma kund and Brahmeswar linga.This Brahmeswar linga was originated from the Brahma Yangna.

The Brahmeswar temple is situated near the Gandhabati river and any person after taking bath in Gandhabati river, if prays to Lord Brahmeswar, he/she would be relieved of all sins committed by him/her during his/her lifetime.

6. Sixth(Sastha) Ayatan

In Sixth Ayatan, there is a temple known as Megheswar temple along with a pond named as "Megha Kund", which is about 400 meters away from the "Kalpa Tree", inside the Lord Tribhubaneswar/Lord Lingaraj temple.

Further towards western side of Megheswar temple, there is a Shivling known as "Lord Bhaskareswar" as this Shivling used to be worshipped by Sun God/Suryadev/Bhaskardev. Towards west side of Bhaskareswar temple, there is another Shivling known as "Kapalmochana". The worshipper attains moksha/nirvana with the darshan of this Shivling..

7. Seventh (Saptam) Ayatan

In Seventh Ayatan, there is a temple known as Alabukeswar temple along with Abulatirtha. If a person, after taking bath in this Abulatirtha, worships Lord Alabukeswar, he /she would go to Nandiloka. It is said that a poor brahmin priest, known as Indrasakha, worshipped Lord Tribhubaneswar/ Lord Lingaraj and prayed for transfer of his beggar's bowl into a pond which would have pure water and would always be beneficial to all. Accordingly this pond is known as "Abulatirtha".

To the northern side of Bindu Sarobar/Bindu Sagar, there is presence of Lord Uttareswar in the Uttareswar temple and this is known as "Maha Samsan pitha/cremation ground". Goddess Uttareswari Devi is also present here.This pitha is very pious and known as reliever of all sins.There is another shivling named as Lord Bhimeswar who takes away all fears from any person.

8. Eighth (Astam) Ayatan

Towards northward direction of Lord Tribhubaneswar/Lord Lingaraj temple (ie. after about 300 meters) and towards southwest direction of Bindu Sarovar, a Shivling famously known as "Rameswar Linga" is present. It was worshipped by Lord Ram during his exile. This is described in the Ekamra Purana.

Lord Ram after constructing a temple near the Ashoka Jhara, requested Lord Lingaraj to oblige him by staying with him in this temple in the form of a Linga known as Rameswar Linga. This temple is known as Rameswar Temple.In this temple, there is presence of other Lingas, such as Siteswar, Hanumantheswar, Labeswar, Bharateswar, Lakshmaneswar and Satrugneswar etc.

Towards south of the Rameswar Temple, there is another temple known as "Gosahareswar temple". From the pond inside this temple, thousands of Cows (kept by Goddess Parvati), used to offer milk to Lord Tribhubaneswar/Lord Lingaraj. In Shivotara Purana, it is mentioned that the temple of Lord Isaneswara is situated at the South-west corner of Lord Gosagareswar.

Towards the South-east direction of Lord Krutibas Lingaraj (ie. after around 700-feet away), a Swayambhu ling named as Lord Sukhmeswar is present in the **"Sukhmeswar temple".** As per legend, if a person offers "Pindadan" / oblation on the southern side of Lord Sukhmeswar, one would get better results from the "Pindadan" than at Gaya and NaviGaya / Biraja ksetra etc.

LAKULISHA SCULPTURE – IN THE TEMPLES OF BHUBANESHWAR / EKAMRA KSHETRA

Lakulisha is a Shaivite teacher and founder of Pashupata sect of Shaivism who resembles Gautam Buddha.

He was a Brahmin from Kayavarohan near Vadodara. The path of the ascetics of Pashupata cult was tough, a path of ruining their ego and annihilating the physical self for nourishing the spiritual self.

As per Vayu Purana and Linga Purana, Lord Shiv revealed that he would make an appearance on earth during the age of Vishnu's incarnations as Vasudeva (Krishna). Lord Shiv indicated that he would enter the dead body of a Brahmin and incarnate himself as Lakulin (ie. Nakulin or Lakulisha, lakula meaning Club). Lakulisha means club bearing deity. He is believed as the 28th incarnation of Lord Shiv.

As per blogger Jitu Mishra, he is seen in the temples of Bhubaneshwar as seated cross-legged in Dharma – chakra – pravartana mudra with a lakuta (stick) held between one arm. He is shown single or with his four disciples-karushya, Garga, Mitra and Kaushik.

The images of Lakulisha is found in the temples of – Parshurameswar, Vaital, Sisireswar, Rajarani, Mukteswar and in the Odisha state museum.

It is opined that this cult reached EKAMRA KSHETRA as it used to attract the followers and teachers of the Pashupata cult for a long time.

As per researchers, the early images of Lakulisha closely resembles Buddha. As Kalinga was a major Buddhist center in the past, hence the temples and sculptures were influenced by Buddhist art and culture.

Similarly the practice of erecting a Stupa enshrining the relics of a dead may have influenced the Pashupatas to erect lingams for their dead teachers. These type of miniature temples with lingams are found in Bharati Matha / other MATHAS.

As per Prof. K C Panigrahi, the temples of Parshurameswar, Kapileswar and MITRESWAR etc are named after the famous teachers of Pashupata cult of Saivasim.

Ekamra Kshetra – As Heritage City –Visa-A-Vis-Similar Important Sites Of The Country/ World

Several Hindu temples and complexes have found their place in the World Heritage List. But, none of them have been nominated as a complete Hindu city, promulgating the ancient principles in city planning and construction as per Vastu Shastra.

Further, Ekamra Kshetra is a living site with several intangible traditions still in place. However, most of the other sites which are included in the list are mostly archaeological parks and groups of monuments.

Ekamra Kshetra can be compared to the following World Heritage sites:

Angkor Wat – Cambodia

It is a much larger site in comparison. But Angkor Wat is an archaeological park with few components of living heritage. Ekamra Kshetra is a living city with a larger historic timeline with continuous traditions and a complete timeline of Kalinga architectural developments.

GROUP OF MONUMENTS-AT HAMPI (KARNATAK) It was the capital city of the Vijayanagara rulers and was established during their brief rule from 14th Century CE – 16th Century AD. Hampi is predominantly an archaeological site that does depict the town planning principles of a Hindu Kingdom but does not follow the Mandala concept in its town planning. Again the strength of Ekamra Kshetra lies in it being a living heritage site with an almost untouched original city structure.

Group of Monuments-Pattadakal (Karnatak) And World Heritage Site Of The Great Living Chola Temples (Of South India-Tamil Nadu)

These are protected archaeological sites with exceptional temple architecture that belong to other eras and have different architectural style and constructions. However, the Kalinga architecture manifested at Ekamra Kshetra is unparalleled.

On a national level, Ekamra Kshetra is comparable to the holy city of Varanasi, Uttar Pradesh.

In EKAMRA KSHETRA, one will find all the three broad orders of Kalinga Architecture, ie. Rekha, Pidha and Khakkhara. Even Hypaethral temple, which rare in the country, ie. circular temple in ground plan without the roof, is found in the city (ie. Sixty four Yogini temple of Hirapur).

Further, EKAMRA KSHETRA can be compared with the pagodas of Bagan in Myanmar.

This temple city is much more when explored.

Ekamra Plan

Modern pathways with ample space around the medieval architecture of Lingaraj Temple has made it attractive. Under "Ekamra plan" steps are taken for reviving the heritage and cultural value of the "Temple City" through an integrated approach. The surroundings of Lingaraj temple have been cleared from the encroachment to create space. Fresh routes, parking, canopy for devotees to enter the shrine have been put in place.

This plan is to create a spiritual and ecological ambience in and around Lingaraj temple. There will be redevelopment plan in the peripheral area of the temple, which is known as "Ekamra Kshetra". There would be Barrier free access between the temple and Bindusagar lake.

Through this heritage redevelopment plan the attraction of Bhubaneswar, the proposed UNESCO heritage site would be enhanced further.

OTHER TEMPLES OF EKAMRA KSHETRA

Although some of the major and representative temples have been described as above for the visitors, however EKAMRA KSHETRA is unique. This is not restricted to some large temples/ temple-complex. There are large number temples which are spread over the EKAMRA KSHETRA area. Some of them are preserved and some of them are in dilapidated conditions/ encroached.

Some of the important temples are described as per Annexure A of this chapter, for further exploration. All these temples contain the carvings of the artisans and heritage of the city is clearly visible in these temples.

As opined by many visitors, "These temples are not only places of worship, showcase of art, culture and thoughts but also these are like thick books which carry many historical incidents, some written, some heard and while some were never disclosed".

DAILY RITUALS AT LINGARAJ TEMPLE

The daily rituals of Lord Lingaraj starts early in the morning and continues till late evening. The temple opens around 5.30 AM to 6-aM.

Everyday, Lord Lingaraj is offered Bhoga (offerings) eight times, which includes five avakasas and three Dhupas. These are – 1) Bala Dhupa / Vala Ballava, 2) Sakala Dhupa, 3) Chatra bhoga (Bhoga Mandap-dhupa), 4) Virakishore Ballava, 5) Madhyahna Dhupa (Dwiprahar Dhupa), 6) Teraphita, 7) Sandhya Dhupa, 8) Bada Singhar.

In the morning the temple is opened by Pharaka (ie. the person having the key) in the presence of Palia Badu (ie. Sevayat) and he sprinkles the water on all the Shivlings inside the temple.

PAHUDA BHANGA

After opening of the inner sanctum, Mangal Arati (ie. auspices waving of light) is performed by a Sevayat and lord wakes up from the sleep. This is known as Pahuda Bhanga.

SAHANA MELA

Thereafter, the flowers and Bilwa leaves are removed from the linga which were placed in the previous night by the Palia Badu and washing of teeth is performed with a twig, Lord is bathed and offered flowers and Bilwa / Tulshi leaves. Lord becomes ready for public darshan. This viewing of Lord is known as Sahana Mela and generally continued from 7.30 AM to 12- noon. However, on special occasions it remains open for a longer period.

MAHASNANA

MAHASNANA takes place after Sahana Mela, which is a purificatory ceremony. The Palia Badu baths the deity and washes the linga pitha with water. For purification, Panchamruta (ie. mixture of – milk, honey, curd, butter/ ghee and jaggery) is poured on the linga.

The linga is dressed and decorated with ornaments, flowers and leaves etc. The hemlock flowers which are generally offered in other Shiv temples, are not offered here. Bela / Bilwa leaves and Tulsi are used in daily worship. MAHASNANA is performed after closure of the doors.

BALA DHUPA / BALA BALLAVA

This is the first food offering to the Lord which consists of items like – Kora Khai and curd etc. which is performed by Panti Badu (ie. Brahmin Sevayat). After this offering is over, Palia Badu cleans the sanctum. Worship of Sun God is performed in the south-east corner of the inner sanctum in the minor shrine and also Dwarpala puja is performed. During this period, half of a ripe plantain is offered to Sun God and other half is offered to dwarpalas.

SAKALA DHUPA

This important offering/ morning meal is offered to Lord in the inner sanctum. It consists of – Rice, khechudi, many leafy vegetables, pitha (cake) and other items. This Dhupa is performed with the co-operation of many sevayats as under:

- The panti Badu decorates the floor with powdered rice.
- Bhitara khuntia stands as the guard at the gate.
- Hadapa Nayak provides water and arecanut (ie. Gua – in Odiya).
- Garabadu provides the Woden seat, water and flowers.
- Patric provides the required 16- upacharas at the disposal of the Panda Brahmin, who conducts actual offering.

- During offering ceremony various musical instruments like – bells, trumpets and other instruments are played by the sevakas.
- Two sevakas hold white umbrella and black umbrella in honour of the deity near the sanctum door.

ARATI CEREMONY

Arati ceremony/ Alati ceremony (ie. waving of light) is performed after Sakala Dhup is over. Camphor, ghee / butter and rice paste fixed with lifted sticks are used in the Arati which is conducted in a rhythmic motion in front of the deity. Sometimes, seven lighted wicks are used in the Arati.

CHATRA BHOGA

This is offered at the Bhoga Mandap. This offering/ Bhoga includes large quantity of food items of Rice, dal, curry and sweet dishes etc., as it is meant for sale among the devotees. The sanctum is purified after this Bhoga is over and the devotees can visit the Lord / sanctum is opened for public.

VIRAKISHORE BALLAV DHUPA

This Bhoga is offered before mid-day meal. The food consists of mainly sweets like Kakara and Tripuri etc. At the time of offering, the Sevayats like – Panda, patri, Gara Badu and other Brahmins should be present.

MID-DAY MEAL (DWIPAHARA DHUPA)

This is offered in earthen pots to the deity. This practice is continuing since 13th century. The inscriptions of Anangabhima Deva-lll refers offering of cooked food in earthen pots (ie. Atika – in Odiya) to the deity. Another inscription also refers the preparation of Nirmalya from Tandula (ie. rice).

There were also endowment of land for the food offering to the deity. The cooked food like – rice, dal, vegetables and other items are prepared in the kitchen complex of the temple. After offering to the Lord, a portion of the offering/ Bhoga is offered to Goddess Parvati in her temple.

MAHASNANA takes place after mid-day meal, the deity takes rest (ie. Pahada) and door is closed to the public.

Teraphala Offering

TERAPHALA offering which consists of mostly different types of cakes are given to Lord and the temple is closed during the period. Thereafter temple is opened for devotees.

Sandhya Arati

This is performed around 6 to 7-pM. During the period the temple door is opened for the evening rituals and public view of the Arati.

Sandhya Dhupa

This is a light meal offering to Lord and is conducted around 8.30 PM. Items like – laddu, Khaja, Arisha pitha and Kharjura etc are offered to Lord during Sandhya Dhupa. After this is over, there is public darshan for a short period.

Badasinghara Ceremony

This is performed before midnight. The offerings of the Badasinghara are items like – Dahi-pakhal, bhaja, khata and some sweet dishes.

The metal image of Panchavakra Mahadev (ie. Bronze image of Mahadev having five faces and Goddess Parvati in his lap) is worshipped and flowers are offered in his honour (ie. Pushpanjali), after which a light food offering is made.

A wooden planquain is laid in the room, incense is lighted, drinking water is served and prepared betel is placed.

Panchavakra Mahadev comes to the palanquin and returns to his own abode after the Arati is performed.

This is the final ceremony and the temple door is closed thereafter.

All the rituals of Lord Lingaraj are in the pattern of Jagannath temple, Puri.

Although the temple is open from morning to evening, however there is intermittent closure in between during offerings (ie. Bhoga) / during rest of the deity.

Four different categories of servitors (ie. Brahman Nijog, Pujapanda Nijog, Badu Nijog and Suara Nijog) are engaged for performing various rituals of Lingaraj temple. They are both from Brahmin and Non-Brahmin communities.

The Badus are non-Brahmin sevayats. They undergo three distinct rites – ie. ear-piercing, marriage and God-touching. They elect their office bearers during Chandan Yatra.

Out of 5-practices of the Badus (ie. Pochha, Pahada, Khataseja, paliabadu and Pharaka), nowadays, only Paliabadu and Pharaka practices are followed. The ablution and dressing of image are also carried by them including dressing of the images of Siddha Ganesh and Gopaluni.

They are assigned their duties by Lingaraj Trust Board and Lingaraj Temple administration. They are enjoying landed properties of Lord.

Chaitanya Mahaprabhu And Lingaraj Temple

Chaitanya Mahaprabhu along with some of his followers had visited Lingaraj temple to worship the Lord. They had taken bath in the Bindusagar lake and after worshiping the lakeside Swayambhu Shivling, had gone to the temple. As per hearsay, after the Darshana of Lord Lingaraj, Chaitanya Mahaprabhu started dancing ecstatically with all the devotees and had spent the whole night there. During dancing before the Lord, he was clapping his hands with chanting the words, "Shiva Rama Govinda".

MAJOR FESTIVALS OF LORD KRUTIBASA/LORD TRIBHUBANESWAR/LORD LINGARAJ OF EKAMRA KSHETRA

In the Lingaraj temple 14-principal Yatras and 12-minor Yatras are celebrated in a year. The year begins from the first day of the new-moon in the month of Margashir (ie. November-December) and festivals are usually calculated from that day.

The festivals which are observed in honour of Lord Lingaraj are known as Yatras. Since the Deity of Lingaraj is solid block of stone and is Swayambhu, it cannot move. It is represented by portable image (ie. Chalanti Pratima).

In Lingaraj temple there are portable images of – Chandrasekhar, Gopalini, Durga, Dolagovinnda, Panchabaktra and Basudev. They are also worshipped in a small temple known as Dakshina Ghar. On some festival days, these portable images, which are of bronze, visit different temples / places as representative of the main God / Goddess. Before departure from the temple / going out, the portable image is taken to the transverse beam by the respective priests. Thereafter, they are taken in a decorated Viman. Before their departure, a coconut is broken in front of Lord Ganesh for smooth journey and performance of the festival. The hereditary officials accompany the deity.

The 14-principal festivals at Lingaraj temple are as under:

1. Shivaratri

This is the main and the most popular festivals of the Lord Lingaraj temple.The Celebrations are held throughout the night and celebrated on the 14th day of the dark fortnight in the month of Phalgun (Feb-March).

It is known as Kala Ratri as per Tantrik worship and it is thought to be consecrated night.

On this day, Large number of devotees visit the temple. They spent the entire day in fasting. Bel leaves are offered to the Lord along with water / milk. They break their fast only after watching the Mahadipa(Divine light) which is lit on the top of the temple. As per belief, worship of Lord Shiv on this day would remove all evils.

2. Ashok Ratha Yatra / Ashokastami / Rukuna Rathayatra

This is one of the major celebration at Lingaraj temple, like Shivratri. It is performed on the 8th day of the bright fortnight of Chaitra Month. This celebration is described in EKAMRA Purana in two sections. The portable deity of Lingaraj (ie. Chandrasekhar) along with Rukmini Devi and Lord Basudev goes to RAMESWAR temple (ie. Maushima temple) in a chariot. The height of the chariot is 35-feet and is pulled by the devotees enthusiastically. Unlike other Rath Yatras / Raths, this chariot never turns back, which is unique. During return journey, devotees push the chariot from behind, hence the proverb, "RUKUNA RATHA UNALEUTA". It is also known as "Papa vinashini yatra" which means, the festival that kills all sins.

The Chariot / Rukuna Ratha

The chariot of the Lord Tribbhubaneswar/Lord Lingaraj is known as RUKUNA Ratha. As per legend, Demon Tripurasura had created havoc on earth. The Gods had constructed a special chariot known as RUKUNA Rath and gave it to Lord Shiv to use the same to kill the demon Tripurasur.

He was accompanied by Goddess Shakti (Rukmini/ RUKUNA). The details are found in Kapila Samhita and EKAMRA Chandrika etc.

Process involved in Construction of the Chariot

On the day of Basanta Panchami, the portable image of Lord Tribbhubaneswar/ Lord Lingaraj (ie. Chandrasekhar) is taken to Badatota in a procession to perform BANAJAGA YATRA for selection of wood for the chariot. Generally, the wood of Mango tree is used for construction of the chariot. The selected Mango tree is marked by a cut on it's trunk.

Thereafter, carpenters (Badheis) are invited by offering Agyana Mala and new clothes. The Bauri sevakas, who are honoured with new cloths, go to the forest before 8-days of Shivratri, cut the selected trees and bring the logs to the temple ceremonially. The wooden logs used for preparation of chariot are consecrated in the Sivatirtha Matha before use by the carpenters. The construction starts after the Shivratri celebrations.

After completion of the construction, the chariot is worshipped like Debadalana / Darpadalana Ratha of Subhadra. A Pratistha Mandap is constructed on the northern side and Kalashas (earthen pots filled with water) are placed on four doors of the Mandap and a Kunda is constructed to perform the Yagnya. These worship are completed on the day of SAPTAMI. After completion of the Yagnya, the side Gods / Goddesses like – Ganesh, kartik, Nandi, Mahakala, one eyed Rudra, Trimurti, Sreekantha and Shikhandi are installed in the chariot in respective places. On the same night (ie. 7th day of the bright fortnight), the chariot is decorated with Umbrella/ roof, Banner, flowers and garlands etc. The banner bears the insignia of Ardha chandra (ie. half moon).

It is a four wheeled chariot of disc- wheels. The two pairs of wooden horses in their riding postures are tied in front of the car.

On the morning of ASHOKASTAMI the four wheels are worshipped along with the four horses.

As per hearsay, the four horses represent 4-vedas. The horse representing Rig Veda is for moving the chariot with force of wind, the horse representing Yayur Veda will bestow the fruits of Bhakti, the horse representing Sam Veda would perform the duties of

Lingaraj and the horse representing Atharva Veda would punish the evil-doers.

Two sets of wooden stallions are tied before the chariot. The height is 35-feet, the diameter of the wheels are 9-feet, the diameter of the hub is 22- inches, the thickness of the wheel is around 10-inches and the separation between the two wheels is 10-feet.

The chariot is decorated with 4-horses, a divine throne, a golden Kalash, sixteen karamandalas, four gates, 21-chhayas and a flag adorned with trident.

The chariot is draped in Yellow, red, white and blue clothes.

Legends

Legend – 1

As per EKAMRA Purana, demon Ravan who was a Brahmin was killed by Lord Ram to rescue Mata Sita and he was afflicted by Brahma Dosha. With the advice of Saint Vashisth, he had worshipped Lord Tribhuvaneswar (Lord Lingaraj) at EKAMRA KSHETRA to get rid of the sin. He had also established 4-Shivlings in his name (RAMESWAR) and in the name of his brothers (ie. Bharateswar, Laksmaneswar and Satrughneswar). As per legend the RAMESWAR temple was constructed on ASHOKASTAMI day.

Legend-2

Mata Sita was confined in Ashok Van by demon king Ravana. During this period of consignment and on the day of ASHOKASTAMI, Mata Sita had offered some Ashoka flower to Lord Shiv with the prayer to unite her with Lord Ram. Hence, as per tradition and to get rid of all their miseries, Hindu wives observe this day by eating eight Ashoka buds with prayer to Lord.

Ashoka buds are also given in each other's mouth to strengthen the friendship between them.

Legend – 3

When Lord Ram was returning from Lanka after victory over Ravana, Mata Sita requested to worship Lord Shiv at the site of this temple. Seeing her devotion, Lord Ram built the lingam at this site, for the purpose of worship. As Lord Ram had built the lingam, it was known as RAMESWAR temple. It is said that, a day before, Lord Shiv comes to visit the temple.

Celebration

EKAMRA PURANA describes in details about the celebration of ASHOKASTAMI. The Khetrabasi Brahmins perform the rituals and the banner is fixed at the highest point of the chariot. This is known as "NETA UTSAV".

On the night of Neta Utsav, the barren ladies bath in the water of the Marichi Kunda of Mukteswar temple, to get children.

After the Neta Utsav, the portable images of Lord Tribbhubaneswar/Lord Lingaraj (ie. Chandrasekhar) RUKUNA (Gopaluni) and Basudev are brought to the chariot.

The four handed image of Chandrasekhar is having Abhaya Mudra in two arms, hatchet (parashu) in 3rd hand and deer in 4th hand.

The image of Vasudev (DOLA Govinda) is having 4-hands with conch, wheel, mace and lotus in his hands. The image of Goddess RUKUNA is having 4-hands with conch in one hand, wheel in another hand and Sula in two hands.

The representative of Lingaraj is Chandrasekhar, Bhubaneswari's representative is Jayadurga (RUKUNA) and Ananta Basudev's representative DOLA GOVINDA.

Gopaluni (jayadurga) is placed in the middle, Chandrasekhar on the south side and Basudev is on the left side of Gopaluni. The three deities represent Shaivism, Shakti cult and Vaishnavism.

The wooden image of Bull and Lord Brahma are in the chariot. The charioteer is Lord Brahma and chariot is pulled by large number of devotees.

The chariot is first pulled in the west direction up to Badhei Banka and from that point towards north to RAMESWAR temple, which is around 2-kms from Lingaraj temple.

The street on which the chariot is pulled is known as Ratha Danda. Earlier, the chariot was drawn by cane ropes and now it is drawn by coir ropes. Large number of devotees pull the chariot. The Dahukas standing on the left side of the Chariot shouts eloquently numerous vulgar couplets which are enjoyed by the crowd.

During procession, the chariot stops at Asur Kiari. The beetle and MUAN are offered to satisfy the demons for safe journey of the chariot.

Thereafter, the chariot stops at Debasabha Batabrukshya. At the end, the images are taken to RAMESWAR temple (ie. known as Maushima temple). The deities stay on the Rath on the first day. On the day of Ramanavami, they are kept at small apartment known as Gundicha Ghar. During these 4-day stay, the devotees perform the rituals. On the 5th day, they return in chariots to the Lingaraj temple.

Like Ratha Yatra of Puri, Goddess Parvati visits on the 3rd day to express her resentment, as Lord has not taken her in the journey.

She breaks (ie. priests represent Goddess Parvati) a bit of the chariot and returns to the temple.

The three Gods begin their return journey on the 5th day, known as Bahuda. While returning back, the chariot is pulled from the back side (posterior).

On the return journey, when the portable image of Lord Lingaraj tries to enter the temple, Goddess Parvati shuts the door and a mock quarrel takes place between two groups of priests (ie. one representing Lingaraj and the other representing Goddess Parvati). Goddess Parvati is placated and the Divinities enter the temple with the end of the celebration.

According to many researchers Rukmini's name, which is one of the names of Laxmi, is never mentioned anywhere relating to Lingaraj. People have changed their names. RUKUNA is not a Laxmi idol, it is the idol of jayadurga, which represents BHUBANESHWARI.

3. Chandan Yatra

This is celebrated for 22-days from Akshaya Tritiya. Everyday the portable image of Lord Lingaraj is taken in a procession to the Bindusagar lake for boating in a custom built decorated boat. The decorated boat is known as "Chapa" and is rowed down around the lake by the sevakas. The deities and the Sevakas are covered with sandalwood paste to protect from heat. The boat is moved in to the Mandap in the middle of the tank. The entire lake is lit up during the period. Dances, community feasts and merrymaking are arranged.

4. Sital Sasthi

This festival celebrates the marriage of Lord Shiv with Goddess Parvati and is observed on the 6th day of the bright fortnight of Jyestha Month.

During this festival, the representative idol of Lord Lingaraj (ie. Chandrasekhar) is carried in decorated palanquin to Kedar Gouri temple, which is the venue of divine wedding of Lord Shiv and Goddess Parvati. The wedding procession consists of members of Lingaraj temple. They chant different names of the Lord along with traditional music.

On reaching Kedar Gauri, the bride's family welcomes the groom's side and the ritual of an Odiya wedding are performed which continues beyond midnight.

One will be delighted to see how the divinity transforms in to mortals and to follow their ways.

5. Damanabhanjika / Damanaka Chaturdashi

It is observed on the 14th day of the bright fortnight of Chaitra Month. It is celebrated before KOTI TIRTHESWAR temple. On this day the portable image of Lord Lingaraj is taken in a procession and worshipped here.

6. Parasuramastami

It is observed on the 8th day of the bright fortnight of Ashadha Month. The portable image of Lord Lingaraj is taken in a procession to Parshurameswar temple for worship.

7. Sayana Chaturdashi

Lord Lingaraj goes to sleep on the 14th day of the bright fortnight of Ashadha.

Hence, this festival is called Sayana CHATURDASHI.

8. Yama Dwitiya

This is performed on the second day of the bright fortnight in the month of Kartika. The portable image of Lord Lingaraj (ie. Chandrasekhar) is taken to Bharati Matha to meet his sister Kamakshi and then to the YAMESWAR temple. He is worshipped according to Yama Mantra.

9. Sunia Divas

SUNIA is celebrated on the second day of the bright fortnight in the month of Bhadrab. It symbolises the beginning of traditional new year as per Odia tradition and some opine that this was the birthday of mythical king Indradyumna and also Vaman incarnation of Lord Vishnu. Therefore, kings and mostly the Gajapati kings celebrate this day as the beginning of the new year. All the Almanac s and palm leaf inscriptions of the horoscopes of the new born carry the name and the reigning year of Gajapati king of Puri.

SUNIA is celebrated in the temple since royal times.

On this day the the servitors of Lingaraj temple, peasant and other holders of temple land offers loyalty and honours to Lord Lingaraj.

10. Utthapana Chaturdashi

It is believed that Lord Shiv goes to bed on the 14th day of the bright fortnight of Ashadha Month and rises up from the bed on the 14th day of the bright fortnight of Kartika.

11. Prathamastami

This is observed on the 8th day of the dark fortnight of Margashira Month (November-december). The portable image of Lingaraj, ie. Chandrasekhar is taken out from the temple in a decorated palanquin in a procession to his maternal uncle's place at Kapila Matha.

His maternal uncle is Lord Baruneswar and aunt is Goddess Banadevi.

Lord is bathed at the Snana Mandap with the holy water of Papanashini tank. New garments are offered by his uncle Maitreswar Dev and his close relative Goddess Kapali Devi. Lord is offered Naivedya (ie. nourishment) / sweets and trailed by Bheta Arati. Lord returns to Lingaraj temple after offering farewell to his uncle and relatives.

12. Pravarana Sasthi / Pravarana Utsav

This is also known as Oghana SASTHI. With the onset of winter, Lord Lingaraj is offered with new pieces of worm clothing. The new clothing is purified on the previous day which is known as Adhivasa. It is offered to Lord on the 6th day of the bright fortnight of Margashir Month. This is used by the Lord as PRAVARANA till Shivratri.

13. Pushyabhiseka

This is observed on the full moon day in the month of Pousha and when it falls on the Pushya Nakshyatra. This day is believed as the birthday day of Lord Lingaraj and is auspicious. During this day the portable deity of the Lord is heavily decorated with flowers, ornaments and dress etc. The deity is taken out in a procession.

14. Handi-Bhanga Yatra

This is connecting ritual between Lingaraj temple and Kapileswar temple.

Handi Bhanga ritual of Lord Lingaraj is observed on the first Saturday after Shivratri. During this Yatra the portable image of Lord Lingaraj visits to Kapileswar temple in a procession to invite Lord Kapileswar. He is taken in a palanquin along with Goddess Parvati. This is an annual ritual.

Lord Lingaraj invites Kapileswar to attend his Chandan Yatra and Sital SASTHI.

It is also believed that Lord Lingaraj visits Kapileswar to get rid of the effects of Shani planet (ie. Saturn).

This is a connecting ritual between Lingaraj temple and Kapileswar temple.

MINOR FESTIVALS OF LORD KRUTIBASA/LORD TRIBHUBANESWAR/ LORD LINGARAJ UNDERTAKEN AT THE LINGARAJ TEMPLE.

Besides the above-mentioned 14-major festivals, there are 12(twelve) minor festivals, which are celebrated at the Lingaraj temple. These are: Dhanu Sankranti, Basanta Panchami, Bhaimi EKADASHI, Kapila Yatra, DOLA Yatra, Naba Patrika, Janmashtami, Ganesh Chaturthi, Durgastami, Sodashadina parva and Kumarostava. All these minor festivals are also performed with much festivities. Some of them are as under:

Pavitra Ropana

This is celebrated on the 14th day of the bright fortnight of Shravana.

Kartik Purnima

Once a year Lord Lingaraj is taken to the jalamandir, which is at the centre of Bindu Sagar lake.

Sailing paper boats /toy boats in Bindusagar and worshipping at Lingaraj temple are the major activities.

Ghrtakambala Ceremony

This is celebrated on Makar Sankranti. The portable image of Lord is taken to Makar Mandap.

Magha Saptami

This is celebrated on the 7th day of the bright fortnight in the month of Magha. This is the day when Sun God is worshipped and is treated as holy.

On this day the portable image of Lord Lingaraj is taken in a procession to the BHASKARESWAR temple.

Dola Purnima

During DOLA Purnima Lord Lingaraj arrives at Sivatirtha Matha to participate in the community launch.

In the month of Shravan, large number of devotees carry the water from the Mahanadi river with chanting of hymns on Lord Shiv and walk all the distance by foot to pour the same over the Shivling.

OTHER IMPORTANT TEMPLES OF THE CITY (OTHER THAN OLD BHUBANESWAR AREA / EKAMRA KSHETRA)

1. Sikharchandi

The temple is situated on a hillock, behind KIIT campus.

This hill is famous for the Goddess SIKHARCHANDI. There are three deities ie.CHANDI, GANESH AND TARINI on the hillock. As per the priest of the temple and hearsay, Lord Ram had performed Yagnya (ie. HAVAN / sacrificial fire) near the Goddess, to save Laxman, who was injured, although there is not any mythological evidence.

One can see, beautiful view of the city from the top.

The place is scenic with greenery all around. One can spend some quality time in the midst of nature.It is a nice place to view the sun rise and sunset in the background of the hill and adjoining areas of Bhubaneswar.

It is a popular spot among the locals. Driving through the lush green trees on all the sides of the road, to reach the temple will be a nice experience. For elderly, the steps are slightly steep with no railings. The hill which was a part of Chandaka forest had eroded with passage of time.

2. Chausath Yogini Temple – Hirapur – A Hidden Heritage

HIRAPUR is famous for Chausathi Jogini Mandir (ie. Temple of 64-yoginis).

Locally, it is known as Mahamaya temple. It was discovered by Sh Kedarnath Mohapatra of Odisha state museum, in – 1953 AD.

This ancient east facing temple of 9th century is surrounded by trees. It is situated in this small village within paddy fields. Gangua river is, nearby. It is dedicated to the esoteric cult of Tantra / occult practices during medieval times.

This is one of the four temples in India and is the second temple in Odisha which is an active temple. It is around 8-ft high and is built with blocks of sand stone.

As this circular temple is open, such type of architecture is known as "HYPAETHRAL" architecture. It is one of the smallest, out of 4-yogini temples in the country.

From the discussions with the priest, it was gathered that Goddess Durga had taken the form of 64-Demi Goddess/ attendants, in order to defeat the demon.

After the demon was defeated, these Demi-Goddesses requested Goddess Durga to commemorate them in the form of a temple. Accordingly, in such type of temples, they are worshipped.

This shrine is open to the sky, as the Yoginis fly outside the room in the night. The yogini centres were used as a place of Tantrik practices. It was an important Tantrik Pitha of the area, as they worship five elements (ie. Panchavut) in the open /without any roof.

During Basanti puja and Dusserha, they are worshipped in the form Goddess Durga.

Inner Portion Of Temple During Puja

It is believed that, the temple was built by queen Hira. The village is also named after her. She was the queen of Shanti – Kara ll.

As per historians, Odisha was ruled by Bhaumakara dynasty between 736- 950 AD. During this period, 6- queens ruled the region with full powers and rights.

The main idol is Goddess Kali who is standing on a human head. There is a Devi Mandap / central pillar with three yoginis, along with four chlorite statues of Bhairabhs (ie. A form Shiv).

It is a circular shrine. The opening is small and one has to bend, to enter inside. A pair of gatekeepers/dwarpals are carved on either side of the door- way. The shrine is having cavities and each cavity contains a statue of the Goddess. They are different forms of Shakti. These images are carved out of fine grained grey chlorite. The statues are less than 2-feet. In line with tantric tradition, skull sculptures are seen in the gear of most of the idols.

Each Jogini / yogini stands on a separate career (Vahan, ie. animals/birds) with different feelings like – sadness, pleasure, Joy etc. The images reflect the role of feminine power.

The yogini cult is a tribal and folk tradition. The Yoginis are portrayed in different shapes like – huntresses with bows and arrows, with faces of horse, rabbit, elephant, rat and decapitated male head, some are standing on a pair of wheels, some are playing drums etc. They are also seen in different postures.

These are adorned with jewellery and their hair style is a one – sided bun or with coronet of curls. Each Yogini exhibits a different hair style.

It is the only yogini temple that has female sculptures on the outer walls.There are nine sand stone statues of female figures, known as Katyayanis in the outer walls.

Many inscriptions are found in the temple, from which it can be inferred that, Yogini cult (ie. esoteric cult of Tantra) was prevalent even in 16th century.

With passage of time some statues are disfigured.

The yogini cult believes that worshiping 64-goddesses and the Goddess Bhairavi would give them super natural powers.

One will also find a lotus filled village pond outside the compound, a small temple near the gate and a Statue of Gopinath. The pond is known as "Mahamaya Gadia".

One should visit this unique temple and sit for sometime in the lawn, looking for the intricacy and architecture of the temple. One can purchase some paintings and artefacts for a memory from the nearby shops. It is a nice place for art lovers.

As per some travellers, when one visits the temple in a winter morning, the fog in the area gives an ethereal feeling. At sunset time the Yoginis appear red with the crimson rays of the Sun. As the temple is situated in a village setting, the tranquility of the temple in the midst of paddy fields has it's own charm.

HIRAPUR village is around 20-kms from Bhubaneswar. One can reach the spot through Bhubaneswar-puri road and has to take a left direction, near a board showing the direction to the temple.

MODERN TEMPLES OF BHUBANESHWAR

Apart from the ancient temples as described above, other important temples were built in recent times like – Ram Mandir and ISKCON Temple etc.

1. Ram Mandir

Ram Mandir of Bhubaneswar is a beautiful and famous temple located in the heart of the city. The temple is home to images of Lord Ram, Laxman and Mata Sita. There are other Gods /

Goddesses like – Lord Hanuman, Shiv and others in the complex. The Architectural beauty of the temple attracts many tourists.

It is one of the pilgrimage places of the state which is well maintained.

The high rise spires of the temple is visible from many parts of the city. The morning and evening Arati /Prayer would attract any visitor. Ram Navami is one of the famous festival of the temple.

The temple is around 1.5 kms from Bhubaneswar Railway station.

2. Iskon Temple

It is one of the beautiful temples of the city. It was built in 1991 AD by Gour Govind Swami Maharaj. The white marble construction gives the temple an alluring touch. The illumination of light on the occasion of Janmashtami is an experience itself in a life time. The delicious prasad is famous in the city.

It is the 108th ISCKON temple in the world. It houses the deities of Lord Krishna, Balaram, Gaur Nitai, Subhadra and Jagannath. It follows the scriptures of Bhagavadgita and Bhagvatham in propagating and imparting spiritual knowledge.

It is on NH – 16, IRC Village, Nayapalli, Bhubaneshwar.

Temple hopping is one of the best things to discover the city of Bhubaneshwar, which one should not miss.

Besides the temples as described above, in the new capital area several religious shrines of other religions have been constructed during last 50-years. There is one Mosque, two churches, one Gurudwara, one Buddha Vihar and one jain temple in new capital area.

Math Culture & Dharamsala

There are several MATHAS and Ashrams in Bhubaneswar. The Kapali Matha near Lingaraj temple and Arakhita Das Matha near Khandagiri are important ones.

As per many researchers, the Mahantas of these MATHAS / Ashrams used to spend their entire life for betterment of the Hindu religion/ spirituality among the people.

Mainly, the MATHAS are/were associated with the rituals of the temples and some of them are/were playing important role during various festivals. Besides playing a great religious role, they had provided shelter / lodgings to the pilgrims. During ancient time they were important centres for imparting cultural and religious trainings.

Some of the important Mathas found in the Old Bhubaneswar area are asunder:

1. Bharati Matha And Temple

This is a unique Matha temple. As per legend this Monastery was established by Yayati Keshari. During initial years, it was used as a shelter home for the artisans who were hired to construct Lingaraj Temple.

This was converted to a Matha which was managed by the Mahantas. As per hearsay, these Mahantas had the power of knowing as to when and where they would die. They used to appoint their successors as and when they foresee about their end. Thereafter, they used to sit in Samadhi, enter in to deep meditative state and eventually, they attain salvation. The locals used to bury them in the said place and construct a small Shiv temple with a yoni pitha. With passage of time, nine small temples were constructed and it was known as Bharati Mata Burial temples.

Temple

This Kalinga style temple is devoted to Lord Shiv and it's period is believed to be of 11th century. It is a part of the cluster of 9-temples (ie. situated towards southern side) as described above under the Matha. This square shaped temple is constructed with coarse grey sand stone and it's height is around 80-feet.

These are one of the best architectural structures of the state although some of them are dilapidated and not functional. There is water accumulation and excessive vegetation growth, which requires urgent maintenance.

It is located next to YAMESWAR temple.

2. Jagannath Matha

It is located south of Lingaraj temple. There are groups of laterite temples nearby.

3. Emar Matha

It is in dilapidated conditions and almost ruined. It is located next to Uttareswar temple.

4. Kapali Matha

Kapali Matha near Badheibank Chowk of old town is a living Matha which is believed to be established during Somavamshi rule, ie. around 10th to 11th century AD.

It is double storied with Pidha DEULA of Kalinga style, as the gateway.

As the presiding deity of the Matha is Kapali, it is known in her name.

ASHOKASTAMI and Prathamastami are the major festivals of this Matha. Lord Lingaraj visits this matha during Prathamastami, as it is the house of his maternal uncle.

Lord Baruneswar and Goddess Bana Devi are the maternal uncle and aunt of Lord Lingaraj.

The deity in Kapali math is considered as the elder brother of Lord Lingaraj.

The deity in Bharati math, Kamakshi is considered as his sister. On Yama Dwitiya and Shiv Chaturthi, it is believed that Lord Lingaraj comes here to have launch with his sister.

The math was the only double storied structure in 18th century in the entire old town area. As per hearsay, drinking water from Papanasini pond which is situated at the premises of this Matha redeems devotees who might have committed sin.

5. Sankarananda Matha /Shivatirtha Matha

This Matha (Monastry) is under "Shankaracharya Sampradaya" and is dedicated to Lord Shiv. There are 13- burial temples in the complex which are square in plan and is arranged in one and half rows. Nine shrines are at the rear end of the complex. Some of the temples situated on the southern side are partly buried. The Matha is famous for Chandan Yatra and Dola purnima. Dola Purnima is celebrated in the belief that Lord Lingaraja visits this Matha to take pankti bhogo(community lunch) on Dola Purnima.The eastern side of the Matha is used as the site for consecration of wooden logs used for construction of the chariot of Lord Lingaraj. After the ceremony, the carpenters use them for construction purposes. The entire area of Shivtirtha Math has rich archeological remains. It is near the northern gateway of the Lingaraj temple.

6. Radhaballav Matha

This matha is loacted towards east of Lord Lingaraj Temple. Prayer and other religious activities are being held here on regular basis.

7. Goudiya Matha

This is located to the south of Lingaraj Temple.The idol of Radha Krishna is worshipped here in a pious surroundings.

8. Baya Baba Matha

It is a beautiful, calm and quiet Matha. It is believed that, Baya Baba who was a Saint has taken Samadhi at this place. There are temples of Lord Krishna, Lord Ram, lord Hanuman, Lord Shiv, Lord Ganesh and other Gods and Goddesses in the premises along with a kirtan area. The kirtan at the evening time is enjoyable.

It is near Rupali square.

9. Gadi Tapovan Ashram – Khandagiri

This is the Ashram, where Sisu Ananta Das resided. It is believed that through his sadhana, he attained mystic powers and he was able to change his form at will.

10. Ramakrishna Math And Mission

The spiritual atmosphere of the city always attracted many saints of Ramakrishna mission.

This is the first branch of Ramakrishna order in Odisha which was started by Swami Brahmananda (ie. direct disciple of Ramakrishna) on 31st October 1919AD.

Daily worship, regular religious classes /discourses are the main activities of the Matha. Celebration of Kali puja and birthdays of the Saints are other attractions.

The mission provides lot of services in the area of education and healthcare.

11. Gopal Tirtha Matha

The Matha is located in front of the Chitrakarini temple. It is a branch of the Gopala Tirtha Matha of Puri. Gopala Tirtha was one of the prominent disciples of Sankaracharya, who commissioned monastic establishments in Puri and Bhuabaneswar. It's period is estimated around 16th century.There are also other MATHAS in the city like – Sarada Matha and Sankarananda Matha etc. which are in a bad state of preservation. Besides the above mentioned mathas, there are two main Dharamsalas situated within walking distance from the Lingaraj Temple. They cater to the needs of the pilgrims such as staying/lodging etc.These are as under:

1. Dalmiya Dhamshala: This was built by Rai Bahadur S Dalmia in 1920 AD. The pilgrims used to stay here during their visit to the temple city.
2. Doodwawalla Dharamshala: It was built by R DOODWAWALLA Bahadur in 1928 AD. It is next to Dalmia Dharmshala.

   With passage of time some of the MATHAS are ruined / in dilapidated conditions and some were demolished during renovation of the temples.

TANKS /PONDS OF BHUBANESWAR

1. Bindu Sarovar /Bindu Sagar Lake

Bindu Sagar is one of the natural heritage and holy pond in Bhubaneswar which is the heart of Old town. Bindu Sagar means ocean drop. It is believed that the water of Bindu Sagar contains the water from all the major Holi pools and rivers of India.

EKAMRA Purana, Shiva Purana, Kapila Samhita, Brahmanda Purana and Padma Purana etc. have described the religious merit of this water.

As per some hearsay Shri Kapila Dev, founder of Sankhya philosophy had advised her mother (Devahuti), how to attain the salvation, at this place.

The tank is spread across 21.7 acres with length of around 1300-feet and width of around 700-feet.

The construction period of the tank was around 7th to 9th century AD and contemporary to many early temples of the city. Some say it was dug during Bhaumakar kings.

The tank which is the largest and oldest waterbody of Bhubaneswar is situated towards the north side of Lingaraj temple.

The temple of Ananta Basudev is on the eastern side, Mohini temple on the southern side, Markandeswar temple in the south-eastern side and Uttareswar temple is on the northern side.

Further, southern side of the tank is used for bathing and religious rites, northern side is having the Bhimeswar and Uttareswar temple complex, western side is having EKAMRA Van and eastern side is the road. The puja Ghat is on eastern side and there are motor-able roads on three sides.

It is surrounded by the archeological brilliance of several temples and shrines and by masonry embankments made up of dressed laterite blocks on all the four sides.

At one time, this largest waterbody of Bhubaneswar was surrounded by more than thousand temples and now more than 500-temples still exists, although some of them are ruined.

It has a tiny Island having some temples in the middle. This small white temple is known as Jagati temple, also referred as Brahma temple. During Chandan Yatra, Lord Lingaraj pays visit to this place by navigating through a boat.

Legend

After marriage, Lord Shiv and Goddess Parvati had settled at varanashi. As it became crowded, Lord Shiv had chosen the new location at EKAMRA KSHETRA (ie. A jungle with a single mango tree) for meditation in disguise. It was known as Gupta Kashi (ie. hidden Varanashi or EKAMRA KSHETRA). Parvati started searching Lord Shiv and she spotted a huge mango tree, where hundreds of cows were milking. She came to know about presence of Lord Shiv at this place.

The cows were coming from Gosagareswar. Parvati disguised herself as a milk – maid to take care of the cows. When she was confronted by two demons, ie. Basa and Kirti, she killed them by crushing them in to ground.

It is believed that the tombs of these demons are found in the Bhabani Shankar temple complex.

It is also said that Goddess fell asleep at the feet of Lord Shiv at this place. As Parvati felt thirsty, Lord Shiv struck his trident at this place and created a spring. This spring water was sanctified by the waters of all rivers and streams and it was converted to a large waterbody.

The lake was formed by the contribution of a drop each, by all the sacred water sources of India. Hence, this waterbody was known as Bindu Sagar.

The pond was consecrated by Lord Brahma and Lord Ananta and Vasudev were appointed to live on the eastern bank of the lake as guardian deities.

According to another hearsay, there is an underground river flowing under the Lingaraj temple thereby forming the Bindu Sagar tank.

As Bindu Sagar lake was created by Lord Shiv by bringing water from all the holy places to quench the thirst of Goddess Parvati, hence it is believed that a dip in Bindu Sagar lake would wash away all the sins and one will be cured from all the diseases by drinking it's holy water. As per Ananta – Vasudev temple inscriptions, it was surrounded by a forest of palm trees. These trees had medicinal value and had power to clean the water.

The water of the lake had unique qualities to cure the physical and spiritual illness, as believed by many.

Other Stories

As per Bhagabata Purana, the lake is encircled by the sacred river Saraswati. Sage Kardama is said to have observed meditation at this place to gain the mercy of Lord Vishnu. When Lord Vishnu arrived, he was so compassionate that, tears rolled out from his eyes. These tears became Bindusagar.

In the past, great sages used to worship the tank. The water of Bindusagar is known as "Sivamrita – Jala and any one who drinks the water of Bindusagar is cured from all material diseases. Lord Kapila had also spoken Sankhya philosophy to his mother Devahuti on the bank of this lake.

All the rituals of Lord Lingaraj is performed with the water of this pond. During ASHOKASTAMI (ie. Annual car festival), the main deity from the Lingaraj temple is carried to the Bindu Sarovar in a procession and given a ritual bath.

Similarly, after bathing in the sacred water, the pilgrims worship Lord Lingaraj.

The Tourism department has launched the musical fountain with multimedia laser show in the lake to make it an attractive tourist spot and to bring back the lost glory of this historical pond. The music fountain is programmed with chants of "Shiv Pachakshyar" and "Shiv Tandav". The amazing laser images of Om and Lord Shiv enhances the beauty and is unique.

It turns in to visual delight when thousands of people set sail tiny boats on the occasion of Boita Bandana / Kartik Purnima, that commemorates rich maritime history of Odisha.

One should visit Bindu Sagar whose tranquil atmosphere would revitalise one's soul.

Bindu Sagar is 4.5 kms from the railway station.

Ekamra Vana

This is on the western bank of the lake. It is believed that the mythological one mango tree was here.

It finds mention in many Puranas /scriptures as an entire forest that comprised a single mango tree and it was the abode of Lord Shiv and Parvati.

It was re-created by the forest department with the help of traditional Craftsmen from the famous craft villages of Raghurajpur and Lalitgiri. It is built with natural stones that is common to hundreds of the monuments of the area.

A variety of plants more than 250, traditionally associated with Hindu Gods /Goddesses and having spiritual and medicinal significance can be found in Ekamravan. There is a nursery that popularises the medicinal herbs and the rare medicinal plants make it as "one-of-it's kind" garden.

There are 3-pindis ie. related to Lord Shiv, Goddess Paravathi and Lord Ganesha which depict the legend behind EKAMRA KSHETRA.

As Lord Shiv is related to agriculture, various medicinal plants related to snake bite and others are found near the Shiv pindi.

Similarly the medicinal plants related to curing of female disease are found near the Parvati pindi.

The plants for improvement of intellect like Brahmi etc. are found near the Ganesh pindi.

The view of Vindusagar lake, Lingaraj temple and other temples from this garden is really awesome and one will like this place who loves solitude. One will feel so much piece and tranquility at this place, which cannot be forgotten.

OTHER HERITAGE TANKS /PONDS

Old Bhubaneshwar was having several water bodies since ages and the city is having a porous laterite soil.

As per the book "Lesser known monuments of Bhubaneshwar" by Prof Sadashiba Pradhan, there were 17- beautiful tanks and were next only to temples. Out of the listed 199 listed lesser known monuments, 160- were temples (80%) and tanks were 8.5%.

When the temples came in to existence and specifically after 6th century AD, almost all the religious places were associated with some waterbody. Water body was always treated as a symbol of wealth, fertility and prosperity. It was believed that water God would clean and purify the worshippers from moral sin and bestow long life.

As per scriptures who digs well for people, half of his sins are absolved and one who digs a pond would be happy for ever and would enter the world of Varun.

It had made the environment beautiful and cooler especially during evening time.

Besides Bindusagar Tank as described above, Bhubaneshwar was famous in the past for many tanks / ponds. Some of the important and holy tanks of the town are –

Papanasini Tank, Ganga Yamuna Tank, Gouri Tank, Brahma Tank, Ramkund (Tank), Sundareswar, YAMESWAR, Bada Kua, Kapila Kunda of KAPILESWAR, Kotitirtha,, Manikarnika, Brahmeswar and GANGESWAR etc.

EKAMRA KSHETRA was conceptualised in the form of Asta Ayatan KSHETRA. The important monuments / water bodies under each Ayatan were – Bindusagar in the 1st Ayatan, Papanasini in the 2nd, Ganga-Jamuna tank in the third, Gouri tank in the 4th, Brahma tank in the 5th, MEGHESWAR temple in the 6th, Uttareswar in the 7th and Ramkunda in the 8th Ayatan.

The temples and pilgrim-routes were symbolically connected to Lingaraj temple and Bindusagar tank.

PANCHA TIRTHA

The tanks of Ganga-Yamuna, Bindusagar, Devi padahara, Kotitirtha and Papanasini are known as PANCHA TIRTHA. The water of these tanks are treated as holy and they are used in funeral rituals (ie. worshipping the forefathers).

The tanks in the Kedar-gauri Temple complex, Marichi Kunda / Tank in the temple complex of Mukteswar and Papanasini Tank have already been described with the respective temples in the earlier paragraphs.

Besides meeting the water needs of the Gods / Goddesses, these tanks / ponds add to the aesthetic beauty of the temple/ area.

Some other important tanks of the town are as under:

2. Devi Padahara

The place where Goddess Parvati is believed to have pushed the demon duo in to hell and the particular place where the demons were buried became famous as Devi Padahara (ie. the area through which the demons were pierced in to hell created this pond).

There are 108-lingas and temples around the pond and is believed to be constructed by Yayati Keshari.

The image of Goddess Parvati is taken out in a procession from Lingaraj temple to the pond on every Durgastsmi.

Similarly on Shivratri, 108-tumblers of water are fetched from the pond for worshiping Lord Shiv. During the period of Chandan Yatra, various religious rituals are performed here.

The idol is also taken here during Holi (Fagu Dashami).

However, almost all temples built inside the pond are damaged and images from some of the temples are stolen.

This large square tank is located behind the market and in front of the Lingaraj temple.

3. Manikarnika Tank

It is located beyond the southern compound wall of Kapileswar temple and on the outskirts of Kapileswar village. It is enclosed by masonry embankments made of both sand stone and laterite.

As per legend Goddess Parvati lost her ear rings (mani – kundal) while fighting with the demon Kirti and Vasa.

This ear ring was discovered by Lord Shiv, when he struck his trident upon the earth near the Kapila – Kunda and Parvati offered the rings to Kapileswar.

Hence, this was known as Manikarneswar Kunda / Manikarnika tank.

Using the waters of this Kunda, kapileswar is worshipped every day.

As believed, one's soul is cleaned, if one takes a dip in this pond during Shivratri and worships Lord Kapileswar.

4. Marichi Kunda

It is nearby Mukteswar temple. It bestows fertility. Barren women hoping to give birth to a son/ child, take a dip in this tank on the night before ASHOKASTAMI which is celebrated during Navaratri.

5. Kotitirtha Tank

It is a PANCHA-TIRTHA tank and it's water is used for various ritual purposes. It was believed as the confluence of ten million sacred pools. It was a natural spring in the past. Kotitirtheswar (Lord Shiv) temple is on the western embarkment of this tank. It is revered for cleansing the sins.

6. Papanasini Kunda

This tank was created with the blessing of Lord Shiv to celanese the sins of human beings.

As per legend, sage Sajoti had performed severe penance to satisfy Lord Shiv. Lord appeared before the sage and asked for the boon. The sage requested for a Kunda that would clean the sins of human beings. Hence this Kunda was known as Papanasini. It is also one of the PANCHA-TIRTHA.

This is located in Maitreswar temple compound.

7. Gosagareswar Pond

This pond is believed to be constructed around 13th century AD and predates the adjoining set of temples. It is a part of Gosagareswar temple complex of 11-temples. It is near Lingaraj temple.

It was fed by a natural underground spring and overflow was discharged in to Bindusagar through a channel on the north-eastern corner. For centuries the inflow and outflow was maintained and water level was constant. Due to various construction activities, the exit channel has been blocked. The water level rises during rains and enters the nearby temple complex. During other period the sacred pond becomes a cesspool of stagnant water and water of the pond is highly polluted.

It requires cleaning and proper maintenance.

8. Bhim Kund

This is situated on the western compound of Bhimeswar temple in kapilapasad.

As per legend, the nearby Shiv temple was constructed by Bhim. There were 5-Shivlings which were established and worshipped by 5-pandavas and later the Bhimeswar temple was built.

It was excavated by cutting the laterite stones and the embankment is also made of laterite stones.

As per some researchers, in the past some of these heritage ponds / waterbodies were fed by a natural underground springs. The inflow and outflow were maintained through different channels. Now, most of these channels are blocked with various construction activities. They are at a stage of advanced decay and some of them have been converted to garbage dumps due to lack of maintenance. They are filthy and polluted.

The above ancient waterbodies which were once having immense medicinal value, are places of monumental beauty and remain in old history books. If developed properly and with beautification, they would be great places for modern Tourists besides supplementing the water resources of the city.

Caves of Bhubaneswar Khandagiri Caves and Udayagiri Caves

Khandagiri and UDAYAGIRI are the oldest monuments of Bhubaneswar and are pride of the then Kalinga empire. These are great historical, archeological and jain religious site of 2nd century BC.

They are two adjacent hillocks with several natural and manmade caves and are amongst few ancient rock-cut caves in the Indian Sub-continent. These are also known as Kattaka caves. As per Hati-Gumpha inscriptions, this was known as kumar giri / Kumari Parvat.

The caves were excavated by king Kharavela. As per historians, some of these caves were rebuilt between 7th to 11th century AD. The activities continued till the time of Somavamshi kings, ie. up to 10th - 11th century AD.

The caves consist of row of cells opened either to veranda or to open spaces in front. In later periods, some of these cells were converted to shrines with minor alterations.

Some are of the view that, there were 113 caves in both the hills. But presently, the remains of 33-caves (18-caves in UDAYAGIRI and 15-caves in Khandagiri) are found.

Majority of these caves originated during the period of Kharavela, when jainsim was the state religion of Kalinga.

The inscriptions also mentions the name of other two rulers of this dynasty, ie.Kudeparishi and Vadukha as donors.

Evidence of illustrious career and conquest of king Kharavela, renovation and building of temples / caves and recovery of Kalinga - Jina which was removed by the Nandas of Magadha (ie. 4th century BC) and it's installation on the Kumari hills by Kharvela, are found from these inscriptions.

The rock cut caves were constructed around 1st-2nd century BC. for the jain monks to live and meditate. These caves are having slanting floors that were used as beds.

The caves were re-discovered and brought under Government control in 1825 AD by A. Sterling.

The above caves are wondrous attractions of the city with a charming garden in the area and with amazing murals surrounding them.

Udayagiri

There are 18-caves in UDAYAGIRI, out of which the main caves are Rani Gumpha, Ganesh Gumpha, Bagha Gumpha and Hati Gumpha. UDAYAGIRI means "Sunrise hill". It is around 35-meter high. This is maintained by ASI.

The details of the caves are as under:

Rani Gumpha (Queen's Cave) – Cave – 1

This is the cave number one and is the most beautiful and the largest. It is double storyed having 32-cells (internal caves) and a spacious courtyard. Two carved gate-keepers (ie. dwarapalas) are at the entrance. Victory march of king Kharavela is found in the lower storey. The people watching the procession from the houses is depicted in the reliefs. It is believed that the queen of lalatendu Keshri had occupied this cave. The pillared hall of the lower story has been collapsed long back.

It has elaborate carvings on historical scenes, dancers and religious functions. There are jain symbols and battle scenes. However, some are eroded beyond recognition.

Bajaghara Gumpha – Cave – 2

This is a simple cave having slanted floors and 4-pillars. It is on the left side of Rani Gupmha.

Choto Hati Gumpha – Cave – 3

This is a single cave having a large rock boulder on the top, which is supported by pillars. There are 6-rock – cut elephants out of which one big elephant is on the top right.

Alakapuri Cave – Cave – 4

It is a double-storied cave having single chamber both on the lower and upper section. These are supported by stone pillars. On the gate of Alakapuri cave, there are statues of elephants.

Jaya – Vijaya Gumpha – Cave – 5

This double storied cave has two female dwarpalas at the entrance. The lower part is simple and rock-cut figurines are at the upper floor.

The interior is having two chambers with decorated top front. There is a Bodhi tree in the central compartment.

Panasa Gumpha – Cave – 6

It is a small cave with two pillars. It is next to the path, that leads to middle portion of the cave.

Thakurani Gumpha – Cave – 7

It is double storied. The lower portion is large and have a carved section on the top left of the bottom section. The upper part of the cave is small. Beyond cave – 7, there is a ramp, which will take one to the next level.

Patalpuri Gumpha – Cave – 8

It is a simple cave with two pillars situated at the top of the slanted walkway. The internal chamber has 4-doors which leads to a single chamber.

Manchapuri And Swargapuri Gumpha – Cave – 9

This cave is having two floors. The lower floor is known as MANCHAPURI having 4-cells.

There is a royal procession and has an inscription believed to be from the time of Kudepasari and Kumara Vadukha (ie. successors of Kharavela).

The upper floor is known as SWARGAPURI and there are many inscriptions. This is believed to be during the period of Kharavela.

The cave is important for it's devotional figures.

GANESH GUMPHA – CAVE – 10

The idol of Genesh is carved on the back of one of the cells. Two elephants holding branches of a mango-tree over a lotus are in the verandah. It is believed that these carvings were added later to the original cave. There are detailed works in the interior. The arched doorway of the cells above the railings are relieved with scenes, like – the abduction scene like that of cave – 1 and the other scenes representing the popular story of Udayana (king of Kaushambi) and Vasavadatta (princess of Ujjain). This is the story of the flight of both the lovers on the back of a female elephant in company of the court jester, Vasantaka. There is a 5-lined inscription of 8th / 9th century AD. It describes the donations by physician Bhimata, son of Nannata, during the reign of the Bhaumakara king Santikara.

This cave is on the extreme right.

Jambeswar Gumpha – Cave – 11

This is situated at the extreme left of Hati Gumpha. This is a simple cave having a pillar at the centre, which divides it in to two sections.

Bagah Gumpha (Tiger Cave) – Cave – 12

It's entrance is in the shape of a head of the tiger. The opening to the cave is through the neck of the tiger and the roof of the veranda is formed by the upper jaw. It is a small cave and the tiger mouth portion is the cave itself.

Sarpa Gumpha – Cave – 13

The shape of the cave is similar to that of a snake. Here, the tiny door is surmounted by a 3-headed cobra.

Hati Gumpha (Elephant Cave) – Cave – 14

Hati Gumpha is famous for the inscriptions (ie. in Prakrit language and in Brahmi script) from which the information about king Kharavela is known. The inscriptions start with Namokar Mantra / religious mantra of the Jains which gives salutations to 24-jain Tirthankars.

Successful military campaign of King Kharavela are known from these inscriptions. There is description about Kharavela 's victory of Kalinga Jina from Magadha emperor Pushyamitra.

There are 17-lines in these inscriptions and from them it is also known that, he was crowned at the age of 24 and Jainism was the state religion during his period. He had also arranged a conference of Digambar jain ascetics. Various works / achievements of King Kharavela are known from these inscriptions. It is mostly natural and is the earliest.

It records the career and achievements of king Kharavela in chronological order and many of his expeditions.

This is the largest cave in the top tier.

Dhanaghara Gumpha – Cave – 15

This cave is having two pillars with a dwarpala on the left. There are some carvings on the top these pillars. This cave is towards extreme right of Hathi Gumpha.

Haridas Gumpha-Cave – 16

The cave has a single pillar. There are 3-doorways in the veranda which lead to a single cave.

Jagannath Gumpha – Cave – 17

It has 3-pillars. There are 3-doors which leads to a single room. However, the doors are netted and there is restriction to enter the cave.

Rasui Gumpha – Cave – 18

This is a simple cave with a single doorway. This is situated on the extreme left. There are also many smaller and mid-size cave like structures around UDAYAGIRI hill.

Apsidal Chaity Griha

From the top of the UDAYAGIRI hill one will see a large stone structure on the ground. As per some historians, it was a jain shrine believed to be of around 2nd century BC.

UDAYAGIRI hill is managed /under Archeological Survey of India. The beauty of Bhubaneshwar city and Khandagiri hill can be seen from the top of UDAYAGIRI, which would charm any traveler.

Khandagiri

Khandagiri means a broken hill. Some of the caves of this hill are natural and some are man made.

This is the adjoining hill of UDAYAGIRI having 15-rock-cut caves. The carvings of 24-jain Teerthankars are found here. As per historians, these carvings appear to be of medieval period. Out of 15-caves, 2-caves are situated in other side of Khandagiri hills.

The details of the caves are as under:

Tatowa Gumpha -Cave – L

This is a single chamber cave having single pillar, two entrances and 2-dwarpalas at the entrance. As the name of the cave, Tatowa signifies parrot, there might be a stone carved parrot at the entrance which might have weathered away with passage of time.

Tatowa Gumpha – Cave – 2

Cave no – 2 is also known as Tatowa Gumpha having the same name as the first cave. It is a single chamber cave having 2-pillars, 3-doorways and remains of stone carvings in the wall.

Ananta Cave – Cave – 3

This is the most important cave of Khandagiri. There are two serpents on the door – aches.

There are three pillars supporting the veranda having 4-entrances.

The carving of Goddess Lakshmi with elephant (ie. Gaja Lakshmi) in a lotus -lake and having stalks of lotus around her arms is an unique architecture. This is the symbol of prosperity among Jains.

Gajalakshmi, Surya, Swastika and Nandipada symbol in Ananta Gumpha in the relief are the important sculptures of early Indian art. There are two inscriptions in the cave.

Tentuli Gumpha – Cave – 4

This single chamber cave having two decorated entrances and has a single column having the symbol of an elephant. It is on the right side of main staircase.

Khandagiri Gumpha – Cave – 5

When one would enter Khandagiri hills after climbing up the stairs, one will find this cave first, which is a simple cave with a restored single pillar and a single open chamber.

Dhyan Gumpha – Cave – 6

This is a simple wide cave towards left of the main staircase.

Navamuni Gumpha – Cave – 7

This is the most important cave of the hill. Although, it looks simple from the outside, but when one enters inside, one will find stone cut panels of jain Tirthnkars.

On the top row of the back wall, there are 7-tirthankars and below these Tirthankars, there are 8- images. The first one on the left is that of Ganesh followed by Yakshi of the individual Tirthankars.

Two Tirthankars, ie. Parashnath and Rishavnath are on the right wall. Chandraprabhu, another Tirthnkar is found on the left wall.

Besides the images of Tirthankars, there are 5-inscriptions around this cave.

Barabhuji Gumpha-Cave – 8

Twelve handed Goddess Durga (ie. BARABHUJI Durga) is worshipped in this cave and large number of devotees visit this place. There are several jain rock-cut panels inside, although BARABHUJI Durga is much prominent.

The depictions of 24-Tirthankars and 12-armed Sasandevis are the importance of the cave. The veranda has the relief structures of 12-armed Chakreswari and Rohini.

Trushula Gumpha-Cave-9

This is on the left of BARABHUJI Gumpha and it's gate remains closed most of the time.

Ambika Gumpha-Cave-10

This cave is converted to a temple and the main cave is collapsed. Three sculptures found in the top are of Rishavnath and the female figure, as understood is of "Amara". This is situated on the left of cave no - 8 and - 9.

Lalatendu Keshari Gumpha – Cave- 11

The original cave is collapsed. On the top portion one can see the sculptures. Two sculptures of Rishavnath and one sculpture of Parashnath are found in the right chamber. Two sculptures of Rishavnath and three sculptures of Parashnath are found in the left chamber.

Unnamed Caves – Cave – 12 And 13

These two caves are on the south side of Khandagiri hills and this is little up and ahead of a rock-cut tank known as Radha Kunda. Only ceilings are found on cave-12 and 13. The remains of the foundation are found in cave-13.

Ekadashi Gumpha – Cave – 14

It is situated on the south-west of Khandagiri hills and near Shyama Kunda.

Unnamed Cave – Cave – 15

It is near Gupta Ganga.

As stated above, these caves which are partly natural and partly man-made are of archeological, historical and religious importance and are the earliest groups of jain rock-cut architecture in India, specially in eastern india. The small caves were used for meditation purposes of jain monks.

However, these caves of Khandagiri are not directly managed by ASI and some caves are used by the locals without understanding the significance of these caves.

Digambar Jain Temple/ Tirtha – Khandagiri

There is a Digambar Jain temple at the top of Khandagiri, which was constructed in late 19th century. It is believed that the original temple and it's constructions were much earlier. The present temple had used the building material of earlier temple. The temple is in the eastern side of Khandagiri.

As per hearsay, 500 sons of king jathard had attained Nirvana (salvation) at this place, hence it is treated as a siddha KSHETRA.

There are 3-temples in the temple complex.

Large black stone idol of lord Parashnath is in the white marble hall of the first temple. The white marble idol of Mahaveer along with number of Jain idols / Tirthankars are in the main temple. Five images of jain Tirthnkars are found in the third shrine.

The temple built in sandstone is of Pidha style while the main temple and Jagmohan are of Kalinga style of architecture. There are no niches for side Gods.

The Rishavnath temple is in the southern directions.

This prominent siddha KSHETRA of Digambar jain community is a peaceful and relaxing place.

Jain Art And Architecture – At Udayagiri And Khandagiri

These two hills are one of the earliest group of rock – cut shelters for Jains in the country.

The sculptures of dancing women, musical instruments, royal procession in Rani Gumpha (ie. queen's cave), sculptures of heavenly creatures, elephants, ornaments etc. in Alakapuri Gumpha, entrance sculpture of Tiger cave and sculptures of elephants and jain Tirthankars at worship in Ganesh Gumpha are found in UDAYAGIRI.

Similarly in Khandagiri, one will find parrot carvings and use of natural colours/ pigments in Totawa Gumpha, jain motifs of Swastiks and servants in Ananta Gumpha, Nine Tirthankars and jain prayers in NAVAMUNI Gumpha, Sculptures of image with 12-arms and reliefs related to Hinduism in BARABHUJI Gumpha etc. prove the rich art tradition of Odisha as well as the cave architecture, rarely found in India.

King Kharavela, being a jain was the harbinger of non – violence and peace and this is reflected in the cave architecture of Khandagiri and UDAYAGIRI in a unique manner.

Jain art and architecture of these twin hills had brought a new dimension to the art tradition of India in their sculptures and ornate splendours.

Heritage Wells / Tanks and Water Management Of Khandagiri And Udayagiri

As per researchers the word "TANUSALAYAPATTA" is found In Hatigumpha inscriptions.

They had decoded it's significance as "TANU (ie. Body)-SALYA (ie. Surgical) – PATTA /BATTA (ie. Waterway). It is identified with an efficient water management system/ ancient aqua duct system of Kalinga in the area.

King Kharavela had constructed/ renovated four water holes in Khandagiri and one waterhole in UDAYAGIRI.

The two water holes of Khandagiri, ie. Gupta Ganga and Akash Ganga were having perennial stream of water and were equated with Ganga.

There are kundas which were created artificially, ie. Radha Kunda and Shyama Kunda in Khandagiri and Lalit Kunda in UDAYAGIRI.

There were concealed over head water connection/ inner water head reservoirs in cave ceilings like – Rani Gumpha etc.

Gupta Ganga

This is situated at a height of around 235-feet. It is excavated conically in to the natural rock. As per locals, water used to flow out from this place around 30-years back. With passage of time, the tunnel in the cave is now closed.

Akash Ganga

It is situated at a height of around 245-feet on Khandagiri hills. It is around 4-meter deep and water is found all round the year. This water is used by the monks and local people.

Radha Kunda

This is situated at Khandagiri hills at a height of around 235-feet. Once upon a time it was used as the royal bath of the queens. There are caves in front of this Kunda with open courtyards. This is the largest Kunda with depth of around 2-meters. It 's size is 10.6 meters by 4.47 meters. Water is available through out the year and is used by the locals.

Shyama Kunda

This is at the extreme end of Khandagiri and is hidden by shrubs / wild growth. It is perennial and bottom of this small pool is visible.

Lalit Kunda

This is the only waterbody of UDAYAGIRI, which is a rectangular rock cut well. There are steps on the eastern side. It's depth is 2-meters and the area is 10-meters by 5-meters. This never dries up and water is used by the locals, sparingly.

From the remains/ damaged portions of Khandagiri and UDAYAGIRI, it is observed that there were water channels drilled through the rocks in caves and some of them are seen in caves like-Rani Gumpha etc. There was also drainage of used and rain water in specific areas of the garden and forest etc. which shows the engineering skill of the people in 2nd century BC.

As per Heritage Odisha, "There are many more surgical incisions on cave body with appropriate gradient for smooth flow of water on both Khandagiri and UDAYAGIRI hills were constructed way back in the 2nd century BC by the great king Kharavela. More research with better equipment shall indeed bring to the fore the details of this Tannusalyapatta or Ancient Aqua Duct system of Kalinga".

These two hills are unique monuments of ancient India and also show the achievements of king Kharavela, the greatest emperor of Kalinga (ancient Odisha).

The pre-historic and man made caves, several inscriptions, engineering knowledge used in that period for better drainage, ventilation in the caves and cave art of various motifs are the monumental treasures of the temple city.

Khandagiri and UDAYAGIRI are located 7-kms west of Bhubaneshwar.

There are also weekly heritage walks on Saturdays at the twin hills of UDAYAGIRI and Khandagiri.

Panchu Pandav Cave

PANCHU PANDAV caves are rock – cut Hindu and Buddhist caves. This Archeological site is under ASI and it was renovated by them.

As per hearsay, five PANDAV brothers along with Draupadi had stayed here, for some period during exile.

It appears the caves adopted their name from this legend.

However, the signage outside the cave tells the date of the cave as 5th to 6th century AD. As Mahabharata was written around 400- BC., it does not match historically.

Although, the place is called Panchu PANDAV, one will find only 3- rock – cut caves in a row. They are having modern brick – built porch and painted in deep red.

The first cave which is the largest is now converted to a temple. The image of Navagraha is at the top of the entrance door. A stone cut Nandi is at the centre and many idols are towards the left. The images of Lord Jagannath, Balabhadra and Subhadra are at the main alter. A Shivling surrounded by many snakes is at the centre.

The stone images of Pandavs, ie. Yudhisthira surrounded by his 4-brothers and Draupadi is sitting next. There is an idol of Durga in the interior.

There is a small chamber to the left of the main chamber which is locked. It looks like a portion of the main chamber.

The second cave is smaller than first cave. It is empty having an iron gate. The depth of the cave is around 10-feet, height is 5-feet and width is around 15-feet.

The third cave is the smallest. It's depth is around 6-feet, height is around 4-feet and width is around 10-12 feet. All the caves are supported by concrete roofs and pillars. As per heresy, there was a underground cave from this place up to Khandagiri, which is closed.

There is a covered well outside the cave. This is believed as the ancient part and was used by the Pandavas.

The area has good landscaping.

PANCHA PANDAV MAHOSTAV is celebrated during winters with folk music and dance by eminent artists. Shivratri is the major festival at this place.

It is situated at Badagada Brit colony, PANDAV Nagar, Bhubaneshwar.

Forts Of Bhubaneswar

Sishupalagarh

This ancient, early historic and ruined fort with large and wide spread structures is a beautiful site of Bhubaneswar.

The name of the fort might have been derived from the name of a small village, Sishupal on the eastern side of the fort.

It was a well planned and square shaped city fort with eight gateways. A Small rivulet GANDHAVATI / Gangua Nala is, nearby.

As per researchers and observation of Paul Yule, a German professor from the university of Heidelberg, "we have one Sishupalgarh in the entire world and we have to preserve it."

Within this ancient fortification, there was having an estimated population of around twenty thousand (ie. one of the largest towns of the time, even greater than Athens of Greece).

SISUPALGARH is believed as the capital of Odisha (Kalinga empire) prior to Mauryan empire.

From the rock edicts of Asoka at Dhauli hill, around 6-kms south-west of this place, where "Chandasoka" was transformed to "Dharmasoka", it is observed that, the inscription in the form of instruction is addressed to the officials posted at Toshali, the capital of Kalinga province.

Some researchers suggest that SISUPALGARH could be Toshali, which is mentioned in rock edicts of Dhauli and Jaugadh.

From the remains and artefacts discovered during excavations, it is assumed that this fort city was between 3rd century BC to 4th century AD.

The first excavation of the site was carried out by ASI under the direction of B B LAL in – 1940AD. As per circumstantial evidence, the site was tentatively identified with Toshali of Ashok and Kalinganagar of Kharavela.

This fort finds mention in the inscriptions of Hati Gumpha of Udaigiri.

As per historians, "according to the inscriptions of KHANDAGIRI-Udayagiri Hills, Kalinganagar was provided with fortifications and king Kharavela repaired the gateway and fortification wall which has been damaged by a storm. He built the Maha Vijaya Prasad (ie. The great victory palace).

Till date, no fortified town of comparable date except Sisupalagarh is known to exist nearby Khandagiri-Udayagiri hills. Further the excavations did reveal a collapse and subsequent repair of the southern gateway flank of the fortifications".

However, no definite evidence is found from the site.

As per historians, the defence system of the fort was the highest, compared to other forts during the then period of contemporary India.

Originally, Gangua Nala was flowing to the west of the fort area, but at the time of construction of the fort, the main current was diverted to all sides forming a sort of natural moat.

The defences were erected in the beginning of 2nd century BC and they comprised a clay rampart.

Subsequently 4 to 6-feet thick covering of laterite gravel was added to the top of clay rampart. The defences were further fortified by baked brick revetments on both sides. The gateway consisted of large dressed stone blocks / larger than usual size laterite stone slabs.

There is a quadratic defensive wall measuring 1200 by 1160 meters and surviving wall as high as 12-meters and water moat on all the sides to protect during invasion.

Sisupalgarh Fort – Remains

During visit, old large pillars as high as 12-meters and queen's palace, will impress any one. The houses were with stones and bricks.

The centre of the fort area is around 500-yards from the western gate. This area is not excavated and contained 16-pillars (sowla Khamba) of the structural hall. 14-monolithic pillars of laterite stone, with socket hole at the top, are found in the rice fields and mounds of earth.

There are stone lined reservoirs, which might have been used for storage/harvesting of water and which was a major significance of this settlement. It was known as Rani Pokhari / Chedi Pokhari.

During excavations some ceramics such as Rouletted ware, knobbed ware and red slipped ware etc. were found and on the basis of ceramic assemblage, the site has been dated between 500- BC to 1st century AD.

R k Mohanty from Deccan college, Pune and Monica Smith from Cotsen Institute of Archeology, University of California, excavated around 18-pillars and found various artefacts like, earthen ware, bangles and other jewellery items.

They found the evidence of an urban settlement and estimated the population of the community at over 20-thousand living in a city having well laid-out streets and houses with 2/3 rooms each.

As per historians it was built over several centuries with additions, alterations and various fortifications.

Sishupalgarh is the earliest known fort of Odisha which remained a model for subsequent forts.

The exact decline of the city / Sishupalgarh fort is not known. As per some researchers the decline may be due to war or natural disasters.

However, some believe that, this fort was continuously occupied, till it was destroyed by Moghul Subahdar Taqui Khan in – 1731-AD.

Further Excavations and more research is required about this fort, to know the history of Odisha during the period and to know the exact period of the fort.

Legend

As per some legends, the fort was constructed by SISUPAL of Mahabharat fame and accordingly, it was known as SISUPALGARH.

Sishupal was a powerful Chedi king. He was associated with Lord Krishna and Mahabharata war. The Kalinga warriors had fought in the side of the Kauravas. Hence, this fort is an antique of the Mahabharata era or may be beyond. However, there is no authenticity about the same. Sishupal was an ancestor of king Kharavela of Odisha.

As per Dr. B K Rath, famous archeologist, the archeological finds from the place like pieces of pottery, vessels and building materials etc. were carbon dated and date back to more than ten thousand years old.

In 1950AD, this fort was notified as a centrally protected monument under ancient Monuments Act – 1904 AD. Government/Archeological department should take immediate steps to save this ancient fort, whose urban planning may be more advanced than that of Harappan. The fort should be saved from encroachment by private builders/ land grabbers.

Even gold coins and pottery found from the site were stolen, as understood.

If urgent steps are not taken, this historical fort which was 562.68 acres in 1947-48 (ie. by ASI) is now reduced to 0.77 acres, may be lost for ever.

It shows how neglect and apathy had almost ruined this fort which was the architectural brilliance of Kalinga empire.

This fort is half an hour drive from Bhubaneswar city centre. It is around 7-kms from Railway station and 10-kms from the airport, in Samntarapur area (ie. South-eastern part) of Bhubaneswar.

DHAULI-BUDDHIST TRAIL

Dhauli – (The Place Where Ashoka, The Emperor Was Reborn And Converted Buddhism To A World Religion)

DHAULI is situated on the left bank of river Daya and consists of three hillocks /3-short rocky ranges running parallel to each other. It was known as Surabha hills. This hilly area is of immense historical significance and was the place where Kalinga war was fought between Ashok and Kalinga state.

The southern range is known as Aswathama, on which the famous Ashokan edicts are found on the north face. These rock edicts are inscribed in a space of around 15-feet long and 10-feet high.

Immediately above the inscriptions is a terrace, on the right side of which is the fore part of an elephant, about 4-feet high hewn out of the solid rock. The elephant has given the name of the hill as Ashwatthama, the famous elephant of Mahabharata war.

From the visit of J D Butler in 1875-76 and R l Mitra in 1880 AD, there were remains of a Stupa, which might be there till 19th century AD.

The present Dhavaleswar temple is standing on the most prominent hill range. It was built on the remains of an ancient temple of 5th centre AD. It is in eastern extremity.

On the western side of DHAULI hill and at the foot hills, the renovated Bahirangeswar Shiv temple and the dilapidated Ganesh shrine are located.

There is a large tank on the east of the hill known as Kaushalya Ganga. The tank was originally a Kosh (4.02kms) long on each side. However, great part of it is silted.

It was the location of the famous Kalinga war, where the banks of Daya had provided the natural boundary line between two armies. As per Ashokan Rock edict – XllI and in Ashoka' own words "One hundred and fifty thousand persons were thence carried away captive, one hundred thousand were there slain and many times that number died". Kalinga war holds a very important position in Indian history, as after witnessing the bloodshed and massacre, Ashok laid his arms to follow the path of Dharma-Vijaya (religious victory). Here, the Emperor Ashok was reborn, accepted Buddhism and converted Buddhism into a World Religion.

Discovery

As described by Kevin Standage, till an employee of the East India Company with a passion for history and archaeology entered the scene during early part 19th century, it was not known to the outsiders.

Kevin Standage has stated inter-alia as under:

"James Prinsep was head of Asiatic Society of Bengal, with a particular interest in the pre-islamic history of India. His close friend Andrew Stirling had heard of some carvings on a rock in the jungle of Dhauli in 1817 and it took a further 20 years before James Prinsep was able to explore this rumour further. Prinsep contacted Markham Kittoe, who was working for the East India Company in Orissa seeking out new coal fields in 1837 AD. Kittoe was also a keen historian and antiquarian, so unsurprisingly he leapt at the chance to become a Victorian Indiana Jones.

Kittoe's attempts to explore the hill did not get off to a good start. He was faced with strong resistance from the local people, finally being assisted by a man from Varanasi who, during the night and with a burning torch, took him to a rock covered with etched text. Kittoe knew immediately that these edicts were excellently preserved and potentially incredibly important.

At daybreak a few hours later, Kittoe hurriedly returned to the rock only to be attacked by a mother bear and her two cubs who were nesting nearby.

Kittoe panicked and frantically climbed up the rock, and from above shot the mother bear dead. On that very spot up on top of the rock, Kittoe made a surprising discovery. Right beside where he was standing was a carving of an elephant sculpted into the rock.

Kittoe climbed down and got to work copying the script carved on the 5m x 3m rock face. It was written in Magadhi Prakrit language in Bramhi script. At that time the text had not been deciphered, so what was actually being declared on this rock was completely unknown.

Prinsep received a copy of the edict text from Kittoe and spent the following year researching this and other similar mysterious edicts that had been discovered on rocks and pillars throughout India and beyond.

Prinsep was ultimately successful, and the great Indian king Ashoka was once again known to the world. His name was getting traced not just in India, but also in Nepal, Sri Lanka and most notably by the Chinese Buddhist monk-scholar Xuanzang (also known as Hiuen T'sang or Husan Tsang) who explored north India widely between 634 and 645 A.D.and documented his travels. "This discovery had changed the history of mankind and cemented Buddhism as a religion of India.

Rock Edicts

The famous rock edicts of Ashok are worth witnessing. Rock edicts l to X and XIV are found here. Edicts XI-XIII are replaced by two special edicts known as Kalinga Edict-I and ll which might have been engraved as per local requirements.

The missing rock edicts XI to XIII are found every other rock edict. These missing edicts speak about Kalinga war and the heavy death toll. This edict was missing as it was sensitive to local population and it might have gone against political wishes.

The rock edicts are protected by a structure and visitors can go up to close to the text.

The special rock edicts are unique as it contains specific instructions from Ashok to his local officials to maintain their conduct, in his newly conquered territory, to earn trust.

ELEPHANT

As described above, the rock – cut elephant was discovered by Markham kittoe in 1837 AD and is above the Ashokan edicts. It is not a full elephant, rather front half of the elephant is protruding from the rock face.

It looks as if, it is emerging from the rock itself. As per some interpretations it is a symbolic representation of Buddha's birth out of his mother's womb. It is unique, no other rock-cut sculpture exists like this anywhere in the world.

Elephant is one of the sacred animals in the Buddhist pantheon.

As per legend, queen Maya, mother of Siddhartha (later known as Buddha) had a dream, where she saw a white elephant entering into her womb.

This was the sign that she conceived Sidharth and thus the importance of elephant in Buddhist religion. This stone elephant is one of the oldest surviving specimen of Indian art considered to be the earliest Buddhist sculpture in Odisha dating back to Mauryan period.

The rock edicts of the bottom carved on stones, contain the instructions of Ashok, to his administrators as to how to rule his subjects.

This proclamation of Emperor Ashok is written in Prakrit language and Brahmi script on the rock of DHAULI on the southern end. Here, Ashoka enunciated the famous doctrine of paternalism, ie. "all men are my children". It is the sheet anchor of Odisha history.

These edicts advise the administrator, "you are in charge of many. You should gain affection of men. All men are my children that they obtain welfare and happiness both in this world and the other world, the same do I desire for all men".

These edicts also shed much light on the miraculous transformation of a great king from a ruthlessly ambitious warrior to a benevolent and highly evolved soul dedicating his later life to Buddhist way of life.

These inscriptions are remarkably clear even after 2-thousand years.

Apart from Ashokan edict, another important inscription is found in one of the caves opposite to the Ashokan edict. It is dated 93- of an unknown era. It may be corresponding to Ganga era. R D Banerjee assigns the inscription to 865 AD. It belongs to the Bhumkar king Santideva (829 AD) and records construction of a Buddhist Monastery named – Arghyka-Varati by Bhimata and his son Loyamaka of Viraja (modern jaipur).

Dhauli Caves

These caves are situated in DHAULI hills. There are many small rock -cut caves.

It is in the vicinity of Daya river. It is famous for ancient sculptures and attractive art works.

Dhauli Shanti Stupa

Dhauli Shanti Stupa, known as "Peace Pagoda", stands majestically commanding a magnificent view of the Daya river below, is an awesome monument.

This peace pagoda was built in 1972 AD by Kalinga Nippon Buddha Sangha in collaboration with Japan Buddha Sangha and with the support of Fuji Guruji and Odisha Government.

It is constructed on the site where famous Kalinga war, one of the bloodiest in the history of mankind, was fought. It commemorates the grand peace that kalinga war achieved.

The Stupa is in the shape of a dome and made up of white marbles. It has four massive idols of Lord Buddha in various postures. Various panels around the periphery of the Stupa, depict Buddha's life episodes carved on stone slabs.

The carvings are elephant – procession, reclining Buddha, sleeping beauty and emperor Ashok giving up war by offering his sword to Lord Buddha etc. Along with episodes from Gautam Buddha's life, one can see the footprints of Lord Buddha as well Bodhi tree over the stone panels.

The dome structure of Shanti Stupa possesses five umbrellas and they symbolise five elements of Buddhism. There are two pillars like Ashokan pillars on the entry with two lions at the top standing as guard to the Lord.

Dhabaleswar Temple

The temple of Dhavaleswar is at a short distance from the Shanti Stupa. This was renovated in the year 1972 AD. This is frequented by the Hindu and Buddhist devotees, which is just behind the Stupa.

Monastery

There is a monastery at the vicinity of Stupa named as Saddharma Vihar Monastery.

It is a place of devotion and worship for various people for different generations.

It is a symbol of peace.

The Shanti Stupa dazzles atop DHAULI hills during the day and transforms in to this canvas for the night that beams laser rays in to surface.

Dhauli – Light And Sound Show

The captivating light show depicts the Kalinga war and subsequent conversation of king Ashok to Buddhism and peace loving ruler with bright and beautiful visuals. It is truly engaging.

It recreates history that immediately transport the onlooker back in to time.

Vairangeswar Mahadev

This is another Swayambhu Shiv temple known as Vairengeswar Mahadev which is facing west.

The main temple is of late Kalingan style dating back to 15th century. The present temple was built during the Gajapati Rulers. A four-handed black chlorite image of Brahma holding Veda and water vessel in upper two hands and rosary, abhaya mudra in lower two hand.

OSA had reconstructed the main shrine. The ground plan of the temple in square shape is visible. Several pillars in dilapidated conditions are found. The temple belongs to Bhaumakar period. A modern temple by the side of Shiv temple now houses the beautiful image of Ganesh. It is similar to Ganesh image found in Lingaraj temple.

The temple is situated on the foothills of Dhauli. It is on the left bank of the river Daya, which is in the south-eastern outskirts of Bhubaneswar and in the village Khatuapada.

Others

Dhauli is an incredible tourist place having Peace pagoda (Shanti Stupa), Ashokan edicts, fore part of an emerging elephant and presence of old temples.

It is the DHAULI hills that adopted the path of Dharma which lets only peace and love enter one's life. Breathtaking view of the city and Daya river below is stunning.

This is situated to the south of Bhubhaneswar and is around 8-kms from Bhubaneswar. It can be easily reached by a short diversion on the Bhubaneswar-Puri highway, just after crossing the Daya river bridge. The drive to the monument in the midst of lush green agricultural lands and river Daya is gratifying and the view of the town from the hill is amazing.

Parks

The charm of Bhubaneshwar goes beyond it's rich heritage. It is known as a family oriented city with a peaceful environment. There are various entertainment options within city bounds and without going too far out of the city. The city offers plenty of options when it comes to places that can be visited by families or group of friends or to spend some time with one's loved one without much hassles.

The following are some of the best places and amusement parks for the visitors. The peaceful environment of these places are for just to unwind and relax. There are lakes / water bodies in many of the parks which provide picturesque view of the surroundings. These are perfect settings to city's historical surroundings and some of them are also major tourist attractions. The decorative lamps adorn these parks which illuminate them in the night.

1. Ekamra Kanan Botanical Gardens

EKAMRA KANAN Botanical garden which is a part of Regional plant resources centre, is the biggest Botanical garden and park in the city which is spread over an area of more than 500-acres. It separates Bhubaneshwar city from Chandaka reserve forest along the backside wall. It is managed by department of forest and environment, Government of Odisha.

Major parts of the park are as under:

A) Glass House And Cactus Garden

A large pyramidal glass house contains many type of cactus plants, known as the cactus garden. This is one of the largest collection of cactus plants in Asia. More than 1-thousand varieties of cactus plants including rare species and succulents (fat plants) are found here.

This green house in the shape of pyramid is the focal features of the park.

B) Main Park

Around the above glass pyramidal house, the main park of EKAMRA KANAN with large green lawn is developed.

There is around 3-kms long walk way with an area more than hundred acres.

Flower garden with different varieties of flowers, medical garden with medicinal plants, large trees, Orchidarium, bamboo garden, fruit garden and a play ground with several swings, slides and ladders for climbing are other attractions.A Musical fountain is present in one side of the park.

The hibiscus garden has 52-varieties of hibiscus, rose garden has more than thousand varieties of hybrid – T and miniature roses etc. It has many rose gardens and nursery.

C) Lake

There is a small lake with boating facilities. The area of the lake is around 45-acres. During winters large number of migratory birds are found in the lake and the surrounding wet land.

D) Ret Garden

One will find 32-varieties of threatened plants in this garden. Botanists, students and conservationists who are interested for bio-diversity of the state would like this garden.

E) Palmetum

Varieties of tropical palms are grown here for conservation and research. It is understood that more than 54-varieties of tropical palm trees are found here.

F) Jagannath Vatika

This is developed in an area of 5-acres. The plants used in the ritual of the Lord are found here. It is understood, there are 125-Species of plants which are used in different rituals, festivals and day to day religious rites of Lord Jagannath and these are found here. One will know the Jagannath culture and tradition by visiting this portion.

Koraput Cofee Outlet

This new Koraput COFEE OUTLET is near the side of the lake. It serves both cold and hot COFEE. One will also get the Ragi cookies and Mandia bread from the Tribal heartlands of Koraput, which is a perfect accompaniment to the COFEE. While taking a stroll through the park, one can enjoy the same. One will get – Espresso, Cappuccino, Café latte, Black COFEE and cold COFEE etc. and these are displayed in a rustic background. One will have a choice of bags of different coffee powders and impressive filters to take home with them.

The flower show held in the garden, in the month of January of every year is another attraction for the visitors.

One should not miss this well landscaped park, which is full of exquisite flora including numerous varieties of roses in the rose garden, cactus plants, musical fountain and lake with boating facilities, as stated above.

However, the aquatic garden requires proper maintenance. There are large number of exotic birds throughout the park. In the early morning and evening hours the chirping of birds would captivate the traveler.

It is around 2-kms distance from NH-16 on the Jaydev Vihar to CRPF square inner road. Distance from Airport and Railway station is around 7-kms.

2. Biju Pattanyak Park/Forest Park

This park is locally known as Forest Park. It is full of nature and is a perfect place for refreshing and relaxing. Floating mountain, jogging tracks, musical fountains, play area for children, rosarium and rookeries etc. make it a sightseeing attraction for the tourists. Palm trees, a modern art structure and well laid out walkways are worth for a stroll.

It has greenery and well maintained plants. This is an old park of the city which has an open gym area and play areas for kids. There is an eatery.

It is very popular among the locals and one will find large crowd of locals relaxing during early morning hours and late evening hours.

Children enjoying boat ride and water sports in this well lit park are other attractions.

It is a prominent land mark of the city and is located centrally, ie. in Bapuji Nagar area and close to Airport. It is spread over in 7-acres of land.

3. Jayadev Vatika Park

This has large varieties of indigenous, exotic flora and medicinal herbs, shrubs, climbers, bamboos having more than 3-hundred species. It is spread over an area of 39-hectares adjoining the foothills of Khandagiri.

Natural topography with hillocks added with creative landscaping with vast expanses of lawn and meadows, lilies and lotus ponds, fountain, waterfall, cascading stream have made it wonderful picturesque landscape park with scenic beauty for the visitors to have mental peace with ecstatic joy.

Creeper huts, sit – out under tile roof shelter, picnic pindis with infrastructure facilities have made it a best outdoor recreation centre for Nature lovers, picnickers and all types of visitors.

As per ecotourism Odisha, "Named after 12th century Saint poet Jayadeva is a jungle away from jungle. Trees, shrubs, herbs, creepers of Jayadev VATIKA are depicted in the Gita Govindam Kabyam composed by the celebrated poet Jaydev of 12th century AD influence the emotions, sensuality and mysticism, aesthetic panorama through different colours like red, saffron, yellow, white colour and aroma of flower of different species. Truly Jaydev Batika serves as a carbon sink cum green lung, creating a micro climate of the capital city of state of Odisha".

As understood, there are 24-grooves in the park planned according to the description of nature and natural beauty in Gita Govinda.

There are artificial water streams, meadows, variety of rare plants and plants having medicinal properties as well. This is a nice place for nature lovers.

It has two artificial waterfalls, pool and many picnic spots.

There are more than 10-thousand rare plants and some of them are having medicinal properties. It is special for botanist and nature lovers.

It is around 4.5 kms from Airport and 7.5 kms from Railway station.

4. Biju Pattanayak Energy Park

This park is managed by OREDA (ie. Odisha Renewable Energy Development Agency) and was set up under special area demonstration programme of Ministry of New and Renewable Energy.

There are different activity zones, like – Urja, Oriana, Aditya, Mitra, Bhaskar and Ishban representing energy resource centre, children's corner, indoor exhibit gallery, conference room and interactive media centre etc.

There are many outdoor exhibits and live demonstrations of working models of different renewable energy devices. They depict the working principles and their applications.

For an inquisitive visitor these activity zones and exhibits have a great deal to offer. There are lot of things to do and learn in this energy park.

One learns about energy conservation, energy efficiency, application of renewable energy and technology. There are many live demos, working models of varied renewable energy and devices exhibited in the park. It is a nice park for kids and for energy lovers and is near kolothia Bus stop, Khandagiri.

5. Buddha Jayanti Park

This park is filled with verdant greenery. This is a large park. Shrubs, trees, flowers, lake and a Buddha Stupa inside the park make it a nice place for visit. The peaceful environment is good for unwinding. There is play area for the children.

This is spread over in an area of around 47-acres. This park is having pathways, lake, abundant trees and flowers. The peaceful environment of the park is all absorbing. This is situated in Niladri Vihar, Chandrasekharpur.

6. Indira Gandhi Park

Indira Gandhi park is spread over in 10.6 acres of land in front of the secretariat. It was inaugurated by the then Prime Minister Rajiv Gandhi. Sprinkles and water fountains are attractions of the park. The statue of late Prime Minister, Indira Gandhi is placed exactly at the spot, where she stood and gave her last historic speech on 30th October, 1984 AD. Here, Indira Gandhi had delivered her last speech, before she was assassinated. Earlier, It was the parade ground. The park has plenty of trees, shrubs, flower garden etc.

7. Mahatma Gandhi Park

It is built in 5-acres of land. It has water fountain with a stream, rockeries, ball fountain and landscape garden. It is near janata maidan and XIMB square. It has some natural sight seeing galleries, play station for kids. One will feel relaxed in this clean and grassy park.

It is around one km from NH – 16 of Jaydev vihar.

8. Madhusudan Das Park

This is a landscaped park named after the great son of Odisha, Kulabrudha Madhusudan Das and is one of the top parks of the city. It is having open gyms, rain shed, yoga places, skating area, pathways, slides and swings for children. In the evening, the lighted park is attractive. There are lot of trees, shrubs and seasonal flowers. It is a good place for all age groups and the best place for spending quality time with family and friends.

Many palm trees add to the beauty of the park.

This is in Pokhariput, Bhubaneshwar.

Besides the above-mentioned parks,there are many other beautiful parks in the city like – Netaji Subhash Chandra Bose Park (ie. with beautiful gardens, flower beds, sprinkling fountains, play areas and spaces for yoga and meditation), Kharavela park in Khandagiri area (ie. well maintained green carpeted lawns, jogging track and separate play area etc.) and IMFA PARK in Sahid Nagar area (ie. having well maintained orderly lawns, separate play section and flower beds etc.) for spending time. Each park has it's own beauty

9. Smrutivan

The Smruti Van (Memory park) is a unique place in Bhubaneswar. Here, one can plant a tree as a loving memory of bereaved one. To plant a tree and for life time care of that plant, one has to deposit certain amount to the authorities of this place.

One can also plant a tree for the memory of a living person or for a memory like the birth of a child etc. There are varieties of plants including medicinal plants in the garden.

For departed soul the "Vatika" is known as Smruti Vatika "and for memory of some happy occasions it is known as "Subha Vatika".

This is a serene and Divine place where, even after end of the life / events, memories last for ever. It requires further development with the support of the public and Government.

This is situated at the outskirts of Bhubaneswar in an area of 17.5 acres in Kalinga Nagar and developed by the forest and environment department of Odisha.

Amusement Parks

The city is home to two wonderful amusement parks ie. BDA NICCO PARK and Ocean World Water Park. Both the parks provide lot of funs and adventures to children as well as grown ups. The Parks are have thrilling water rides. These are places to enjoy unlimited fun with family and friends. One should go out to enjoy a whole day of fun at these water and amusement parks and this will awake the thrill seeker in you.

1. Bda Nicco Park

It is spread over an area of 25-acres and is one of the best amusement parks in the city. This was designed and built in association with NICCO, Japan and is having beautiful and well maintained gardens.

An artificial lake runs through the centre of the park. It is filled with seasonal flowers and the Musical fountain in the middle, adds to it's beauty.

Thrill lovers would like this place which is packed with water rides and games for all ages.

One can enjoy various rides like flying Saucer, Moon Raker, Twist and Turn, striking cars, caterpillar and pirate ship etc. and the water rides like Pedal boating in the artificial lake.

There is a mini golf course located at the premises and those who have Interest in golf can enjoy the same. This mini golf course attracts both experienced players and ammetures.

The complete entertainment zone of the park would engage one to have a fun full day.

One can try in the multi-cuisine fast food centre which serves delicious foods.

It can be visited with family and friends which is one of the quick gateways for a day out in the city.

It is in Madhusudan nagar, Bhubaneswar.

2. Ocean World Water Park

It is planned similar to the concept of "Water Kingdom" of Mumbai and "Aquatica" of kolkata. It has rides and attractions designed to thrill visitors of every age.

It is a nice place to have fun with family and friends in an amazing wave pool.

Although it is a small place, the slides are enjoyable. Apart from water rides, roller coasters, it is a good place for weekend relaxations especially with children and a great place for photo shoot.

The rain dance can inspire to shake a leg with one's partner under the falling drops of water. There is something romantic.

It has an amusement park with number of dry rides to keep one fully engaged. There is also a Ayurvedic message centre and food court.

Although it is at Kuranga sasan, Phulnakhara, GANGESWAR of Cuttack District, this water park is in the middle of the twin city and is around 22-kms from Bhubaneswar.

Museums

The museums represent the material and cultural history of a society. These are important places for researchers, students, teachers, historians, travellers and common people, as they are repository of historical elements, materials and cultural traditions.

Bhubaneshwar boosts of many museums and galleries and they house some of the finest collections. One's time will be well spent by taking glimpses of such classic treasures.

Some of the important museums of the city are as under:

1. Odisha State Museum

This is the oldest museum of the state which was started way back in 1932 AD from Ravenshaw college, Cuttack. The foundation stone of the present museum at Bhubaneshwar was laid on 29th December, 1957AD by Dr. Rajendra prasad, the first president of India.

This is a huge museum spread over multiple sections and has an exclusive collection of some unique and ancient art and craft objects. It is divided in to eleven segments of galleries including galleries for anthropology, manuscript section and the archeology section etc.

It's galleries display some of the most interesting archeological remains, fine arts and other timeless antiquities. One can find Buddhist sculptures, jain sculptures, inscriptions from times of Kalinga war and medieval period, musical instruments both folk and traditional, copper plates, jewellery, paintings, epigraphy, numismatics, Anthropology, primitive weapons, primitive coins, palm leaf manuscripts, scientific tools and natural history etc..

The collection includes stone sculptures, bronze coins, armours, pre-historic metal plates, rare inscriptions in delicate and rare palm leaf, bamboo leaf and manuscripts in Ivory etc..

The museum also collects and displays documents. They preserve documents, antique items, maintain journals, facilitate research on art, history and organises exhibitions and seminars.

It is home to more than 56-thousand rare antiquities. This is a perfect place to explore some of the incredible rich culture and heritage of Odisha. The unique traditions of paintings, sculptures and handicrafts that reflect a long diverse cultural heritage would be liked by any visitor.

By visiting it, one will have an idea about the evolution of culture, art, language, architecture, religion of the state, the history of Odisha and Bhubaneshwar and several dynasties and kingdoms who had ruled over Odisha since ancient times.

There is proposal to develop a comprehensive master plan for a world class museum complex with different facilities for history, art and culture etc. as as the state is the repository of rich cultural and artistic heritage.

KALINGA ART GALLERY

This is the largest Art Gallery which is situated in the premises of the State Museum. This was established along with 5- regional Art galleries at 5-districts (ie. Chhatrapur of Ganjam, Puri, Balasore,

Sambalpur and Koraput) with the initiative of the Odisha Lalita Kala Academy and was inaugurated by the then Chief Minister Naveen Pattanayak.

As per the CM "Kalinga Art Gallery will be a power house of art and artists of the state. It will be a confluence of artists from different regions including artists of National and international repute. It will help Art loving citizens and the tourists to learn about the glorious artistic traditions".

These art Galleries are focal point of interaction among the young and budding artists. It encourages local youths to display their artistic creativity and it promotes local art form.

It is situated on the Lewis road, Kalpana square, BJB Nagar.

2. Regional Science Centre

This was established on 18th September, 1989 AD to inculcate scientific temper and to popularise science and technology in all walks of life, especially among students. It is having 3-galleries, ie. Motion gallery, Mathematics gallery and popular science gallery.

It is an incredible science centre with many gadgets and machines showing how different things work scientifically. There is a 3-dauditorium, where one can see 3-dmovies related to science and technology.

The Tara Mandal Area showcases different planets, stars and constellations. The centre had a lovely park with ducks. In the park centre one can see exotic plants, one can understand the underlying principles of action from molecular level to motion of planets.

In the pre-historic life park, one can come face to face with 3-dimensional figures of animated dinosaurs models synchronised with a story-telling and light and sound show.

It is spread over 8-acres of land. Around 84- interactive exhibits help people to understand and appreciate the role of science on global and local scale. This is a popular place for science enthusiasts and kids.

It is situated at Pandit Jawaharlal Nehru Marg, Bhubaneshwar

3. Insects Museum

This museum is located in the campus of Odisha University of Agriculture and Technology.

It has 4367 specimens of insects. These insects generally attack and affect the crop plants. This helps the students and research scholars to identify the various species which may help in protecting the plants from attack of these insects. This was established with the financial help of Indian council of Agricultural research, New Delhi.

4. Museum of Tribal Arts And Artefacts / Museum Of Man

This was established in 1953 AD to protect and promote the tribal culture of the state.

It is divided in to 5-Separate halls. More than 4-thousand tribal artefacts are displayed in these five halls. The halls are digitised and are provided with interactive touch screen.

There is a fully air conditioned auditorium for staging tribal dances and exhibiting tribal films.

In the courtyard of the museum 14-tribal shrines are displayed where the tribal deities are enshrined. It gives a divine touch.

This museum houses the collections from 62-tribes of Odisha and their costumes, accessories, jewellery, farming equipment, weapons and gear etc. are found here.

There is a new PTG gallery showing 3D representation of their unique life style.

Seven replicas of tribal huts along with life size sculptures of tribal men and women are also seen.

The tribes such as – Santhal, Juanga, Gadaba, Saora and Kandha, Gond and Chuktia Bhunjia are found in their traditional style. The artefacts collected from different tribal groups including those from the PTGs (primitive tribal groups/ particularly vulnerable groups) are displayed in the tribal huts, which is open to the visitors. It provides the knowledge covering different human species in totality.

This is a hub for the people having interest in Anthropology. The tribal life style, especially cultural heritage of 13-pVTs of Odisha, such as Bonda and Saora etc, personal and house hold belongings of Tribals, instruments used for haunting, fishing, dance and music and Dhokra items etc. would attract any traveler. There are tribal food court and souvenir shop.

This museum is one of it's kind for preservation, documentation, display and demonstration of rich tribal heritage of Odisha. It is conceptually labeled as "Museum of Man".

It is one of the best tribal museums in the country and in 2010AD, it was recognised as the best among 21-tribal museums in India by UNESCO.

If one likes to explore the tribal culture and traditions of Odisha, this museum is a must visit.

It is spread over 12-acres of land and maintained by Tribal Research and Training institute.

This is situated at Unit-8, CRPF Colony, near CRPF Square, Nayapalli.

5. Regional Museum of Natural History

Regional Museum of Natural History is a good place for visitors who are interested to know about the historic and prehistoric flora and fauna specially of eastern India.

First thing which attracts the visitor at the entrance is the skeleton of an elephant, named Shankar. (ie. kept in a huge glass box and a bullet stuck near it's neck portion). The bullet embedded inside the rib was a country made ball like bullet weighing 32-grams, which was recovered from the inner part of the second vertebrae while cleaning the bone.

When one will listen the story of Shankar, whose habitat was nearby Chandaka – Dampara sanctuary, one would know how man and animal conflict ends of in loss of many innocent lives.

Similarly, the skeleton of baleen whale installed in the museum (ie. 47.1-feet which was brought from Gopalpur, Odisha), is supposed to be the largest for any museum in India.

The visitors are taken through fascinating bio-diversity galleries, a separate section dedicated to North-eastern biodiversity, African gallery, insect corners, well stocked library and a discovery centre etc.

The exhibits of plants and animals found around the country, taxidermy gallery with exhibits of various animals like – Cheetah, deer, Hyena, rhino, elephants, skeletons of baleen whale and dolphins are major attractions. There are display of models that represent the eco-system, skeletons of animals, stuffed animals, varieties of floral species. There are preserved butterflies, reptiles and moths with detailed information.

These precious items which are collected, preserved, documented and exhibited in different galleries emphasise the conservation of nature, natural resources and depict the ecological interrelationships among plant and animals.

The museum also organises out-bound programmes for schools and colleges, film shows on nature and environment and exhibitions on wheels which are mobile exhibitions.

It has incredible collection of exhibits which would be liked by the visitors of all age groups, especially children. It is a great informative place with blend of education and entertainment. It is understood that it is the third best regional museum of natural history in India because of varieties of huge collections.

It is located near Acharya Vihar square and near planetarium.

6. Kalabhoomi – Odisha Craft Museum

This is a craft museum and is spread over 12-acres of land. It is divided in to two blocks (ie. Museum having display area and a live section). This is built using local raw materials like Laterite stones etc.

There are eight galleries which showcases handicrafts and handlooms of Odisha.

The handicrafts galleries are on terracotta, traditional paintings, stone, wood carvings, metal crafts including tribal crafts, Pattachitra, Dhokra and bell metal crafts etc.

The handlooms galleries display unique and antiques raw materials and rare old equipments. Different handloom sarees produced in different parts of the state, like – Khandua, Tusser, Sambalpuri, Bomkai, Berhempuri silk, kotpada sarees and Maniabandha sarees etc. are displayed here.

The galleries are housed in Odiya style houses with sculptured terracotta styles of western odisha and traditional courtyards. The outer walls are painted with Pattachitra paintings and Ushakothi paintings etc. The items/ collections in the galleries like – pre-weaving, tribal art, Handlooms, modern gallery, dance costume and gallery on Jagannath culture are exceptional.

The live section is having separate workshop, an outdoor amphitheater and children's play area.

Kala Bhoomi Store

This store sales items like – Terracotta, Stone, Wood Carvings, Appliqué and Handloom products of the state. It promotes welfare of the artisans. One should purchase some mementos from this store as a memory or as a gift for a loved one.

The museum also provides guided tours / museum trails / museum walks and workshops on different crafts. The EKAMRA walk on Sundays in this campus (museum trail) would be liked by many visitor.

There are also cultural events on some occasions.

This is located at Pokhariput.

7. Sudarshan Art and Craft Village

This is one of the best stone carving crafts making points of the state which is owned by Padmashri Sudarshan Sahoo.

Art work such as stone carvings from granite, black marble, red stone and soap stone sculptures of all sizes are available in a garden like setting. Here, one can meet people who give life to the stones. Many artists are trained and hundreds of Craftsmen and sculptures all over the state have got training from this place.

One will observe how the ancient Guru – Sishya system is prevalent in the premises. The training is imparted free of cost and after completion the artisans are free to open their workshop.

Two years course is also provided under the development commissioner of the handicrafts, Central Government. The centre is having workshop, art gallery, tool room, hostel and other facilities.

This crafts centre showcases the living heritage of Odishan art and crafts at Bhubaneshwar. It is a great place for visitors to see, feel and to buy some stone carvings / sculptures.

It is situated at Nadankanan Road, Jayadeva Vihar.

8. Jain Heritage Museum-pratap Nagari

Jain heritage Museum at Pratapnagari is situated in the middle of the twin-city near Goddess Dhakulei, NH -16, although the place is in Cuttack District. (covered by the Author in the book -EXCITING CENTRAL-COASTAL ODISHA, under Cuttack District).

Seven jain sculptures were recovered during digging of the kakatpur Branch Canal during 1970's. Subsequently 9-jain sculptures were recovered from the nearby agricultural fields of the locality. The museum was established in 2005-AD to place these sculptures.

The museum has sculptures of Rishavnath (1st Tirathnkar of the Jains), Parsvanatha, Mahavir, Ambika and Gomedha etc.

As per historians these sculptures which are of black stone, may be of 9th / 10th century AD. It is believed that there was a Jain temple near Kuakhai, which might have been destroyed by natural calamities or by the invaders. Further research required in the matter. The museum requires infrastructure development.

This museum is set up to preserve the ancient Jain sculptures recovered from the nearby areas of Kuakhai river.

9. Kalinga Rail Museum

The Kalinga Rail Museum showcases the history of Indian Railways, especially of the East Coast Railways . Many untold stories and achievements of the railways in general and East Coast Railways in particular would charm any visitor. The old coaches, engines including steam, diesel and electric, railway equipments, instruments, technology devices, signalling systems and models enlighten the public about the railways. There is an impressive display of artefacts and photographs, various documents, old manuals, railway maps from early days, postage stamps and logos etc. in the indoor section, which meticulously present the real history of the railways.

Coach restaurant and toy train are other attractions.

Visit to this museum would facilitate any visitor to enhance one's knowledge about heritage of Indian Railways and it's operation.

This is situated at Rail Kutir, Chandrasekharpur.

PLANETARIUM

Pathani Samanta Planetarium

PATHANI SAMANT PLANETORIUM named after great naked eye astronomer Mahamahopadhyaya Chandrasekhar Simha Harichandan Mohapatra Samanta (ie. Popularly known as PATHANI Samanta and famous for his classic-Siddhanta Darpana), was built by the science and technology department of Government of Odisha. It is a dome shaped building, where one can witness number of programmes associated with astronomy. It has a 12-diameter dome with sitting capacity of 178-persons.

It spreads awareness about the study of astrophysics, astronomy and space sciences. It has rich collection of books on science and technology.

Inside the PLANETORIUM one can learn from the audio visuals. There are many poster shows where one can participate. The main highlight is the night sky gazing and observing the astronomical objects and their position in the space. "Safe sky watch" programmes are also conducted during solar and lunar eclipse and on the days of rare astronomical events.

It is a favourite for science lovers.

This is built in an area of around 5-acre with a well maintained garden around it. It is near Acharya Vihar square.

Art Gallery

Visit to Art Galleries of Bhubaneshwar would enhance one's knowledge about various art forms both contemporary and traditional, popular tribal and folk paintings and relationships between human and nature. Besides the Kalinga Art Gallery as described under Odisha State Museum, some of the important Art Galleries of the city are as under:

1.Odisha Modern Art Gallery

This is known for boosting Odisha art of modern times, where one will find both ancient as well as contemporary artworks.

The exhibits of some brilliant works of art on wood carvings, sculptures, oil and water work etc. are the attractions. It provides a platform to local artists.

Creation of various artists of state and national level and large collection of Odisha's art and craft are found here. One can buy the wonderful creations. Special art camps and imparting training to children for various art tricks are other specialities of this art gallery.

It is situated in forest park, Bhubhaneswar.

2. Buddha Art Gallery

Buddha Art Gallery is one of the biggest art galleries in the state which was established with the initiative of Government of Odisha.

Some of the innovative tribal art forms, traditional art and contemporary art and the painting of eminent artists like Siba Panigrahi and DN Rao are found here. Although, the visitors cannot buy the artwork directly from the gallery, they can contact them directly to buy the exhibited sculptures and paintings.

It is situated in Buddha Jayanti park, Lumbini Vihar, Chandrasekharpur.

3. Subhadra Art Gallery

It deals in both traditional and contemporary forms of art and craft. This is one of the most precious art galleries of Bhubaneshwar. One will find diverse portfolio of art and crafts of traditional painting, magnificent sculptures, fascinating painting made by use of acrylic, charcoal, oil etc. It is a hub of artists, collectors, curators and art patrons. It also outsources creations of senior artists of the country and abroad.

The gallery also hosts workshops, art camps and exhibitions to promote the contemporary art of the state and country all around the globe.

It is located in Tankapani road, near Radhika tower.

4. Gallery Oic

The Gallery of OIC (ie. Odisha India Craft Gallery) is an overseas initiative which deals with painting created by various artists of the state.

One can find traditional paintings such as Pattachitra, Saura tribal and palm leaf paintings along with modern art including canvas paintings. It is functional in digital mode. It is in N 2/ 117A, IRC village, Nayapalli.

Bhubaneshwar As Sports Capital Of India

Odisha Government has invested substantial amount for development of Bhubaneswar as a sports city, which is a premium site as a sports destination.

In 2018 AD, the then FIH and IOA President Narinder Dhruv Batra regarded Bhubhaneswar as the "Sports capital of India". As per Sh Batra, "While Delhi is the political capital, Mumbai the financial capital and Bengaluru the IT capital of India, Bhubaneshwar is undoubtedly the Sports capital of the country".

Odisha, which is the cradle of Hockey was the first state to sponsor National Hockey Team. The sponsorship is applicable for both mens' and womens' team besides the junior boys' and girl's team.

Odisha was the first state to organise Tribal Sports Meet in 2017, Champions Trophy Hockey Tournament in 2014 AD, FIH Hockey world league final – 2017, Indo – Japan Hockey series-2015, Hockey India League – 2014, 2015, 2016, 2017 AD, Asian Athletics Championships – 2017 AD and ITF Men's Futures – 2018 (Tennis).

Further, Indian arrows adopted Odisha as their home ground for the U-15 I – League. Asian Rugby 75- U18 Women's Championship-2018, Indian Super league – 2018 (football), Indian Super cup – 2018 (football), I-league matches – 2018 (football) FIH Hockey World Series Finals and the Biggest Sporting extravaganza Hockey Men's World Cup – 2018 were held here.

MOU have been signed with several corporates and Sports persons to set up high performance centres in – Hockey,Athletics, swimming, weightlifting, shooting, Sports climbing, Football and for different other sports. Sports has become an important part of the culture of the state and Bhubaneswar city plays an important role.

Besides Field Hockey, other sports like – Tennis, Rugby sevens, Football and athletics are now becoming the most popular sports of the state.

As per the then Chief Minister Sh Naveen Pattanyak, "we want Odisha to set a benchmark in global sports arena and it is hoped it will take the state to the next level".

Bhubaneshwar has emerged as a major sports destination on the world map.

There is a great potentiality to project Odisha internationally.

Even as per some sports reporters / professionals, Odisha has the capacity and infrastructure to pull off Olympics very well.

Kalinga Stadium

It is a multi – purpose stadium in Bhubaneswar which is situated near Nayapalli area / Jayadeva Vihar fly over.

It's foundation stone was laid by former Chief Minister of Odisha, late Biju Pattanayak in 1978 AD. It is the home stadium of Indian Men's and Women's National Field hockey and also Kalinga lancers, that performs the Hockey India league.

The sports complex have 10-high performance centres. It has facilities for athletics, football, badminton, hockey, swimming, Basketball, Table Tennis, sports climbing, sports science and sports management. The stadium has 8-lane athletics track, gymnasium and sports hostel for players.

India's first Olympic standard pink and blue water based AstroTurf is present here.

The capacity of the Hockey stadium is 15-thousand with 4-grand stands. It is one of the best Hockey stadiums in the world with upgraded pitch lights and broadcast cameras. It has the facilities for locker rooms, goalkeeper equipment rooms, umpire changing room, media tribune and broadcaster's room.

The Naval Tata Hockey High Performance Centre and Abhinav Bindra Targeting Performance Centre (ABTP) would be liked by any sports personality. The stadium has a sitting capacity of 16-thousand.

Due to infrastructure available in the stadiums like Kalinga stadium of the city and as per Survey, Bhubaneshwar was ranked third among five cities of India in terms of Sports Ecosystem and ability to host mega sporting events.

Wild Life Sanctuary

A) Nandan Kanan Wild Life Sanctuary

The entire landscape which includes Nandan Kanan Zoological Park, the Kanjia Lake and the State Botanical Garden has been notified as Nandan Kanan Wild life Sanctuary. Nandan Kanan signifies Garden of Gods.

Nandankanan Zoological Park

This Zoo was carved out of Chandaka forest. The centrally located Kanjia lake separates the zoo from the botanical garden. It was established on 29th December, 1960 AD to ensure that flora and fauna can be thrived in a natural habitat. It is spread over an area of around 437-hectares. Nandan Kanan means garden of pleasure. Out of total area of 4.37 square kms, 1.64 square kms are used for tourism. The road coverage for Tourism is around 8-kms.

This is home to diverse range of wild life which includes flora, fauna and mammals.

There are more than 3-thousand animals with around 158-Species. Which includes more than 634-mammals, 812-birds and 134-reptiles.

It is famous in the world for it's white tigers and white tiger Safari, now known as Tiger Safari. It is the only Zoo in India that is home to Patas Monkeys, Eastern Rosella variety of Parakeet and open billed stork.

The natural forest area of Nandan Kanan is home to free living wild animals including 13-species of mammals, 15-species of reptiles, 179-species of birds, 20-species of Amphibians, 96-species of butterflies and 51-species of spiders.

The Zoo had created history, when in 1967 AD a wild female tiger climbed up the concrete wall and leapt down in to the tiger enclosure of the Zoo, thereby perhaps becoming the only wild animal in existence that has ever opted to join in a zoo.

As per National Geographic, "Odisha must be the only place in the world with enough sophistication to have a modern well designed Zoo and enough tigers to stock it by voluntary membership!"

Here animals are kept in their natural habitat. Tigers, lions, coloured leopards, black panther, European brown bear, Himalayan black bear, gharials, Indian Python and king cobra are the attractions of the zoo.

The zoo contains several rare and endangered species such as white tigers, Asiatic lions, crocodile, Indian pangolin, 34 aquariums that contain several species of fish / aquatic animals. In the aquarium both fresh water and marine species are found. The Sucker fish would attract any visitor.

Nature interpretation center, water bird aviary, lake view, nature trail, Reptile park, Nocturnal house, Aerial rope way, Aquarium, toy train, boating and elephant ride etc are added attractions. The local forest area is having more than 700-Species of plants.

All larger animals like – Carnivorous and Antelopes etc. have huge enclosures.

The section of Nocturnal birds and animals is quite dark / dim – lit and are specially designed. These are specious naturalistic enclosures stimulating their natural habitat with species-specific enrichment to fulfil the biological needs.

All the 3-types of crocodiles found in the country along with varieties of turtles are there.

The aviary for exotic birds is a unique exhibit of it's kind in the country.

The aviary has-tree dwellings birds, land dwellers and water birds.

The rare birds are housed species wise in dedicated enclosures. The chirping of love birds in varieties of colours are the attractions.

Non indigenous flightless birds like Emu and Ostriches etc. add to it's beauty.

The reptile park has a gigantic dinosaurs at the entrance and having many varieties of reptiles. The Amphibian exhibits are attractive.

Nandankanan Zoological Park is a premier large zoo of India. Unlike other Zoo s in the country, this Zoo is housed in a forest. The animals are housed in enclosures with green surroundings with a feel of real forest.

The tourists can take a tour on foot to enjoy the wild life in their natural habitat. This zoo is the first in the world – to have bred Melanistic and white tigers successfully, the first zoo in India where endangered Ratel was born in captivity, only conservation breeding centre of Indian Pangolins in the world, only zoo in India to have an Open-top Leopard Enclosure and second largest heronry for Open Billied Storks in Odisha

As understood, this is the only zoological park in India to become an institutional member of World Association of Zoos and Aquarium (WAZA) and only zoo in India after which an express train Puri-New Delhi express has been named as "Nandankanan Express".

While visiting Nandankanan Zoo, one should visit the following centres with the permission of the Zoo Authorities.

A) Breeding Of Water Monitor Lizard

This is a breeding centre for water monitor lizards and they are bred regularly since – 2012 AD. Through artificial incubation, the Zoo has hatched the water monitor lizard eggs, successfully. It is understood more than 27-births had taken place in the zoo.

B) Gharial Breeding

This zoo is famous in the world for breeding of the Gharials in captivity for the first time, during 1980 AD. Hatching of crocodile eggs both in artificial hatchery and naturally inside the enclosure was successful in the same year and was continued in subsequent years.

During the year 1986-87 AD, 81 Gharials were first released in Mahanadi river system. As understood, more than 578 Gharials were released in nature and 64 were transferred/ exchanged to other centers/ Zoos till date. Zoo is also making efforts to incubate the available eggs artificially in sand cubes with proper monitoring and regulating the temperature and humidity.

C) Indian Pangolin Breeding

As understood, with the efforts of the breeding centre some pangolin babies were born.

The study is being carried out under the surveillance of installed CCTV cameras inside the enclosures which are capturing the activities in the form of videos during the night time also. This is unfolding the secrets of the life of the pangolins. S

D) Conservation Of Vultures

Nandankanan is among the six participating zoos for the conservation breeding of White-backed vulture for which an enclosed area of 0.3 acres and surrounded by around 7-acres undisturbed forest area has been constructed. This satellite campus has all the basic facilities. The centre was established with objectives to develop protocol for captive management and breeding of long billed vultures for reintroduction and release in to wild and to generate awareness about the conservation need of the vultures and their role in the ecosystem.As per Authorities of the Zoo, "The centre presently has one colony aviary (100'X40'X20'), two nursery aviary (10'X12'X8') and a laboratory complex with observatory room for CCTV monitoring, laboratory for analysis of biological samples, incubation room and biologist chamber.The aviaries are large enough for the vultures to perform wing exercises by flying from one end to another and to feed communicably on carcasses, exactly as they do in the wild, thereby minimising the human contact with vultures.

It also has species specific enclosure enrichments like naturalistic nesting platforms and nest baskets, adequate perches in vertical and horizontal positions from the walls and water pools. All the perches are wrapped with coir ropes to prevent bubble foot disease. Aviary doors open to galleries which provide double door protection which provides birds from accidental escape.

All the vultures are marked with leg bands for individual identity. Their activity pattern including mating is being monitored through two fixed angle and one PTZ camera with infrared facility."

Safari Inside The Zoo

The Bear Safari (covers an area of 5-hectares), Lion Safari (covers an area of 20-hectares), Elephant Safari, Unique White Tiger/ Tiger Safari (covers an area of 12-hectares) and herbivorous Safari (covers an area of 21-hectares) are the hallmarks of the Zoo. The lion Safari made inside the zoo is one of the largest in India. The vehicles carrying visitors along with guides roam inside the tiger Safari, lion Safari and Safari containing the deer, bisons, sambars, four horned antelope, wild boar, pea fowls and jungle fowls etc. in natural environment. Here, the visitors are confined in a vehicle and the animals roam in the open jungles. The Zoo had introduced an innovative concept, ie. "Adopt-An-Animal" programme to mobilise resources. The visitors to the Zoo have the benefit of a sanctuary. If one is interested for Nature and wild life, this is the best place in the city. There are well laid out path ways with signage and the map ie. "you are hear map of the park".

Nandankanan is 15 kms from the Bhubaneswar city centre. The Bhubaneswar railway station is at a distance of 18 kms and the Biju Patnaik International Airport is at a distance of 20 kms. Tourist cottages inside Nandankanan are available for accommodation, only during day time, on prior reservation from the office of Deputy Director, Nandankanan Zoological Park.Uniqueness

Kanjia Lake / Nandankanan Lake

This natural lake is spread over an area of 75-hectares and is declared as the wetland of National importance. It is on the northern outskirts of this historical city.

The wetland covers an area of 105-hectares and road divides the wetland. The zoological garden is on the south side of the lake and the botanical garden is situated on the northern side.

It has a rich ecosystem that consists Nandankanan Bio-logical park and Botanical gardens which are adjacent. One can explore the same, after exploring the lake.

The lake has the opportunity to indulge in waster sports and it provides recreational boating. Paddle boats and motor boats playing in calm waters is entertaining and one of it's kind experience during sunset in the midst of Zoo, the vast greenery of Botanical garden and hippos in the lake water.

It is home to many local migratory birds and a nice spot to watch large number of migratory birds during winter months.

It has rich collection of aquatic flora and the floral diversity consists of 10-Submerged macrophyts, 14-Species of floating macrophytes and 24-Species of emergent macrophytes.

The faunal diversity includes 39-Species of avi-fauna, 14-Species of reptiles, 10-Species of amphibians, 46-Species of fish fauna and 3-Species of prawns.

Rapid urbanisation in the area has taken a toll on the inlets and outlets of the lake and it is facing threat.

The water level has decreased substantially due to weeds and sedimentation.

As per Tourmyindia.com, "It is one of the famous tourist spot of the country because of the surreal beauty that girdles it. Complementing the quiet and charming views of the lake, the green clad hills in the backdrop make a surreal ambience at Kanjia lake for all the travellers to admire".

It is on the boundaries of Nandan Kanan Zoological Park and the Botanical garden.

Botanical Garden- Nandan Kanan

The State Botanical Garden is situated inside Nandankanan wildlife sanctuary and is on the other side of the zoo.

It is situated between the wetlands of Kiakani lake and Kanjia lake. Kiakani Lake with an area about 25 hectres is located inside the State Botanical Garden.

The Botanical Garden was established in the year 1963 and was initially under the management of Horticulture Department. The management of the State Botanical Garden was transferred to Nandankanan wild life sanctuary on 1st August 2006.

It is one of the pioneering plant conservation and nature education centre of the State and provides memorable experience to the green enthusiasts.

The main objective of this unique Botanical garden is to spread awareness among the public and to preserve the plant species. More than 750-species of plants have been documented. The State Botanical Garden is spread over an area of 75 ha (around 173 acres). It is a part of the moist deciduous forests and has preserves of varieties of indigenous plants.

Details

The Botanical Garden covers 24 different satellite gardens and parks, like –

Butterfly garden, Rose garden, Medicinal garden, Japanese garden, Bougainville garden, Heritage garden, dry garden, evolution garden, Arboretum park (Botanical garden for trees) and Mogul garden etc.

There are facilities for Forest Rest House (FRH), Pindis for picnics and interpretation center etc. The details of the gardens and other facilities as observed and understood from the officials of the park are as under.

Glass House

A spacious glass house of 2013 square ft. has been developed for housing succulent plants. A variety of succulents add beauty to the Glass House. One can enjoy blooming ornamental plants during the period from November to March.

Cacti House

A 1080 square ft. Playhouse houses important species of cacti plants. A rich collection of more than 1200 cacti are available in the Cacti House.

Bonsai

A rich collection of more than 300 numbers of bonsai of 55 varieties are available.

Philodendron House

More than 2000 numbers of 5 varieties of philodendron are available.

Dry Garden

A garden of xerophytes plants has been developed over an area of 0.65 Acre in front of Glass House. The entire garden has been designed with loose stone work to give it exclusive look of dry zone which attracts the visitors.

Green House

A state of art green house of 5200 Sq ft. houses the of 60 species of indoor plants like Aglaonema, Philodendron, Calathea, Cordyline, Diffenbachia, Spathophyllum, Peperomia, Monstera, Hemigraphis etc..

Butterfly Park

Butterfly Park, an interesting option among visitors has been developed over an area of 36,590 sqft. The garden has a unique landscape with 6400 butterfly dependant plants. The garden has one cascading waterfall with 170 sqft. flowing water channel, fountains and artistic bridges. One can sight more than 81-Species of butterfly, here. The visitor will get the fragrance of beautiful flowers and feel the beauty of flying jewels of nature. The newly created Butterfly Park was opened to the visitors in February, 2014.This Butterfly Park also contain a butterfly interpretation centre. The Centre spreads over an area of 800 sqft, has been developed near the Butterfly Park. The newly opened centre has colourful pictorial display boards to disseminate information on butterfly to the visitors. The main objective of the centre is to provide latest information on various aspects of butterfly. A short documentary about butterfly is an added attraction. The Interpretation centre was opened to the visitors in March, 2015.

Rosarium

It is one of the richest collections of 1200 Rose plants belonging to 55 varieties grown over an area of 1.5 acres of land. The garden is liked by the visitors most and has maximum foot fall during the winter.

Orchid House

This is the largest orchid house of the State which spreads over an area of 5000 sqft. and displays more than 1000 orchids of 57 varieties belonging to 37 species. One can enjoy the orchid in bloom round the year displaying various colour of nature.

Medicinal Garden

A well laid medicinal garden spread over an area of 2.26 acres which displays of rich collection of 225 species of trees, shrubs and herbs.

Japanese Garden

A state of art Japanese Garden in Tsukiyama-niwa style with flowing streams and other typical features is a star attraction. It covers an area of 0.50 acres.

Mughal Garden

Mughal Garden covering an area of 1.01 ha. has a cascade of flowing water and flowering plants both seasonal and perennial on both the sides give a look of gardens of Mughal era. The garden is liked mostly by the young people and has maximum foot fall during winter.

Evolution Garden

The newly constructed Evolution Garden covering an area of 0.77 ha. gives complete information about the evolution system of plant kingdom. The one way path takes a visitor from lower plant groups like Algae, fungi, Bryophyta, Pteridophyte to evolution of large plant groups like Gymnosperm and Angiosperms. The concept of such garden is very informative for the students and researchers.

Heritage Garden

The Heritage Garden covering an area of 1.2 acres is situated adjoining to the Evolution garden with natural rock and old Banyan trees. A Tulsi (Ocimum sanctum) garden containing six varieties of Tulsi plant with models of monk, live size cow and tribal hut are the attractions of the garden.

Landscape Garden

It is a model landscaping having different elements like lawn, trees and shrubs spread over an area of 1.6 acres. 1000 trees of different species have been planted to maintain the rhythm.

Palm Garden

Palm garden is an amazing site to see varieties of common and rare palms. A collection of 29 varieties of beautiful palms have been planted over an area of 15000 sqft. One designed water body along with 15000 sqft grass carpet has been developed inside the Palm Garden for the public.

Bougainvillea Garden

One Bougainvillea garden has been developed over an area of 21400 sqft. inside the State Botanical Garden. More than 1000 Bougainvillea plants of different colours (8 varieties) have been displayed in the garden. A series of creepers raised on the back of the garden add beauty to the park.

Arboretum

The Arboretum spread over an area of 4 ha. has been established with collection of more than 234 species (from 49 families) found in the eastern Zone forests. A minimum of 10 nos. of each species has been planted with signage displayed. A network of paths have been made through the plantation which will be an ideal walk way for botanists / trainees / students.

Hibiscus Garden

A garden has been developed over an area of 11000 sqft. located in between glass house and Palm garden. More than 130 numbers of plants of 27 varieties have been planted in the garden.

Carnivorous Plant Garden

The garden established inside the state botanical garden covering an area of 800 sqft. is intended to exhibit carnivorous plants. Nandankanan is 1st of its kind to display carnivorous Plants.

The garden has been developed initially to accommodate 4 species of carnivorous plants with provision of naturalistic landscape. It was opened to the visitors in March 2016.

Children's Park

A niche for the kids has been created within the natural setting by providing swings, merry-go-round, sliding chute etc. The gallery located nearby is filled with ornamental plants and enhances beauty of the Park.

Buddha Park

The park has been developed over an area of 12000 sqft. and is located near the scenic beauty of Kanjia Lake. It features a beautiful Buddha Statue as its centre place. Rain shelter, sit outs and ornamental flower beds are other attractions.

Artificial Zoo

Models of different animals are used to explain the ecological niche with an objective to generate awareness among the children.

(source – Botanical garden)

This vast garden is an unique destination and the charm of visiting Bonsai collections, Medicinal garden, Mogul garden for rich colours of flora, Rose garden for blooms of various colours, Japanese garden for advanced techniques of grooming plants and others cannot be forgotten in this hideout of Mother Nature.

B) Chandaka – Dampara – Wild Life Sanctuary – Carbon Sink Of The Twin City

The sanctuary is spread over an area of 193-square kms. It covers a boundary line of around 170-kms and is spread over Cuttack and Khurda districts. It is divided in to 2-ranges, ie. Chandaka and Dampara and is having a common boundary with Nandan Kanan Zoo. There are 7-reserved forest blocks, 5-demarcated protected forest blocks and proposal to include another 6-proposed forest blocks.

It is in the North-western periphery of Bhubaneswar. This sanctuary is for conservation of elephants and is an important elephant reserve of the country.

Many rare species of Flora and fauna are also found here. The Flora consists of semi evergreen forests with thorny bamboo, planted teak, coastal Sal, Jamun and Karanja etc. Common medicinal plants like – Patal Garuda, Shatavari, guduchi lata and Kurchi etc are found plenty. There are few species of ground orchids, ferns and lichens etc.

This sanctuary is famous for wild elephants, popularly known as pachyderm country. It was declared as an Elephant reserve in August-1982 AD. Chital, Wild pig, barking deer, Indian civet, Mongoose, sloth bear and wolf etc. are also found here.

Until 1960 s, there were tigers in the sanctuary. As understood, the last tiger of the area took his last breath in 1967 AD. Although the forest guards speak about presence of tigers, it is yet to be established.

Many avian species like, – peacocks, owl, eagles and many duck species are found, here. During winter as water bodies are nearby, migratory birds are seen.

This sanctuary is home to reptiles like – Rock Python, common krait, turtles and cobras etc.

As per zoological survey of India, there are 37-Species of mammals, 167-birds, 33- reptiles, 13-amphibians and 28-fishes in this sanctuary.

This is a nice place to visit, where elephants are conserved somewhat successfully, although Man-Animal conflict is a common event in this area and the sanctuary is reeling under human pressure.

There are number of watch towers for the visitors. Charichhak, Pitagadia and Kochilaberana are good for observing the Elephants / animals and birds.

Some of the places/ spots, like – Bharatpur reserve forest (ie. wild elephants can be seen from the watch tower in it), Kasuria water source in Bharatpur for wild animals, Godabhangatangar for natural water flow, Kumarkhunti watch tower near water reservoir for wild animals, Salabari for dense sal forests, pithakhia under Akhanga protected forest for natural beauty and Jhalara under Baharpita reserve forest for peacocks and jungle fowl etc. are excellent.

Other Important Spots /Places Inside The Sanctuary

Goddess Ambakali

She is the living Goddess of the area. She is the symbol of love and unity among the inhabitants of the forest and the nearby areas. This is a small temple which opens once in a year.

Bualigarh, Naharthali and Baunsaberena

One will find the remains of the fort which was built by Chodaganga Dev between 1078- 1147 AD. The main palace of BUALIGARH is in the centre of the sanctuary. There is a hill top nearby where one may visit through the forest path of around 1-km.

In the rainy season, one will observe a waterfall from the hillock and it remains almost dry throughout the year. The Baunsaberena water harvesting structure is nearby the fort and is the main attraction of the wild life.

Sunakhani and Dholakatha

The fire clay of this area is famous in the state / country. In the SUNAKHANI demarcated and protected forest one may observe the life style of the ancient people/ tribals.

Madua

This is situated in the Tadakai reserve forest and is famous for the minor irrigation project. It is an amazing place to watch the wild animals.

Salabari

Thick Sal forests is the specialty of the place. During visit a huge and old Sal tree can be seen. As understood from the guard, the tree is more than hundred years old and is around 12-feet diameter.

Mantu

This is situated in Akhanga protected forest. The tranquility of the place and scenic view of Mahanadi river at a distance would mesmerise any visitor. This was the haunting place of the Dampara kings in the past. Pithakhia area of this forest is full of natural beauty.

Godibari entrance is one of the main entrance, to this sanctuary. The cave gate with elephant structures on the top of the entrance gate is an attraction at this place. Godibari is in between Daspur and Bhola forests.

There is a training centre to train the elephants at this place (ie. Named as – Kumki elephant training centre).

This is an enchanting forest reserve. The area is full of lush green dense wood and tall trees. The nature is in abundance in this forest area. This is surrounded by the mountain hills of Cuttack and khordha area.

Private vehicles are not allowed in the sanctuary area. One can walk few kms in the safe zone of the sanctuary. One can also avail the elephant ride.

Safaris

One should enjoy jeep safaris (vehicles which are generally 8-12 seater) in the forest and can explore the jungle and see the wildlife, birds and many others in their habitats.

One can stay at Deras Nature camp and Godibari Nature Camp (ie. both are 5-kms apart) where the visitors can enjoy the beauty of the reservoirs and the sanctuary. The Kumarkhunti watch tower (ie. near the water reservoir) and Ambilo watch tower (ie. under kodamunda reserve forest) are nearby where one can watch birds and wild animals/ elephants without disturbing them.

The animals are generally found during morning / noon hours. Nature trail near the camping site are an added attraction.

It can be visited any time other than monsoons. However, monsoons have it's own charm.

The forts like Chudanga Gada, Buali Gada and caves like – PANDAV Bakhara are part of the forest. (This is covered by the author in the book – Exciting Central – Coastal Odisha, under Cuttack district.)

There are shops and snacks counter and rest shed etc. near the entrance of the sanctuary. One can purchase some mementos here, for a memory.

Others (Visit / Safari At Bharatpur And Chudanga)

There is proposal to develop Chudanga and Bharatpur forests of the sanctuary to showcase the Eco – Tourism asset of Bhubaneshwar. There is plan for two more safaris in Chudanga reserve forest and Bharatpur Reserve forest. Bharatpur is a part of the Chandaka – Dampara sanctuary covering an area of around 1-thousand hectares. Besides wild animals, there are several waterbodies in these two areas, which add to it's beauty.

One can also visit these forests to feel the wilderness

There are two entry points, ie. Godibari and Kantabada / Near Dearas dam to enter the sanctuary.

Tribal Village

The visit to the sanctuary will not be complete without visiting a tribal village nearby. The visitor can have experience of tribal life, their culture, bamboo weaving and their rural life etc.

There are five hamlets inside the sanctuary inhabited by mostly the Shabar tribes and their population is around 6-thousand.

Immediate steps are required to check the encroachment of the sanctuary, from the real-estate developers/others, to safeguard it's eco-system, which is very near to Bhubaneswar. Everyone should try to preserve this beautiful sanctuary.

Dams

Deras Dam

This dam is situated in Chandaka-Dampara elephant sanctuary/ national park. There are cottages on the hill top with provision of guided safari.

One will find bamboo-houses of different styles. The beautiful bamboo huts / twin log hut of Baunshghara in Barhapita reserve forest are the best places for the nature lovers.

The scenic view of the sanctuary can be seen from these cottages and one can see the animals in night. The water flows of the dam, during July to October, will charm any visitor in the lush green surroundings.

The forests, hillocks and calm water would enchant any visitor. The environment is fresh. One can spend some quality time in this silent area, far from the madding crowd. One can see the rich fauna of the area through the watch towers.

One has to take tickets to visit this place near the check post.

The closing time of the dam is 5-pm.

It serves as a water source for the animals of the sanctuary and elephant herds can be seen on some occasions. One can have the nature trail by the side of the dame for around 6.5 kms.

It is a nice place for nature lovers and a great day – long-break, at a peaceful place, near Bhubaneswar.

It is around 20-kms from Bhubaneswar, main bus stand (Baramunda).

Jhumka Dam

This is close to DERAS on the CHANDAKA – DAMPARA WILD LIFE SANCTUARY boundary. No permission is required to visit the area.

Three thick forested hills encircle the dam with water up to the horizon. This place is not far from the city, but filled with some adventures.

The area around the dam is nice and cosy to escape from the boredom of everyday city life. The place is ideal for nature lovers and other visitors to sit back and to enjoy the surroundings.

One has to move on the JHUMKA dam road from Kantabada, after Godibari nature camp. It is around 18-kms from Bhubaneshwar, main bus stand.

All the above three places (ie. DERAS, JHUMKA AND THE SANCTUARY) are close to each other on the KHORDHA – Chandaka Road, where on can spend some time in a relaxing atmosphere inside the jungles. It would be really rejuvenating.

Food / Unique Food Items Of Bhubaneswar

The city is cosmopolitan in nature and people from all parts of the state and country reside here. Hence, culinary lovers would like the city for varieties of appetising cuisines as the city has some of the finest dining experiences.

The special street foods of the city are – Bara-Ghuguni, Arisa pitha, Gupchup, (ie. Gol Gappa in North, Pani-Puri in West and Puchka in West Bengal), Dahibara – Aloo dum, Chat, rolls, momos and sweet dishes like – Rasgulla, Chenna Poda, Chhena Jhili, Malpua and Rasabali etc.

Classic Sweet Dessert

Chenna poda which is burnt cheese cooked with cashew, nuts and sugar, is the most traditional sweet dish of Odisha. It is a must try for any one having a taste for sweets, which is somewhat crispy on the outside and soft on the inside and having a distinctive taste.

Chenna Jhili prepared in fried cheese and sugar syrup is also a popular sweet dish of the city, although it's origin is from Nimapda.

The sweet dish Rashabsli which is originated from Kendrapara, is made using cheese curds and is soaked in flavoured milk and garnished with cardamom.

Bikalananda Rasgulla which is originated in Salepur of Cuttack is a must try for any visitor.

There are many Khau – Gallis (street food lane) in the city. In some of the streets, like – near the Ram Mandir and Patia (ie. near Infosys) and CRPF square etc., one will find rush for street foods during evening hours.

There are many street vendors on the road sides all over the city, especially near colleges, offices and markets. These street foods are not only delicious but also are linked with culture. One has to explore.

Other unique food items of Bhubaneswar are as under:

A) Kora-Khai

Bhubaneshwar is known for it's Kora – Khai which is a traditional food item, mainly served as an offering (prasad) in the Lingaraj Temple / other temples of the city.

These are made up of Khai (Lia, ie. puffed paddy), jaggery, pepper, cinnamon, cashews and coconut pieces. It turns hard and crunchy, when dried. The mouth watering taste and crispness upon biting are it's speciality. These are available in packets and one may carry them on way back to home.

One should visit Baya/ Baiya Kora Khai Shop, near Lingaraj Temple which is famous for it's excellent quality Kora Khai. This jaggery coated flavoured puffed rice is prepared in quality Desi Ghee and mixed with small fried coconut pieces. This is also very popular at various places outside the state.

B) Traditional Odiya Snacks

Pitha is the famous traditional dish/ snacks item of Odisha. This dish has many variants like: –

Enduri pitha, Chitau pitha, Poda pitha, Kakara pitha, Manda and Arisha Pitha etc., which are some of the best Odiya delicacies.

One will be amazed to watch how Enduri pitha (ie. also known as Haladi Patra pitha) is served after unwrapping the same from the turmeric leaves. This is prepared from rice flour and are stuffed with wonderful ingredients like-coconut, jaggery and black Gram etc.

Similarly Chitau pitha / Chakuli pitha is like a sweet variation of Dosha but without any inside stuffing.

Kakara pitha is made from semolina, cardamom and grated coconut etc.

Poda pitha is baked cake – style Odiya dish and famous for it's nice smelling aroma.

Manda pitha is prepared from rice flour with coconut stuffing inside. It resembles Modak of Maharashtra.

Generally, Pitha is cereal based cake which is mostly steamed / boiled.

Although these dishes are prepared during festival time, they are now easily available in many shops. These are tasty snack items to connect with the locals.

Authentic Odiya Cuisine

Visitors should try the dishes like – Dalma (ie. Dal with mixed vegetables), Santula (ie. cooking different types of vegetables togather/ the dish having more greens and fewer spices), Macha Besara (ie. fish cooked with mustard sauce), Pakhal (made from soaking cooked rice) with Badichura (ie.crushed fried Badi / crushed Sundried red lentil dumplings) and Pulao (a sumptuous rice dish) etc. for an authentic ODIYA food experience. These are available in most of the restaurants both big and small. One will also find all the above food items in every traditional ODIYA home.

C) Pahal Rasgola

Pahal is situated in the middle of twin city, Cuttack – Bhubaneshwar. One will find several shops selling, mainly same product of Pahal Rasgulla on both the sides of NH – 16.

This traditional Odisha Rasgullas are softer and creamish in colour. Here, each shop has it's kitchen at the back. If one goes during early morning hours one will get hot Rasgulas, straight from the Kadai. These are also having different sizes.

The Rasgola is very light and somewhat spongy with less sugar / milder sweetness compared to normal Rasgulla.

Besides this famous Rasgulla, one will find Chenna poda and Chenna Gaja.

The locality is synonymous for traditional and unique sweets of Bhubaneswar and Cuttack.

D) Abhada

The ABHADA of Lingaraj temple and Ananta Vasudev temple is the most sought after holy meal in Odisha, after "Mahaprasad /ABHADA" of Lord Jagannath of Puri. This is also taken by the devotees which is considered as a vegetarian culinary delight.

Bhubaneshwar based start-up of the techies have developed an application through which the "ABHADA BHOGA" is delivered at the doorstep, at click of the mouse.

This prasad (ABHADA) is the first choice for many festivals/ religious functions/ festive meals on different occasions. Only seasonal ingredients and indigenous to the country are used.

E) Bamboo Chiken /Bamboo Mutton and Matka Biriyani

Bamboo Mutton / Bamboo chicken is a specialty in some unique restaurants of Bhubaneshwar/ Twin city. Small pieces of Mutton /CHIKEN is cooked inside the bamboo stem and simmered in the oven.

As per Times of India, "The succulent meat carries a burnt flavour which provides earthy smokiness to the dish. It is very popular and sought after in Bhubaneswar".

There are some restaurants like – Jungle View restaurant at the outskirts of the city and some restaurants inside the city which are famous for their indigenous preparations.

F) Koraput Coffee (Ekamra Kanan Botanical Garden)

This outlet provides the best quality coffee produced from the tribal heartland of Koraput district. As opined by many, "Got a craving for coffee? Do not think much, just head towards EKAMRA KANAN and fall in love with Odisha's own coffee, Koraput Coffee".

Nimantrana – Promoting Culinary Tourism

NIMANTRANA restaurant is located on Janpath, near Ramadevi Women's University. This is the first "NIMANTRANA" chain of Restaurants of OTDC. Similar restaurants are opened at Blue Flag Beach, Puri and Rani Bukhari (Queen's palace) of Sambalpur.

It serves authentic Odiya cuisine and Odia cuisine lovers would have one stop destination in the capital city.

One should visit this restaurant to get a taste of authentic Odiya dishes and to get a sense of knowing about the area and it's people.

Others

Most of the people of the city are non-vegetarian and dishes made from fish, crabs, Mutton and chicken are popular. The city is having many famous restaurants which serve flavoured and delicious foods including – Traditional Odisha Cuisine, North Indian, South Indian, Chinese, sea-food, vegetarian dishes / meals, Italian, Mexican and other regional/ continental dishes.

Sea-food, scrummy and mouth watering street foods form an integral part of local cuisine.

While visiting Bhubhaneswar one should have a taste of the same and in every shop there is something to try or just a place to pass one's time.

As described above and for the best eating experience, the city has lot to offer to culinary tourists.

Exhibitions / Fairs / Important Festivals

The cultural heritage of Bhubaneshwar which is more than two thousand and five hundred years old and which is prominently displayed in the architecture of temples, caves and hills has been described in earlier pages. The city provides complete records of Kalinga architecture almost from it's nascent stage to it's culmination.

The vibrant culture of the city can be best enjoyed during religious and cultural festivals.

Further, the spellbinding Odisha dance forms an integral part of the city's culture. This is performed in different festivals, cultural events and functions in various auditoriums Like – Rabindra Mandap and Bhanja Kala Mandap etc.

The famous Odishi dance is also accompanied by classical Odiya songs and Odishi music as well.

Numerous exhibitions, fairs and festivals both religious and cultural are held in the city and every one of them is distinct and is having their own speciality. These are great attraction for the visitors, which are celebrated with great fanfare and enthusiasm.

Religious Festivals

As Bhubaneshwar is a city of various religions and tribes, one will find the celebration of almost all festivals of different religions and tribes.

The major festivals celebrated by the Hindus of the city are- Raja, Maha Bishub Sankranthi, ASHOKASTAMI, Makkar Sankranthi, Magha Saptami, Chandan Yatra, Snana Yatra, Rath Yatra, Durga puja,

Lakshmi puja, Kali puja/ Diwali, Ganesh puja, Nuakhai, Janmashtami, Kartik puja, Shivratri, Holi and Saraswati puja etc.

The Muslim celebrate the festivals like – Eid, Muharram, Eid-al Fitr and Ramzan etc. and Christian celebrate the festivals like – Good Friday, Christmas and New Year etc.. The tribal festivals like – Chaitra Parva, Magh parab and kedu festival etc. are celebrated by various tribes of the city.

It is a city of diversity and here, all the festivals are celebrated with great joy.

Cultural Festivals

The city hosts a number of cultural festivals/ series of fairs which promote the culture, cuisine, martial arts, classical and traditional musics of Odisha.

The vibrancy and spirit of the city can be experienced through these cultural events. The folklores and traditions that are reflected in these festivals would mesmerise any Traveler.

Some of the major fairs/ cultural festivals of the city are as under.

1. Adivashi Mela

This is one of the oldest Tribal fair (Adivasi Mela) of the country which is conducted annually.

This Mela was started with the initiative of the ST and SCRTI Department to popularise the art and craft, folk songs, music and dance of the indigenous communities / Tribals of Odisha under one roof.

Large number of Tribal SHG s also participate in the fair. The products sold here are of genuine quality at a very reasonable price.

The specialty of the festival is the unique tribal jewellery of different tribal communities. Tribal apparels and handicrafts from bamboo and cane etc. are other attractions. It showcases tribal food, tribal agriculture produces, forest products and cultural programmes of the communities.

It is a rare occasion where the unique tribal culture of Odisha can be felt and to learn the life style of the tribal people.

It is held at Adivasi exhibition ground during January/ February for around 15-days.

2. Sisira Sarasa Mela

This fair is organised by ORMAS (Odisha Rural Development and Marketing Society) with the purpose to create market linkage of rural producers with Urban consumers. Large numbers of SHGs also participate in the festival.

This mela which is of National level provides a large platform for display of items and provides opportunities for sale of products by the PGs and SHGs.

Most of the states of the country participate in this event. The art and crafts of North-East like bamboo crafts, decorative flowers, from UP crafts like – silk, wrought iron work and handlooms, Tassar from MP and CHHATISGARH, household decorative items from Gujarat and Rajasthan, food items from Maharashtra, handlooms and home furnishings products from Andhra Pradesh and Tamilnadu, Phulkari Garments from Punjab, woollen and dress materials from Jammu and Kashmir etc. are the attractions of the mela.

All the districts of the state also participate with their products including terracotta products.

Food and spices items from Rayagada, Kandhamal, Nuapada, forest products from Koraput, Kalahandi, Malkangiri, Sabai work from Baripada etc. are special.

There are various cultural programmes in the evening including Odishi dance and folk dances. This mela is like mini India and is organised for around 10-days at Exhibition ground near Ram Mandir, during the month of January.

3. Bali Yatra-Bhubaneshwar

Bali Yatra is organised at Jaripatna, near Patia at the outskirts of the city on the banks of the river Kuakhai.

Although Bali Yatra of Cuttack is famous, recently it is held in Bhubaneswar.

This is observed around 8-days from Kartik Purnima (ie. around October/ November).

Food and household items, varieties of swings and amusement rides are the attractions of the mela. There are toy stalls, giant wheels and different games which are the attractions for the children.

There are cultural programmes in the evening to showcase the maritime history of Odisha.

4. Ekamra Utsav

This is celebrated for ten days which is dedicated to Lord Shiv. The UTSAV has derived it's name from the word "EKAMRA" meaning mango tree and linkage of the place with Lord Lingaraj (ie. Shiv) and his consort Parvati, as per legend.

It is a combination of – Food festival, National Handloom exhibition, Folk Dance festival and National Handicrafts Exibition.

Earlier, it was known as "FEST".

Food fiesta, story telling, trails and performance of celebrities in different areas are the hallmarks of the festival.

Food festival offers several kinds of cuisines of the state. In the street food festival several states and foreign countries also participate.

One will listen to the famous story tellers and their troupes.

Theme based walks are organised to give tourists and locals an opportunity to explore the city.

The celebration which focuses on multiple activities also aims to boost the rich textile industry and the cultural heritage in the most colourful way. The textile exhibition exhibits fabrics gathered from the famous textile centres of Odisha.

National handicrafts exhibitions is the other attraction.

The folk festival shows regional shows that depicts scenes from Ramayan and Mahabharat etc. The distinctive dance performances like – Danda Nrutya, Ghoda Nach, Chhau dance, Akhada, PAIKA dance, Ranapa, Sambalpuri dance and Ghumura are the highlights.

It is organised by BDA in association with Odisha Tourism around December/ January.

5. Mukteswar Dance Festival

It is celebrated in the courtyard of Mukteswar temple, which is one of the most prominent and well preserved temple complex of the city. The temple is famous for it's stone archway and ceiling with eight petal lotus.

The festival was initially started in 1984 AD and was made an annual cultural event from 2004AD.

It concentrates exclusively on Odissi dance where artists of National and International repute participate. This is a good platform for Odissi dancers to showcase their talent.

Solo, duet and group performance of young and senior artists with their classic attire and graceful movements with tapping of their feet to the strokes of accompanying instruments mesmerises the audience. The temple at the backdrop adds beauty to the festival.

It is a 3-day festival organised by Odisha Tourism in association with Odisha Sangeet Natak Academy and OTDC and is held in 2nd / 3rd week of January (ie.generally 14th to 16th January). It showcases the cultural heritage of Odisha to the world.

6. Rajarani Music Festival

This music festival is celebrated against the backdrop of the architectural beauty of Rajarani temple, which is a monument in the absence of any presiding deity. However, the temple is famous for it's 8-digpalakas (ie. guardians of 8-cardinal directions) and sculptures.

The key objective of the festival is to promote the Indian classical and traditional music. Music artists including vocalists, instrumentalists and dancers come from different corners of India to participate in this festival. This festival cherishes various classical dances including Odissi, which is the soul of Odisha.

The festival which popularises the glorious tradition of Indian classical music is celebrated during 2nd / 3rd week of January for three days and is one of the top festivals of the state. It would be liked by any visitor and it attracts large number of National and International tourists.

It is organised by Odisha Tourism department in collaboration with other organisations like OTDC and Odisha Sangeet Natak Academy and Union Ministry of tourism.

7. Dhauli Kalinga Mahostav

DHAULI KALINGA MAHOSTAV showcases a wide range of rural art, Martial art forms and cultural events. It brings together classical, folk, martial and various art forms under one platform.

Dhauli Festival was launched by Odissi dance Guru Gangadhar pradhan in 2003AD.

Kalinga MAHOSTAV was conceptualised by Bhubaneshwar based Italian Odishi dancer Ileana Citaristi as an exclusive martial arts festival highlighting the victory of peace over violence and was staged atop DHAULI hill.

These two independent festivals were brought under one umbrella in 2011 AD with the intervention of Tourism Department of the Government of Odisha and was renamed as Dhauli-Kalinga MAHOSTAV.

Besides promoting cultural tourism, the festival aims to showcase Odisha as one of the most preferred tourist destinations and to place it prominently on the domestic and international Tourism map. It creates awareness among youths, particularly the students about the cultural heritage and traditions of Odisha. One will find hundreds of youths from colleges as the audience.

The Venue DHAULI hills alongside Daya river is the place, where emperor Ashok is believed to have fought Kalinga war and embraced Buddhism.

This is also the festival of martial dance which is celebrated to mark the major victory of peace over war when Kalinga witnessed the battle during the reign of Ashok. The festival encourages people to follow the path of peace and calm, rather than fighting amongst themselves.

Martial artists from all over the state /country participate in the festival. This festival helps in keeping alive the vibrant martial arts forms of the state / country, like – PAIKA Nacha from Odisha and Thang Ta from Manipur etc.

It is celebrated during February.

This festival shows the beauty of Odissi dance and music, folk dances of the state and Cultural dances of other parts of the country. It is a treat for commoners and connoisseurs alike.

It is organised by Odisha Tourism and Odisha Dance Academy for 3-days in the month of February (ie. around 1st /2nd week), at the foothills of DHAULI Shanti Stupa.

8. Khandagiri Mahostav And Kharavela Mela

This Mela starts on the auspicious day of Magha Saptami (7th day of the bright fortnight in the month of Magha). It is also known as "Khandagiri Kumbha Mela" / MAGHA MELA where a large number of saints, religious people and others from various parts of the country participate.

Tradition

A Yagnya is performed in front of the Ananta cave. On first day of the mela PANCHA SAKHAS are installed and Ram Charit Manas is read.

On the second day, a lamp is lit in front of Barabhuja Devi and at the end of Mela, it is dedicated in the Yagnya.

In the evening the locals of Jagmara (ie. a settlement at the foothills of Khandagiri) take out a procession with the deity of Lord Ananta Keshari in a palanquin and walk up to the foothills of UDAYAGIRI. The deity is taken to Rani Hanshpur of UDAYAGIRI hills and after worship is over, the deity is brought back to Naga Math of Jagmara.

As per locals, the Ratha Yatra of Ananta Keshari Dev was celebrated every year from Magha Saptami to the full moon day of the month. Ananta Keshari Dev used to travel to Maushi Maa Temple, known as Naga Matha (ie. at jagmara village) for 9-days, like Rath Yatra of Puri.

At the time of British attack, Lord Ananta Keshari was shifted to Jagamara village from Khandagiri. After mela, he is brought back to jagmara village. The system is changed and now Lord Ananta Keshari is brought to Ranihanshpur of UDAYAGIRI instead of Khandagiri for a day as stated above.

Khandagiri Mela is both a religious and a cultural fair. Both sides of the road towards Khandagiri Chowk are decorated with lights.

Traders and Craftsmen from various parts of the country assemble during the period to sell their products.

Many Craftsmen assemble with their bamboo, clay and stone crafts. Varieties of local handmade products especially from the rural areas are displayed for sale.

Many food kiosks, performance of Jatra, craft items including sell of household items are other attractions.

Jatra is the main focus of the mela.Generally 12-major Jatra troupes perform on 6-Stages during night time. Delicious foods in many stalls are liked by all.

During this period and in the evening hours, Festival of Indian classical and folk dances is organised.

This cultural and religious fair is celebrated with much fanfare for 10-days at the foothills of Khandagiri and UDAYAGIRI hills.

This is organised by the state culture and Tourism department, Bhubaneshwar Municipal Corporation and Odisha Tourism Development Corporation.

There is proposal to shift this Mela (ie. other than religious part) to some other parts of the city.

9. Toshali National Craft Mela

This is one of the most popular handlooms and handicrafts fairs in Eastern India.

The artisans, weavers and sculptures etc. showcase the best of handlooms and handicrafts from across the country. Odisha textiles and crafts would attract any visitor.

The vision of the mela is to strengthen the position of the weavers and artisans who are economically weak by creating market for their products.

The mela creates awareness among the visitors on the skills and creative intricacies involved in making the product.

As per the organisers, this Mela is accessible, inclusive and sustainable, a differently abled and senior citizen friendly event. Many people visit the mela to buy artistic products at a very reasonable rate.

Cultural programmes are performed by the artists/ troupes from different parts of the state /country. The folk dance and folk music performed during the Mela are other attractions.

This is held generally during winter months (ie. November to February) at Janata Maidan.

10. Gurukul Mahostav / Vrindavan Mahostav

This is performed during Holi and has become a permanent fixture of the vibrant events calendar of Odisha Tourism.

It was founded by renowned flautist Pandit Hariprasad Chaurasia. Many internationally acclaimed artists participate in this annual musical extravaganza. It also gives platform to the students to showcase their skill.

It is a joint initiative between Odisha Tourism, Vrindavan Gurukul and other institutions. It's purpose is to bring Indian classical music maestros from across the globe on a single platform.

Trade Fair

Bhubaneshwar is a fast emerging market in Eastern India. Various trade fairs in the city provides the opportunity for wide range of business possibilities. These exhibitions and trade fairs help in expanding the market and bring all the potential buyers and sellers to a single platform. By visiting these fairs one will get the benefit and learn through live demonstrations, product launches, networking opportunities and seminars related to entrepreneurship. It provides platform to expand business contacts.

Many trade shows / fairs like – Fashion and life style exhibitions in hotels like MAYFAIR, India International Travel Exhibition, Make in Odisha Conclave, Indian Fashion exhibition, Odisha Travel Bazar, Holiday Expo, Indian Tourism fair, career fair, National Philatelic exhibition and Home-Décor exhibition etc are held during different period of the year.

However, some of the major trade fairs of the city are as under:

1. India International Mega Trade Fair and Home Décor Exhibition

This trade fair is one of the biggest exhibitions in the area of household consumable industry in India.

Different states and many countries participate in this mega fair. Diverse range of industries showcase their unique products in different stalls.

This fair gives an impetus to builders, home decorators and other traders. This is generally organised by the Confederation of Real Estate Developers' Association of India (CREDAI) in collaboration with Odisha Chamber of Commerce and others.

It is generally held at Janata Maidan during January-February.

2. Msme Trade Fair

Startups, Food processing units, Mission Shakti and PSU units etc. are the participants of this festival. It provides open platform for demonstration of machineries and new technology. Special emphasis is given to Women entrepreneurs and Mission Shakti Groups for socio-economic development of the state.

As many PSU s and potential entrepreneurs participate to locate potential vendors, the scope for extension and expansion of MSME is immense through B2B and B2C meetings etc. It is generally held during January-March at IDCO EXHIBITION GROUND.

Book Fairs

Book Fairs are knowledge fairs which reunites the publishers, writers and book lovers. Such fairs add new horizon of knowledge among the public. They provide interactive space for writers and book lovers. Such type of events provide platform for intellectual discussion. In various book fairs of the city, a lot of literary persons come in the evening and they discuss and give insight on a lot of topics. The major book-fairs of the city are as under:

1. Rajadhani Book Fair

Rajadhani Book fair is generally held in the Exhibition Ground, Unit -3 during winters (ie. around December/ January) which is attended by large number of booksellers, publishers, distributors and agencies from different parts of the country. One will find varieties of books on religious scriptures, science and technology, culture, politics, astrology, sports, fiction and non-fiction books, competitive books for students, text books and material in CDs etc. It attracts large number of book readers.

In the evening culture programmes, seminars and various competitions are held.

This book fair owes it's origin to Children's Book Fair during – 1999AD at Soochana Bhavan under the leadership of Dr Upendra Kumar Jena. This was later converted to Rajadhani Book Fair with the participation of more publishers.

Many corporate houses, Government organisations and Universities also participate in this popular fair.

This fair receives good response and large number of people visit it.

2. Kalinga Book Fair and Sishu Mahostav.

This book fair is organised every year by the ladies of Bhubaneswar/ State (started under the direction of the founder/ secretary Mrs Renuka Mishra) for children.

This is organised for more than 25 years.

The first children's book fair was held in the year 1996 AD at Kasturaba Nari Mahal, Bhubaneshwar, by original founder late

Purnendu Mishra, writer and the then secretary of the NGO named SISHU MAHOSTAV.

In the year – 1998 AD, after the death of the founder "Children's Book Fair" was given the new name as "Kalinga Book Fair" and was organised by the women members in a new venue at "Soochana Bhavan".

With the participation of more publishers from the state / country, it is being held in the EXIBITION Ground, near Ram Mandir, since – 2003AD.

Besides various book stalls mainly related to children, the students and experts of the state used to discuss various issues and review the books.

The books published in different categories are selected for the annual Kalinga fair award and Purnendu Mishra Memorial Award.

Hundreds of book publication houses participate in the fair. This apart various competition such as poetry, reading, essay and other contests among the Children are organised, every evening. On some occasions, one will find interesting toys of children which help them in cognitive development.

This is generally held in the month of November.

3. International Book Fair

The International book fair is held at the exhibition ground where hundreds of book publishing houses from the country/ world participate.

This is being organised by the Odisha Language, literature and culture department. Besides the book release function, cultural programmes are organised every evening.

4. Walking Book Fair

Bhubaneshwar is also famous for the walking Book Fair which is an independent bookstore, library, publisher and bookmobile based in Bhubaneswar.

It was started in 2014 AD by Akshaya Bahibala and Shatabdi M to take books to different states of India and make them available at affordable rates. They have partnered with Speaking Tiger, Harper Collins India and Pan Macmillan India.

It is a van full of books (book mobile) with the purpose of making them available to more people. It also provides space for the youths to debate about the issues around through poetry and books. This is unique.

The Department of Odiya language Literature and Culture of Odisha Government organises The State Book Festival (ie. Akshara Book Fair) at EXIBITION Ground, Unit-3.

In the age of digital, these book – fairs are a rare treat for those who enjoy and appreciate the wonders of written words. While in Bhubaneswar during this period, one should visit these fairs not only for purchase of good books but also to discover new books and authors.

Education Hub

Bhubaneshwar is an education hub of the country and specially in Eastern India due to presence of many institutions of National eminence / many Universities/ higher learning institutions/ Technical institutions both under public and private management.

The major institutes present in the city / suburbs are – AIIMS, Institute of Medical Sciences and Sum Hospital, Kalinga Institute of Medical Sciences,

Hi-tech Medical college and Hospital, Dr. Abhin Chandra Homeopathic Medical college and Hospital, Indira Gandhi Memorial Ayurveda Medical College and Hospital, Utkal University, RD Women's University, Odisha University of Agriculture and Technology, Utkal University of Culture, Siksha-o-Anusandhan University (SOA), Xavier University, Kalinga Institute of Industrial Technology University (KIIT UNIVERSITY), IIT, NISER, Institute of physics, Institute of Mathematics and Applications (IMA), Institutes of Minearals and Materials Technology, Central Institute of Fresh water Aqua Culture (CIFA), National Institute of Fashion Technology, Regional Research Center, KISS, Utkal Sangeet Mahavidyalaya, Guru Kelucharan Mohapatra, Odissi Research center, Bhim Bhoi school for the blind, BJB Autonomous College, College of Engineering and Technology, Central Institute of plastic Engineering and Technology, Regional Institute of Education, Regional Medical Research centre and many private Engineering, Management, Computer, life science, law colleges, Teacher training institutes, Diploma / polytechnic colleges and other institutions of fine arts.

These institutions provide quality education to the students on various disciplines and throughout the country. Some of them are premier institutions of the country.

Marketing

Bhubaneshwar has a lot of options to shop unique handicrafts and handlooms of Odisha. There are also many shops from where the silver filigree items and tribal jewellery can be purchased. Some of the important market places of the city are as under:

Ekamra Hat

This shopping hub is spread over an area of around 5-acres. Here, one will find various types of handicrafts, quality handlooms and various other items produced by the artisans of the state.

This traditional handicrafts produced by local artisans and weavers would be liked by any visitor.

One can taste the local cuisine or enjoy one's leisure time in the open air theatre or enjoy the sight of beautiful water fountain.

It is situated in Madhusudan Marg, Unit-3, Bhubaneshwar.

Utkalika

This is one of the popular shops to get unique textile items of the state, brass and bell metal items, appliqué works, tribal jewellery, terracotta products.

It is a one step shop for buying exotic Odisha handicrafts and handlooms.

This is owned and managed by Odisha state co-operative handicrafts corporation and one will get wide range of handicrafts and handloom items of the state.

It is situated in Market building, Unit – 2 of Bhubaneswar and in Sahidnagar.

Market Building

It is one of the oldest shopping place of the city where one will get most of the items. There are separate shops for various items. The market is famous for clothing, footwear and souvenirs etc. The local food stalls are added attractions. It is one of the busiest street markets in the city / state. This market is crowded all the time and has a separate charm.

It is situated in Unit – 2, Ashok Nagar.

Master Canteen Area

This is one of the oldest shopping place of Bhubaneswar. This area is having several gems -jewellery shops, saree shops selling wide range of sarees, filigree items and local handicrafts / other crafts of the state. Many people visit this area as the shop keepers will make you happy with the one that you are looking for, as wide range of items are found here.

There are other markets in the city, like – Bapuji Nagar (famous for electric/ electronic items), Sahid Nagar (various artefacts with many designs and colours, computers and mobiles etc.) and Chandrasekharpur area for wide range of products.

Bhubaneshwar is also having many shopping malls like – Esplanade One Mall-Rasulgarh, BMC Keshari Mall-Ashok Nagar, Pal Heights – Jayadeva Vihar,

DN Regelia Mall – Patrapada, Utkal Heights – Kalpana area, which are also good options for shopping in a spacious and airy atmosphere. One will get the best National and International brands under one roof. The food courts and well known food chains in these malls are added attractions. These are nice places to spend time with family and friends and for a better shopping experience.

Others

Ekamra Walk / Heritage Trail

This is a heritage walk to explore the heritage trail of Bhubaneshwar which is a guided walk through the old town Bhubaneswar. It starts every Sunday morning around 6.30 AM.

This is a weekly heritage walk to rediscover the city.

The famous four routes under heritage walk are as under:

- Route – 1: It covers 8-temples, ie. Brahmeswar, Bhsakareswar, Rajarani, Taleswar, Parshurameswar, Daiteswar, Mukteswar and Kedareswar temples. They are lying at a walking distance of 2.5 kms.
- Route – 2: It covers 23-temples, ie. Mukteswar, Daiteswar, SWARNAJALESWAR, Subarneswar, Brahma temple, Vishnu

temple, Gourishankar, Chitrakarini, MAKARESWAR, Vaital and Sisireswar, Taleswar, Kedareswar complex, Kotitirtheswar, Sampurnajaleswar, Ananta Vasudev, TIRTHESWAR, Kainchi temple, Papanashini, Bharati Matha, Uttareswar and Parshurameswar. It covers around 2.2 kms.

- Route – 3: It covers 11-Shrines, ie. Laxmaneswar group of temples, Rameswar, Gosagareswar, Vaital, Bharati math, MAKARESWAR, Papanashini, Chitrakarini, Kainchi, Vimaleswar and Lingaraj temple. It covers around 2-kms.
- Route – 4: It has 11-heritage temples, ie. TARESWAR, Dwarbasini, Brahma temple, Ananta Vasudev, N-E corner shrine, Suka-Sari complex, Mohini, Markandeswar, Vaital, Chandan Mandap and Uttareswar temple. It covers around 2.2 kms.

Visit to these heritage sites and the beauty of these majestic monuments would enthral any visitor.

Some of the heritage trails start from Mukteswar temple and terminates at EKAMRA Van.

One can also decide one's own route to feel the pulse of EKAMRA KSHETRA.

The EKAMRA walks takes one along the dusty alleys of old town across the time less temples. One can travel back in time through the living traditions of the local settlements along with their customs, costumes, colour, cuisine and experience the glorious history of EKAMRA KSHETRA.

The heritage trail which is trending as EKAMRA walk has welcomed more than thousands heritage lovers.

These weekly walks are organised around temples of old town, covering destinations of great historical and cultural significance.

Flower Show-at Ekamra Kanan

A flower show is organised in the EKAMRA KANAN in the month of January, every year. Large varieties of flowers in the show would attract any visitor.

To encourage the residents for raising garden, there is garden competition for the residents.

The plant bazar is another attraction of the show, where the public can buy varieties of saplings/ flowering plants, garden tools, fertilisers and pesticides etc.

This is organised by the plant lovers association in collaboration with Regional plant resources centre, Odisha Tourism and Horticulture department.

VINTAGE AIR CRAFT AND VINTAGE CAR

The Aircraft D -185 Twin Beech at the entrance of Mayfair Hotels is the first Aircraft owned by an Odia (Maharaja of Mayurbhanj, a former princely state of Odisha). As understood, it was probably the first to touch the soil of Odisha in 1945 AD. There are also display of specially curated collection of vintage cars in the premises of the said hotel. This would be liked by any visitor.

Miniature Book Collector / Museum

One should visit the miniature book museum of Siddhartha Mohanty having more than 4-thousand books. There are more than hundred Geeta and bibles and dictionaries for than 300-languages and 300-miniature Shakespeare's books etc... This is unique.

Unique Ganesh Idols (In-House Gallery)

In the house Er. Kshitish B Swain one will find more than three thousand unique Ganesh idols.

The idols and images vary from different types of stones to brass, copper, steel, wood, paddy, grains, coconut, ceramic, charcoal, glass, silver filigree, bamboo and many other materials. In this home gallery one will find artefacts and utility items featuring Lord Ganesh.

His house is in Brit colony, Nayapali.

Sister Cities

Bhubaneshwar and Cupertino were officially approved as sister cities in August-2012 AD.

It is a community based non-profit organisation to develop positive multi-cultural interaction and understanding through art, culture and education by exchange of student programmes, government delegations and Rotary club etc.

Cultural Corridor

The cultural heritage of Bhubaneshwar is best reflected in various art -stone cultures, wood carvings, paintings, bamboo basketry, silver filigree and papier mache among others.

There is a proposal to set up "Cultural Corridor", one of it's kind initiative in the city. It would promote and display rich and diverse art and culture of the state. The city's prime business corridor will be converted in to cultural corridor where special kiosks will be put up to showcase and to sell famous items/ indigenous products of the state – like – Koraput coffee, Kandhamal Turmeric, appliqué handicrafts of Pipili etc. This would also provide livelihood for many people besides making the city attractive to the visitors/ tourists.

Miscellaneous

Odisha Krushi Bhavan built in 2018 AD in an area of around 1.30 lac square feet has received the World Architecture Award for it's construction and architecture.

Eastern and western tower which is a first generation building, used to be the most happening place of the capital city during 50's when the new city was established. There was a round market in front of it / left of capital police station.

The old secretariat is an outcome of Shaivism, Budhisim and Jainsim. The new secretariat is a mixture of Lingaraj temple and Portuguese Architecture.

One should visit and explore the beautiful places of the city. It will enthral the visitor with it's rich historic culture.

ANNEXURE-A

Other Heritage Temples / Structures Of Bhubaneswar

Bhubaneshwar was the ancient capital of the Kalinga Empire and the architectural legacy of the city is its greatest attraction. As stated earlier, this area was known as Ekamra Kshetra which can be loosely translated to mean an 'area (kshetra) adorned with one mango tree (ekamra). As per researchers, the old city was of "Asta-Ayatan" in concept. Asta-ayatana is an ancient Hindu system of reference such that shrines are located at the four cardinal points and at the four intermediate points of cosmos. The eight sectoral regions that emerge are guarded by their respective gods. Further, city was having many "Mandals". As per experts, Mandala is a spiritual and ritual symbol in Hinduism and Buddhism that represents the Universe. Graphically, it denotes any plan or chart which symbolically represents the cosmos. The basic form of most mandalas is a square with four gates containing a circle with a center point. Mandalas often exhibit radial balance.In the past, the city was having thousands of temples, earning the tag as the 'Temple City of India'. Only some temples survive today and some of which are really magnificent. These temples are mostly built in Kalinga style of architecture with a pine spire that curves up to a point over the sanctum housing the presiding deity and a pyramid-covered hall where people sit and pray. The entrance in some of these temples are of very short height. As understood the motive behind such entrances are that people can kneel down before the Lord. The temples in Bhubaneswar are having mostly saivite influence. The Ananta Vasudeva Temple is the only major temple of Lord Vishnu in the city of Shiva. Generally the rituals in most of the Shiv temples are almost same. The lingam is offered milk and water many times to keep Lord Shiv cool. As per belief, Lord Shiv is having third eye on the forehead and it emits fire, if opened. Hence, flowers, milk and water are offered on the forehead to cool it. The major festivals in all these temples are Maha Shivratri, Janmashtami, Shiv Vibaha, DOLA Purnima and Chandan Yatra etc. Various social events like – marriage, sacred thread ceremony and engagements etc. are performed in many temples. Although historical significance and architectural beauty of the major temples like – Lingaraj, Kedar Gauri, Mukteswar and Parshurameswar etc. have been described / covered in earlier pages, but there are large number of lesser known monuments/ temples in the city. Each of them are having interesting stories and some of them can spellbound any visitor. These monuments hold value for all.

Prof. Sadasiba pradhan (Head of postgraduate department of ancient Indian history, culture and archeology of Utkal university) has documented 199-monuments in a book published by the INTACH and all the monuments are listed with their location, address, traditions and legends, age and significance etc.

However due to rapid urbanisation, many temples/ monuments of the city are suffering. Many of the temples are buried and swamped by residential buildings and no consideration was given to save them. Many of them are not visible due to new high rise around the temples.

Unauthorised construction near water channels around the temples, blocks the water and water spills over to road as well as temples. The temples remain submerged during rains. Due to constant contact of water, the monuments are eroded. In some cases the level of nearby road had already been raised. There were many unknown ancient structures that have been lost/ sealed by net work of roads and densely packed properties of old town area. Many of the temples are in the process of rapid decay due to cracks in the walls, stagnant water inside the sanctum and growth of vegetation etc.

As per Jitu Mishra, "in the whole old town region, there could be thousands of buried temple remnants. Wherever we dig, we could find something".

As per UNESCO, These temples are still functional and home to many intangible living traditions, rituals, festivals and other observances believed to be centuries old.

Some of the prominent temples of the city are as under:

Aisanyeswara Shiv Temple

This temple is situated near the western compound wall of Lord Lingaraj temple. It is a 13th-century Hindu temple dedicated to Lord Shiva. Lord Lingaraj visits this shrine after the 6th day of Shivratri. Various rituals like – Rudrabhisekh and jalabhisekh are performed here. This is a saptaratha temple with Viman and Jagmohan. It is situated back of Lingaraj temple, next to BMC Hospital of old town.

Akhandachandi Temple

The temple is surrounded by Bindusagar tank in the east, Markandeya temple in the west and private residential buildings in the southern side. Mahishamardini Durga is the presiding deity of this south facing temple.

This Kalinga style temple is constructed using coarse – grained sand stone. The main temple is rectangular in plan and is a khakhara DEULA. Besides the main entrance, there are two other gateways to the temple. The Doorjamb is decorated with plaster design.

Baidyanath Temple (Kharakhia Vaidyanath Temple)

This Shivling is in open. As the Sun rays fall directly on the Linga this is known as Kharakhia. It is a small temple situated in the Kapileswar temple complex. It believed that the temple was constructed during 18th century AD

Bakresawr Temple

This east facing temple is having a DEULA and Jagmohan. It appears to be of Saptaratha style of construction. It is opposite to YAMESWAR temple.

Bharateswar Temple, Lakshmaneswar Temple And Satrugneswar Temple

Bharateswar temple along with Laksmaneswar temple and Shatrughaneswar temple (ie. opposite to RAMESWAR Temple/ Maushima temple) are believed to be oldest survived temples of Odisha, built during Shailodbhava rule around 6th centuryAD.These temples are aligned north-south (ie. Lakshmaneswar is in north, Bharateswar in middle and Satrughneswar in south). These were built in sandstones with Rekha Viman archetecture. The Shivling is installed in circular yoni pitha in each of these west facing temples.

The entrance to these temples are very short height and T-shaped. The temples are built in Tri-Rath plan. The carvings like – Nataraja, Harihar, Kartikeya, Ardhanareeswarar and Surya etc. would attract the visitor.

Bharati Matha Temple

This 12th century temple built by king jajati keshari is dedicated to Lord Shiv. The deity of Lord Vishnu is also there. Hence, people from all the sects visit the temple. This also works as a monastery and it is three storied.

This west facing temple is built with coarse grey stones. The temples are in dilapidated conditions.

However, it is having link with Lord Lingaraj and Lord Lingaraj visits during Prathamastami festival.

Details of Bharati Math which is situated in Badheibanka Chowk, is described under the Maths of Bhubaneshwar of this chapter.

Bahirangeswar Shiv Temple

It is located at DHAULI, ie. 8-kms south of Bhubaneshwar. It is one of the most visited Shiv temples in the city of Bhubaneshwar and is an ancient temple.

This is covered under Dhauli of this chapter.

Bhimeswar Temple

The temple is situated immediately north of Uttareswar temple. The presiding deity is Lord Shiv and is situated within a circular Yoni pitha.

Bhrukuteswar Shiv Temple

This north facing temple is believed to be constructed by Keshari kings. Lord Shiv is the presiding deity and is enshrined in a circular Yonipitha. This is a single structure Pidha DEULA with a frontal porch.

It is situated in YAMESWAR patna and west of Teleswar temple and east of Bakreswar temple.

Byamokeswar Shiv Temple

This west facing temple is believed to be constructed around 10th century AD.

The Shivlings is inside a circular Yonipitha and the inner sanctum is now below the ground level. This living temple was a buried temple which was recovered recently. It is situated in the left side of the eastern gateway of Lingaraj temple across the road.

Budha Deula

This is behind Mohini temple on the southern embankment of Bindusagar. There are two Shivlings within a circular Yonipitha. There are also 4-Small Shivlings between the two. It is understood, the Shivlings were recovered from the Pond and is worshipped here.

Bhabhani Shankar Temple

This temple is in Trirath style and is believed to be built around 14th century AD. It is on the southern side of Bindusagar and near to Lingaraj temple.

As per legend the temple was built at the spot where Goddess Parvati took rest at the feet of Lord Shiv after crushing both the demons underground/ where demons were buried. Bhabani is another name of Goddess Parvati. The temple was built to consecrate the event and it was known as Bhabani Shankar.

Chakreswari Shiv Temple

This temple is believed to be built around 10th / 11th century and the presiding deity Lord Shiv is within a circular Yonipitha. Chakreswara pond is in the west and temple is on a low platform. The Viman of the temple is of Rekha order and is of Pancharatha plan. There is a renovated frontal porch.

The temple is having some special features like – four armed Ganesh in Lalatbimba in place of Gajalakshmi and images of Parvati, Kartikeya and Amalaka stone in the southern side of the temple. The images of Surya with lotus in his hands, Rahu with half moon and Ketu with serpent tail are unique. There are Saivite dwarpalas in the doorjamb. It is situated in Hatiasuni lane of Rajarani colony.

Champakeswar Shiv Temple

This 13th century temple is having a Swayambhu Shivling and is believed as the abode of Champa Nag. Accordingly, the deity is named as Champakeswar. It is Pancharatha in plan having a Viman and Jagmohan.

The temple built with laterite stones is on the western side of Parasuramesvara and on the right side of the Kotitirthesvara lane leading to Bindu sagara.

Chandrasekhar Mahadev Temple

This 19th century east facing temple dedicated to Lord Siva is situated in the village Patia, on the southern outskirts of Bhubaneswar. The enshrined deity is a Siva lingam within a circular yoni pitha. It consists of a Viman and a hall in front of it. As understood, Chandrasekharpur area of Bhubaneshwar is named after the Lord.

Chintamaniswar Shiv Temple

It is located at the end of CHINTAMANISWAR road towards west. It is believed to be constructed in13th / 14th century. It was built in sandstones which is now whitewashed. It is a Rekha style temple with a square sanctum.

There is a beautiful rectangular pond with large fish population in the premises. As per locals, it was constructed during the period of Keshari kings and is fed by a natural spring with water from underground.

Marriage ceremony and thread ceremony are performed in the premises of the temple. The Shivling is within a circular yoni pitha.

It is at CHINTAMANISWAR, CHINTAMANISWAR road, near Railway station, Bhubaneshwar.

Dakara Bibhishaneswar Temple

The temple is believed to be built by Vibhishana, brother of demon king Ravana. It's construction period appears to be around 13th century AD. The temple has a deity, who is known as the messenger of Lingaraj.

Debasabha Temple

This 14th century east facing temple is abandoned and without any deity inside it. It is a Rekha temple built with laterite stones and devoid of any decoration. The Viman is squarish with a shallow frontal porch. The temple is Pancharatha in plan. As per legend, this was the assembly place of all gods and goddess for which it was known as Devasabha.

It is situated within the premises of Kharakhia Vaidyanatha temple.

Disheswar Temple / Dishisvara Shiv Temple

Lord Shiv, the presiding deity is inside a circular yoni pitha. Although It was a popular temple, now it is dilapidated condition. This was built with laterite stones.

This 15th-century, privately owned temple is situated within a private compound surrounded by private residential buildings on three sides of east, west, south and the road on the north.

As per some, the temple dates back to 8th century AD.

Dologovinda – Vaidyanath Temple

This is a 15th century structure and is mainly known as Vaidyanatha Shiv. As it is situated near the DOLA MANDAP across the road, it might have been named as above.

It is situated near Rathagada Chowk.

Dula Devi Temple

The presiding deity of the temple is the four armed Mahishamardini Durga. This 18th century temple built by Bhoi rulers, is located on the right side of Duladevi Chowk in the village Kapilesvara in Bhubaneswar. It is 100 metres south east of Kapilesvara Siva temple.

Ekamreswar Temple

This Shiv temple was built around 11th century AD. This temple was almost buried, which has been unearthed by removing the earth. This west facing temple constructed with sand stone and ochre is near the Lingaraj Temple. The inner sanctum of the temple, which is below the ground level is empty. The mythological stories of Lord Vishnu are displayed in the temple walls. From these displays and the dwarpalas in the doorjambs, it is believed as a Vishnu temple. It's construction period is believed around 12th /13th century AD. It is situated on the right side of the temple road from Garage Chowk to Lingaraj temple and near the front entrance of Lingaraj temple.

Gangeswar Shiv Temple And Yamuneswar Shiv Temple (Ganga – Yamuna Temple)

These two temples are situated on either side of Ganga – Yamuna road and near Ganga – Yamuna tank. The Yamuneswar temple is built in grey sand stones. This 15th century temple has statue of Nayikas on it's walls. As per legend, after killing the two demons, Goddess Parvati became tired and rested at the feet of Lord Shiv. The trident of Lord Shiv was struck in to the earth nearby the Yamuneswar temple and a stream was emerged. To bless this stream of water, Goddess Ganga and Yamuna were summoned. The presiding deity is Siva lingam within a circular yonipitha. It is a living temple and maintained by the Ganga Yamuna Sangathana. It was constructed around 13th to 14th century. There is a water tank in the compound and it is believed as holy.

Gokarneswar Shiv Temple

It is in close proximity to the ancient fort of Sisupalgarh, which is identified as the Kalinganagari of king Kharavela of the 1st century BC. As per the local legend, the temple is believed to be very old and some assign the period as 1st century BC (ie. period of king Kharavela). However, as per some researchers, the temple fragments, however, do not agree to such an early date (ie. after technical examination). It is a peaceful place.

Gopal Tirtha Matha

The Matha is located in front of the Chitrakarini temple and it is a branch of the Gopala Tirtha Matha of Puri. Gopala Tirtha was one of the prominent disciples of Sankaracharya, who commissioned monastic establishments in Puri and Bhuabaneswar. It's period is estimated around 16th century.

Gosagareswar Temple

This Shiv temple is around Lingaraj temple. This west facing Shivling is at the center of a circular yonipitha inside the sanctum, which measures around 1.10 square metres

Legend

As per local legend once Lord Siva killed a calf inadvertently. In order to cleanse the sin of killing the calf he had to take a bath in the Gosagaresvara pond and worshipped the lord Gosagaresvara. In keeping with the tradition, even today people suffering from the sin of killing cows, take ritual bath in the tank and worship Gosagaresvara to cleanse the sin

The Gosagareswar complex consists of 11-temples dedicated to various Gods / Goddesses. Some of the other temples are – Ishaneswar, Narashimha, Paradeswar and the Saniswar temples. Lord Shiv is the presiding deity in all these temples. Three temples are abandoned. There is also a large Mandap.

Due to constant accumulation of water of the nearby pond, the foundation of the main temple has become weak and many cracks have developed in these temples. Water seeps in to inner sanctum of all the temples. The Mandap has also leaned.

However, it's original stone walls are whitewashed. Immediate measures are required to save the structures.

Gourisankar Shiv Temple

This temple painted in orange- red is known as the" Traffic Mahadev" by many. The temple is buried from 3-Sides and one has to pass flight of steps leading down to the entrance. The Siva lingam is inside a circular yonipitha in the sanctum. As per some researchers the temple appears to be of 8th / 9th century AD. It is near Tirtheswar Temple and Bhabani Shankar Temple complex on Bindusagar road.

Jaleswar Shiv Temple

The temple is situated on the western embankment of Jaleswar pond at Kalarahanga, near Patia railway station and 6-kms south of Chudangagada. It is known as "second Lingaraj".

As per legend, the temple was established by Keshari kings (ie. Padma Keshari) who was an ardent devotee of Lord Lingaraj. The area was surrounded by water in all directions and it was difficult to visit Lord Lingaraj everyday, during monsoon months. Lord Lingaraj appeared in his dream and asked him to construct the temple at the centre of the lotus pond. Accordingly, the king constructed this temple and had given land to Brahmins of Rahanga Sasan, puri to worship the Lord. The place was known as Kalarahanga. It was believed to be constructed around 12th century.

The temple has a Viman, an Antarala, Jagmohan and Nata Mandir. The niches have idols of Lord Ganesh in south, Kartikeya in east and Mahisha-Mardini in the north. The head of the temple is around 8-feet tall. Chaitya motif which is flanked by two conches and surmounted by a Gajakranta above two miniature DEULAs. The image of flying Hanuman carrying a hillock in the right hand is above the Gajakranta. It is constructed in Lingaraj temple style.

The temple of Goddess Mangala is inside the complex. The presiding deity is a Siva-lingam within a circular yonipitha inside the sanctum, which is 1.15 meters below the chandrasila. The Sanctum measures 2.00 square meters. It is a living temple having a beautiful entrance.

Kartikeswar Temple

This temple was buried. The temple is renovated to some extent. It is believed to be built around 13th century. It is built in sand stones. There are many nice carvings in the exterior.

It is around 120-meters east of the main entrance to the Lingaraj temple and Ekamreswar temple is 100-meter west from this temple.

Kuseswar Temple And Labeswar Temple

The twin temples of Kusheswar and LABESWAR are situated on both the sides of the roadn(ie. separated by a road) almost opposite to each other in close proximity, to the east of Ramesvara temple (ie. Maushi Maa temple).

A small complex of 3-temples of Bharateswar, Laxmaneswar and Satrughnesvara, which are considered to be the oldest temples of Bhubaneshwar in existence today, are also nearby.

These are living temples and facing towards west. The enshrined deity is a Siva lingam within a circular yonipitha inside the sanctum.

These are situated near the road leading from Kalpana square to Bindhu Sagar.

Ladu Baba Temple (Known As – Kainchhi Temple)

As per researchers this east facing temple was constructed by Gangavamshi kings around 13th century AD. The inner sanctum is empty and there is no presiding deity. Although this is not a living temple, there is a 4-armed Ganesh with partly broken trunk standing on a lotus pedestal and is in the western niche. It is Pancharatha in plan having a square Vimana with a frontal porch. From the sculptural embellishments, it is believed that the temple was originally dedicated to Lord Shiv. As per local legend, the deity was rescued and shifted from Ravana's Lanka to Ekamra Kshetra during the conflagration of Svarna Lanka on the eve of Rama-Ravana war. It's period was estimated as 15th century. The temple is partially buried and swamped on three sides by residential buildings. It is opposite to Chitrakarini Temple and on the right side of Ratha Road leading from Lingaraj market.

Lakheswar Shiv Temple

Lakhesvara Siva temple is located in the right side of the Ganges–Yamuna road, behind the Lingaraja market complex, Old town, Bhubaneswar. It is situated at a distance of 70 metres north east of Lingaraj temple and at a distance of 10 metres south of Gangesvara and Yamunesvara Siva temple across the road. It was constructed around 13th century.

Lakheswar Temple

LAKHESWAR Mahadev temple is situated between Bhubaneshwar and Cuttack, near Phulnakhara around 100-meters from NH-16. It is surrounded by lush green fields with spacious parking area. The architecture of the temple is attractive.

Lakheswar Temple

It is situated at Barimund, Patia, Bhubaneshwar. It is believed that this temple was built by Somavamshi kings around 12-hundred years ago. The statue of Ganesh and Kartikeya are well crafted and are made of single granite. The peaceful environment and natural surrounding would attract the visitor.

Lakhmaneswar Temple

Details of this 6th century temple which was built during Shailodbhava rule has been described with Bharateswar temple and RAMESWAR temple (ie. Maushima temple) in earlier paragraphs.

Madaneswar Shiv Temple

The temple dedicated to Lord Siva was built around 12th century. It is situated on the left side of the Mahavir Lane branching from Garage Chowk in Santarapur to Sisupalgarh. The enshrined deity is a Siva lingam within a circular yonipitha (basement). It is a broken shrine, and at present, only the Pabhaga portion is available.

Makareswar Temple

It is situated next to Maitreswar temple but without any indication. There are two structures in the temple premises and not maintained properly.

Mangaleswar Shiv Temple

This 14th century east facing Shiv temple is located in the precinct of Papanasini tank and is on the southern embankment of the tank.

The deity is in a circular yonipitha and the Lingam is absent. The temple is 1.60 metres below the present road level.

The Viman is Rekha DEULA type and Jagmohan is Pidha DEULA type. It has a square Viman of around 3.30 square meters and square Jagmohan of around 4.50 square meters. There are Saivite dwarpalas (ie. with trident in left hand and Varada mudra in right hand) in the doorjambs. Goddess Laxmi with lotus in her both hands are at the lintel. There is a carved Navagraha where Ravi holds a lotus, Rahu holds a bow (ie. half moon) and Ketu in serpent tail. Some beautiful carvings can still be seen on the exterior of a temple which is ruined and adjoining to this temple.

Mitreswar Temple

It is in the vicinity of YAMESWAR temple. As per Prof. KC Panigrahi, this temple is named after Mitra, who was one of the four principal disciples of Lakulisha. It is believed to be constructed around 12th/14th century AD during Gangavamshi kings.

This is a Lakshmi temple with Pancharatha style having Viman and Jagmohan.

Papanashini tank is situated in the temple compound.

Mohini Temple

This temple is dedicated to Goddess Chamunda. It was built around 9-10th century AD and is situated on the southern bank of Bindusagar. This is a Tantric site. The 10-armed Goddess is seen in dancing posture standing on corpse. In the corner of the premises, many Tantric statues are seen.Some others also opine that this temple is dedicated to Mohini Avtar of Lord Vishnu. It was built by Mohini Devi, the queen of Bhaumakar king Subhankar-ll and is named after her.

Nageswar Temple / Nabakeswar Temple

It is a plain temple without any decorations and is believed to be constructed during the period of Somavamshi kings around 10th century AD.

It is a west facing temple of Rekha Vimana architecture without the Jagmohan. Nageswar Shivling is the presiding deity.

The images of Ganesh, Kartikeya and Parvati are found in the exterior niches of the walls. There is a subsidiary temple/ small shrine nearby where many idols are stored.

There is a well maintained garden near the ancient tank. It is also known as Nabakeswar temple.

This ancient Shiv temple was renovated recently. There is an old water tank in the compound which was dug through the rock bed.

It is towards north of Parshurameswar temple and is around 300-meters away.

Pabakeswar Temple (Daiteswar Temple)

The temple is believed to be constructed around 10-11th century AD. It is almost hidden between two houses and trees. However, there is a sign board which informs the construction period of the temple.

The temple has a Viman with a renovated frontal porch. The doorjambs are decorated with a single vertical band of scroll work. Gajalakshmi is sitting in lalitasan in a full blown lotus and in lalatbimba. The dwarpala niche is crowned by a Chaitya motif. There is a Shaivite dwarpala that holds a trident. Above the door there are traditional Navagrahas.

It is adjacent to Parshurameswar temple.

Pabaneswar Temple

The presiding deity is a Sivalingam within a circular yonipitha inside the sanctum. It is a living temple. The 10th century temple is surrounded by private residential buildings and market complex on three sides and the road on the south. The temple was rebuilt or renovated sometimes back as it appears from the second phase of building from above the pabhag. This temple is near Parshurameswar temple. It has a Viman with a renovated porch. Lord Shiv is the presiding deity and is inside circular yonipitha in the inner sanctum.

Papanashini Shiv Temple

This 14th century south facing temple built in sandstone and of Kalinga style architecture is located at Badheibanka Chowk. It was constructed in dry masonary style and it's height is around 45-feet. This is an abandoned temple and both the sanctum is empty and the niches are empty. The temple is having only Viman and the porch is missing. However, the fineness of the sculptures would interest the visitor.

Parameswar Temple

It is near Mukteswar temple. It is a small and beautiful carved temple of Lord Shiv. The sculptures of amorous couples, animals and floral motifs are attractive. It is believed to be constructed around 7th century.

Pataleswar Temple

This small Shiv temple located on the banks of Bindusagar is almost buried below the road. The construction period is believed to be around 10/11th century.

Purveswar Shiv Temple

The temple is situated towards the east of Lingaraj and according to local tradition, the presiding deity is known as Purvesvara. It was constructed around 13/14th century.

The enshrining deity is a broken Lingam within a circular Yonipitha at the centre of the sanctum, which is 1.07 metres below the present ground level. It is a living temple and now under the care and maintenance of Purvesvara Temple Development Association of that locality. It is at Kahcha sahi in Bhubaneswar.

Sarvatreswar Shiv Temple

This temple was constructed around 10th century AD. It is a Swayambhu Shivling which is within a circular yonipitha inside the sanctum. It is a living temple. The temple is located on the right bank of Gangua stream.

Satrughaneswar Temple

This temple, one of the oldest temples of Bhubaneswar, was constructed during Sailodbhava Rule, in the later half of 6th century. It is covered under RAMESWAR temple (Maushimaa Mandir) and Bharateswar temple.

Sisireswar Temple

This Shiv temple is situated in the compound of Vaital temple and believed to be built around 8th century AD. It is a Rekha DEULA and Jagmohan with flat roof. This temple contains Mahishamardini image in the northern central niche of the Viman. As per archeologists, the temple is of the same period of architecture as that of Vaital temple.

Subarneswar Shiv Temple

This 10th century east facing temple is opposite the Nageswar temple. It is situated on the left bank of Lingaraja west canal, which can be approached through Kotitirthesvara lane leading from Parasuramesvar temple to Bindu sagar. The presiding deity is a

Shivling which is within a circular yoni pitha in the sanctum measuring 2.35 square metres and is 1.20 metres below the chandrasila of the door.

Swarnajaleswar Temple

This is a Trirath type temple with a single Viman. It's construction period is estimated as 7th century AD during the period of Sailodbhava kings. This ancient Shiv temple is known for beautiful depictions of the popular epic Ramayan. The northern and western walls of the temple exhibit- Rama killing the golden deer, Bali's death at the hands of Lord Ram and the fight between Lord Shiv, disguised as Kirata and Arjuna. On the northern side, the worship of linga and marriage of Shiv and Parvati are also depicted. Other unique feature of the temple is the Naga holding Purna GHANTA (full jar). It is a nice place to visit for it's unique features. This is situated along the Kotitirtheswar lane.

Subarnajaleswar Temple

This is a Pancharatha type temple. The original temple was damaged and is now renovated. The specialty of this temple is that Shiv and Parvati are found in the door jamb. There is an attached porch. The construction period is believed as 9th / 10th century AD.

Suka And Sari Temple

There are 3-temples in the premises. West facing Sari temple is the main structure and Suka temple is smaller which is towards the south-west of Sari temple. The third temple is partially ruined. Sari temple is believed to be constructed around 13th century by Gangavamshi kings and is having wonderful ornamented carvings of human figures, Gods and Goddesses and floral motifs. Due to soft sand stone, many carvings are weathered. As per Alice Borner, the Sari temple is constructed in Ratnasara style and the Shikhara is of ten tiers.

The image of Goddess Parvati is the only surviving side Goddess of this temple.

West facing Suka temple which is contemporary to Sari temple was dedicated to Lord Shiv. There are remains of carved masonry in front of this temple, which suggests the existence of Jagmohan in the past. Although many of the carvings of this temple is weathered, still there are some excellent carvings which would attract any archeologist/ historian.

The details of the third temple are not known properly. Some opine that it was originally a part of Bindhyabasini temple.

These temples are abandoned and not in use.

Legend

Lord Shiv had noticed a pair of parrots on the branch of a tree, who were listening to his conversation with Goddess Parvati about the essential truths of life. This tree was near Bindusagar. Lord Shiv was pleased with the parrots and immortalised them in the temple nearby, which was known as Suka-Sari temple.

During beautification drive and while digging up the area, the floor of a temple which is believed to be part of ancient structures in and around the Suka-Sari temple was found. The temple floor was discovered at the north-west corner of Sari temple.

Two other structures have also been partially exposed which could be remains of small shrines. The upper portion of the temple was destroyed during demolition drive.

From the remains of some other structures/ temples during excavations, the archeologists believe that the Suka-sari temple complex could have been built in the Panchayatan style (ie. main temple surrounded by four sub-shrines) like nearby Chitrakarini temple or might be a Saptaratha structure. The smaller structures buried are believed to be of 7th century AD. It 's construction might be around 10th century AD by Somavamshi kings, earlier than Lingaraj temple. It is next to Lingaraj temple near Bindusagar.

Sukuteswar Temple

The presiding deity in this east facing temple is a Siva-lingam (Lord Shiva) situated at the centre. It has a Viman and a frontal porch. In the lalatbimba there is a Gajalakshmi image seated on a double petalled lotus and flanked by two elephants. Navagrahas seated in Padmasan are above the doorjambs. The temple observes various religious rites like Mahasivaratri, Chandipatha, and Rudrabhisekha. Temple is used mainly for community gathering.It is on the right side of Ganga-Jamuna Road and behind Lingaraj market complex.

Swapneswar Shiv Temple

This east facing temple is Pancharatha in plan with a square Viman and a frontal porch facing east. It is a Rekha temple with usual Bada, Gandi and Mastaka. The niches are devoid of ornamentation and vacant without any side Gods / Goddesses. The doorjambs and lintel of the temple are renovated recently. It is constructed with light grey sandstones and technique used was of dry masonary. The temple is renovated completely. The temple is surrounded by private residential buildings. It is in Gouri Nagar close to the Purvesvara Siva temple. It was constructed around 13th century and difficult to locate. One has to approach from the main road to reach the temple.

Shyameswar And Nilakanteswar Temple

This ancient Shiv temple is situated next to Kharakhia Vaidyanatha temple. It is in old town Basisthanagar area. It is believed to be constructed around 12th / 13th century AD.

Teleswar Shiv

The Talesvara Siva temple is one of the smallest temples of EKAMRA KSHETRA. It has a small single room only. It is believed to be built around 9th century AD. Some others believe the construction period between 6th to 9th century AD. It is a living and east facing temple and built with laterite stones. It is Trirath in plan. There are dwarpala niches at the base of the doorjambs and these are Saivite dwarpalas. The right side niche houses four armed dwarpalas. They wear sacred threads, jata Mukut and Padma kundal. They are having lotus stalk, trident in 3-hands and the upper right arm in Varada mudra. The river Goddess niche is beyond the dwarpala niche. The image of Yamuna with a small female figure and the image of Ganga with the upper part missing are found in the river niche. It is situated in Gouri Nagar, Old town, Bhubaneshwar.

Tirtheswar Temple

It is opposite to Bhabani Shankar temple. It was built around 14th century AD. It is at Kedar Gouri lane, Gouri Nagar, Old town.

Uttareswar Shiv Temple

Uttaresvara Siva temple is situated on the northern embankment of Bindusagar tank in the Nalamuhana Sahi, Kedara-Gouri Chowk, Old Town, Bhubaneswar. The presiding deity in this temple is a Siva lingam within a circular yoni pitha at the centre of sanctum. It is surrounded by nine other smaller shrines. It is believed as a Tantra pitha.

The original temple has collapsed, as evident from the renovation work above the pabhaga. There are presence of cult images of earlier phases in different parts of the temple walls without conforming to the chronological prescriptions.It's architecture is of Kalinga style and the temple is believed to be constructed around 12th /13th century. The flat roofed Jagmohan of the temple without any carvings is similar Parshurameswar temple. On the exterior walls, the images of Ganesh, Kartikeya and Kama Dev with Rati and Preeti are seen. The temple has been built in Trirath style with Viman and Jagmohan. This is a Chamunda temple. It is situated near entrance of Bindusagar lake, where the Gods play the watersports. Before ASHOKASTAMI, Lord Lingaraj, Jagannath and Kapileswar are taken in a decorated boat on Bindusagar. The Godavari pond is near Uttareswar temple. As per legend, taking a dip in it is equivalent to a dip in Godavari.

Vishnu Temple

It is situated on the eastern embankment of Bindu Sagar at Talabazar, on the right side of the Talabazar road leading from Lingaraj temple to Kedara-Gouri lane. The temple faces west and the Sanctum is presently used for storage purposes. The sculptural embellishment on the outer wall and the parsavadevatas in raha niche suggests that the temple was originally dedicated to Vishnu. It was constructed around 12th century AD.

The devotees treat the temple of Uttareswar as Tantra peetha, Kharakhia BAIDYANATH as Yoga peetha, Lingaraj as Bhoga peetha and Kedar Gouri as Siddha peetha.

Temples / Structures In The Kapileswar Temple Complex

KAPILESWAR is one of the ancient temple of the town and the state. Details of the main temple has already been described under the important temples of the town in earlier paragraphs of this book. It is believed that Lord Shiv roams inside this temple complex. There are many Shivlings and small temples inside it. Idols of Lord Ganesh, Jagannath, Shani, Kali, Navagraha, Parvati and Radhakrishna etc are found. The pond and the well with lot of fish in it are an added attractions. Some of the major shrines/ structures of Kapileswar temple complex are as under:

Baidyanath Temple

It is small Shiv temple and date of construction was around 18th century.

Bhaskareswar Shiv Temple

It is Pidha type temple and was constructed by Somavamshi kings around 10th / 11th century AD.

Chakreswara Shiv Temple

The temple is believed to be built by Somavamshi kings around 10th /11th century. It's elevation is Tringabada and the Viman is of Pidha order.

Dakshin Kali Temple

The presiding deity is the 4-armed Goddess Kali. It is believed that the temple was built by Gajapati kings. The temple has a Pancharatha Viman and saptaratha Jagmohan. It has a Rekha Viman.

Dula Devi Temple

Four armed Mahishamardini Durga killing the demon is the presiding deity. The temple was built by Bhoi kings around 18th century AD.

Dutiya Kapileswar Temple

The temple is having Pidha Viman and a flat roofed Jagmohan. The Shivling is the presiding deity. It was built during the period of Gajapati kings around 15th century AD.

Ghanteswar Shiv Temple

The temple is of Trirath in plan and the Viman is of Pidha type.

Gupteswar Shiv Temple

The temple was constructed during the period of Gajapati kings around 14th /15th century AD. It is Trirath in plan and Triangabada in elevation. The Viman is Pidha type.

Jareswar Shiv Temple

Shivling is the presiding deity. The Viman of the temple is of Pidha order. It is Pancharatha in plan and Panchangabada in elevation. It was built by Gajapati kings around 16th century.

Kalika Shiv Temple

The Shivling is in the inner sanctum. It is believed to be constructed around 11th century.

Laxmi Narayan Temple

The Viman of the temple is of Pidha type. The images of Lord Vishnu and his consort Goddess Lakshmi seated on the lap is found in the inner sanctum.

Shaneeswar Shiv Temple

Shivling is the presiding deity. It's Viman is of Rekha type. It is Trirath in plan and Triangabada in elevation.

Siddheswar Shiv Temple

The temple is of Pancharatha in plan and panchangabada in elevation. It's Viman is of Pidha order. The presiding deity Lord Shiv is placed in the inner sanctum. The Viman is of Pidha order. The images of Ganesh, Kartikeya and Parvati are in the niches.

It was constructed around 15th century during the period of Gajapati kings.

Somabareswar Shiv Temple

The presiding deity is the Shivling. It is Trirath in plan and the Viman is of Pidha order.

Vishnu Temple

This temple is having two images of Vishnu and the images of Lord Jagannath, Balabhadra, Subhadra and Buddha. The other structures found in the Kapileswar temple complex are as under:

Bada Kua

This is a square shaped rock-cut well. Some images like – Varaha and Vishnu are found in the niches. It is believed to be constructed by Gangavamshi kings around 13th /14th century AD.

Beharana Mandapa

There is a wooden ceiling in the Mandap which is carved with various designs and decorations. It is believed to be built around 18th century AD.

Hazara Mandapa

There are 16-pillars in this Mandap. It was constructed around 13th century.

As per IGNCA, there are many other temples like – Amunha temple, Arjuneswar temple, Baleswar temple, Baneswar temple, Dhabaleswar temple, Durga Shrine (Pancha goan), Dutiya kedareswar temple, Gandhi Garabadu precinct Vishnu temple, Gupteswar temple, Hanuman temple, Jagannath temple (Patia), Kala Bhairavi temple (Patia), Kalika Devi temple, Kedareswar temple, Kukuteswar temple, Loknath Shiv temple, Manibhadreswar Shiv temple, Mahakal – Mahakali temple, Narasimha temple, Panchanan – Akhandalamani Shiv temple, Paradeswar temple, Paramguru temple, Paschim Somnath temple, Sahasralinga temple, Saniswar Shiv temple and Sundareswar Shiv temple (Sundara pada)etc, which are situated mostly in the old town area. Large number of devotees visit some of them and steps are also required for proper maintenance of these temples.

SPECIAL ACT

For proper management of the religious ceremonies, performance of the rituals, to solve the problems of the Sevayats and to manage properties of different temples, a special Act was passed, to start with, for 66-temples including Lingaraj temple and other temples (ie. like – Brahmeswar, Karataleswar, Kotitirtheswar, Ganeswar, Jatileswar, Yamuneswar, Dakara Bibhishan, Tirtheswar, Natakeswar, Nileswar Dev, Nilakantheswar, Paschimeswar, Parshurameswar, Purbeswar, Varuneswar, Maitreswar, Balunkeswar, Vaidyanatha Dev, Bhabanishankar, Bhairabeswar, Manguleswar, Lakshyeswar, Ladu lavaneswar, Chakreswar, SIDDHESWAR, Suvarna Jaleswar, Suvarna Mukteswar, Akrameswar, Ganeswar, Kusheswar, Shubheswar, Gosagareswar, Ananta Vasudev, Kukuteswar, Labeswar, Dhaneshwar, Mukteswar, Sukhmeswar, Uttareswar, Ananta Dev, Jambeswar, Kedareswar, Ma Ambika, Char Narayani, Jageswari, Vindhyavasini, Sathidushi THAKURANI, Ramayani, HARACHANDI, Kapali THAKURANI, Kanika THAKURANI, Gopaluni, Mahadei, Savitri

Devi (Astamuurti), Lavaneswar, Markandeswar, RAMESWAR, Laxmaneswar, Bharateswar, Satrughaneswar, Sukeswar, Pavakeswar, Ma DAKSHIN Chandi, Bhimeswar and Kapileswar etc), Ten TIRTHA Kundas (ie. Kotitirtha, Gaya kunda, Ganga Jamuna, Godavari, Gosagareswar, Devipadahara, Papanashini, Bindusagar, Mukteswar, Marichi kunda, Dusti Bhajan TIRTHA kunda) and Three Mathas (Shiva TIRTHA, Shankarananda and Gopalatirtha).

It is believed that with the promulgation of the above Act, various heritage structures (ie. at least the structures as stated above) like – temples, ponds and Mathas of EKAMRA KSHETRA would be managed properly.

The temples like – Akhandachandi temple, Arjuneswar Shiv temple, Bahirangeswar Shiv temple, Bata Mahadev, Baneswar Shiv temple, Buddhanath temple, Chakreswari temple, Dwarbasini temple, laxmi-Narayan temple, Mahakala-Mahakali Mandir, Manibhadreswar Shiv temple, Megheswar temple, Narayani temple, Nilakantheswar Shiv temple, Paradeswar Shiv temple, Parvati temple, Paschimeswar temple, Taleswar temple, Tirtheswar temple and Vishwanath Shiv temple etc. are in dilapidated conditions.

Further, many temples are in bad state of preservation and are deteriorating day by day. Superstructure in many cases are collapsed / disfigured by unauthorised elements. These temples which are great historical monuments require urgent maintenance.

Visit to some of these temples in this important pilgrimage centre of the country will take one back to more than thousand years old.

Narrow and winding roads may pose a problem, however when navigating through getting lost is a good thing in one's trip. Hence, one should visit during morning hours.

ANNEXURE-B

History behind Naming Different Parts Of Bhubaneshwar

Every city has its own story and the name of different places in any city often stand testimony to some important personalities or events of the past. Similarly the smart city Bhubaneswar has it's own story to tell. The name Bhubaneshwar is the combination of Bhuban (ie. area / earth) and Ishwar (ie. almighty).

Although modern city of Bhubaneshwar was planned by German urban planner Otto Königsberger in 1948 AD, the history of the areas in and around the present city can be traced to 3rd / 4th century BC. The city which is more than 2500 – years-old has derived it's name from Tribhubaneswar (Lord of the Three Worlds). Historically, it has been known by different names such as Toshali, Kalinga Nagari, Nagar Kalinga, Ekamra Kanan & Ekamra Kshetra etc. The city has evolved through the centuries and has spread out it's branches in different directions although the backbone structure still remains the same.

The city is divided mainly in to-Old town area (ie. which is mainly EKAMRA KSHETRA), the planned city, added areas and grater Bhubhaneswar area.

The city is further divided as per geographical locations as under:

A) North Bhubaneshwar: The areas lying north of National Highway-16, up to Baranga, which are developed later, are mostly part of North Bhubaneshwar. The areas covered under it are – Chandrasekharpur, Vani vihar, Salia Sahi, Jayadev Vihar, IRC Village, Patia and nearby villages like – Barimund, Raghunathpur, Tangibanta, Jaripatna, Kalarahanga, Injana, Singda, Rokat, Kalajhari, Barang (part), Pathargadia, Chandaka and Andharua etc.

B) Central Bhubaneswar: Central Bhubaneswar (Acharya Vihar to Forest Park) is a planned area and localities are named after various personalities or landmarks (ending with either Nagar/ Vihar /Units).

   The areas covered under it are – A G Colony, Acharya Vihar, Ashok Nagar, Bapuji Nagar, Bhauma Nagar, Bhoi Nagar, EKAMRA Vihar, Forest Park, Ganga Nagar, Keshari Nagar, Kharavela Nagar, Madhusudan Nagar,

   Master canteen, Nayapalli, Saheed Nagar, Satya Nagar, Surya Nagar and Unit-1 to Unit-8.

C) South Bhubaneshwar: This area covers – BJB Nagar, Rajarani colony, PANDAV Nagar, Samantarapur, Lingaraj nagar, Gouri Nagar, Bhimtangi, Kapileswar, Brahmeswar Bag, Old town and Uttara etc.

D) Western Bhubaneswar: These areas are both planned and unplanned. This is also relatively new part of Bhubaneswar. The localities like – Delta colony, Gopabandhu Nagar,

Baramunda, Surya Nagar, CRPF, Jagmara and Khandagiri etc and nearby areas like – Pokhariput, Palaspali, Bhimtangi, Dumduma, Sundarpada, Gandamunda, Balabhadrapur, Kantilo,Ebaranga, Patrapada, Tamando,Kalinga Nagar, Ghatkia, Janla and UDAYAGIRI vihar etc. are covered under it.

E) Eastern Bhubaneswar: This part covers the areas like – VSS Nagar, Rasulgarh, Mancheswar, Palasuni, Satya Vihar, Jharpada, Laxmi sagar area and Pandra etc.

Other than planned localities, the additional areas are basically nearby villages/mouzas and are added subsequently. They still hold their original names. The areas like- Bapuji Nagar, Saheed Nagar and Ashok Nagar came in to existence, when Government intervened in the allotment of lands to residential areas.

However, there are some interesting stories behind some of the localities in Bhubaneswar, which are as under:

Irc Village

This posh locality is near CRPF Square. It was named after the Indian Road Congress (IRC) convention that was held in this previously open field in Bhubaneswar, in the 1980s.

At that time, due to non-availability of enough quality hotels in the city, tents were erected in the open field for stay of the delegates. Hence, the site was known as IRC Village (ie. like Asiad Village in Delhi).

Master Canteen

It is said that initially there was a singada (ie. samosa) and snacks counter or canteen, which was opened by a teacher (ie. customers fondly called him as "master") and thus the name – Master Canteen came in to existence.

In later years, Master Canteen became "Master General Store". It was the only shop in the locality, ie. outside Bhubaneswar Railway Station, at one time.

As per another version of Syed Maqbool Ali (renowned engineer Syed Mumtaz Ali's son), Master Canteen was named after one of the elder Hans (early Bhubaneswar business family), who was a tailor (the term "Master" is used for a head tailor too).

Former Chief Minister, late Biju Patnaik had commended this "Master" for stitching him a bandhgala coat overnight (ie. an impossible feat in those days).

Now, a fast food chain under the brand name "Master Canteen" has been opened just outside Lalchand Market Complex to revive the old era. Its branches are opening across Bhubaneswar.

Bapuji Nagar

When the local government planned to designate specific areas for residential purposes, systematic allotment of plots were carried out in newly created nagars like Ashok Nagar, Saheed Nagar and Bapuji Nagar. And, nobody knew that these purely residential areas will one day turn into business hubs. While the names of some nagars can easily be traced, Bapuji Nagar's case was different. Bhubaneswar's foundation stone was laid by Pandit Jawaharlal Nehru at a place near the existing Durga Temple in Bapuji Nagar. The stone was later shifted to the State Assembly complex. There was a suggestion to erect a huge statue of Mahatma Gandhi (fondly called Bapuji) here. It was later planned to shift it to an area like Market Building, but that never happened.

Barang

Barang (near Nandan Kanan) evolved from Chudanga (garh), the fortified area made by King Chodagangadeva, which itself was previously known as Sarangagarh (due to abundance of waterlilies around).

Dhauli

Dhauli hillock evolved from Toshali/Toshala, the capital city of the erstwhile Kalinga.

Similarly, nearby Kausalyaganga is a combination of Kausalya+Ganga. It was named by King Chodagangadeva (of the Ganga dynasty) after his Queen Kausalya when he converted a huge area of land into a scenic lake. Now CIFA (Central Institute of Freshwater Aquaculture) is located here.

Old Town

Old Town is a typical name and this area/ part is historic/ original core of the city / town. It is across the railway line.

In Bhubaneswar, Old Town is the oldest part of the city (starting from BJB Nagar to Kapileswar). It is characterised mostly by the Shaiva heritage temples and holy ponds. The rest of Bhubaneswar may be termed as New Town. This area is famous for large number of ancient and beautiful temples including Lingaraj temple. ASHOKASTAMI, Shivratri and Sitalsasthi are major festivals of the area.

It has all the important temples of the city and always brimming with activities from very early in the morning. It is also identified with original EKAMRA KSHETRA.

Poonama Gate

The railway level crossing at Palaspalli, on which a new flyover has been built, is said to be named after Poonam, a girl from the Bhimtangi area who is said to have committed suicide in that area. Several other stories, too, revolve around Poonama Gate.

Jagamara

Jagamara hamlet was originally a part of Bechhapuri mouza and a dwelling place for travelling Jain/ Buddhist monks, who used to visit Khandagiri caves for meditation and for performing yagyas. On one occasion the sadhus were disturbed by non-followers while they were performing yagya. The name Jagamara has probably been derived from the term Jagyanmara (when a yagyan becomes impure/ disturbed in the middle).

Rupali Square

This famous junction at Saheed Nagar was named after a small restaurant called Rupali (some argue it was Rupali Hotel) started by a family of three from Balasore at the very place where Pathik Hotel stands now. Rupali was the only destination for foodies from newly-settled Saheed Nagar residents at that time.

Rajmahal Square

This busy square was named after Hotel RajMahal (still running), opened around 60 years ago near the chhak by Raju Sahoo (RajKishore Sahoo), who had initially started a street-side joint, selling vadas. It is said to be the first hotel-cum-restaurant in the city and is still in business.

As per Discover Bhubaneshwar, "60-years ago, this busiest square of the city used to be an isolated and eerie land where no one dare to step just after 6-pm in the evening. The only attraction that took the attention of a passerby was a man preparing "Bara" the famous Odiya street delicacy.

The man Rajkishore Sahu, popularly known as Raju Sahu suddenly became a live example of a rags-to-riches story among the then city inmates. From a small road side stall to a roadside dhaba and then one day, the first high class restaurant and hotel of the city, Raju Sahu made it big within a span of just 10-years and materialised a whole new concept. Rajmahal restaurant used to be a matter of pride and luxury during that period as only upper class could afford it.

And no other building in the vicinity, the square was identified as "Rajmahal" after the first hotel-cum-restaurant in the town and still continues to be.

Kalpana Square

It was named after the nearby Kalpana Theatre (the first theatre of Bhubaneswar and an important landmark during that time). It is said that Kalpana was the name of the daughter of the theatre owner. It is demolished now. As per another version, "Kalpana" was actually the dream business (ie. Kalpana means – dream in Odia) of Sri Padmanabha Nanda, who started the theatre business with the name Kalpana Theatre.With passage of time Kaplana Theatre became a landmark and the chhak was named Kaplana Square. The theatre does not exist any more.

Chandrasekharpur

Chandrasekharpur is said to be one of the largest residential locality in the country, at one time. It was named after the ancient temple of Chandrasekhar Mahadev in Patia. It has attracted many institutions of higher learning, like IT, higher management institutes, a number of good Hospitals and IT hub having complexes of INFOSYS, TCS, MINDTREE, WIPRO and Tech Mahindra etc.

Laxmisagar

King Chodagangadeva had constructed/ had dug a pond and had named it as "Laxmi sagar" after Laxmivati, one of his queens. The pond is now called Bada Pokhari and still exists near Chintamaniswar.

But it is not in a good condition. It can also be approached from the Laxmisagar side.

Pandav Nagar

Pandav Nagar is named after the Panchu Pandav caves inside the colony. It is believed that the Pandav caves were built in the seventh century for the Lakulish (Shaiva) sadhus to reside in. Currently, it is being renovated/preserved as a park by ASI. Many also link the caves with PANDAVs.

Sisupalgarh

It is one of the earliest fortifications of ancient India and one of the earliest planned cities in the world. As per hearsay, it was built by Chedi king Sishupal of Mahabharata fame.

Some also believe that the name is derived from the small village 'Sishupa' located nearby.

Patia

Patia is the short name for Patiagarh, the erstwhile princely state, towards Nandankanan Zoological Park, Bhubaneswar.

Satya Nagar

It is said that Satya Nagar has been named after Satya's family, one of the earliest residents there. Further, the goddess at the local Kali Temple is called Maa Satyakali.

Khandagiri

The ancient name of Khandagiri & Udayagiri hills was Kumari Parvat, Kumaragiri & Skandagiri (as per Lord Kartikeya). Probably, the term Skanda was known as Khanda with passage of time. The road between the twin hills was built by the Britishers in 19th century, to make way for better connection with Chandaka and Baranga.

Nayapalli and Jaidev vihar

This area is famous for the location of many corporate offices and star hotels like – Mayfair, Trident, Swasti and other hotels etc.

Buddhist Influence

Buddhism was quite prevalent in ancient Kalinga, including this part of the kingdom. Hence, Buddhism has greater influence on the earlier known names of Bhubaneswar and its nearby areas.

Chandaka is derived from Lord Budhha's divine charioteer Chhandaka, Santarapur is Samantaraypur, which is said to be derived from a combination of the names of two Buddhist deities, Shyama and Tara.

Some opine that Samantaray is a popular surname in Odisha and the locality was known in the surname of some Samantray, who might be a popular person or zamindar of the area.

Bhubaneswar is linked with Lord Buddha. The area where Gautam Nagar is located has a Mausima temple (Rameswar temple complex) and the area opposite to it is Buddha Nagar. The nearby temple is Buddheswari (a female equivalent of Buddha). Palasuni was a Buddhist deity. Delang derived from Buddhist scholar Acharya Dignag, is said to be teaching at Aragada monastery.

Other Names

Sripur, spelled as Siripur, Sundarpada, derived its name from the original Sindurapada (ie. which is linked with Sindureswar temple). Damana might be from Maa Damanei. Dumduma from an old Panthei devi temple and

Gangua canal from River Gandhavati & Ganga Nagar from Chodagangadeva, Sridevi Chhak (Tankapani Road) from a cloth store by its name. Lewis Road from British Governor Howthorne Lewis or his better half, popularly known as Lady Lewis in the locality, for their good works. Rasulgarh from Wasuligarh, a toll gate made to collect tax from passersby during Mogul period in Odisha.

The name of the places like Ganda Munda and Baramunda might have been originated from some tribal habitations / leaders.

One should explore different parts of the city to know the curious stories of various localities.

CHAPTER 2

Puri

PURI – JAGANNATH DHAM

From the time immemorial, Puri is known as "Srikshetra Dham", "Sankha KSHETRA", "Neelachala Dham", "Jagganath Dham" and "Purusottama Dham" etc. Puri was known as "Bhogakshetra", ie. land of enjoyment.

Jagannath temple at Puri is called "Yamanika TIRTHA", where as per belief, the power of "Yama" (ie. God of death) has been nullified due to presence of Lord Jagannath.

In puri, not only the temple is holy but the whole of it's surroundings is treated as grand and splendid, ie. Lord Jagannath is the Lord of Universe and He is Great in all respects: His temple is the Great Templa (Bada Deula), the road that he travels during the Car festival is the Grand Highway (Bada Danda – Grand Road), the sea is Mahodadhi (Great sea) and His prasad (offering) is Mahaprasad

(Unique and the Best food)." The city hosts more than 24 festivals each year with the Ratha Yatra as the most impressive/ grandiose.

Lord Jagannath is the embodiment of all the Gods and Goddesses rolled in to one and Jagannath culture is beyond ordinary comprehensions.

The social, economic and cultural life of the city revolves around Lord Jagannath, Balabhadra and Subhadra and the Jagannath temple. The temple is the heart of the city and is built in Pancharatha plan following Kalinga style of architecture. The city is therefore referred as Jagannath, Puri or Purusottama Puri.

Geographically, it is bounded by the sea to the South, Musa River to the North, Mangla River to the West and the Balukhanda Reserve Forest to the East. The city stands on a bed of alluvial formations which are not consolidated.

The Musa River is known to have been connected with the sacred tanks in the past which formed a network of water systems. There are several ponds found in many Jagagharas which are located towards the western part of the city.

The Balukhanda forest reserve which is located on the eastern edge of the city is traversed by the rivulets such as Nuanai, Kusabhadra, Kadua and Prachi. It extends from Banki muhan of Puri to Keluni muhan near Daluakani.

Chakratirtha and Baliapanda areas are sweet water zone of puri.

Mythologically it is believed that the city was planned in the form of a conch (ie. Sankha) which was spread around 5-koshas (ie. around 10-miles) out of which 2-koshas were submerged in to the sea. On the centre of the city was a hillock, known as Nilagiri, on which the temple of Lord Jagannath is situated. The spine/ axis of the conch was the "Bada Danda" (ie. grand road) which connects the Jagannath temple and the Gundicha temple.

Eight sahis or precincts are radiated from it and each is having a presiding Shiva Temple. These eight Shiv temples are guarding the eight directions/ quarters.

The temple of Lord Loknath is at the western side which was the broad end of Sankha KSHETRA. The temple of Nilakantha and Indradyumna Tank are at the tail end of Sankha KSHETRA.

As per many researchers, the initial period of settlement of Puri town area goes back to the period of Rigveda. The fishermen were living near the Sea-Shore and Shabar tribes were living in the forests.

Although the existence of Puri is attributed to the Jagannatha Temple, it is not certain when the temple was first established and the settlements came into being.

The original history of Jagannath Temple goes back to Mahabharata period, according to which the temple was constructed by the king Indradyumna on the daru (ie. wood) floating in the eastern coast, which was believed as the form of Lord Krishna who was killed by a Shabar tribal, known as Jara.

The early history of Puri is therefore shrouded in mystery, which are based primarily on hypotheses and disputed by some.

The spirituality and holiness which pervades in the city goes back to as early as the 4th Century AD, ie. to the period of Garuda Puran, which describes Puri and ranks it amidst the likes of Ayodhya, Mathura, Gaya, Kasi, Kanchi, Avantika and Dvaravati / Dwaravati as one of the holiest places in India.

In 9th century AD, Shankaracharya had visited Puri and had named the place as one of the four shrines. King Yayati Keshari had built the second temple of Lord Jagannath around 10th century AD, as the original temple was dilapidated. The construction of exiting temple commenced during the rein of King Chodaganga Deva in 12th century AD (ie. the construction period is believed to be around 1135 AD during his rule between 1112 AD-1147 AD) and his grandson completed the temple.

Being a Hindu religious centre, its planning is said to be based on the Vaastu Purushu Mandala and with consideration of many meta-physical aspects in the town's design. The built heritage of the city is the culmination of close knit residential quarters that have grown surrounding the abode of the city's presiding deity – Lord Jagannatha, and a plethora of temples, mathas, ashramas, akhadas, jagagharas, mandapas, gosalas, pokharis / ponds and other religious structures that one encounters at every turn, featuring prominently among other heritage buildings.

As the English word (ie. born out of the Rath Yatra experience) – 'juggernaut' suggests, the city of Puri is a phenomenon of momentous cultural implication that has a potential which once initiated cannot be stopped.

The initial growth of the town occurred with Jagannatha Temple as its epicentre, along a sandy tract known as Ganjam road and up to Matiani stream. With the drying up of this stream, the direction of city's growth was changed towards Gundicha temple.

Eight colonies known as 'sahi's radiated outwards from the temple, housing a number of religious structures such as mathas, ashramas, jagagharas, pokharis and residences of priests and other members of the society that take part in the temple's day-to-day activities and provide services for its smooth functioning.

These eight earliest sahis were – Harachandi Sahi, Baseli Sahi, Kundhei Benta Sahi, Haragouri Sahi, Markandeshwar Sahi, Choudanga Sahi, Bali Sahi and Matimandap Sahi.

These historic sahis are characterised by a distinctive spatial pattern, open spaces, water harvesting and storage elements, heritage buildings connected with streetscapes and street network with chhaka or chowks. These streets were of two types: narrow residential lanes and mixed use streets with wider streets.

PORT

The ancient port of Puri was a prominent participant in the maritime trading activity that occurred in the Eastern coast of India from the 3rd century B. C. to the 3rd century AD. According to Cunningham, "Chelitola" was the present town of Puri.

Even during British period, Puri was a sea port and trading activities were undertaken in this port mostly during September to March. It was a minor port and mostly country barges were used for the activities. Shipment of rice was the main activity of the port which was sent to Madras and Mauritius etc.

There is no port at present.

Initially the settlements of Puri were inhabited exclusively by those associated actively with the temple. However, with the growing popularity of Rath Yatra and the city itself, as a holy centre, the region saw a large influx of permanent population. At present, though 80% of the economy is generated by the temple, other industries also exist and tourism features prominently among them.

TEMPLES

Puri city is having approximately 112 temples among which Shri Jagannatha Temple is the most significant. This temple occupies the central position in the history and cultural traditions of Puri.

The several other shrines in the city add to the sacred geography of Puri i.e. the sankha kshetra area. All other temples are located around the main temple and these are Shiva temples, Sakti temples, Nrushingh temples and Hanuman temples etc.

Apart from Shri Jagannatha temple, there are five main Shiva temple of immense religious significance and are locally known as Pancha Pandu or the five pandavas. These are – Lokanatah Temple, Yameshwar, Kapalmochana, Markandeshwar and Nilkantheswar Temple. Mythologically, there are eight incarnation of Lord Shiva known as Asta Sambhu (ie. Asta – means eight and Sambhu-means Shiva) who guard the sacred land (khsetra) and are marked by eight Shiva temples and correspondingly eight Goddesses of Chandi or Kali also protect the holy Kshetra. These eight Shiva and Kali / Shakti temples are as under:

Shiv Temples

Kapalmochana, Kama, Khetrapal, Yameshwara, Markandeshwar, Biswesra, Nilakantha and Bateshwara

Shakti Temples

Dwarabasini, Mahabajreswari, Swanabhairabi, Bhadrakali, Bedhakali, Bhubaneshwari, Sitala and Jagnyeswari

Shri Jagannatha Temple is an example of a distinct style of architecture which is remarkable in its plan, elevation, scale. The details of construction and decoration are unique.

Among 112 identified temples listed by INTACH and IGNCA, Jagannatha Temple is a notified monument by Archaeological Survey of India. It is managed by Shri Jagannatha Temple Administration along with the Gundicha Temple.

Other temples such as Loknatha Temple is managed by Loknatha Temple Trust and the local elected representative of the sahi.

Puri is famous mainly for the Jagannath temple and the Sea Beach. Puri Dham is unique amongst the four Dhams (shrines) and is one of the best-known pilgrimage sites of India. It is also the foremost proponent of Jagannatha culture in the world, which is the assimilation of all sects and does not belong to any sect.

The city attracts millions of devotees, onlookers and tourists – both domestic and international – throughout the year and on various occasions.

For a visitor, the main religious, historical and archeological places of the city along with the beaches are as under:

SEA BEACH-PURI

Puri is the most popular sea-Side destination of the country to experience the roaring waves, radiant colours of the sky and the golden sands of the beach.

Long and wide waves break in at the beach. The sun rise and sun set are other attractions of the beach. Sea shells in different shapes and sizes would attract the visitor.

The enchanting Puri beach is running a length of around 9-kms. The beach is long and sandy. It forms entire south eastern edge of the city and is a popular place for relaxation for both domestic and international visitors. Standing at this lovely beach and looking at the unending horizon, one will have incommunicable bond with the sea. The beach is mesmerising. The MUHANA / MOHONA (estuary) is one end of Puri beach and the other end of the beach is "Penthakata".

In many of the sea beaches of the country, taking bath in the sea is risky due to under currents, depth and tides. However, the beaches at Puri are long and sandy. The sea bath at these beaches are enjoyable.

Further, out of Pancha TIRTHAs of Puri and as per Hindu belief, the sea of the town is the holiest. The beach is continuing as a divine venue for maximum number of pilgrims coming to Lord Jagannath, puri. For countless years, Puri is the venue for taking the traditional purifying dip by the pilgrims.

The fine golden sands and the roar of the breaking waves from the Bay of Bengal would fascinate any visitor time and again. The marine road passes through a series of beaches.

Visit to Puri beach is always enjoyable whether with school / college friends or a family trip with grand parents. It is considered as one of the safest beaches.

Golden Sea Beach

This 900-meter stretch between Mayfair Hotel and Gandhi Park is known as the golden beach. This beach is having the Blue Flag certification due to it's Eco-friendly environment, tourist friendly amenities and cleanliness etc.

There are pedestrian track, deck chairs, proper sanitation and solid waste management facilities. For beach illumination there are solar street lights.

There are no vendors to disturb the visitors. There are cafeterias and the beach is plastic free.

An area of around 200-meters stretch has been earmarked in the beach for the tourists to have sea bath. There is a clean bath complex to change clothes after sea bath.

Certain amount of fee is collected from the visitors who wish to spend time at the golden beach.

The Author with Family at Golden Sea Beach-Puri

Nimantrana Restaurant

For authentic Odia cuisine from various districts of the state, one can visit this restaurant of OTDC. This is facing towards the blue flag beach (ie. golden beach). There is an entrance from the blue flag beach to have food there. This restaurant is inside the Panthanivas complex. This local cuisine would also help any visitor to understand the place, community and the culinary legacy of the state.

Niladree Beach

This beach is adjacent to blue flag – Golden beach. The surrounding grassy park and beautiful flowers, beautiful wall paintings on the wall and handcrafted architecture carved in stone with soothing light are the attraction. It is nice to see as to how on a pole, different beaches of Odisha are directed along with multiple small umbrellas.

Although there are beach front chairs, however these are reserved for the guests staying at the beach front hotels / properties.

This beach is clean and nicely maintained. As the entrance is not on the main road, it is less crowded.

Beach At Chakratirtha Road

It is situated towards northern end of Puri town. This is also famous for Lord Vishnu who is worshipped as Chakra Narayan, where he carries Sudarshan Chakra. The Chakra is also worshipped along with Lord Vishnu. Three forms of Lord Nrusingha is worshipped here, ie. Abhaya Nrushingh, Chakra Nrushingh and Laxmi Nrushingh.

This beach is near Sonar – Gouranga and is clean, calm and quiet. It is also known as Puri new sea beach.

There are less number of visitors in this beach. Here, the waves are huge and wild. The shore of the beach is elevated. As observed by some tourists, "one will be awestruck with the calm beauty of the beach. If one wants a beach gateway alone and to spend some time embracing one self with the sea, this is the best beach. There are some food stalls and shopping stalls in the beach. As the height of the waves increases in night, the beach is good for day time visit. This beach will give a thrilling experience.

Soft sand, worm Sun, the bright clouds, cool breeze, the roaring waves, the gigantic boats, the blue sky, the camels, the vendors and the people of this Puri new sea beach cannot be forgotten".

The foreigners prefer this beach to take Sun-bath, water sports, body message and swimming etc.

As this is near CHAKRATIRTHA road, there are large number of hotels on either side of the road and also in the connecting lanes.

Banki Muhana

This portion of Puri beach is linked with many myths / legends and also linked to the origin of Lord Jagannath.

This is the place where the extinct river Malini (ie. this river, which was a tributary of Bhargavi, was previously separating the Bada Danda – Grand Road) meets the sea. As per some researchers, Sardha Devi, wife of the then Puri king Gajapati Narasingha Dev had closed the mouth of the river Malini and the river was filled with sand. This closed mouth is called BANKI MUHANA.

It is told that, when poet Balaram Das was not allowed to have holy glimpse of the Lord on the chariot, he came to Banki MUHANA sea beach and built 3-chariots of Trimurti on sand. This was also the early phase of Sand Sculpture.

This portion of the beach was in the news in 2017-aD, when renowned sand artist Sudarshan Pattanyak had staged 5-days dharana to draw the attention of Government to save the beaches and sea from pollution.

This river mouth is also selected for development of first ever sand – art park of the country.

Penthakatta

This is at the end of CHAKRATIRTHA road and is the last fishermen's colony inside Puri town. Large number of fishermen stay in this area. If one is interested, one can watch the activities of the local fishermen as to how they catch the fish, mend their nets, comes back from deep sea and pull their boat to the sea shore. When a boat returns from the sea and unloads the fish over the sand, it is surrounded by the traders and buyers and after sale, it is transferred to the truck which might be waiting in the road side.

They take visitors inside the sea to watch the sunset and act as life guards.

One can see and enjoy the traditional fishermen playing their catamarans or sail boats and drawing their nets with rich catches of prawn, pampfret and other fishes in this long and wide beach extending for miles.

However, the beach is not clean. On the beach one will find large number of colourful fishing boats.

The construction of these boats are made of solid tree trunks and are heavy. They are made in two or 3-pieces and split longitudinally. When not in use, they are found in the beach. This is also the sitting place for many tourists.

The best time to visit the beach is around early morning hours or in the afternoon when the fisherman return to the shore in the background of colourful rising and setting sun.

It is around 5-kms from SWARGADWAR, puri.

Swargadwar Beach

This beach is running along the marine drive of Puri. It is in front of the SWARGADWAR crematorium.

This beach is always full of exuberance and bustle and is the throbbing heartbeat of the city. It is crowded throughout the year.

Thousands of visitors come here daily to take bath in the sea to get the thrill – some experience.

This beach is enjoyable with family and friends any time of the day. In the morning and noon hours for bathing and in the evening time to watch the sunset and to spend some quality time while some big waves of the sea come and make the feet wet.

Tube swimming with life guards in deep sea will give a thrilling experience in this beach. Kids can play with their toys at the long and sandy beach.

There are also chairs on the beach where one can seat by paying Rs15/ 20 per hour and the sea waves and the breeze would cool one's mind and soul.

This beach is dotted with numerous stalls selling local handmade products, seashells and jewellery etc. Many stalls can be found for variety of fast food and snacks. There are many restaurants in SWARGADWAR locality that specialises for many varieties of fish dishes and is a heaven for sea-food lovers.

In the SWARGADWAR lane, there is a small Jagannath Temple.

This beach is around 4-kms from the main centre of the town.Here, one can enjoy camel ride and horse ride besides shopping and taking sea food.

Baliapanda Beach And Light House

This is one of the best beaches, if one likes to enjoy the sea without crowd. It is well maintained and clean.

There is a light house at this place. The light house remains open during afternoon/ evening time. From the light house one can see a spectacular view of the sea and Puri city. One can also enjoy the cool breeze. The sun rise along with the scene of the fishermen catching the fish in their boats can be seen early, in the morning.

It is somewhat isolated, cleaner and less crowded. One can reach the top floor of the light house through stair-cases. This revolving light house is the best place to capture the unhindered view of beautiful sun-set.

Dhaudia River Muhana

Many people do not know about this place, which is known as MUHANA by many people. This is an estuary where river DHAUDIA meets the Bay of Bengal.

This is the west end of Puri sea beach, just near Baliapanda.

As many people do not visit this area, here, the beach and the water are clear. The DHAUDIA river is flowing over the sand. During high tide and low tide, the water level and flow direction of the River DHAUDIA changes. The view is scenic.

During low tide one may cross the river with knee deep water. Here, there are large areas of clean sand to roam around.

One will find large number of jelly fish and sea shells in the beach. One can stand for hours while water flowing over the feet and sand flowing away from the beneath.

The sun rise at this place is really amazing and truly golden.

Lovely morning walk on this beach and reflection of morning sun over the water and making the water shine like a sheet of diamonds would charm any visitor.

This is around 4-kms from Golden beach of Puri and near the sterling resorts.

To enjoy the serenity and beauty of the beaches, one should visit the pilgrimage town Puri.

Besides the above beaches in the city, the district is having at least 7-enchanting beaches, ie. Chandrabhaga (Konark), Balighai, Ramchandi, Astaranga, Bali Harichandi and Rajhans (Chilika). These beaches are covered by the Author under Puri District and Chilika lake in a separate book, ie. Charming South-East Odisha.

Sand Sculpture

Puri beaches are famous for the sand sculptures. Although the sculptures are temporary and can be washed and blown away, these are eye catching. This is also popular among the tourists.

The hypnotic sand art done at the sea shore by sand artists with some strong social and public awareness are a treat to watch.

The sculptures created by famed Sudarshan Pattanayak is very famous.

He holds many limka records and Guinness record. He had also created the world's biggest sand art of 43.2 feet long and 35-feet wide chariot at Puri Beach. Pattanayak with his students had created this 3-dsand art.

He spreads awareness on many issues through his sand art. Odisha, specially Puri has acquired a unique distinction in the field of sand – art.

Saradha Bali

Saradha Bali is situated near Gundicha temple in Puri. The vast land extending from Sri Gundicha temple to Bada Sankha is known as "Saradha Bali".

Thousands of devotees gather in Saradha Bali to see the Trimurti during 9-day Ratha Yatra festival.

Mr. Naik, the then registrar of NISER had described, "like one cannot count the sand grains of Saradha Bali, the miracles of Lord are innumerable".

As per many researchers, there was a river named Malini, a tributary of Bhargavi/ branch river of Sankhua, which was flowing between Jagannath Temple and Gundicha temple separating the Bada Danda (grand road). In the past, 6-chariots were used for Ratha Yatra (ie. 3-chariots on each side of the river). The images were carried to other side over a makeshift bridge for mounting the chariot on the other side.

Saradha Devi, the queen of Puri king Gajapati Narasingha Dev, was ordered by Lord Jagannath in the dream to have single Rath Yatra. As a result, the queen filled the mouth of the river and the entire river with sand. The mouth is known as Banki MUHANA and place is known as Saradha Bali / Saradha Setu.

As per Sanskrit scholar Surendra Mishra, there used to be seven chariots during Rath Yatra (ie. 4- on one side and 3- on the other side). The musicians were utilising the extra chariot up to Malini river.

As per his version, the Tri-Murti used to dismount at the location which is now known as Saradha Bali. The place of dismounting of the Lord was a place of reverence and it was known as Saradha (ie. from Saradha/ Sradha – in Sanskrit) Bali. As the buried river started flowing again during 16th century, it was again filled up with the orders of Gajapati king Ramachandra Dev.

Due to filling of the sand in the river, three chariots were/ are used for journey of the Lord. The chariots of Tri Murti stops at Saradha Bali and Lord Jagannath and others are taken in a "pahandi" (ie. ceremonial carrying of the Lord by Daitapati servitors on their shoulders) for placing them in the sanctum sanctorum in the Gundicha temple known as Adap Mandap.

The sand of Saradha Bali is also known as Bajra Dhuli. However, now it is almost a barren area.

Puri Beach Festival

This is a week long beach festival generally held during Month of November. This annual beach festival holds various events and exhibitions along with other events like fashion shows, adventure sports, art and craft, cultural theme from different parts of the state and cuisine/ food festivals.

Diverse range of folk dances of the state, beautiful handloom products and Pattachitra would attract any visitor.

Further, the sand art made by the artists add to the charm of the festival.

Beach kabaddi by girls, county boat race among Nolias and beach volley ball etc. would make the tourists busy.

It is organised by the Hotel Association of Puri along with Ministry of Tourism and Department of Tourism and Culture. It was started on 29th October, 1993 AD by the then CM, late Biju Pattanayak.

This is a favourite gathering place for both Indian and foreign beach lovers. This is a carnival that one cannot miss, which is one of it's kind.

Sarvatirtha (Assimilation Of All The Tirthas)

The sea of Puri is known as Sarvatirtha Maya, ie. assimilation of all the TIRTHAs. In other places of the country, the rivers like – Ganga, Yamuna, Saraswati, Godavari, Krishna and Kaveri etc. are considered as TIRTHAs. As all these rivers flow in to the sea, hence, sea is considered as "Sarvatirtha Maya" (ie. TIRTHA of all TIRTHAs).

Further the wood (ie. DARU) of Lord Jagannath, Balabhadra and Subhadra was collected from the sea at Puri on the 12th day of the bright fortnight of Phalgun month (ie. Govinda Dwadashi). Hence, sea at Puri is considered as the most important TIRTHA.

Marine Drive

This is 35-kms long Puri-Konark road. The drive on this road passes through the beautiful sea on one side and coastal forests of Balukhanda sanctuary on the other side. If one is lucky one can see some wild animals and deer crossing the roads. The area is calm, soothing and not crowded.

There are many resorts on this road. On the way, one can stop and pay homage at Ramachandi temple, Panchamukhi Hanuman temple and Gupteswar temple.

Near Ramachandi temple and beach one can play water sports. The confluence of the kushabhadra river and sea at this place provides a panoramic view.

One can stop at any point and any picnic spots on the road to take beautiful pictures for a memory and enjoy with family and friends.

The sandy beaches near the road are home to Olive Ridley turtles, although found in less numbers.

Enroute the marine drive one can visit some stone carvers and may purchase some mementoes available for any range.

One will be astonished to know about some artists, who claim themselves as the descendants of the carvers of Konark temple.

This is a perfect and smooth road in the midst of casuarina and cashew plantation for an awesome drive and is one of the best marine drives in India.

As per some visitors, if one can pair one's time with sun-rise or sun-set, one will have the most memorable time in the midst of fresh and cool breeze.

SUDARSHAN ART AND CRAFT VILLAGE

This is one of the best places in the city for any art lover and to capture special moments in a camera.

This museum was established by Padmashree Sudarshan Sahu, the renowned sculpture and designer of the state.

One will be astonished to see the intricate carvings in stone, wood, fiber glass and various paintings. The Japanese architecture of Buddhist temples would charm the visitor.

As per Travel Odisha, "Amusing characters, fabulous designs, colourful landscape and ambient music would refresh one's soul".

It is situated at the station road, at a distance of around 2-kms from Puri Railway Station.

HERITAGE ZONE OF PURI

Puri town is famous for the temples, MATHAS, Akhadas, Jagagharas, holy tanks and vernacular / traditional buildings.

As per PKDA (Puri-Konark Development Authority), the exclusive blend of heritage elements are found in seven Zones of the city as under:

Zone – 1

This is the epicentre of the KSHETRA and it houses the idols of Lord Jagannath, Balabhadra and Subhadra on the divine platform.

Zone – 2

This is the second fold which is hexagonal in shape and houses the 4-goddesses of power, two TIRTHAs, two sacred trees, Garuda and the top of the hill in the form of the tortoise shell.

Zone – 3

This is the outer layer of second fold and is the central part of lotus like structure having 8-petals, which houses an idol of Shiv and Goddess in each petal.

Zone – 4

This area comprises of the space between the inner compound wall and the outer compound wall.

Zone – 5

The eight incarnations of Lord Shiv, ie. Astasambhu which are guarding the sacred land and Goddess Chandi or Kali is protecting the holy KSHETRA in different names. These are old shrines having ritualistic connections with the Jagannath temple. These are placed carefully with link roads to approach them.

Zone – 6

This zone is having the sacred TIRTHAs, the tanks and also the ocean Mahodadhi. It is believed that visiting these sacred places in Puri is equivalent to visiting the three sacred places in India, ie. Gaya, Kashi and Haridwar.

Zone – 7

This is the outermost zone and consists of the sentries of Sankha KSHETRA, Puri and two pilgrim centres which are as under:

- Nilakantheswar (Governor of KSHETRA)
- Narisingha (place where yajna is performed)
- Ardhasosani (guardian of night)
- Bileswar (apical region of Sankha KSHETRA)
- Lokeswar (the basal region of Sankha KSHETRA)
- Kapileswar (watchman of the KSHETRA)
- CHAKRATIRTHA (pilgrim centre of unique merit)
- SWARGADWAR (the passage to heaven)

The areas around Jagannath temple, the stretch of Grand road and the SWARGADWAR road are the three major nodes where the ancient and heritage structures of the city are situated.

Jagannath Temple

Lord Jagannath temple is the centre of the town and the area around it is most important for any visitor.

This majestic structure stands at the heart of the city. The activities of the temple are immense and they create enough interest for all. Further Lord is not only the God of the Hindus or Indians, but also the Lord of entire humanity.

This is a place, where on one platform, the rituals are performed by Aryan Raja (Gajapati king, which represents Indradyumna),

Daitapati (representing Shavara Shresta – Biswabasu) and Brahmin (representing Bidyapati).

As per Madala Panji, official Almanac of the temple, Yayati Keshari of Keshari dynasty had constructed a small temple of Purushottama Jagannath along with two other shrines of Goddess Vimala and Goddess Laxmi.

It is believed that the temple was built on a huge sand dune resembling a blue hillock known as NILA SAILA (ie. Nila – means blue and SAILA – means Hill) / NILA GIRI (ie. Nila – means blue and Giri means – Hill). The temple surface is around 20-feet above the surrounding area / grand road.

The construction of present Jagannath Temple commenced during the reign of king Ananta Varman Chodaganga Dev (ie. beteween 1112 AD-1147 AD) and the construction of the temple was completed in 1197 AD during the period of Anangabhima Dev - ll. However, different chronicles variously mention the date of construction and completion beteween 1112 AD to 1216 or 1226 AD etc.

This east facing temple consists of 4-Structures – ie. Viman (sanctum), Jagmohan (porch), Nata Mandap (Dancing hall) and Bhog Mandap (Hall of offerings /Refractory. These four structures are in axial alignment.

The temple is PANCHARATHA in plan. The temple of Lord Jagannath is the highest among the existing temples of the state. It is around 214.8 feet high from the grand road level.

The Viman and Jagmohan were built during 12th century. The Nata Mandap was constructed during the reign of king Purushottama Dev (1461- 1495 AD) and Bhoga Mandap was added during the reign of Prataprudra Dev (1495-1522 AD).

The base of Viman and Jagmohan are square and the erected part of Viman up to Kalash / Chuda (ie. top) is circular.

Viman / Bada Deula / Garva Gruha / Main Temple

This is Pancharatha in plan and is divided in to five parts in both horizontal and vertical directions.

The 5-parts of the horizontal order are – Bhumi, Bada, Gandi, Mastaka and Dhwaja and each part is vertically divided in to several portions.

The Viman is also constructed in Rekha order, ie. a type of temple with curvilinear super structure. The Rekha Gandi is also divided in to 5-parts (ie. Paga) vertically. The middle one is known as Raha Paga (Ratha part). Both the sides of Raha Paga is known as Anuraha Paga and two corners are Konika. Some of the component parts are linked to human body.

On the three sides (ie. north, south and west) of the tower, there are three miniature shrines for side Gods of Varaha (on the south), Nrushingh (west) and Trivikrama (north). They are of black granite.

These are of Pidha order and also known as Nisha Temple. During deplastering of these temples, the popular 24-forms of Lord Vishnu, carved one above the other on both sides of the wall are found.

On the Varaha side out of 8-forms, seven of them are identified as – Madhava, Samkarsana, Damodar, Trivikrama, Kesava, Vishnu, Madhusudan and one is mutilated.

In the side of Nrushingh shrine, out of 8-Sculptures, only two of them are identified as Sridhar and Hrishikesh and other 6-are mutilated. In the side of Trivikram, out of 8-Sculptures, six of them are identified as – Padmanava, Achyut, Janardan, Krishna, Pradyumna and Vamana and two are hidden. Each image is standing on double petal lotus and all are artistically carved with Nupur, armlets, necklace sacred thread, jewels and Kirit Mukut on head etc.

This is unique and is an important discovery, as for the first time all the 24-forms of Vishnu are depicted together in the form of sculptures. Out of thousand names of Vishnu only 24- names were selected through skill full alteration of the four Chief attributes of Lord Vishnu (ie. Sankha, Chakra, Gada and Padma – held in four hands).

It is also heartening to know that the number of possible formulations of 4-attributes taken over at a time is exactly twenty four. Further no where in the country, all the 24-forms of Vishnu are depicted within any known temples either in south or north.

The several sections as stated above are superimposed one over the other tapering to the top where the great Amalakasila and Kalash are placed. The Amalakasila keep the structure properly balanced. The sila is supported by dopicha lions at the corners and figures of Garuda in between them. A hole is created in a stone placed in the

Kalash to hold up the Ayudha, ie. Sphere known as Nila Chakra (blue wheel).

Nila Chakra (Blue Wheel)

It is made up of Astadhatu (ie. eight different metals). It is installed on the Kalash (ie. Dadhinauti) on the top of the temple. The height is 12-feet, diameter 7.6 feet, thickness 2- inches and it's weight is 1500 Kg. It is a duel of inner and outer circles having spokes. There are 8-axles in the sphere and the length of each axle is 1.10feet. Flags of different colours, usually white and yellow with a mark of half moon are placed in Nilachakra with a bamboo stick.

The flag of Nila Chakra is known as "Patitapabana Bana" and there are number of songs eulogising the glory of the flag.

If the flag is is lost due to some untoward incident, offerings are not made to Lord. People who could not come to the temple to visit the Lord, they feel the presence of the Lord by seeing the flag from a distance. They also offer BHOG / prasad at that place, which is known as "Chakramanohi".

As per custom, after offering prayer to Nilachakra, one has to move towards the south from the temple of Pataleswar and proceed to Jagannath temple, climb 7-Steps of the gate of Nata Mandir in the northern side and enter the Natamandir of Jagannath Temple. One has to move straight to the back of Garuda and see the Lord.

Garuda Pillar

It is situated in the Nata Mandir. Garuda, the carrier of Lord Vishnu is seated with folded hands on the top. It is placed at such a level, so that Garuda can point his eyes to the feet of Lord Jagannath at the Ratna Vedi / Ratna SIMHASANA. From this place one can view Lord Jagannath, Balabhadra and Subhadra. Devotees embrace the pillar and offer prayers to Lord. Some people believe that they can get relief from incurable disease, if one touches the pillar. It is understood, Chaitanya Mahaprabhu used to offer prayer to Lord from this place.

The figure prints of Chaitanya Mahaprabhu is also seen in the gate of Bhoga Mandap. It is believed that the stone of Bhoga Mandap became soft with the devotion of Chaitanya Mahaprabhu and as a result his finger prints are imprinted.

Garbha Gruha (Sanctum Sanctorum)

The interior of the Viman is plain and is of 3-tier structure. The ground floor is 30-feet by 30-feet and 48-feet high. The first floor is 30-feet by 30-feet and 33-feet high. The second floor is 28-feet by 28-feet and 30-feet high.

Ratna Simhasana / Ratna Vedi / Bejewelled Platform

This is in the middle of GARBHA GRUHA and in the middle of the room. The images of lords have been installed on it. It is 16-feet long and 13-feet wide. The height of the throne is 4-feet and there is sufficient space for devotees to perform circumambulation. A wooden structure of Kanakamundi has been installed in theRatnasimhashan. The lower portion of kanakamundi has been covered by a large appliqué. Three round shaped black granite blocks are kept on the Ratnasimhasan.

The wooden images of Lord Balabhadra, Goddess Subhadra and Lord Jagannath are seated from right to left. The emblem Sudarshan (ie. in the form of wooden log) is placed on the left of Lord Jagannath. Shree Madhav (a small image of Lord Jagannath, placed at the back side of Shreedevi), Shreedevi (golden image of Goddess Laxmi) on the left side of Lord Jagannath and Bhudevi (a silver image) on the right side of Lord Jagannath are also on the Ratna Vedi. These seven deities are called "Saptada Vigraha" (ie. seven-in - one).

This has only one door leading to the Jagmohan and is known as Kalahata DWAR (door).

Chaturdha Murti

Shree Jagannath, Balabhadra, Devi Subhadra and Sudarshan are known as Chaturdhamurti. Lord Jagannath is the main attraction of the temple who is the master of the universe. He is described as Sripurushotttama (supreme entity) in various religious scriptures. He is the origin and the end of the Universe. Balabhadra is considered as an incarnation of Lord Shiv. Plough (Hala) and mace (Mushala) are his sacred weapons. He is known as Lord of farmers, elder brother of Lord Jagannath and incarnation of Mahakala / Maharudra.

As per mythology, he is the Seshanaga / seshadeva who is holding the earth in his hood. Goddess Subhadra is believed as the willpower of the Lord and she curbs the pride and arrogance of any one and inspires them for a better life. She is the Adyashakti.

According to Ray Ramananda-Balabhadra, Subhadra and Jagannath (trinity) are one and same.

Sudarshan is placed to the right of Lord Jagannath. It is believed that he is the source of energy of Lord Vishnu.

Jagmohan (Audience Hall)

It is a Pidha DEULA. It has horizontal platforms (Pidhas) which are receding in size, as they go upwards. It is described by some as pseudo – Pancharatha temple and which may be called a Tri-Ratha Pidha temple. The main shrine and the porch were constructed during the same period. The height of Jagmohan is 120-feet.

The roof of Jagmohan stands on four pillars. Although it is believed that Jagmohan stands on a platform like the Viman, however it is not visible. The Bada consists of usual 5-divisions, ie. Pabanga, Tala jangha, Bandhana, Upper Jangha and veranda. The Gandi is made up of 13-pidhas arranged in 2-tiers, ie. seven in the lower and six in the upper and these are diminishing in size as they proceed from bottom to top.

There are erotic figures, Gajasimha motifs and damsels playing with various kinds of musical instruments.

It has four doorways and the west door is known as Kalahatadwar. It is the only entrance to the sanctum. It is 14.4 feet by 8.10 feet.

As Lord is the embodiment of 16-virtues (Kalas), the doorway is believed as the junction of all these Kalas.

Jaya Bijaya Gate

The doorway opening to the Nata Mandap is known as Jaya and Vijaya which is 14-feet by 7-feet (ie. This gate connects Nata Mandap with Jagmohan). Jaya and Vijaya are celestial creatures of heaven who guard the Ratna SIMHASANA. It is of saptabandha (ie. 7-layers) and all aspects of Rasa Lila have been depicted here on the upper side of the door. This doorway is one of the finest specimen of Kalinga architecture. There is an idol of Navagraha on the door.

On the side walls of the doorway, there are inscriptions of Prataprudra Dev which is written in ODIYA language.

Before the rituals start in the temple, these door keepers are worshipped. Similarly in the night, before the Sayan Thakur goes to sleep, he comes to this place. Green coconut and flowers are offered to Lord.

After crossing Jaya-Vijaya gate one goes to Jagmohan. This is known as outer Pokharia. In the past, Devadasiss used to perform their dance at night at this place, when God goes to sleep. Cots are placed here for Sayan Thakur to sleep.

The southern doorway is 13.8 feet by 6.5 feet and on the porch there are two important figures, ie. figure of Lord Brahma with four heads and kamandalu in hand and one nicely carved image of Lord Shiv.

The northern doorway leads to Ratna Bhandar (ie. strong room of the temple which is the repository of valuables). The images of Astashakti and the image of Lokanath, the Treasurer of Lord Jagannath are installed here.

Nata Mandap (Dancing Hall)

Architecturally, Nata Mandap is different from the Viman and Jagmohan and was constructed at a later date. It is squarish in plan measuring 69-feet by 67-feet from the inside and the outside being square of 80-feet. The famous Garuda pillar is at the eastern side and is placed inside the Nata Mandir.

The front view of the deities can be seen from this place. The height of Nata Mandap is 30-feet.

The Devadasis used to dance at the time of Sakala Dhup (morning food offering) and various functions in the temple.

There are four small rooms attached to the sides, may be for orchestra/ worshipping some deities. There are five water spots on the flat roof, shaped like the mouth of a crocodile.

There are sculptures representing the scene of Kanchi – Kaveri expedition and it contains two mounted cavaliers (ie. Jagannath and Balabhadra) with a milk-maid Manik standing before them carrying a pitcher on her head. There are some other paintings including the picture of Shankaracharya offering obeisance to Lord Nrushingh and Ten incarnations of Lord Vishnu etc. which are more prominent.

There are seven steps in north gate, known as "SATA PAHACHA". During Ratha Yatra the deities move through theses steps (pahachas) and in the last step (Pahacha), they are decorated with Tahia.

Nowadays, Nata Mandap is used as Jagmohan (Audience Hall).

Bhog Mandap

This is immediately east of Nata Mandap. The building is of square in structure measuring 58-feet by 56-feet. It is constructed with yellowish sand stone and is red due to ochre paintings. The structure stands on 4-pillars. Although there are no decorations in the interior, the exterior walls are well decorated. The Chlorite figures in the niches of upper jangha depicts many mythologies scenes and are the most finished styles of Kalinga art. The height of BHOG Mandap is around 30-feet.

It has four openings. One, to the east side and other, to the south side is connected with the gateway from the kitchen leading to Nata Mandap. The other doors are to the north and to Nata Mandir. When BHOG is offered, the door connected to the Nata Mandap is opened to enable to see the picture of deities in brass mirror for the purpose of offering. It is understood that the number of Chlorite sculptures preserved in the niches of the outer wall were brought by the Marathas from the Konark temple.

Scroll works are found extensively. Rows of elephants, mounted cavalries, bridled tiger mounted by human figure having kilted legs and erotic sculptures are other attractions.

There are interesting sculptures like – king is worshiping Durga, Shivling and Lord Jagannath, marching of royal army, king's coronation, Lord Krishna dancing with Gopis while playing the flute, Ramabhiseka and Lord Shiv dancing over the bull etc.

Sayan Thakur

This is a tiny gold image and is a combined form of Laxmi and Narayan. It's right half represents male and left half as female. It is an Ardhanareeswarar form. The two bodies of Vishnu and Lakshmi are combined as one. There are eight hands. The attributes of Lord Vishnu, ie. Conch, wheel, club and lotus and attributes in the hands of Laxmi are – manuscript, lotus, mirror and a pot fitted with gems. This type of metal image is not found in the state.

This image, known as "Sayana Thakur" is brought from the store (Bhandar) by Bhandar Mekapa. It is anointed with sandal paste and placed in the SIMHASANA, near the image of Lord Jagannath. The holy beds (Ratna palankas) are placed in front of the deities and devotional songs are sung by the MAHARI along with the sound of lute.

The Sayana Thakur is brought to Jaya – Vijaya DWAR and is made to sit on a dambaru. After offering of the green coconut water, camphor Arati and puspanjali etc, the Sayana Thakur is made to sleep in the bed of Lord Jagannath and thereafter taken to store room. The temple doors are closed and the premises are cleared of. This is known as Pahuda, Muda and Sodha.

This ritual is performed in the late evening after Badasimhar Dhupa.

JAGANNATH TEMPLE COMPLEX

The area of the temple complex is around 10.734 Acres and is surrounded by two big concentric boundary walls. The outer wall is known as" Meghanada Prachir (ie. 665-feet by 640-feet) "and the inner boundary wall is known as" Kurma Prachir (ie. 420-feet by 315 -feet). The height of outer wall varies from 20-feet to 24-feet. Although the period of construction of these boundary walls are not known, some are of the view that it was constructed not earlier than 15th century.

The strong boundary walls also prove that, the temple was serving the purpose of a fort. As per historians, the civilians as well as soldiers had taken shelter inside the compound at the time of Muslim invasion in the past.

Aruna Stambha

This Sun Pillar (Aruna STAMBHA) with height of around 33.8 feet from the ground is in front of the entrance to the eastern gateway. This pillar was originally stood in front of the Sun temple at Konark and was shifted by the Marathas. This is a monolithic pillar with 16-Sides and made up of Chlorite.

It is in two parts, ie. the pillar of 25.2 feet in height, 2-feet in diameter and 6.3 feet in circumference stands on a carved Chlorite pedestal of 7.9 feet square and 6-feet high and has a capital on the top with height of 2.5 feet.

The praying Aruna in squatting position is at the top. The capital is formed of two rings and surmounted by a series of lotus petals.

Although the pillar is present here for around 2-centuries, it's original construction dates back to early part of 13th century.

GATES WITH TEMPLES NEAR OUTER COMPOUND WALL (MEGHANADA PRACHIR WITH NEARBY TEMPLES)

There are four gates in the outer compound wall as described below which are opening out to four principal directions. These four gates represent-dharma (west gate known as Tiger gate), Artha (North gate known as HASTI DWAR), Kama (ie. south gate known as ASWA DWAR) and Mokshya (Simhadwar – lions gate). Some others opine that these four gates of the Lord represent-kama (lust), lova (greed), Moha (delusion) and Mascharya (jealousy), which are to be conquered to reach the Lord.

The architecture of Navagrahas (nine planets) are found as architecture of all the gates and the gates are ornamented.

EASTERN GATE – SIMHA DWAR (LION'S GATE)

This is the most important entrance to the temple and it faces towards DOLA Mandap Sahi, where the residents are Suaras, Daitas and Puja Pandas. They are important functionaries in different rituals. Some important monasteries like – Emaar, Radhaballav, Mangu and Navaldas etc. are present which are having direct and regular ritualistic connections with Jagannath Temple.

Two lions are standing on each side.

ENTRANCE TO THE TEMPLE THROUGH LION'S GATE /SIMHA DWAR.

The gate is ornate beautifully with the image of Nine planets on the upper part. The image of Mahalaxmi is above the Navagraha. The idols of Jaya – Vijaya (door – keepers) are in front of the gate. There are two fold doors covered with brass plates and a small door on the right big door for the use of the Sevayats, when door is closed.

In the intervening portion of the lions gate and before reaching the 22-Steps, one will find the image of PATITAPABANA (ie. picture of Lord Jagannath) carved in the wall in the right side and image of Hanuman in the left side.

Patitapabana

This image on the right side was carved during the time of king Ramachandra Dev (1726 AD – 1736 AD) to enable him to see the Lord from outside, as he became an out-caste because of his marriage with a Muslim girl. He had married the sister of Taki khan, to protect the temple from Muslim invasion. This image also helps the devotees to see the Lord, who cannot enter in to the temple.

Fate Hanuman

This idol of Hanuman having 12-hands is placed in the left side and in a small place. It is believed that the image was placed around 14th century, by Ramanandacharya who was a worshipper of both Lord Ram and Hanuman.

He had established centres at 5-places to train youths to protect Jagannath Temple from Muslim invaders. Fate Hanuman is the protector of the eastern side gate of the temple.

22-Steps (Baisi Pahacha)

Through Lion's gate one has to climb 22-Steps to reach the inner compound of the temple. The steps are constructed with felsper and Khandolite stones. These steps were constructed by king Bhanu Dev.

Legend

King Bhanu Dev had no sons. He had prayed Lord Shiv (Jambeswar) of the temple and with his blessings he got a son. As per the predictions of an astrologer, he came to know that the life period of his son was around 22-years. Again king prayed to Lord Shiv for the long life of his son. Pleased with his prayer, Lord Shiv advised the king to build 22-Steps inside the temple and the boy has to roll down 22-Steps before Lord Jagannath for his long life. Accordingly king constructed the 22-Steps and rolled his son. This custom is continuing and people roll down their children in these 22-Steps to increase their life span.

The name of the steps are – Triba, Kumudbati, Manda, Chandobati, Dayabati, Ranjani, Ratika, Rodra, Krodha, Badrika, Prasarani, Brati, Marjani, Kshyati, Rakta, Sandipani, Ajapani, Mandanti, Rohini, Ramya, Ugra and Ksyovini.

The presiding deities of the 22-Steps are – Maya, Chetana, Budhi, Nidra, Kshyudha, Chaya, Trushna, Kshyanti, Jati, Lajya, Shanti, Kanti, Bruti, Smruti, Daya, Tusti, Bikri, Mata, Bhranti and Pragyana.

It is believed that "Yama Shila" is placed in the second step and devotees have to touch this stone, before visiting Lord Jagannath and they will be relived of unnatural death.

Each step is having height of around 6 to 7- inches, breadth is around 6-feet and length is around 70-feet. The breadth of the 18th step is 15-feet. Through 19th and 20th steps which are semi circular, one can enter the Ananda bazar. SHRADHA ceremony for the ancestors are also performed on these steps. The Chaturdha Murti is taken to the chariot through these steps during Rath Yatra.

As per Yoga Shastra, a yogi has to cross 22-para Prakriti to see the Lord.

There are some other beliefs about these steps, which are as under: –

One has to cross – 7-patalas (ie. Atal, Sutal, Bital, Talatala, Mahatala, Rasatal, Patal), 7-lokas (ie. Bhu, Bhuba, Swaha, Maha, Jana, Tapa, Satya) and 8- Baikunthas (ie. Sri Baikuntha, Kaibalya Baikuntha, Sesasai Baikuntha, Karnarnaba Baikuntha, Swetadeep Baikuntha, Parabyoma Baikuntha, Garbhodaka Sai Baikuntha and Kailash Baikuntha) to reach Lord Vishnu, hence 22-Steps.

- The 22-Steps symbolises – PANCHA ATMA, PANCHA BHUTA, PANCHA VIJA, PANCHA DEVA and both Jiva and Param.
- It is the symbol of 22-tIRTHAs of Srimad Bhagabat with Ten Gods (ie. Basudeva, Narayan, Madan-Mohan, Rama - Krishna, Sridevi, Bhudevi, Bimala, Bhubaneswari and Pacharasa, ASTA SATWIK BHABA, TRI BIJA, TRI SHAKTI and TRI GUNA.
- The total legs of the ten incarnations of the Lord Vishnu are twenty two and accordingly 22-Steps.
- These twenty two steps symbolises 22-tIRTHAs and 22-Bhabas (ie. feelings).

One has to sacrifice the evils / sins while climbing this 22-Sacred steps to see the Lord with liberated body and mind.

The devotees while climbing, touch these steps in hand and many children / many people are seen rolling on these steps.

The temples of – Kashi Vishwanath, Ramachandra and Nrushingh are situated on the southern side of these 22-Steps. Earlier Mahaprasad was sold in the 22-Steps which is now shifted to Ananda Bazar.

Kashi Vishwanath Temple

This west facing small temple is situated at the east corner and on the third step of the 22-Steps. The idol is of marmar stone. The construction period of the temple is not known. However, as per legend, lord Shiv appeared at this place satisfied with the devotion of Chakrapani Khuntia, a Sevayat. The devotees get the benefit of worshiping Vishwanath of Kashi, by worshiping at this place.

It also shows the co-existence of Vaishnavism and Saivites.

Rama Chandra Temple

This is very near to Kashi Viswanatha temple. Ramayan is recited at this temple, as Lord Shiv is fond of hearing Ramayan and the temple is nearby.

Nrushingh

This is known as Goudiya Nrushingh temple and is very close to Ram temple. As per hearsay, Chaitanya Mahaprabhu could not climb 22-Steps, as he had not taken permission from Lord Nrushingh. Hence, Goudiya Vaishnavas worship the Lord and seek permission to enter the Jagannath temple.

Western Gate (Vyaghra Dwar-tiger Gate)

This gate faces Baseli Sahi and is in the south-western side of Harachandi Sahi. The temple functionaries like – singharies, Puspalakas., supakaras, Maha Supakaras, Madeli, bazanitri and Maharies etc. stay in these area and it stretches up to Loknath temple.

On each side of the gate there is a figure of tiger made up of mortar. One has to climb 11-steps to reach the inner compound of the temple.

One has to visit the following deities in the west gate.

Durga Madhav Temple

This is situated on the south-western corner of outer wall.

Siddheswar Mahadev Temple

This temple is on the way to the flower garden of the Lord (Neelachal Upavan) and on the western side. It is believed that by worshiping the Lord one get Siddhi.

Chakra Narayan Temple

It is near SIDDHESWAR temple and there is a Mandap in front of the temple.

Char Dham Temple

This temple is near SIDDHESWAR Mahadev. The deities of 4-important shrines of Hindu Religion (ie. Badrinath, Dwaraka, Jagannath and RAMESWAR) are present in a small temple. It is believed that, those who cannot visit the 4-dhams (shrines) can get same results by worshiping the deities, here.

Mahavir Temple

The temple of Hanuman is on the left side of western gate. He is the protector of 4-dhams (four sacred places) and is known as Vir Vikram Hanuman.

Hasti Dwar – Northern Gate

The area around it is known as Markandeswar sahi due to presence of Markandeswar temple and tank. This tank is one of the 5-tIRTHAs of puri.

One has to climb 13-Steps through this gate to reach the inner portion of the temple.

On each side of the door a big elephant is found. During Muslim invasion, this was disfigured. These figures were repaired and plastered with mortar at a later date and were placed at the northern gates of the inner compound.

The following temples are near the north gate.

Sitala Temple

This north facing small temple is situated on the right side of the north gate. The Goddess is holding Kula in her hand. It is believed that the deities meet Lord Jagannath in a Mandap situated in front of the Goddess. The Golden well (SUNA KUA) is situated in front of the Temple. On Snana Purnima day (bathing ceremony) water is taken from this well to bath the Trimurti.

Jhadeswari Temple

This temple is on the northern side of Sitala temple.

Bedha Lokanatha

This is situated on the east of Sitala temple.

Ganesh Temple

This is situated near Bedha loknath temple.

Parasunatha Temple/ Kasinath Temple

This is situated on the south of Ganesh temple.

Dhabaleswar Temple

This temple is situated near the Parasunatha temple.

Baikunthanath Mahadev Temple

This is situated on the way to Koili Baikuntha. The temple is in dilapidated condition.

Arpana Gopal Temple / Bardhaman Radhakrishna Temple

The temple is situated on the right side of the entrance to Koili Baikuntha.

Tapaswi Hanuman Temple

This temple is close to Arpana Gopal Temple. As per legend, this place was given to Lord Hanuman by Lord Jagannath to worship him.

Vaman

This temple is close to Tapaswi Hanuman temple. It is in dilapidated condition.

Lakshmi Nrushingh

This is close to Vaman temple. Laxmi in the lap of Nrushingh is worshipped here.

Uttarayani

This is known as Uttar Durga. The temple is close to Laxmi Nrushingh temple.

Isaneswar Temple

This Shiv temple is situated in the corner of inner wall and outer wall. Lord Shiv is placed 20-feet below the temple surface. As per Madalapanji, this temple was constructed by Dhruba Keshari and is older than Jagannath Temple. An image of Hara – Paravati is installed on the way to the temple. It is believed that river Ganga flows through this temple and Lord is the Ishana Guru of Lord Jagannath. Shivratri is the major festival of this temple.

ASWA DWAR – SOUTHERN GATE

One has to climb 10-Steps of Khandolite stones to reach the inner portion. There are two galloping horses with Lord Jagannath and Balabhadra on their back and it shows the martial glory of the Lord.

The following deities/ temples are situated between the outer compound (Meghanada Prachir and inner compound (Kurma Bedha).

Nrushingh Temple

This north facing temple is situated in the right corner entrance of south gate. The Puranas are recited in front of this temple.

Sadabhuja Temple

This west facing temple is near Nrushingh temple. Wooden image of Chaitanya (Gouranga) with 6-hands (Sada Bhuja) and in a standing position is found here.

This temple was constructed at a later stage.

As per hearsay, A Sevayat (Ananta Mahapatra) had seen Chaitanya with 6-hands in the dream and he was ordered to install this type of image by cutting a 6- branched Neem tree found near a pond known as Babaji Pokhari. The Sevayat had informed the king about his dream. As per order of the king the tree was cut and wooden image of Chaitanya Mahaprabhu was installed.

Sri Ramachandra Temple

This temple is near the Chaitanya temple. Lord Ram is worshipped with Laxman, Sita, Sugriva and Hanuman. Sampati, a large bird, putting 8-Soldiers on it's back is in standing position.

As per legend, before the expedition of Lord Ram to the kingdom of demon king Ravan, this bird by putting 8-Soldiers of Lord Ram on it's back had shown the kingdom of Ravan, which was on the sea shore.

THE FOLLOWING TEMPLES ARE FOUND ON THE LEFT SIDE OF THE ENTRANCE OF THE SOUTH GATE.

Barabhai Hanuman

Twelve soldiers of Lord Ram (ie. 12- brothers of Lord Hanuman) are worshipped in this temple.

Gurundi Gopal

The early stage of Lord Krishna (ie. in creeping position) is worshipped in this temple. It is near Bara Bhai Hanuman temple.

Purana Nrushingh

It is near the GURUNDI temple. Lord Nrushingh, known as Nrushingh of Kalki Incarnation (ie. Purana Nrushingh) is worshipped. The idols of Saint Suka preaching Bhagabata to King Parikshit are also found.

Budhi Maa

This is near the Nrushingh temple and She is worshipped during the small pox epidemic.

PLACES / STRUCTURES BETWEEN OUTER COMPOUND WALL(MEGHANADA PRACHIR) AND INNER COMPOUND WALL (KURMA BEDHA)

One may visit and should know the following places between the outer compound wall and inner compound wall.

Temple Kitchen

This is situated at the east-south corner of outer compound wall. This was built during the period of Dibyasimha Dev (1682-1713

AD). The roof from temple kitchen to Bhoga Mandap was built by Harekrushna Dev (1720- 25 AD). It's area is 150-feet by 150-feet.

These are specially made and are 6/7 feet high from the ground level. In the same oven 9-earthen pots are placed and cooked simultaneously which is unique. After fire worship, the cooking is started.

The temple cooks are known as Supakaras and they have special skills. The clay pots used are made by Kumbhara (potters) who stay inside the town.

Around 500-people and 1500-helpers work daily in the kitchen and there are up to 750-chulas (stoves). After completion of all procedures, the cooked materials are offered to the deities as prasad / BHOGs. After puja, the prasad is again taken to the sanctum of Goddess Vimala and is offered to her. It becomes Mahaprasad after that.

Ananda Bazar

It is situated on the north-east side of outer compound and is close to Snana Mandap. The sacred food (Abhada / Mahaprasad) offered to the deities are sold to the devotees/ visitors, at this place. Two kinds of Maha Prasads (Dry Maha Prasad) and Anna Mahaprasad are sold to the people.

It covers an area of 250-feet by 250-feet. This is one of the biggest open air and holy hotel in the world, where thousands of people buy and eat various types of food.

Chahani Mandap

It is situated on the east-south of Ananda Bazar. The return journey of Lord Jagannath (ie. Bahuda) is witnessed by Goddess Laxmi from this place.

Snana Bedi

This is the bathing platform of Trimurti and is situated in the North – East corner of outer compound wall. It is squarish with 75-feet by 75-feet.

During Snana Purnima (fortnight before Rath Yatra) the three deities take annual bath at this place. As this platform is high, devotees can watch the function from outside the temple.

Koili Baikuntha

This is situated in north- west corner of the temple between inner circle and outer circle. This is the burial ground of the lord.

During Nabakalebara, the old images are buried here and new images are carved at this place along with Nabakalebara rituals. It is around 9-feet deep and covered by Malati creeper.

It is the most ancient place.

As per hearsay, the dead body of Lord Krishna was set on fire at this place. Here, Nila Madhav was worshipped by a Sabar tribal devotee. However, there is no mythological evidence.

Koili is interpreted as "Jiba" (soul) and here, as Jibatma meets Paramatma(supreme soul – lord), it is known as Koili Baikuntha.

Niladri Vihar

It is situated in the west-north corner between Kurma Bedha and Meghanada Prachir. It is close to western gate. Various sports of the Lord are depicted through the idols.

Nilachal Upavan

This is situated in the southern and western corner of the temple between outer compound and inner compound. This is the flower garden of the Lord. One can enter the garden on the passage in front of Vir Vikram Hanuman Temple, near western gate. The temples of Chakra Narayan, SIDDHESWAR and DHABALESWAR are in the garden.

Temples In The Inner Compound Wall (Kurma Bedha)

The inner boundary wall is known as "Kurma Prachir" is constructed in two parallel walls (ie. 420-feet by 315-feet) with a narrow pass between the two.

There are 6-opening, ie. 4-corresponding to four outer gates, one opening leads to Ananda Bazar in the North-East corner and one opening leads to the covered passage of the kitchen in the east – south corner. After climbing 22-Steps one will enter the kurma Bedha.

The temples of the inner compound are as under: –

Agniswar Mahedev

This is situated on the way to kitchen. When one enters the inner compound from the side of 22-Steps, one has to turn left towards south to visit Lord Shiv of this temple. He is the protector of the fire in the temple kitchen and due to his grace half cooked food becomes full cooked, when it passes in front of him.

By visiting the Lord one will be freed from all sins.

Sataya -arayan Temple

Lord Satyanarayan is the synthesis of Hindu and Muslim religion. Hindus worship him as Vishnu and Muslims worship him as Satya pira. Although the prayers are having in Odia script but the verses are of Urdu and Bengali.

As per some researchers, Satyanarayan was installed inside the temple as an assimilation of Hindu and Muslim religion at the time of frequent Muslim invasion of the temple.

The temple is situated in the east – south corner of the inner compound. This is an image of Lord Vishnu of Khandolite stone and holds conch, discuss, mace and lotus in his four hands. During Snana Yatra 108-pots of water from Suna Kua are kept here and people also prepare flower garlands for the Lord, in the vacant place in front of the temple.

On the occasion of birthdays of their children, devotees worship Lord Satyanarayan.

Radha Krishna

This is near Satyanarayan temple. Two north facing temples of Krishna and Radhakrishna are there.

Hari Sahdeva

He is the protector of the cows of the Lord. People worship the Lord to get the benefits from cattle rearing. This is a small temple.

Bata Abakasha / Bata Jagannath Temple

Lord Jagannath is worshipped with Goddess Laxmi. Here, Chaitanya Mahaprabhu had met Jagannath Das, while he was reciting Odia Bhagabat.

Some opine that this image of Lord Jagannath was kept here in the south gate during Muslim invasion to protect the Lord. This is a small temple.

Kalpa Bata, Bala Mukunda, Bata Ganesh, Bata Mangala

These four temples are near the kalpa Bata. These group of temples are in front of Bata Jagannath.

Kalpa Bata

This holy banyan tree is standing in the temple complex from time immemorial. As per hearsay, this tree was not destroyed during pralaya(ie. dissolution of the universe). Devotees tie up red thread with stone for fulfilment of their wishes. When wish is fulfilled, they open the thread and offer Maha prasad to Brahmins. This tree is described in Kapila Samhita and skanda purana. Any one who stands under the tree or circumambulates it, all his sins are cleaned.

Bala Mukunda

This small temple is at the eastern side of Kalpa Bata. Lord Krishna as a child is sleeping on a banyan leaf with his head towards south. As per skanda purana, at the time of Pralaya (complete destruction) Child Krishna had invited Sage Markandeya, who was floating in water, to take shelter near him.

Bata Ganesh

The temple is situated on the south of Kalpa Bata. This is a 3-feet idol with white face and red body and a small stone mouse as carrier in his front.

He is holding different attributes in his 4-hands (ie. Mala – in right upper, one destroyed tooth – right lower, sword – upper left and laddu (sweet) – in left lower hand). As understood from the priest, if one puts the hand on the body. One can feel thorny projections on the whole body.

It is believed that, the king might have worshipped Lord Ganesh at this place before installation of Lord Jagannath in the main temple.

Bata Mangala

This west facing temple is on the north of Kalpa Bata and back of Ganesh temple. The temple is having both Viman and Jagmohan. A small statue of Sarba Mangala with 4-hands, is in the inner sanctum.

She holds trident and mace in two hands and the other two hands are in Abhaya and Barada mudra.

The Goddess is related to Tantra and during Durga Puja she is worshipped for 16-days. For entering the temple of Lord Jagannath, the devotees have to pray before her and take permission.

Pancha Pandav

These are 5-Shiv temples in front of Bata Mangala Temple (ie. Sri lokanath, Sri Yameswar, Sri Nilakantha, Sri Markendaya and Sri Kapal Mochan). These 5-Shivs are the guardian deities of Srikshetra. They are also known as PANCHA MAHADEV.

As per legend, Pandavas had visited this place during their incognito exile. They had stayed here for one night and worshipped Lord Vishnu for blessings. The 5-Shiv temples are constructed inside the Sri Mandir to commemorate their stay at Puri / Jagannath DHAM.

Markandeya Temple

The temple of Sage Markendaya is near the Bata Mangala temple. The Shivling is 7/8 feet deep from the base level. As per Skanda Purana during the period of total destruction, the sage was floating on the water. He was advised by Lord to stay at this place and to worship the Lord. A Madhav idol is found inside the temple as a symbol of the incident.

Indra

This south facing temple is situated on the south door of Nata Mandir. Indra temple is not found anywhere in the state. The presence of these temple, who is the king of Gods, might be to perform the function of gate keeper and to protect.

Ananta Basudev

This small temple is situated near the south gate of the inner compound. The front portion (Mukhashala) of the temple is larger than the main temple. Lord Vishnu is sleeping on the lap of Ananta Naga (serpent king), laxmi is sitting near and messaging feet, lotus is coming out from the naval portion and Lord Brahma is sitting on the lotus. This represents the early position before creation of world.

Kutam Chandi

The Goddess is placed on the west side wall of Ananta Basudev temple. The body portion of the Goddess is like a dog and the face portion is like Shakti. As Jagannath was worshipped as Tantric God, a portion of prasad is offered to Swarna Bhairavi after the puja. As per researchers, the image of Kutam Chandi was earlier near the Ratna SIMHASANA and with the Vaishnava influence, the idol was shifted from the temple and was placed, here.

Digapala

This temple is situated on the western side of Ananta Basudev temple. The guardian of ten directions are worshipped here. Each God has to supervise and guard one direction.

Surya Narayan Temple

This temple of Sun God is situated towards north of Digapala temple. Yantra of Sun God is worshipped here and every day the Puja Pandas worship at this temple first, before starting any ritual in the temple.

Kshetrapala Mahadev Temple

Lord Kshetrapal is the protector of Sri Mandir. Devotees worship Lord Shiv of this temple and seek permission to visit the Jagannath temple. This temple is near Ananta Basudev temple and was constructed during the time of Anangabhima Dev.

Mukteswar Mahadev Temple

This temple is at the side of Mukti Mandap. It is believed that by reciting Maha Mrityunjay Mantra before the Lord, the devotees get libertarian.

Maha Bajreswari

The Goddess is also known as Indrani and is the shakti of Kshetrapal Shiv. The temple is situated near the Jagmohan of the temple.

Mukti Mandap

It is the seat of Brahmin Pandits of Puri. It is a square type pedestal having a single platform and 16-pillars. The side of the square is 38-feet.

It is understood that the present Mandap was built during the period of Raja Ramachandra Dev, as per request of the queen of Raja Mansingh, who was in charge of Puri and Jagannath temple during the period of Mughal king Akbar. King Ramachandra Dev had also allotted 16-pillars to 16- Brahmin Shasans for smooth Administration of the temple. They were authorised to sit in the Mukti Mandap.

Shankaracharya of Puri is the president of Mukti Mandap Pandit Sabha. Temple priest, the Rajagurus of the king are also authorised to sit.

Presently, Brahmins of 24-Brahmin Sasans are authorised to sit in Mukti Mandap. Subsequently, further 6-villages were also authorised to sit (ie. total 30-Brahmin Sasans). The Pandit Sabha has also a library of it's own which has various religious books, mostly of Sanskrit texts.

The Brahmins sitting on the Mandap helps in resolving the disputes relating to rituals and also advise the common people as to how to get relief from the sin committed by them as per religious scriptures.

The deities are placed in this Mandap on a hanging swing during swing ceremony (Jhulan Purnima), which is celebrated from the 11th day of the bright fortnight of Shravan Month to full moon day. The entire Mandap is decorated with light and flowers.

As per legend, Lord Brahma sat at this place and had instructed Demi Gods to perform the incarnation ceremony of Lord Jagannath.

Yajna Nrushingh

This is situated in front of the south door of the main temple and near the Mukti Mandap.

As per the inscription found in this temple, it was built by king Chodaganga Dev. He had placed Lord Nrushingh at this place, before construction of the main temple. This is one of the oldest temples in the complex.

As per Skanda Purana, Lord Jagannath had appeared in the form of Nrushingh and king Indradyumna was terrified by seeing the furious form of the Lord. Lord Brahma prayed lord to take a graceful form and Lord appeared in the present form. Lord Nrushingh also plays an important role during Nabakalebara and it is performed by reciting Nrushingh Mantra.

Rohini Kunda

This is situated in the north – west side of Nrushingh temple. As per some religious scriptures, this Kunda was earlier under Kalpa Bata and there were steps to go inside.

The present Rohini Kunda is a symbol of earlier one and glorifies the virtues.

A Sphere, believed to be the replica of Sudarshan Chakra of Lord Vishnu and one image of crow, named Bhusanda Kaka are present here.

As per Skanda Purana, a crow named Bhusanda fell down from Kalpa Bata and was immersed in Rohini Kunda. This crow had taken the form of Vishnu with four hands and this incident was witnessed by Lord Brahma during his visit to Nilachal KSHETRA.

It is believed that, if any one takes the water of the Kunda, one will get rid of all the sins.

Nrutya Ganapati

This south facing temple is near the Rohini Kunda. Lord Ganesh with eight hands and on the back of mouse (carrier) stands in the pose of a dancer. He holds one serpent in upper two hands, head of a snake in one hand, garland in two hands, a broken tooth, an Ankush (weapon) and Laddu (sweet) in different hands.

Goddess Vimala

This temple is situated in the south – west corner of inner compound. She is the presiding deity of Sri KSHETRA and Lord Jagannath is her Bhairav, as per Tantra.

The temple consists of – Viman (main temple/ inner sanctum), Jagmohan(audience hall), Nata Mandir (Dancing Hall) and BHOGA Mandap (hall of offering). The main temple appears to have been built around 13th century during the period of Gangavamshi kings. It is believed that it was constructed over the ruins of an earlier temple. As per Madalapanji, first temple was constructed by Yayati Keshari.

The BHOG Mandap was constructed by the king of Paralakhemundi during the period of Dibyasimha Dev (1703-1720 AD).

The paintings of Dasa Mahavidya are found in the walls of Nata Mandir. DAKSHIN KALI is worshipped in the south-west corner of

Jagmohan. The idols of Ganesh and Kartik are in the standing position at the entrance of Nata Mandir.

As the foot of Sati fell here, Puri became the Pada Pitha (seat of Foot) of Sati and Goddess Vimala is known as "Pada Pitheswari".

As per Tantra Chudamani, this is identified with Naval Pitha of Sati. In the description of "Upapitha", it is identified with "Ucchistha".

Goddess

Goddess is standing on a lotus and is having four hands. She is holding Akshya Mala / Aksamala in upper right hand, Ring (pasa) in upper left hand, Sudhakalas (pot of nectar) in left lower hand and blesses the devotees on one hand showing Abhaya Mudra (fearlessness).

She holds Kalapasa (which is the weapon of Maha kali), Sudha Kalash (Relates to Maha laxmi) and Aksamala (related to Saraswati) which represent qualities of 3-goddesses.

As per researchers, Goddess Vimala is the synthesis of Maha Kali (Klim), Maha Laxmi (Hrim) and Maha Saraswati (Srim).

She is the most important Goddess in SRI KSHETRA. During Durga puja, she is worshipped for 16-days, (ie. from the 8th day of the dark fortnight of Ashwin, it continues till Mahanavami ie. Ninth day of the bright fortnight of Ashwin).

During the 16-days of Durga Puja ceremony, Goddess is decorated in different Besas, like – Vana Durga (4th day), Bhubaneshwari (5th day), Narayani (6th day), Bagalamukhi (7th day), Jaya Durga (8th day), Ugratara (9th day), Matangini (10th day), Dasabhuja (11 th day), Raja Rajeshwari (12th day), Harachandi (13th day) and Simhavahini (14th day).

During Durga Puja, a special kitchen is arranged for her and non-veg food(fish) is prepared for her offering on Maha SAPTAMI, Maha Astami and Maha Navami days. Goat was sacrificed during Durga Puja in front of Vimala Temple in the past. Now the offering (Naivedya) on these 3-days are khichadi and fish curry. This is cooked in an exclusive kitchen built for the purpose in front of the Vimala temple. The cooking starts after the principal deities of the main temple go to sleep (ie. Pahad).

This is unusual in the premises of a Vishnu temple.

Further, at the commencement of the worship, the metallic image of Durga stored in the temple is given bath with one thousand pitchers of water and is symbolically awakened from sleep. The unique feature of the worship is the tying together of the metallic image of Durga and the wooden image of Madhava.

The metallic image of Durga and Madhav (a small wooden statue of Lord Madhav) sits in the hall of offering (Bhoga Mandap) for first 8-days, out of 16-days ceremony during Durga Puja.

For rest eight days, these statues are kept in Sakta Gundicha temple of DOLAMANDAP SAHI (ie. in the temple of Narayani).

Further, Durga-Madhav photograph is placed in various ceremonies of the Hindus.

Maha Prasad

After each sacred food is offered to Lord Jagannath, these are again offered Goddess Vimala. The prasad after being offered to Goddess Vimala, becomes Maha Prasad.

No separate food is offered to the Goddess. It is understood from the priest that She is "KAIBALYA LOLUPINI" (ie. too much attached to Mahaprasad).

As a famous Shakti Pitha, the name of Vimala and Purusottama are found in the Matsya Purana and in various other Puranas.

Benu Madhav

This east facing temple is near Vimala temple. The images of Jagannath, Balabhadra and Subhadra are found in this temple. Here, Lord Jagannath is worshipped as Benu Madhav (Flute in hand).

Mandani Ghara

This is near Benu Madhav temple. Many idols like – Gopeswar, Nanda-Yashoda, Basudev, Devaki, Dama – Sudam, Rama Balaram, Gopal, Nrushingh, Ramachandra, Hanuman, cows and calves etc. are found.

Sakhi Gopal

Lord Krishna and Goddess Radha are worshipped in this temple, which is close to Mandani Ghara. Initially, the image of Sakhi Gopal was placed here by Gajapati king Purusottama Dev, which was brought from Kanchi after his victory. Later on, this was placed in

Barabati fort. After shifting to many places, it is now placed at Sakhigopal Temple, which is around 20-kms away from Puri.

As a token of these idols, Sakhi Gopal (Krishna and Radha) are worshipper here.

Kanchi Ganesh

This temple is close to Sakhi Gopal temple. This is a rare image made up of granite stone. It will be observed that his trunk touches the genital of Siddha Devi, who is sitting on his lap. It has four arms and he holds broken tusk, rosary, battle axe in 3-hands and in the 4th hand, he holds the testicles.

This Kanchi Ganesh is also known as Kamoda Ganesh, Bhanda Ganesh and Uchhista Ganesh etc.

This idol was brought from Kanchi by Gajapati king Purusottama Dev by defeating the Kanchi king. It is just behind the main Jagannath temple.

Khirachora Gopinath

This temple is next to Kanchi Ganesh Temple. It is a replica of the Khirachora Gopinath of Remuna, Balasore. As the Lord had stolen Khiri for a devotee, known as Madhabendra, he was named accordingly.

Pancha Shakti Temple

This temple is close to Khirachora Gopinath Temple. This is also known as Bhubaneshwari Temple.

The temple consists of – Viman, Jaganmohan, Nata Mandir and Bhoga Mandap. There are 5-goddesses in this temple, ie. Bhubaneshwari, Saraswati, Sasti, Sabitri and Gayatri.

Bhubaneshwari

She is placed in the main temple. She is also known as Kamala. She is having 4-hands and 3-eyes. She holds pasa in one hand and Ankush in another hand and other two hands are in Abhaya and Barada Mudra.

Saraswati

She is installed in a small temple and she is the Goddess of learning.

Sasti

She is the Goddess of children and is two handed. The parents worship her for the welfare of their children and for their long life.

Sabitri

Women worship her, for the long life of their husband. She was the wife of Satyaban. She had taken back the life of her husband (ie.As Satyaban was dead in the forest) from the clutches of Yama (God of death).

Gayatri

She is known as Veda Mata and Gayatri Mantra is the core. She leads the path for uniting the devotees with the Lord.

The images of Sasti, Sabitri and Gayatri are placed in small cave like structures.

Goddess Saraswati is placed on the left side and Goddesses Sasti, Sabitri and Gayatri are placed in the right side.

Nila Madhaba

It is near Bhubaneswari temple. It is believed that Nila Madhava is the original deity of Nilachala.

The researchers interpret Nila Madhava, as the combination of 3-deities, ie. Nila (means blue- which signifies Lord Jagannath), Ma (ie. Goddess Subhadra) and Dhaba (means White – which represents Balabhadra).

Bhadrakali / Bedha Kali

This east facing temple is towards the northern side of Nilamadhaba temple.

This is a wooden idol of around 3-feet, having two hands. She is holding sword in one hand and human skull in another hand. Garland of human skulls are seen in her neck.

It is understood, the real idol is in the back of the present idol. In the past people were fearing to visit the area which was full of weeds and due to presence of Goddess Kali. One Tantrik (Baba Brahmachari) gagged the mouth of the Goddess through Tantrik rights. From that day, this wooden idol is placed in front of the original image.

There is a hole towards right of the present image. Flowers and sandals are placed everyday through this hole for her worship. If wind blows through the hole, the sound of flute comes out, as heard by many.

Laxmi Narayan

This small temple is near Bedha Kali temple and Laxmi Narayan are worshipped.

Mahalaxmi Temple

This temple is situated in the north – west corner of inner compound. The temple consists of – Viman, Jagmohan, Nata Mandir and Bhog Mandap.

The temple was constructed during the time of Jagannath Temple. This was protected through lime plastering. However, during deplastering process, beautiful architecture/ sculptures of the temple are found.

The paintings of Ganesh, Hanuman, Nrushingh, Baraha and Laxmi Nrushingh are found in the Jagmohan.

An idol of Nrushingh, holding Laxmi in his lap and an image of Saint, believed to be Adi Shankaracharya is found in the Jagmohan.

Goddess

She is the Goddess of wealth and Shakti of Jagannath (Narayan). She is having four hands and is sitting on a lotus. Lotuses are held by her in two hands and other hands are in Abhaya and Barada mudra. Water is poured on her head in golden pitchers by two elephants.

Puri is named in her name as Sri KSHETRA (ie. Sri – Signifies laxmi).

There is a special kitchen for Maha laxmi and different kinds of cakes are prepared for her offerings.

She is associated with the Lord in all festivals. Mahalaxmi is the cook in the kitchen of Lord Jagannath and prepares food for the Lord, everyday.

She remains absent during Dhanu Sankranti to Makar Sankranti and during that period, the food is prepared by the mother of Jagannath.

Legend

As per Laxmi Purana, Lord Jagannath had banished Laxmi from Sri Mandir as per advice of Lord Balabhadra, as she had gone to the house of Sriya Chandaluni, (a low caste lady) to accept her offering. After her departure from the temple, both Jagannath and Balabhadra suffered a lot. At last both of them had accepted their fault and Goddess Laxmi returned to the temple.

Every Thursday, her house is visited by Lord Jagannath, other than EKADASHI day.

Similarly, during Ratha Yatra, on Heera Panchami (ie. 3rd day of festival) she goes to Gundicha temple and breaks part of the Rath, as Lord Jagannath had not taken her with him.

When Lord returns to Sri Mandir during Bahuda Yatra, Goddess Laxmi shuts up the door of Sri Mandir for a short period to convey her anger and grievances.

After consoling by Lord Jagannath, Goddess allows the Lord to enter the temple.

Mahalaxmi is also worshipped in the main temple with Lord Jagannath as Sri Devi Sayan Thakur (ie. who daily sleeps in the cot). This is also a combination of Laxmi and Narayan (ie. Eight hands and Ardhanareeswarar idol of Laxmi-Narayan).

After circumscribing the temple, the devotees usually sit a while in the Jagmohan of the Goddess/ temple premises to seek her blessings.

Nabagraha

This temple is situated on the north side of Maha Laxmi temple. Nine planets are worshipped from right to left, ie. from Rabi to Ketu.

The idols of Lord Ram, Laxman, Sita, Hanuman and Samaleswari are worshipped along with nine planets.

Satya Narayan Temple

This temple is close to Navagraha temple. Towards last part of the temple Laxmi and Narayan and Radha Krishna are worshipped.

Surya Narayan Temple

The temple of Surya Narayan is close to Laxmi Narayan temple and towards east.

Sun is worshipped while sitting on a chariot and drawn by seven horses. As per Madala Panji, this idol was brought from Konark during the period of Raja Narasingha Dev of Bhoi dynasty for worship.

The temple is having 3-structures, ie. -viman, Nata Mandir and BHOG Mandap.

There is another idol of Indra behind the idol of Surya Narayan. Some other idols are also worshipped in this temple.

The temple has a separate kitchen. Special puja is performed in this temple on Sunday, on lunar and solar eclipse days and Samba Dashami.

On the 6th day of the bright fortnight of Magha Month, the car festival of Sun God is also performed.

The temple is famous for marriage negotiations. Parents of both the bride and bride groom take an oath before Sun God to get their children married with each other.

Dadhi Vaman Temple

This is near Surya Narayan temple. Lord Krishna is worshipped here. The image of Gajalakshmi is on the wall.

Sri Ramachandra Temple

This temple is towards east of Dadhi Vaman temple. The images of Lord Ram, Sita, Bharat, Laxman and Satrughna are worshipped here.

Pataleswar Temple

This temple is towards eastern side of Sri Ram temple. The Shivling is beneath the surface of the temple, hence Lord is known as PATALESWAR.

It is around 20-feet below the inner courtyard of Jagannath Temple. One has to enter the temple through steps.

As per legend, when Vaman incarnation of Lord Vishnu, had put his third leg on the head of Vali and pressed him to Patal Lok (ie. nether world), Bali stayed here by becoming PATALESWAR Shiv.

The inscriptions during the period of Anangabhima Dev-lll are found in the door entrance of the sanctum.

As per custom, the devotees after visiting Lord PATALESWAR turn their face towards south to see the Nilachakra (flag of the main temple) and pay their respects to Lord Jagannath. Some others opine that, devotees look towards treasure house (Bhandar Ghar) of the Lord and think about their duties towards maintenance and preservation of this great heritage.

Patitapabana (Protector Of Downtrodden)

Lord Patitapabana is the sole entity of Lord Jagannath. He is worshipped in many temples across the state.

There are 5- images of Patitapabana in the Jagannath temple premises, ie. at lion's gate, Bata Patitapabana in front of Bata Ganesh, Purana Purusottama Patitapabana at Purana Panda Ashram near Nata Mandap, Anandadata Patitapabana at the temple of Sri Nilamadhav and Mokshyadata Patitapabana at the Chari Dam temple.

As per researchers, Lord Jagannath is worshipped in 64- names, out of which the names of – Shree Dadhibamana, Shree Bhagabat and Shree Patitapabana are important and worshipped in many places.

Lord Jagannath is the Lord of the suffering humanity. In mythology "Patita" signifies as a state of mental deterioration and not caste and only way to elevate one is to pray the Lord. Patitapabana worship in the temple is very old.

Hanuman

As described above, 4-hanuman s are guarding the temple in 4-cardinal directions, ie. Lion's gate (east – Fate Hanuman), western gate (kanapaa Hanuman which is around 4-feet high), Southern gate (Bara Bhoi Hanuman, whose height is around 7-feet) and Northern Gate (Astabhuja Hanuman who sits in Lotus position and holding Chakra in 4-hands).

Nine Baikunthas

As per religious scriptures, the place where Lord Vishnu stays is known as Martya Baikuntha (ie. Baikuntha on earth). In Sri KSHETRA there are nine Baikunthas which are as under:

Niladri Baikuntha

The area of Ratna SIMHASANA, where the Lord Jagannath is installed is known as Niladri Baikuntha. It is very sacred.

Leela Baikuntha

The area between Garuda stamba to Jaya – Vijaya DWAR is known as Leela Baikuntha. Rituals are performed in this area, when Lord returns to Ratna SIMHASANA during Ratha Yatra.

Purba Baikuntha

This is the first entrance to the temple through Aruna Stambha. Patitapabana is worshipped at this place. Lord Jagannath is taken out through this route and also he enters in to the temple through this route, during Ratha Yatra.

It is believed that when the devotees enter the temple through this first entrance they experience the Lord.

Brahma Baikuntha

The Mukti Mandap area is known as Brahma Baikuntha. As per religious scriptures, Lord Brahma resided at Brahma Baikuntha on king Indradyumna's invitation during establishment of Sri Mandir. It is believed that any devotee, who prays here get the blessings from Lord Brahma.

Paschima Baikuntha

The stretch from Nrushingh temple to Jagmohan of Laxmi temple is known as paschima Baikuntha. Here, the secret union of Madan Mohan (representative idol of Lord Jagannath) and Sri Devi (laxmi) takes place.

Patali Baikuntha

The northern stretch from Mahalaxmi temple to Ananda Bazar entrance is known as PATA AGANA. it is believed that during Vaman incarnation of Lord Vishnu, he had put his foot on Bali on the northern side of PATA AGANA. Hence, it is known as PATALI BAIKUNTHA.

Amar Baikuntha

This is located outside Sri Mandir, at SWARGADWAR. It is the path to salvation. It is believed that one attains salvation after his body is cremated at SWARGADWAR.

Ananta Baikuntha

This is the place where Lord Jagannath had appeared. It is known as Ananta Baikuntha, Adap Mandap / Janma MANDAPA.

Koili Baikuntha

It is on the northern side of Sri Mandir. It is also known as Kaivalya Baikuntha. As Lord performs his Kaivalya Leela during Nabakalebara at this place, it is named accordingly. As per Tantrikas, it is the burial ground of Lord during Nabakalebara.

The Jagannath temple of Puri is constructed in such a way that, one will find temples of Lord Shiv, Nrushingh and Hanuman on the way of each gate, ie. Kashi Vishwanath (Shiv), Goudiya Nrushingh and Fate Hanuman in the east gate, RAMESWAR Mahadev, Nisa Nrushingh and Bira Vikram Hanuman in the west gate, Bedha LOKANATHA, Ishaneswar, Parsunath, DHABALESWAR (all SHIVA s), Laxmi Nrushingh and Tapaswi Hanuman in the north gate and SIDDHESWAR Mahadev, Baikuntheswar Mahadev, Purana Nrushingh and BARABHAI Hanuman in the south gate.

Holy Circumambulation (Sri Mandir Parikrama)

As per many researchers and work of Dr. Ramachandra Mishra, generally a pilgrim should undertake the following order (holy circumambulation) while visiting the Lord –

- Before entering the temple one should wash his hands and feet and thereafter stand behind Aruna Stamba and pray respect to Lord looking at the Nila Chakra (Temple sphere).
- Enter the lion's gate and pay respect to Patitapabana and Fate Hanuman at the entrance gate.
- To climb 22-steps (Baisi Pahacha) and visit-Kashi Vishwanath, Ramachandra and Nrushingh on the left
- Enter the kurma Bedha (inner enclosure) after climbing 22-Steps and keep to the left
- Visit Agniswar Mahadev and Satyanarayan temple
- Proceed to see Bata Ganesh, Bata Krishna, Bala Mukunda, Hari –Sahadev (left), Bata Avakash (Bata Jagannath), Siddha Ganesh / Siddha Vinayak /Sweta Ganesh

- Proceed to right and see Bata Mangala and on the way left PANCHA PANDAV SHIV (Markandeya, Lokanath, KAPAL MOCHAN, Nilakantha and YAMESWAR)
- Ananta Vasudev and Kutam Chandi
- Proceed to see Mukti Mandap and on the side to Adi Nrushingh and Mukteswar, which are situated towards last of Mukti Mandap
- Proceed to see Rohini Kunda, Dancing Ganesh in front of Vimala temple
- Goddess Vimala, Veni Madhav, Nanda Maharaj, Sri Ram, Sakhi Gopal
- Bhadra Ganesh and Kanchi Ganesh
- EKADASHI Devi in front of Bhadra Ganesh
- Khirachora Gopinath
- PANCHA Sakhi temple (Bhubaneshwari, Saraswati, Sasti, Sabitri and Gayatri)
- Nilamadhav
- Bedha Kali
- Laxmi
- Navagraha
- Suryanarayan, Sri Ram temple
- PATALESWAR temple
- Thereafter Jagannath temple should be approached through northern inner gate. One has to climb 7-Stairs and after entering the temple, one had to stand near Garuda pillar and have a glimpse of the Lord.
- Enter to inner part (near Garva GRUHA) to see the Lord from nearby.
- Come back outside the temple and move to extreme east and north corner and to Satyanarayan and Mahalaxmi
- Enter Ananda Bazar and take Mahaprasad and leave the temple.

The circumambulation path described as above are tentative and is of general in nature. However, as Lord is omnipresent and omnipotent, a devotee can see/ visit the Lord in any manner he likes.

Mandir Parikrama (Heritage Corridor) And World Heritage City

The foundation stone of the ambitious Shree Mandir Parikrama project was laid by the Gajapati king Dibyasingha Deva in the presence of the then Chief Minister Naveen Pattanyak.

There will be an unobstructed 75-meter corridor around the Meghanada Prachira (outer wall of Jagannath temple). This will also provide amenities for devotees and strengthen security.

This will be divided in to 9- zones on the western, northern and the other sides. There would be 7-meter green buffer zone adjecent to Meghanada prachira. The deities 'ceremonial procession will be conducted in 10-meters. There will be inner "pedestrian only" path for use of general public for clockwise circumambulation. A 14-meter landscape zone with a garden of local varieties of shrubs and tree, important in Jagannath culture will be there. Trees will also line the eight meter outer circumambulation path. There will be 10-meter public convenience zone comprising of drinking water, fountains, rest rooms and information-cum – donation kiosks. There will be queue management facility along with security checking. The Matha and temples within the 75-meter Shree Jagannath Heritage corridor will be redeveloped in the Kalinga style of architecture in general and with specific Matha traditions.

There is proposal for 600-capacity reception center, Jagannath culture center including Raghunandan Library, the grand road heritage landscape, Sri Setu, Jagannath Ballav pilgrim center, SWARGADWAR development, Pramod Udayan, Gurukulam, Mahodadhi market, beachfront development, Musa river revival plan, information and donation center, renovation of 18-mathas adjecent to the temple, Atharanala development and housing for Sevayats etc. so as to make Puri a World heritage city.

Sebayats

The Seba Puja (ritual services) of the temple starts from early morning to late evening. Specific ritual services are performed for the deities and the temple has an elaborate system of daily worship. It is believed that the ritual services were started during the period of Gangavamshi kings which are continuing till date.

The people assigned to different sebas are known as sevakas (servitors) There are sevakas for each and every seva of the Lord. In the past, communities from almost all categories/ castes were involved in the traditional system of Sevakas.

Initially there were nine Sebakas and they were called Charu Hota, Patra Hota, Brahman Acharya, Pratihari, Pushpalaka, Daita, the washerman and the barber. The services of the sebaka were later extended. It is believed that Anangabhima Dev had introduced 36 categories of servitors known as Chhattisa Niyogal Nijoga involving number of nijogas. They were mainly:

Pratiharinijoga – They were responsible to maintain law and order inside the temple premises and enforce discipline among the visitors and devotees within the walled compound of the temple.

Besides they are also assigned with the specific duties of messenger between certain temple functionaries. Until they formally invite the kitchen mates, they cannot bring Bhoga (food for the Gods) to the main temple.

Suar or Mahasuarnijogas – They were for preparation of bhoga and to look after the maintenance of the temple kitchen.

Bhitarsebaknijoga – They look after the smooth functioning of the sebapuja, opening of the temple gates in the morning and check the seals on the doors.

Pujapandnijoga and many others – They are association of priest Sebakas who can offer priestly services to the deities.

The head of the nijogas is called Nayaka. Chhattisa Nijoga is headed by Chhattisa Nijoga Mahapatra who enjoys authority over the temple functionaries. He supervises the execution of all orders by the temple authorities. He belongs to pushpalaka category of Sebakas.

C Grome, the then Collector of Puri had submitted a list of 250-categories of Sevakas in 1805 AD.

The temple record of rights (ROR), 1952 recorded 119 categories of Sebakas. However some sevas / Nijogs are not functional and presently, on an average 75-Sevakas perform ritual services.

Some of the main Nijogas are:

Raja Of Puri

He is the foremost sevaka of Lord Jagannath. He performs the sweeping of three chariots during car festival, performs certain duties during Chandan Yatra, Snana Yatra and DOLA Yatra etc. He is the Chairman of Shree Jagannath Temple Managing Committee.

Mudiratha

If king can't perform his duties due to some reason, he officiates for the Raja in sweeping ceremony and other Yatras.

There are many other Nijogas, like – Bhitarchha Mahapatra (for purity of Bhog and opening of door), Talichha Mahapatra (sealing the door at night and purity of kitchen) Chhatisa Nijoga Nayak Patajoshi Mahapatra and Bhandar Nayak (to see that all sevakas perform their duty and performs Sari Bandha ceremony), Bhandar Mekap, Parichas, DEULA Karana, Brahmins / Purohit, Pujakas consisting puja pandas, Daitas, Patis, Duttas and many others.

They do not have any monthly salary and each of them get some portion from the Raja Bhoga / Kotha Bhoga (ie. known as-khei). Some also get rewards in cash / kind.

All these Sevakas are important for Seva puja and management of the temple.

The services were designated/ entrusted to particular families / communities by the Gajapati king and are hereditary in nature. These are continuing for centuries.

Warja System / Pilgrim Management Of The Temple

The term Warja means archival items and is a local word for a note or a diary.

In the past, the pandas and Pratiharis of the temple used to keep contact with pilgrims in different parts of the country. Some of them were employing pilgrim agents / Gumastas. These pandas, also known as TIRTHA GURUS knew different languages and were able to communicate with the pilgrims in their native language. These pandas were also visiting their respective areas and were preaching the philosophy of Jagannath cult.

As they were bringing pilgrims from different parts of the country to Puri they were known as BATUA (Journey men) or SATHUA (fellow travellers).

They used to gather pilgrims and escort them to Puri. The pilgrims were using the services of their pandas/ Purahit / priest of the area. The pandas used to take care of the pilgrims from arrival to departure. In olden days no pilgrim used to cook his own food at

Puri during their stay and they were wholly dependent upon the Mahaprasad of the Temple being supplied by the Pandas.

The pilgrims were treated as a member of their family and the pilgrims also respected the pandas. They were provided accommodations either in their residence or Dharamshalas.

The Pandas used to make all arrangements and take personal interest for their stay at Puri. Even the Pandas were bearing the cost, if the pilgrims fall short of funds for their stay and return journey. They used to stay3/4 days. During Rath Yatra and other festivals large congregations of pilgrims were felt.

At the time of return journey, the pilgrims used to offer an "Annadan Atika BHOG" amount and secret donations to the Panda and they used to receive Nirmalya / Dry Prasad, in return. This ATIKA BANDHA is performed at Koili-Baikuntha and the pilgrims were persuaded to pay a round sum to feed the Brahmins, ascetics and the beggars.

If the devotees could not pay the secret money / donations, the Panda or his Gumasta (employee) would visit his home place to collect the promised amount.

The name and detail address of the pilgrims and their pre and post generation were being recorded in a binding register known as "Warja "and in some cases, pilgrims had put their signature/ thumb impressions in the register, so that future generation of the pilgrims could recognise the Tirthagurus of the area / family. It is the record of information about the pilgrims over generations.

Initially, their complete address was written in Palm – leaf manuscripts. Subsequently, the complete records of all pilgrims and in some cases with their signature were being kept in the register. This is like a mini archive for the pilgrims. This relationship between Tirthagurus / panda with pilgrims was a long term relationship like a trade family business.

It is a part of the system of the temple activity. According to the pandas, they maintain "warja" as a way of service to the God.

In the temple usage, service to the god is called seba and the person who performs this seba is called sebaka. Each of the panda has a hereditary seva to the God and maintaining warja is an additional duty for them through which they earned further opportunity to offer their services to the lord.

Presently record keeping and maintenance of the warja has been largely institutionalised that operates through formal bodies.

Rituals Of The Lord

The details of the rituals of the temple are recorded in the Record of Rights of the temple. These are also found in the sacred texts like – Niladri Mahodaya and Purusottama KSHETRA Mahatmya etc. The Devine Leela of the Lord includes both Aisworya Lila (Lila of a king) and Madhurya Lila (ie. as a child of Vrindavan).

Further the Temple rituals / Nitis of the Lord are classified as – 1) Daily Rituals, 2) Special rituals according to speciality of certain days 3) Various festivals observed during the year.

Daily Rituals Of The Lord

The daily rituals of the Lord are as under: –

- Opening Of Door: First ritual starts in the early morning with the opening of the doors of the temple. The Bhitarchha Mahapatra accompanied by Palia Mekap, Pratihari, Akhanda Mekap and Muduli (ie. all are different Sevayats) examine the seal put on the Jaya – Bijaya DWAR by Talicha Mahapatra in the previous night. If the seal is alright, he breaks it, unlocks the padlock and opens the door.

  The door of inner sanctuary is opened in the same way. They enter inside the main temple and clean the inner sanctum and put the things in order.
- Mangal Arati: Mangal Arati is performed with the chanting of the hymns and playing of Mangal Vadya (ie. auspices music) after lamps are offered to three deities.
- Mailam: The dresses of the deities which were worn in the previous night are changed. Tadap and Uttariya (a kind of dress) are given to the deities to make them ready for next ritual, ie. cleaning of teeth, bathing and dressing etc.

The above process is known as Mailam (ie. change of dress).

Abakasa (Cleaning Of Teeth, Bathing And Dressing)

The priests pretend to clean the teeth by sitting in front of three brass mirrors in which the images are reflected. Tooth sticks and tongue cleaners are shown to the deities as symbol of brushing and cleaning the teeth.

They bath them by pouring water on the 3-mirrors. Holy water mixed with camphor, curd, Amala mixed with sandal paste is poured on the brass mirrors.

After bath, deities are dressed in Pattabastra (ie. a type of new cloth), flowers and ornaments.

A temple astrologer reads the probable happenings of the day and Akhanda Mekap (Sevayat to light the lamp) lights the lamp near the jewel pedestal. It continues burning till the doors are closed in the night.

Sahana Mela (Opening For Public Viewing)

The devotees are allowed to enter inside and have a closer view of the deities.

After Sahan mela is over the deities are again dressed with ornaments.

Performance Of Fire Sacrifice In The Kitchen, Sun Worship And Worship To Gate Keepers (Jaya And Vijaya) And The Carrier (Garuda)

Every day before preparation of rice offering, fire sacrifice is performed in the kitchen to purify the place. Sun worship is performed and puja is offered to Jaya, Vijay and Garuda to keep them alert all the time.

Gopal Ballav Bhoga

By way of early breakfast, Gopal Ballav consisting of sweet meets, fruits and curd etc. are offered to the deities. It is offered outside the inner door. It is also known as Anabasarpindi.

Sakal Dhupa / Raj Bhoga

This is the first morning meal which is offered to Lord at about 10 AM. This is also known as Raj Bhoga. It is offered near Ratna Vedi.

This generally consists of 13 items including the Enduri Cake and Mantha Puli.

The temple administration bears the entire cost and the prasad of the Lord is distributed among the temple functionaries for the duties performed. Betel- nut is offered to the deities at each meal time.

Next follows the change of dress and then the Bhoga Mandap Bhoga.

Bhoga Mandap Bhoga

It is done to facilitate the pilgrims, Mathas, private individuals and other institutions. As the Bhoga offered in the morning meal is scanty and not available to public for sale, this Bhoga Mandap Bhoga is meant for them.

The offering inter-alia consists of Pakhala with dahi and Kanji Payasa. The offering is made at the Bhog Mandapa, about 200 feet away and in front of the Ratna Vedi. This is called Chatra Bhog and was introduced by Adi Shankaracharya in the 8th century to help pilgrims share the temple food.

During heavy demand, there may be 2/3 Bhoga Mandap Bhogas. However, it is not a part of compulsory ritual.

Mid-Day Offering (Madhyahna Dhupa)

This Bhoga is offered near Ratna Vedi around 1-pm and is offered after Bhoga Mandap BHOG.

After mid-day meal, the deities change their dress and enjoy a siesta occasionally. Cots are taken from the store room and placed in front of them. Betel-nut, green coconut and perfumed water are kept by the side of the cots and Arati is performed.

The doors are then closed. The doors are again opened in the evening with the same procedure as in the morning.

Sandhya Arati

In the evening, light offering of the deities are performed. On ordinary days light offering is made after the change of dresses. During the month of Kartik (October- November), when doors are closed for sleeping of the deities, evening light offering is done when the doors are opened.

Sandhya Dhupa

This puja is performed near Ratna Vedi. During this Dhupa, sweet preparations with water rice are offered to the deities.

After conclusion of Puja, light offering (special Aratis) to the deities are performed. This light offering is known as "Jaya Mangala Arati", which is performed for benefit of the humanity.

Thereafter inner sanctuary is thrown open to the public.

Chandan Lagi (Smearing Of Sandal Paste)

The dress of the deities are changed after evening puja. Sandle paste mixed with camphor, Kesara and Kasturi are offered to the Lord.

Badasimhar Vesa

This is a flower based decoration. In the night, the deities are dressed in Patta Vastra (silk cloth) woven with slokas of Gita Govinda of Jayadeva wrapped on them. The deities are dressed with long garlands (Jhara), flower pendant in left nose (Nakuasi), Adharmala (long garlands to touch the base), Padaka (A circular flower work with jack fruit leaves and decorated with Ketaki flowers and Tulsi leaves) and Kara Pallaba (flower ornaments resembling the fingers of the Lord). The deities are decorated to appear like a lover (Sringaraka). This is performed around 10.30 pm.

Badasimhara Bhoga

This Bhoga is offered after floral decorations are over. In this Bhoga, items like cakes, watery rice, cakes of plantain pulp and few other items are Offered to the Lord. It is offered around 11.30 PM. No light offerings are made.

Going To Bed

This is a symbolic ritual. The Sayana Thakur (sleeping deity), a combined image of Laxmi and Narayan comes from store house and takes a seat in Ratna Vedi. Green coconut, betel and camphor are offered the deities.

The Devadasi (temple dancer) sings devotional songs from Gita Govinda in the Hall of dance. The last rituals are Gana, Khata seja lagi, Puspanjali, Pahuda, Muda and Sodha. The couches are put in front of Ratna Vedi. Three green coconuts are placed close by with some betel-nut and Flowers. The Gods are left to the slumber. The doors are then sealed by Talichha Mahapatra with his seal. Other than watch and ward staff to guard the temple, all others leave the premises.

However, the timing of these rituals change in case of exigencies and on special occasions.

Special Rituals

Special rituals are performed in the temple on special occasions, like –

Thursdays, New moon days, EKADASHI (11th day of the dark and bright fortnight), Solar eclipse, lunar eclipse and when temple precincts are defiled due to death etc.

On every Thursday, a special bath, decoration, puja, turmeric rice and grass (Duba) offerings are performed to Madanmohan and Laxmi (ie. representative deity) by placing them in Marjana Mandap (pedestal near main temple). On this day Lord Madan mohan goes to Laxmi temple for union. After light offering, turmeric rice and grass offering, he comes back with Laxmi and is placed in the south side temple. However, this union does not take place if Thursday is EKADASHI, 11th day of the bright fortnight of Bhadrab Month, Devi puja period, Birth day of Lord Ram in Chaitra Month and Nanda Utsav etc.

On EKADASHI day sandal paste is smeared on the entire body of the deities and after evening puja, a torch (Mahadipa) is placed at the top of main temple. The Sevayat also sings in praise of Lord and king Indradyumna.

If EKADASHI falls on Monday then the deities – Madan mohan and lokanath visit loknath temple and after meeting they return to original place. This ritual shows the union of Hari and Hara. Birthday of the deities are performed with offering of rice pasted with turmeric and grass.

On each Wednesday, the face of the deities are coloured with local herbal colours and the Sevayat, Dutta paints the face. During the time of paintings, the doors are closed and devotees are not allowed. Doors are opened after completion of painting. This is known as BANAKLAGI / SRI MUKHA SIMHAR.

During eclipse, the deities are bathed and special Bhoga is offered.

Special rituals are also performed during Anabasara and Nabakalebara which are confidential.

In winter months from Odhana SASTHI (6th day of the waxing moon of Margashir Month) up to Basanta Panchami in the moth of Magha, the deities are dressed in warm garments. These are known as Ghodalagi.

Kartik Month And Bala Dhupa

During Kartik month (October- November) large number of devotees congregate and special offerings, Special Beshas (attires) and special rituals are performed in Sri Mandir. During this month, an additional special offering known as Bala Dhupa (Bhoga) are offered to deities.

As per legend, once Gajapati king was sick for many days and could not visit the Lord. However, he reached the temple when the deities were in ABAKASH Besha ritual. As there was no flower garlands in the body of the lord, a Sevayat (named Balabhadra Puspalak) gave flowers to the king from his head as the prasad. As there was hair in the flower, the king was angry. Out of fear, the Sevayat told the king about presence of hairs on the head of the Lord. The king wanted to see the hair in the head of the Lord in next morning. The servitor prayed Lord to save him for his false utterances. When king arrived to know the truth and the flowers were removed, bunch of hairs came out from the head of the Lord. The king could not believe. Suddenly blood oozed out from the head of the Lord and king was frightened. The blood stopped with the prayer of the servitor. During night, the king had a dream, where he was advised to offer special BHOG known as Bala Bhoga. The king promised before the deities to start this special Bala Bhoga and this special offering is continuing in the month of Kartik.

MAHAPRASAD /ABHADA (FOOD OFFERING OF LORD JAGANNATH)

Four important shrines (Dhamas) are located at different parts and directions of the country, ie. RAMESWAR, Badrinath, Puri and Dwaraka.

It is believed by many that Lord Vishnu takes his bath at RAMESWAR, meditates at Badrinath, dines at Puri and retires at Dwaraka. Puri is also known as Bhoga KSHETRA. Therefore much importance is given to the temple food of Lord Jagannath, at Puri.

The holy food which is served to Lord Jagannath as Bhoga (offering) is known as Mahaprasad / Abhada.

As per "CITY HRIDAY PLAN FOR PURI" (HRIDAY-heritage rejuvenation infrastructure development augmentation Yojana)

"The Mahaprasad, the only one of its kind in the world and considered most divine than all other prasads, is also known as Chhappanbhog as it is said to consist of 56 food items".

These items, each a delicacy in itself, are supposed to derive their taste from the fact that Mahalakshmi, wife of Lord Jagannath presides over the kitchen herself. Strictest of adherence is followed regarding the cooking ritual and following of instructions, to ensure that the consistency of taste remains unwavering through generations. On days when the food is not cooked to perfection, a black dog is said to appear in the kitchen periphery as a warning from the Lord. In such cases, all the items cooked are disposed of immediately and the entire procedure is repeated from scratch.

The 56 food articles, reflecting the culinary culture of the state and the Vaisnavite food habit, have been enumerated by scholars as follows.

Annabhoga (Offerings Of Rice Items) :-

Abhada Anna 2. Ghee Anna 3. Kanika 4. Khechudi 5. Dahi Pakhala 6. Mitha Pakhala 7. Ada Pakhala 8. Oria Pakhala 9. Thali Khechudi Mitha Bhoga

- *Offerings Of Sweet Items:* 10. Khaja 11. Gaja 12. Ladu 13. Magaja Ladu 14. Jira Ladu 15. Jagannath Ballav 16. Khuruma 17. Mitha Puli 18. Kakara 19. Marichi Ladu 20. Luna Khuruma Pitha
- *Offerings Of Cake Items:* 21. Suara Pitha 22. Jhadeineda 23. Jhilli 24. Kanti 25. Amali 26. Chakuli 27. Poori, 28. Keli 29. Bara 30. Dahibara 31. Arisha 32. Tripura 33. Rosa Paika
- *Milk Product Offerings*: 34. Khiri 35. Papudi 36. Khua 37. Rasabali 38. Tadia 39. Chhena Khai 40. Papudi Khaja 41. Khua Manda 42. Sara Puli
- *Offerings Of Delicacies And Cuisines*: 43. Dali 44. Biridali 45. Arhad dali 46. Mung dali 47. Dalma 48. Mahura 49. Besara 50. Saga 51. Potala Rasa 42. Goti Baigana 53. Khata 54. Raita 55. Pita 56. Baigini

Legend

As per legend Lord Krishna had hold the Govardhan Mountain to protect the people from the anger of Lord Indra. As a symbolic compensation for the 8 daily meals, that he missed every day, (ie.

when he was holding the mountain) for 7-days, the 56-items were presented to Lord.

Mahaprasad is cooked only in earthen pots and fire wood is the medium of fuel.

Once the steam cooked food is ready, it is first offered to the Jagannath Temple, known as Sankudi Bhoga and then to Goddess Vimala of Maa Bimala Temple, after which it is turns in to Mahaprasad.

It is said that on the way from the kitchen to the temple, no aroma rises from the offering. It is only after the Lord has partaken of it, that it's fragrance becomes perceivable.

After it has been offered to Lord and Goddess Vimala, a portion of it is sent to the families of the temple's servitors, and the rest is sold at Ananda Bazaar – a market on the North-eastern corner of the temple. This Mahaprasad is freely taken by people of all castes and creeds without any discrimination.

Mahaprasad is also known as Anna Brahma or Nirmalya. It's significance and the comparison was narrated by Sage Vasishta to legendary king Indradyumna quoting Lord Brahma. It is also described in "Shree Jagannath Charitamruta" written by Dibakara Das.

The virtue earned by Japa (prayer), Homa (fire sacrifice), Brata (regular religious act of devotion) and Tapasya (penance) is obtained/ achieved by consuming Nirmalya.

However, during the 21 days preceding the Rath Yatra, the offering of Mahaprasada does not take place, as the Lord is said to be taken by high fever during this time. Further upon initiation of the Rath Yatra, the earthen portion of the entire kitchen is broken down, and built anew. During this period, the kitchen and the Ananda Bazaar are both relocated at the Gundicha Temple.

Mahaprasad has also influenced the food habit of Odisha, particularly the vegetarian cuisine of regions in and around Puri, Bhubaneswar and Cuttack. It is said that, "Mahaprasad consolidates human bond, sanctifies sacraments and grooms the departing soul for its journey to heaven."

Kitchen And Cooking Of Mahaprasad

As described earlier, the Temple kitchen is known as The roshaghara. It is located in the south east corner of the temple precinct within the boundary wall. It is one of the largest kitchens in the world serving up to one lakh devotees per day on some occasions.

It was built afresh by Shri Dibyasingha Dev between 1682 and 1713 AD, as the previous kitchen, located behind the Laxmi Narayan Temple was small to handle all the requirements.

The kitchen operates under a code of strict confidentiality that has been handed down through generations to the Suaras, Mahasuaras and Supakars. They are God's own cooks and are hereditarily connected to the Shree Jagannath Temple service for centuries through the Sevayat system.

At present, there are more than 500 cooks, and 300 assistants and porters for the carriage of raw materials in the kitchen. No one can enter the kitchen other than the specific Sevayats as stated above.

It is believed that Goddess Laxmi looks after the kitchen and prepares the food for the Chaturdha Murti.

It is estimated that the kitchen covers a quadrangle with sides of around 150-feet in length, 100-feet in breadth and the height is around 20 feet, at an elevated level above the ground. There are ten rooms in the kitchen and this signifies ten Digpalas, ten incarnations and ten Maha vidyas. The temperature of the kitchen is around 15 to 20-degrees higher than the outside temperature. It is also believed that Goddess DAKSHIN kali protects the cooks and other Sevayats of the kitchen.

The number of chulhas or cooking stoves are estimated to be around 243, however some say it is anything up to 742.

There are three kinds of cooking stoves (Chullas), ie. Anna Chuli (cooking place for rice items), Ahia Chuli (improvised oven dug for temporary cooking ie. generally cooking place for vegetables / other items) and Pitha Chuli (cooking place for cakes).

The cooking stoves (Chulas) are made as per Vedic rules. As Fire Goddess is having 7-tongues, the chulas are having 7-faces and one earthen pot is put in each face of the Chula. Upon these chulhas, earthen pots are stacked up to 7-layers, with the steam from each pot being used to cook the one above.

The top most earthen pot is cooked first. Surplus water from the pots, once cooked, is removed by an expert by piercing the earthen pots by an iron spoon.

As per religious scriptures, Goddess DAKSHIN Kali is the protector of the kitchen.

The chullas are also divided in favour of the names like – Goddess DAKSHIN Kali, Raghav Das Matha, Odia Matha, Bhitaracha Mahapatra and Emaar Math etc.

As outsiders are prohibited to enter in to the kitchen, the information is generally known based on hearsay and as understood from temple functionaries.

MATHAS – IN DAILY RITUALS OF THE LORD

Large number of religious monasteries / Mathas are located in Puri. Most of them are connected to perform different Sevas / duties in the temple. Some Mathas are also directly involved in various rituals and celebrations during the festive occasions.

The lands were offered to the Mathas by the donors with the specific purpose of offering some Bhogas or performing certain sevas in the temple of Lord Jagannath or for performing other acts of charity.

In the past different Gajapati kings had also given them rights through Sanandas / royal charter in favour of some Mathas. As per Record of Rights under the Puri Shri Jagannath Temple (Administration) Act, 1952, details of rituals to be performed by certain Mathas are enshrined.

Some of them are as under:

Gobardhan Matha

This was established by Adi Shankaracharya. It plays an important part in the rituals of the temple.

Shankaracharya of this Math is the head of Mukti Mandap and he has the authority to offer his opinion on the ritualistic system of the temple. The Khei granted to this Matha is unique and rarely enjoyed by any other Matha. Shankaracharya is also given special privilege by the temple administration.

It provides Panti Bhoga at the Baishi Pahacha on Ratha Yatra day. It gets offerings of the Lord on some occasions.

Jagannath Ballav Matha

Jagannath Ballav Matha is one of the most renowned Math of Puri. This is the pleasure garden of Lord Jagannath. The representative images of the lord visit this Math on different festive occasions, like – Basanta Panchami, on the 1st, 4th, 5th and 12th days on the bright fortnight of Falguna. This Matha supplies flower ornaments like – Tilak and Jhumpa for Badasinghara Besha and supplies "Kora"(ie. sweet food) for "Kaliya dalana" and "Pralambasura badha" Beshas. It also supplies "Dayana" for "Dayana Chori" ritual. It offers Panti Bhoga on Heera Panhami.

Jatia Baba Matha

This is one of the preserved MATHAS of Puri near Narendra Pond. This Matha supplies the silken rope (Pattadori) for the Chandan Yatra.

Emar Math

It was established by Saint Ramanuj and is one of the biggest MATHAS. Chandrika and Chausar made of flowers for Bada Singhar Besha of the Lord is supplied by this Matha. It offers "Pan Bhog" during Chandan Yatra. "Chakata Bhog" during Anasara period and "Bala Bhog" during Kartik month are supplied by this Matha.

This Matha provides Tahia on Snana Purnima, Ratha Yatra, Bahuda and Niladri Bije days. It supplies part of Hathi Besha, Tuli for Pahandi and certain amount of sandlewood for Sarbanga Neeti on "Khalilagi EKADASHI, flower garlands for Nabanka Bedha and offers "Adhar pana Bhog" and "Panti Bhog" on certain festive days.

It is situated near southern gate of Jagannath Temple.

Odiya Matha

This was set up by Atibadi Jagannath Das, a great poet and Saint of the state, in early part of 16th century.

It supplies "Trimundi chandua" and silk clothes for "Chaka Apasara", repairs

"Kanaka mundi", supplies Til / Phulari oil oil for "Phuluri Neeti", Oil and ghee etc for "Deva Deepavali", "Chakata Bhoga" on Anasar, "Adharpana Bhog" and "Panti Bhog" on certain days. The Mahanta of this Matha makes marjana of Ratnavedi on "Niladri Bije Day".

This Matha makes arrangement for the Pankti Bhog in the Jagmohan during Rukminiharan festival and supplies Black saree to

Goddess Vimala. This Matha also clears the Ratnavedi and supplies canopy and pillows for the Lord.

Bada Chata Matha

It is situated in front of the temple. This Matha performs "kirtan" at the time of "Mangala Arati", "Pahuda Arati" and "Bala Dhupa". This Matha does the "Padma Besha" of the Lord and offers "Kshiri Bhog".

Mangu Matha

This is located on the side of EMAR Matha. This Matha is associated with the memory of Guru Nanak. In the past, this math was supplying a Ram for sacrifice before the Goddess Vimala, each year on Maha Nabami night.

Gopal Tirtha Matha

Gopaltirtha Matha supplies a part of 'Hati besha' on the Snana Purnima day and ' makara chaula' on the Snana Purnima and Makara sankranti days and offers panti bhog at the temple of Lord Jagannath.

Some other Mathas provide services like – Radhakanta Matha (kirtan service in front of chariots, cleaning of the temple and lighting of Masal), Sanachhata Matha (Alata Chamar service), Papudia Matha (Panti Bhoga and Aalata Chamar service), Janjhapatia Matha (kirtan service at inner compound and Samarjana of Gundicha temple), Chhauni Matha (Panti BHOGA service and Aalata Chamar service), Jayadev Dasavatar Math (cultural functions), Kapadia Matha (dress), Kotha Bhoga Matha (kotha Bhoga), Suna Goswami Matha (flower garlands), Siva TIRTHA Matha (tooth brush), Trimali Matha (Mohan Bhoga) and Kanika Rani Matha (provide Madhabi flower) etc.

There were some other Mathas, who were connected with the rituals of the Jagannath temple, like – Chaitanya Gaudiya Matha, Purusottama Goudiya Matha and Punjabi Math etc. Some of these Mathas have stopped performing the rituals and those who perform are doing this in a limited scale as many of them have not sufficient income/ they are not in a position to collect their income from land.

COSTUMES (BESHAS) OF LORD

The religious rites of the temple are modelled like a human. The images change their clothes and wear different kinds of ornaments as many as eight times during a normal day. The servitors, mainly – Puspalaka, Khuntia and Changeda Mekap are involved in daily decorations of the Lord. The Palia Puspalakas used to decorate the deities on every occasion. The specific category of servitors are experts in decorating the deities on every occasion.

The deities are decorated mainly in three ways, ie. Puspa Singhar (with flowers), Vastra Singhar (with clothes) and Alankar Singhar (with ornaments). Except festive occasions, they are attired in "Vastra Singhar" and "Puspa Singhar".

The cotton and silken clothes, namely-tadapa, Uttariya, Paharana, Phuta, Sri Kapada, Baralagi PATA, Srimukhabala, Chadara and Gita Govinda PATA etc. are used. Garlands and other floral ornaments, namely – Adharmala, Chandrika, Gava, Alaka, Kara Pallava, Hruda Padaka, Kaustava Padaka, Guna, Makara Kundala, Tadagi, Nakuasi and Sri payara Mala etc. used and are made from specific flowers, Tulshi leaves and leaves of jack fruit etc.

Sandal paste, camphor and some times precious musk are used in daily and periodical rituals. There are 36- Beshas of the deities out of which 18- Beshas are important and which attracts large number of people/ devotees.

Some of these Beshas are related to Lila of the Krishna (ie. Banabhoji, Kalia Dalana, Pralambasura Badha, Rama Balaram, Bali Bamana, Radha Damodar, Trbikrama, Bankachuda, Adikia, Sraddha, Nabanka, Makar, Gaja Udharan, Chacheri, Kundala, and Raja) which are described in Srimad Bhagabata Purana. Some of the Beshas related Lord Ram are – Pushyabhiseka (Rama Raja Besha), Rama (Sri Ramnabami), Sradha (where Lord Jagannath offers pinda to Dasarath and Kaushalya) and Parshuram Besha, which are described in Ramayan.

Vijayadashami Besha related to Shakti cult and Ganapati Besha on Snana Purnima is related to Ganapati cult. Some Beshas are also made keeping in view the time / seasons of the year.

Daily Beshas

Abakash (Tadap Uttari Besha)

This Besha is done every day, immediately after Mangal Arati. The clothes worn by the deities are Tadap and Uttariya. ABAKASH relates to brushing of teeth and bathing ritual of the deities.

After bath, deities are dressed with silk clothes. Silk clothes of the deities are changed every day with different colours, depending upon the day of the week. The dresses are also changed after each Bhoga.

Sadha Besha

The three deities are dressed every day from Sunday to Saturday with different silken clothes, known as Baralagi PATA. They are – Red (on Sunday), white cloth with black spots (Monday), Pancharangi clothes, ie clothes mixed with 5-colours (Tuesday), sky blue (Wednesday), yellow (Thursday), white (Friday) and violet (Saturday).

Bada Singhar Besha

This Besha is done every night before the deities are retired to bed. This is the last Besha of the Lord. This is made up of different floral ornamentation and with Gita Govinda Khandua PATA. The puspalak Sevak adorns the head with Srikapada, (ie. another cloth) by ascending the pyramid ladder and Palia Pushplak sevaka helps him.

They are adorned with Karapallava (ie. hand like decoration with leaves) and Padak (circular lotus like decoration with flowers). The deities are decorated with number of garlands / floral ornaments like – Aadhar, Jhumpa, Chandrika, Tilaka, Guna, Gava and some of the garlands are also inter-mixed with Tulsi leaves.

This Besha is very attractive and devotees wait eagerly to see this Besha in the midnight. This Besha relates to peaceful sleep of the deities and sandalwood paste is smeared in the body as coolness is required for proper sleep.

Beshas On Various Festive Occasions

As Jagannath cult is a synthesis of various cults like – Vaishnavism, Saivsim, Shakti, Ganapati and tribal forms of worship, therefore the deities are decorated in different forms and on different occasions to satisfy different groups. The Sevayats like – Palia Puspalak, Bhitarchha Mohapatra, Talichha Mahapatra, Daitapatis, Khuntia and Mekup are involved in decorating the Lord during these Beshas.

Some major Beshas of the deities are as under:

Chandan Besha (Baisakha Month – April-May)

This is generally performed in Baisakha Month during Chandan Yatra, which starts from Akshay Trutiya and spreads over 42-days. The sweet scented sandalwood is smeared on the Devine body.

Gajanana / Hathi Besha / Ganesh Besha (Full Moon Day Of Jyestha Month – May-June)

This is performed on Snana Yatra (bathing ceremony) which falls on the full moon day of Jyestha (May-June). The deities are taken to the Snana Vedi (bathing platform). After ceremonial bath, the deities are dressed like an elephant (Hathi / GAJANANA). Generally the annual cycle of festivals of the temple begins from Bathing festival and it is the general practice to worship Lord Ganesh at the beginning of every religious rite.

Legend

Ganapati Bhatta, of Karnatak, a devotee of Lord Ganesh came to Puri on the day of Snana Yatra. He was disappointed, as he could not see the image of Ganapati in the bathing platform. The Lord had appeared in the form of Ganesh to satisfy the religious sentiment of the devotee.

Since that day, the GAJANANA / Hathi Besha (ie. in the form of Elephant) is observed on the Snana Purnima day (bathing ceremony). This is performed by Palia Puspalak, Khuntia, Mekapa and Daitapatis on this day.

Suna Besha / Bada Tadhau Besha

This is performed in the month of Ashadha (June – July), when the deities return to the main gate of the temple after Ratha Yatra (ie. 11th day of the bright fortnight of Ashadha / Ashadha Sukla Ekadasi). They wait for 2/3 Days in the chariot. The gold ornaments like – golden hands, golden feet, golden crown, golden ear ring, golden peacock feather, a half square shaped golden aura (Rahu Rekha) and golden necklace are worn by them.

Lord Jagannath holds a gold disc in his right hand and silver conch in the left hand. Lord Balabhadra is decorated with golden plough in the left hand and a gold mace in the right hand.

This Besha is also done on – Dussehra, kartik Purnima, Pousha Purnima and DOLA Purnima.

Lakhs of devotees visit during this period to see the Lord in the Ratha.

On the 15th day of the dark fortnight of Shravan (July-August), Chitalagi Besha and the 5th day of the bright fortnight of Shravan Rahurekha lagi Besha are performed.

The following Beshas, like – Banabhoji, Kaliyadalan, Pralambasura Badha and Krushna Balaram Besha are observed around the birthday celebrations of Lord Krishna. It is believed that Lord is also a form of Krishna / previous incarnation of Lord Krishna.

Bana Bhoji Besha (Bhadraba – August-September)

This is performed on the 10th day of the dark fortnight of Bhadraba Month. The deities are dressed like cowherd boys, as if they are going to attend the picnic.

Many Gopis, Gopals, cows, birds and peacocks are displayed which are made from Sola. The whole Ratna SIMHASANA area is decorated. The devotees celebrate the picnic of Lord Jagannath in the style of Lord Krishna.

Kaliya Dalan Besha

This is performed on the 11th day of dark fortnight of Bhadrab Month. Lord Jagannath is dressed like Lord Krishna killing the KALIYA serpent. Lord Jagannath holds on to a huge snake made up of Sola that circles over his head.

As per Puranas, KALIYA, the venomous serpent was living on the banks of Yamuna river. People were fearing the snake and he was of great danger to the local people. Lord Krishna had killed him.

This Besha of the Lord is to commemorate the said incident and it is a reenactment of that episode. The actual scene is also dramatised in the Markandeya tank.

Pralambasura Badha Besha

It is performed on the 12th day of the dark fortnight of Bhadraba Month.

A demon Pralamba who was messenger of king Kansa was killed by Balaram. Lord Balabhadra wears this Besha. Lord Jagannath watches the same surrounded by cows.

Krushna Balaram Besha

This is performed on the 13th day of the dark fortnight of Bhadraba Month. In this Besha Lord Jagannath and Balabhadra are dressed like Lord Krishna and Balaram. These are made of Sola and two brothers put their arms over each other's shoulder.

It is believed that this Besha was started by Jagannath Das, writer of Bhagabat in ODIYA around 1524 AD.

The Beshas like – Banabhoji, Kaliyadalan, Pralambasura Badha and Krushna Balaram Besha show the impact of Krushna cult in Sri Jagannath Temple.

Baman Besha

This is observed on the 12th day of the bright fortnight of Bhadraba Month. Lord Jagannath is dressed like Baman, 5th incarnation of Lord Vishnu. The Besha is made in such a fashion that, Lord Jagannath looks smaller.

Raja Besha

This is made on the 10th day of the bright fortnight of Ashwin Month (September- October). This is a royal Besha of the Lord.

Lord Jagannath is believed as the incarnation of Lord Ram and as Ram defeated Demon king Ravana on Vijaya Dashami day, Lord Jagannath is decorated accordingly. Bow and arrow are added to show Lord Jagannath as Sri Ram.

Further, Lord Jagannath is regarded as the king of Odisha and this Besha is continuing since the period of Gangavamshi kings.

Radha Damodar Besha

This is performed from the 11th day of the bright fortnight of Ashwin Month to 10th day of the bright fortnight of Kartika Month.

As per mythology, Akrura on his way to Mathura had witnessed this form of the Lord while bathing in the river Yamuna. Lord Jagannath and Balabhadra put on "Trikachha". They hold pair of Nalibhuja in their hands. They also wear different types of gold ornaments, ornaments of flowers and different type of cloths. This is performed in Ratna SIMHASANA. This Besha is also witnessed by Large number of devotees during Kartik Brata.

Harihara Besha

Harihara Besha of Lord Balabhadra is performed on each Monday during the time period of Radha-Damodar Besha. The Besha is done for a fortnight till the full moon day. Half of the body of Lord Balabhadra looks blackish while the other half looks whitish. It indicates that one half of his body is Vishnu (Hari) and the other half is Shiv (Hara).

TRIVIKRAM BESHA/ ADAKIA BESHA (KARTIK MONTH – OCTOBER – NOVEMBER)

This is performed on the 13th day of the bright fortnight of Kartika. As Jagannath is the Lord of 3-worlds, ie. heaven, earth and hail, he is given heroic dress with his attributes of Conch, sphere, mace and lotus. This was started by the Panchasakhas.

Laxmi – Narayan Besha /Thiakia Besha

This is performed on the 11th day of the bright fortnight of Kartika. As per researchers this Besha gained popularity in the temple since the visit of Ramananda.

Bankachuda Besha

This is observed on the 12th day of the bright fortnight of Kartik month. This is similar to Laxmi – Narayan Besha. However, golden head gear is an addition in this Besha.

Nrushingh Besha / Laxmi – Nrushingh Besha / Dalikia Besha

This is observed on the 13th day of the bright fortnight of Kartika Month. Here, Lord Jagannath is dressed as lion to celebrate the Nrushingh incarnation in Satya era.

Rajeswari Besha / Raja – Rajeswar Besha

This is performed on the full moon day of Kartik month.The deities are dressed in royal dress. Lord Jagannath is dressed as Lord Krishna with flute in hand. This shows, Lord as king Krishna.

Nagarjuna Besha / Parshuram Besha

This is performed on the 13-14th day of the bright fortnight of Kartika Month. This Besha is performed occasionally, ie. when there are 6-days in Panchak(ie. an extra day) as per Almanac instead of 5-days.

On this day Lord Jagannath and Lord Balabhadra are dressed like Nagarjuna, who was a military general.

Ghodalagi Besha

This is observed from the 6th day of the bright fortnight of Margashir Month (Nov – December) to Basanta Panchami (5th day of the bright fortnight of Magha). The deities on the Ratna

SIMHASANA are covered with specially designed winter dresses. Generally a cotton cloth is used to wrap the deities in addition to usual dress.

Jamalagi Besha

The deities wear modified winter dress from Basanta Panchami to DOLA Purnima. This is known as "JAMALAGI BESHA".

Shradha Besha

This Besha is observed for three days during Deva Deepavali occasion from 13th day of the dark fortnight of Margashir to 15th day / new moon day. These are observed for the fore-fathers.

On the 13th day, SHRADHA is offered to Kapila and Aditi, on 14th day SHRADHA is offered to Dasarath and Kaushlya and on the 15th day SHRADHA is offered to Basudev, Devaki, Nanda, Yashoda and king Indradyumna.

Special rites are observed in the temple for these 3-days. The deities wear white cloths on this occasion.

Raja Besha/ Deva Abhiseka Besa (Pousha Month – December-January) / Pushyabhiseka

This is observed on the full moon day of Pousha Month. Some say, it was the date of coronation of Lord Ram. This is also known as Pushyabhisekha. However, this day is said to be the day of first installation of the deities. They are dressed in gold ornaments like a king.

Padma Besha (Magha Month – January-February)

This is performed on the second day of the bright fortnight of Magha Month.

It is understood that, it is observed during the month of Magha in any Saturday/ Wednesday between new moon day of the month and Basanta Panchmi. It is performed during Bada SINGHAR ritual at night. The deities remain in this Besha throughout the night. Big lotus petals adorn the faces of the deities in the shape of a disc. Fresh pink and white lotus garlands are spread across the arms and lotus petals made of Sola are on their heads. The sides of the deities are decorated with various art motifs made of Sola.

Four swans are projected in this Besha and are seen with lotus stalks. The materials for the Besha are provided by the Bada CHATA Matha.

The Matha also provides khiri (ie. one kind of sweet dish prepared from rice) which is distributed among the Sevayats.

Legend

Manohar Das, a devotee of the Lord, of Village Sahapur, near Rushikulya river had a strong desire to meet Lord Jagannath. He started his journey with a basketful of lotus flowers covering it with a wet towel. While coming, he used to pluck lotus flowers from the tanks, found on his way. He also used to spray water on the old flowers to keep them fresh. After reaching Puri and before visiting the Lord, he stayed at Bada CHATA Matha. Thereafter, he went inside the Jagannath temple and requested the priests to offer the flowers to the Lord. However, as the flowers were stale, the priests threw the rotten flowers and beat him cruelly. He was unconscious. The inhabitants of Bada CHATA Matha brought him back and put him to rest.

The then Gajapati king had a dream at that night, where he was instructed by Lord Jagannath to treat Manohar with all kindness. The king advised the family priest to take Manohar inside the temple. The thrown way flowers were collected and offered to the deities to fulfil the wish of Manohar. Astonishingly, the flowers became fresh and there was sweet fragrance. The blessings of the Lord on Manohar was heard from the void.

To commemorate this incident, the Padma Besha is performed every year during the period as stated above.

Makara Besha

This is done in Makar Sankranti. Flower decoration and large amount of Tulasi leaves are used in this Besha.

Gaja Uddharan Besha

This is performed on the full moon day of Magha. This Besha is to inspire a sense of devotion to the grace of God. The deities are given hands and legs with Sola. The figure looks like rescuing the elephant from the dreaded crocodile.

This Besha, celebrates the incident regarding the saving of a helpless elephant, from the jaws of a crocodile, who prayed the Lord earnestly. The sincere prayer of the elephant moved the Lord and out of compassion, Lord Vishnu hurled his disc to strike the attacking crocodile and turn it in to pieces.

Chacheri Besha (Phalguna Month – February-March)

This is celebrated from the ninth day of the bright fortnight to full moon day in the month of Phalgun, except on 14th day. During this period people play with coloured powder. As Lord Jagannath is supreme Lord of the people, Lord is seen sharing the experience of the people by playing with rosy red powder (known as Phagu / Abhir).

KUNDALA BESHA is celebrated from 10th day of the bright fortnight to 14th day and Raja Vesha is performed on DOLA Purnima day.

Ram Raja Besha (Chaitra Month – March – April)

This is celebrated on the 9th day of bright fortnight of Chaitra Month.

Lord Ram is remembered in this Besha. The deities are dressed as Rama, Sita and Laxman. The bow and arrows are with Lord Ram. Hanuman and monkeys are also displayed. The representatives/ images were done in Sola. Because of cost factor, this Besha is discontinued. This was last held in the year 1805 AD.

Nabanka Besha

This Besha was started by Chaitanya Mahaprabhu to arouse nine kinds of devotion in devotees. Lord Jagannath is dressed as a lover (ie. Nayak). The long white cotton cloth with red boarder is used. This is folded in such a fashion that the red boarder frames the face.

Generally there are no special Beshas during April, May and August.

Various Beshas (attire) are performed on specific occasions and on specific days as stated above. As per researchers, many of the Beshas are introduced by different rulers in different period of time.

Among all the Beshas, the Suna Besha (ie. golden costume), which is also known as "Bada Tadhau Besha", is more dazzling, where the deities are decked with gold and diamonds while sitting on the chariot and public can view the Lord. Many people visit the city during this period to see the Suna Besha of the Lord, which has a special attraction.

The Suna Beshas are also named differently according to the style of the arrangements. The Beshas like – Thiakia Laxminarayan Besha, Adakia Trivikram Besha, Dalikia Laxmi – Nrushingh Besha, Bankachuda Besha / Vamana Besha are also related to Suna Besha.

Although all Raja Beshas are Suna Besha but in Raja Besha, there are more use of ornaments including gold.

Some historians believe that this Besha was started by Anangabhima Deva, while establishing the temple and some others are of the view that it was started during the period of Kapilendra Deva, the great Gajapati king of Odisha.

As per many historians/ researchers many of the great rulers of Kalinga had always given supremacy to Lord Jagannath (ie. Lord was greater than the king).

They had always offered their wealth to Lord Jagannath which they had collected after their victory in the war.

Almost all the Beshas are performed inside the temple, excepting- Suna Besha, Hathi Besha, Bada SINGHAR Besha and ABAKASH Besha, which takes place outside the temple during Snana Yatra and Ratha Yatra.

After the Besha is over, the devotees keep the used flower / garlands and Tulsi etc. with reverence.

The Beshas of the Lord bring centuries of unforgettable traditions, which were introduced by different rulers and saints from time to time and who wanted to see the Lord in unique way.

FESTIVALS

There are 12- important festivals in the Jagannath temple, which are performed as under: –

Chandan Yatra

This is observed in the month of Vaisaksha / Baisakh and continues for long 42 days. But, generally speaking it is a Festival of first 21 days only. The first period of 21 days is known as "Bahar Chandan"or outer Chandan. During this period, the representative images of Rama, Krushna, Madanmohan, Sridevi and Bhudevi are taken in a procession to Narendra tank.The images of Siva from 5 - Siva Temples known as "Pancha Pandavas" also accompany them to the Narendra tank. At Narendra tank, the images play in well decorated boats and are worshipped.

The second period of 21 days is known as "Bhitar Chandana" and it is celebrated inside the Temple. The rites observed during this period are not as popular as Bahar Chandan" enjoyed.

Snana Yatra

This Festival takes places in the month of Jestha. it is popularly known as the Deba Snana Purnima.This is the first occasion in the course of a year when the deities Jagannath, Balabhadra, Subhadra along with Sudarsan and Madanmohan are brought out from the Temple and taken in procession to Snana Bedi located in the North East corner of the outer compound. The deities are bathed there with 108 pitchers of water drawn from a well (Suna Kua) near the Northern Gate. Here, Jagannath and Balabhadra are dressed like Lord Ganesh with the head of an elephant.

Ratha Yatra

Ratha Yatra is the most important festival of the Lord and is the grand culmination of a series of celebrations spread over the summer and the monsoon months. Lord Jagannath is the Lord of the Universe. During this festival, Lord comes out of his sanctum sanatorium to give DARSHAN (audience) to all devotees belonging to all sects and communities.

As per Kathopanishada, body is the chariot and the deity is the soul in the chariot. Wisdom is the charioteer that controls the minds and thoughts. Akshaya Trutiya tithi marks the beginning of the construction of the Rathas (chariots) for the ceremonial journey and sojourn of Lord Jagannath, Balabhadra and Subhadra to the Gundicha Temple for a week.

The three Chariots of Balabhadra, Subhadra and Jagannath are constructed each year with Sal/ other woods, customarily brought from the ex-princely State of Dasapalla and nearby areas by a specialist team of carpenters who have hereditary rights for this.

Every year, on the full-moon day of the month of Jyestha (May-June) in the Snana Yatra (ie. the Bathing Festival), the three deities move in colourful processions to a platform in the outer enclosure of the temple, the Snana Vedi (ie. the bathing platform), where they bath with one hundred and eight pitchers of perfumed water drawn from a temple well. After the ritual bath, the deities assume the special elephant form, recalling the legend of the Lord's affection for a devotee, whom He proved that he was in fact another manifestation of Lord Ganesha.

At the end of the Snana Yatra day, the holy triad, supposedly afflicted with fever, does not return to their pedestal in the sanctum. They stay away from the public view for a period of fifteen days, called Anasara. There after, they appear in the Navayauvana Vesha (ie. renewed youth) on the new moon day of the Month of Ashadha. During this fortnight the images get a fresh coat of paint which gets washed out on the day of the Bathing Festival. During this period the deities eat only fruits, other restricted diet and soft drinks. Cloth paintings representing the deities called Anasara Pati, are displayed beyond the enclosures hiding the deities from the devotees to see and worship.

Then the Ratha Yatra falls on the second day of the bright fortnight of the month of Ashadha, when the three deities come out of the temple in a spectacular procession called Pahandi. The deities, which are colossal wooden statues, adorned with giant floral crowns, called Tahias, are literally pulled, pushed and dragged in rhythmic movement to the accompaniment of the beat of cymbals, drums and chanting of their names in chorus by devotees in frenzied ecstasy.

The Gajapati King comes from his palace on a richly decorated palanquin. He is the Adya sevaka of Lord Jagannath (ie. foremost servant of God). He performs the Chhera Pamhara (ie. the ritual of sweeping of the chariots with a golden broom by the Gajapati King of Puri). It is a symbolic rite which proclaims that the King, like others, is a humble servant of the real sovereign, ie. Lord Jagannath.

All the deities are seated in their respective chariots after Pahandi is over.

The most exciting part of the Rath yatra is the pulling of chariots by thousands of people who lay their hands on the sturdy ropes and drag the massive structures along the Bada-Danda (ie. grand road).

The chariot of Balabhadra moves first, followed by those of Subhadra and Jagannath. The chariots move forward slowly until they reach the Gundicha temple and the three deities rest for a night at the entrance on their own chariots. They enter the Gundicha temple on the next day in the usual Pahandi style and stay there for seven days. Goddess Laxmi, who gets angry for being left out at the temple, proceeds to the Gundicha temple to meet her Lord, Jagannath, on the Hera Panchami day (ie. the fifth day of the fortnight). After having a stealthy look at her Lord, she returns to the temple, damaging a part of Jagannath's chariot in anger and disgust.

The deities, after the seven-day stay at Gundicha Temple (their garden house), commence their return journey. It is called Bahuda Yatra. It is observed on the tenth day of bright fortnight of Ashadha. The return of the chariots take place in the same order as in the Rath Yatra. Balabhadra's chariot moves first, followed by those of Subhadra and Jagannath. On the way back, the chariot of Lord Jagannath stops for a while at Ardhasani temple, popularly called Mausi Ma temple or the temple of Aunt. He accepts from the aunt his favourite rice cake, Poda Pitha.

The three chariots pulled by thousands of devotees, reach back the Simhadwara in the late afternoon of the Bahuda day and the deities remain seated on their chariots. On the next day, known as the Bada Ekadasi, the three deities are attired in costumes of glittering gold and are worshipped by thousands of devotees. This form of the deities is known as the famous Suna Vesa. On the Dwadasi day, the three deities go back to their original place, the Ratna Simhasana (ie. the jewelled platform), with the usual fanfare and the Pahandi style. Their arrival into the Sanctum sanctorum marks the end of the Ratha Yatra (ie. grand chariot festival).

Chariots

As stated in earlier paragraph, three Chariots of Balabhadra, Subhadra and Jagannath are constructed each year with Sal wood, customarily brought from the ex-princely state of Dasapalla and nearby areas by a specialist team of carpenters who have hereditary rights for this.

Lord Jagannath's Chariot is called Nandighosa. It is 45.11 feet high and 16-wheels each of 6-feet diameters. It is decked with red and yellow coverings of cloth. There are yellow stripes on the canopy of this chariot.

The Chariot of Lord Balabhadra, called the Taladhwaja, has fourteen wheels, each of 6.6 feet in diameters and is covered with red and green cloths. The chariot is 46.4 feet high.

The chariot of Subhadra is known as Debadalana. It's height is 42-feet and has 12-wheels. The diameter of each of the wheels is 6.8 feet. It is covered with red and black cloth.

There are nine Parsvadevatas (ie. the guardian deities), and four horses around each of the Chariots. Each chariot has a charioteer called Sarathi. Matali, Darruka and Arjun are the charioteers attached separately to the three chariots of Jagannath, Balabhadra and Subhadra.

Navakalevara

As a man discarding worn out clothes takes other new ones, so does the embodied soul, casting off worn out bodies enters into others which are new. In the light of this truth of the Bhagavat Geeta, Navakalevar can be interpreted as a ceremony for entering into new bodies, when Lord Jagannath, Balabhadra, Subhadra and Sudarshan cast off their old bodies and take new ones. It is called Navakalevar. The year which has two months of Ashadha is regarded auspicious for Navakalevar ceremony. It usually occurs after a duration of 8, 11 or 19 years. The new bodies of the deities are made out of the newly cut neem trees.

Dakshinayana Yatra

This festival is performed on the day of Karkata sankaranti. Sandle paste is offered to them and the deities are decorated with boirani cloth. Cooked rice is offered to the surrounding Digapalas. When the deities are on the Rath, plain rice is offered instead of cooked rice.

Parswa Parivartan

This festival is performed on the 11th day of the bright fortnight of Bhadraba Month. On the evening of this day, after the usual rituals of the deities are performed, the deities are made to sleep on the other side on which they were laid previously. Before this day, they were facing south. Now their side is turned and they face to the north. After Vandapana / salutations (ie. waving of auspicious light), the door is again closed.

Vijaya Dashami

On this day, worship of different weapons and Vijaya Dashami celebrations are performed.

Hari Utthapana Ekadashi / Prabodhana Yatra

This is observed on the 11th day of the bright fortnight in the month of Kartik. The Gods are awaken from Devine slumber. The Sayana house is opened and the deities are prayed to awake from the sleep with Arati and pushpanjsli.

After MAHASNANA, the deities are placed in Ratna Singhasan and are decorated with sandal paste, clothes and ornaments are offered to them. After camphor Altai/ Aarati is over, the SAYAN DEITIES are placed in the store house of the temple and Pahuda (sleeping) is performed thereafter.

Pravarana

From the 6th day of the bright fortnight of Margashir Month, deities are covered with warm clothes till Basanta Panchami. Thereafter, they are covered with light clothes up to DOLA Purnima.

Rajaviseka

This is also known as Pusyaviseka and is performed on full moon day in the month of Pousha (January). Special and sacred ablutions are performed on the reflection of lord's image in a brass mirror. The Ram aspect of the Lord and his coronation at Ayodhya is highlighted in this festival.

81-pots of perfumed water and 21-pots of ghee are brought before the Lord from Bhogamandap for the ritual. Goddess Laxmi also comes here and offerings are made to both. A Sevayat representing Laxman holds aloft the umbrella made of appliqué and in another clutches the handle representing Hanuman. The deities are armed with floral bows and arrows. The deities are worshipped in Sodash Upachar Puja and thereafter the auspicious light is waved (Bandapana). The movable image of the Lord, ie. Raghunath goes to the temple of Mahalaxmi. The grand bath of both the deities are performed. After performance of the ritual, Lord Raghunath returns.

Makar Sankranti

Special rituals are performed in the temple. On this day uncooked rice mixed with cheese and milk etc. are offered to the Lord. Uttarayan Yatra is performed on the this day when the Sun moves towards vernal equinox.

Dola Yatra

This is celebrated from the tenth day of the bright fortnight of Falguna up to the full moon day. The representative deities Dologobinda, Bhudevi and Sreedevi are taken in a procession to Dolabedi located outside the outer compound wall of the main temple and special rites are performed.

This is also known as Vasantotsava. The coloured powder known as Fagu is sprinkled on the deities.

Damanaka Yatra

This is celebrated on the 13th and 14th day of bright fortnight of Chaitra. The representative deities of Lord Ram and Lord Krishna are taken in a procession to the Jagannath Ballav Math. A scented plant known as Dayana is brought by stealing it. This is offered to Lord by observing elaborate rituals.

Temples Inside Puri

There are many temples scattered around the Jagannath temple related to many other deities, ie. Shiv, Shakti (Goddess), Nrushingh, Hanuman and Radha Krishna etc...

As per Skanda Purana, Sri KSHETRA Puri is like a Dakshinabarta Sankha (ie. Conch). Pleased with the Prayer of Lord Shiv, Lord Jagannath allowed Shiv to be in Nilachal by surrounding the temple. Hence Lord Shiv is surrounding the temple in the form of Astashivas (in the form 8-SHIVAS), ie. – Kapalmochan, Kama, Khetarpal, YAMESWAR, Markandeswar, Bisweswar, Nilakantha and Bateswar.

Similarly to protect the Ratna SIMHASANA, Goddess Parvati in the form of 8-Shaktis seat in different directions of the temple, ie. Mangala (near Kalpa Bata), Bimala, Sarvamangala, Ardhasini, Lambha, Kalaratri, Marichika and Chanda Rupa. The throne of the Lord is protected by these Goddesses.

Originally, lord had appeared in the form of Nrushingh. Hence, Nrushingh temples are found in different directions of Srikeshtra. Beside many Nrushingh temples, ie. Adi Nrushingh in the north, Pandu Nrushingh in the south, Chakra Nrushingh in the east and Nisa Nrushingh in the west, are found.

Jagannath temple of Puri was attacked time and again by several Muslim invaders. To protect the temple, a group of young boys were trained through Akhadas / Jaga gharas. As Lord Hanuman is the symbol of hero worship, many Hanuman temples are found in different places around the temple. Some of the famous Hanuman temples are – Bedi Hanuman in the east, Bargi Hanuman in the west, kanapata Hanuman in the south and Siddha Hanuman in the North.

Due to influence of Chaitanya Mahaprabhu and other Vaishnavite saints, many temples were established by many devotees to worship Radha and Krishna.

As per many researchers like four gateways of the temple, one will find temples of Lord Shiv, Hanuman and Nrushingh in all the four directions of the Srikeshtra.

Gundicha Temple

This is the most important temple of Srikeshtra, next to Jagannath temple.

It is named after Gundicha, the queen of Indradyumna who built the temple.

The distance between the lion gate of Jagannath Temple and the Gundicha Temple is exactly 2,688.0696 meters (8327 feet). Both these temples are located at either end of the Bada Danda (Grand Road) which is the route of the famous Puri Rath Yatra.

The temple is having Viman, Jagamohan, Natamandap, and Bhogamandap and is constructed in the style of Lord Jagannath temple of Puri.

This is a Pidha type temple with height of around 75 feet and having a base of 55 feet by 46 feet outside, and 36 feet 8inches by 27 feet inside. It is connected with kitchen rooms, by a narrow passage.

There is a plain raised seat, 4 feet high and 19 feet long, made of chlorite and this is called the Ratnavedi – the throne on which the images are placed when brought to the temple.

It has two gates, ie. western gate and eastern gate. The deities during Ratha Yatra enter the temple through west gate, which is the main gate and they come out through east gate (ie. known as Nakachana gate) during Bahuda Yatra (ie. Return car festival).

The temple stands in the middle of a beautiful garden, with walls on all the sides.

There are traces of several plastering and are carved in places with obscene figures in mortar.

The Gundicha temple has no activity throughout the year except for the nine-day period when the Rath Yatra is celebrated in Puri. During this period Lord Jagannath is worshipped here and they stay here for seven days.

Bhogas are prepared in the kitchen, in the same style as is done in Jagannath Temple.

Foreigners who are prohibited from entering the Jagannath temple are however allowed inside this temple during this time.

A day before the world-famous Ratha Yatra in Jagannath Puri, the Gundicha temple is cleaned (ie. known as Gundicha marjana) to welcome Lord Jagannath, Baladeva and Subhadra.

This temple is known as the Garden House of Lord Jagannath. It is believed that one will get salvation by witnessing the Lord once in this temple. Further visiting the Lord once in this temple is equivalent to visiting the Lord for hundred years in Srimandir.

The ceremonies like – Hera Panchami, Navami Darshan during Ratha Yatra, Dakshina Moda and Bahuda Yatra are visited by large number of devotees.

A small team of servitors look after the upkeep of the Gundicha temple and the temple is under the management of Jagannath Temple Administration.

It is located at Gundicha square, Badasankha, near Bus Stand.

Maushi Maa Temple / Ardhasini Temple

This Temple is in between, 'Gundicha Temple' and 'Singha Dwara'. This is the shrine of the Goddess, Ardhamsini or Ardhasini, popularly known as Mausima (aunt) of Jagannath. The idol of the Goddess is like the idol of Subhadra.

It is stated in the Skanda Purana, Vaisnava Kandha that during the deluge, when the sea over flooded Puri, this goddess drank half of the flood water and saved the town from drowning due to floods.

As per legend, when Lord Jagannath and Balabhadra were banished by Goddess Laxmi, they left the Srimandir. During this period Goddess Subhadra stayed in this temple/ with the Goddess.

Here, the Lord takes the bhoga / prasad of 'Podapitha" (ie. one kind of burnt cake / a special cake), during return car festival. The chariots halt here and the prasad is taken as a token of love from their Aunt / Maushi.

It is also believed that, Goddess Ardhasini along with KAPAL MOCHAN SHIV are the guardians of Jagannath temple and Puri town during day and night.

Shiv Temples Of Sri Kshetra

It is said that there are one crore Shivlings in the Srikeshtra. LOKANATHA, Markandeswar, Kapalamochana, YAMESWAR and Nilakantha are known as PANCHA PANDAV S. These temples are present inside Jagannath temple complex and in front of Mangala temple.

These five Shiv temples along with the temple of Ishaneswar and PATALESWAR are deep below the ground level. Therefore, it is believed that Srikeshtra, Puri was a Saiva KSHETRA.

The main Shiv temples of SRI KSHETRA are as under:

Kapal Mochan Shiv Temple

This temple is situated on the south side of Jagannath Temple. It is a small temple in the immediate neighbourhood of the Alabukeswara in the Manikarnika Sahi. The sacred pool of Manikarnika is also located here. The Shivling is situated much below the ground level.

There are 12-steps to go inside the temple. The side Gods / Goddesses are – Kartikeya, Haraparvati, Ganga, Mahavir, RAMESWAR and Kali etc. Everyday rice is offered as Prasad in the temple. The idol of Lord Ganesh is without mount of mouse. This shows the antiquity of Lord Ganesh.

Puranic Connection

Lord of this temple finds mention in Skanda Purana. As per said Purana, Lord Shiv gave a slap to Lord Brahma out of anger. Lord Brahma was beheaded and his head was attached with his hand. Lord Shiv worshipped at many places and many Gods to get rid of the head. When he came to Sri KSHETRA, the head of Brahma fell down from his hand. The place where the head touched the earth, Lord Shiv sat there and worshipped Lord Jagannath.

The place became a holy place and was known as Manikarnika TIRTHA. Now, a well is present here.

As per Skanda Purana, the place where Lord Shiv sat is situated in the second round circle of the conch. The devotees who worship the Lord at this place, become free from the Brahma Hatya Dosh (ie. sin due to killing of a Brahmin).

Lord became famous in the name of Brahma KAPAL MOCHAN Shiv / KAPAL MOCHAN Shiv.

The temple is also having connections with certain rituals, like – Chandan Yatra, Sital SASTHI of Jagannath Temple.

Markandeswar Shiv Temple

This temple is situated in the Markandeswar street and in the north side of the Jagannath temple. It is situated near the side of the Tank in the same name.

Puranic Connection

During destruction (ie. Pralaya) of the universe, Sage Markendaya was floating in the water. He saw a banyan tree in Srikeshtra and he reached that place for help. He heard a voice which instructed him to come to his side to take rest. When sage reached that place, he saw Lord Krishna as a child was sleeping in a leaf of the banyan tree.

The sage requested Lord Krishna to permit him to stay at Srikeshtra, so that he can worship him. He excavated a tank which was known as Markendaya tank and he remained in the side of the tank as a Shivling to worship Lord Jagannath.

As per scriptures, if the devotees take bath in the Markandeswar Tank and worship Lord Markandeswar, they will get the benefits of a horse sacrifice (Ashwamedha Yagnya).

The temple is connected with the rituals of Chandan Yatra, Balabhadra janma, Ashram Bije of Laxmi on the day of Rishi Panchami, Sital SASTHI and KALIYA DALAN rituals of Lord Jagannath.

Inscriptions

There are stone inscriptions in the temple which describes the glory of Ganga dynasty. There are stone images of SAPTA MATRUKA in the gate way of Markandeya tank.

Yameswar Shiv Temple / Jameswar Temple

It is located on the extreme end of Harichandi Street and towards south of Jagannath Temple. The construction period of the temple is believed to be around 11th century AD.

The Shivling is below the ground level. One will find the synthesis of Hari (Vishnu) and Hara (Shiv) at this temple. The temple has both Garuda (carrier of Lord Vishnu) and Bull (carrier of Lord Shiv) seated side by side.

Eight Shiv images are found inside this temple, ie. Kapalmochan, Markandeswar, Nilakantha, Visweswar, loknath, Sovhakeswar, Angeswar and YAMESWAR himself. On the steps of this temple, a big Mahavir image is found.

There are some similarities in the rituals of both the Lingaraj Temple and YAMESWAR temple, ie. like – use of both Tulasi leaves and Bela Patra in puja, offering of cooked Rice as prasad and car festival during Sital SASTHI.

This temple is also connected with the rituals of Jagannath Temple, like – The moving deity participate in Chandan Yatra, Sudarshan of Jagannath Temple visits Lord Shiv of the temple on the birthday of Lord Balabhadra and he also calculates the income and expenditure of Jagannath temple etc.

Puranic Connection

As per Skanda Purana, Lord Brahma while worshipping at Srikeshtra found a crow was drowned in the Rohini Kunda of Srikeshtra and he took the form of 4-armed Vishnu and sat near the Lord.

In the meantime, Lord Yama (God of death) prayed Lord Jagannath to relinquish him from his role as a God of death, as he could not perform the same at Srikeshtra. Lord Jagannath was satisfied with his prayer and advised Goddess Laxmi to reveal the glory of Srikeshtra.

Lord Jagannath also advised him to to leave the Srikeshtra for the devotees and to rule in other places. Further, satisfied with the prayers of Lord Yama, he was allowed to stay and to worship him. From that day, he remained in Srikeshtra.

As per another legend, Lord Jama (ie. God of death) tried to disturb the meditation of Lord Shiv. Lord Shiv was angry and defeated Lord Jama in the war. From that day, Lord Shiv of this place was known as Jameswar and he is protecting Puri from the wrath of Lord Jama.

When the devotees worship the Lord, they could achieve the benefits of worshipping crores of Shivlings in many places.

This place is known as YAMESWAR TIRTHA. Lord Shiv protects this holy land from the influence of Yama.

From various historical evidences and analysis, one can get a lot of evidence of the culture of Puri from the activities of this temple.

Nilakantha Shiv Temple

This temple is situated in the backside of Gundicha temple. The height of the temple is 12-feet, Jagmohan is 15-feet and Nata Mandir is 20-feet. The seated image of Kali is found in front of Lord Shiv in the Nata Mandir.

There is another Nilakantha temple at Labnikhia Chowk, where the representative deities of the temple are also found.

Cooked rice is offered to Lord as prasad. The temple and the Lord is also connected with Chandan Yatra and Sital SASTHI rituals of Lord Jagannath.

Puranic Connection

As per Skanda Purana Lord Nilakantha is situated in the upper side of Sankha KSHETRA. From the churning of sea by both the Gods and demons when poison came out, Lord Shiv consumed the poison to save the world. From that day Lord Shiv was known as Nilakantha.

Lokanatha Shiv Temple

This famous temple of Puri is located about 3-kms away from the Jagannath Temple, towards the western end. The Temple is believed to be built during 10th-11th century A.D. The main temple is of Rekha style and is around 30-feet. The porch in front of the temple is of Pidha Style.

This Shiv temple is ranked next to Jagannath temple in importance.

The Shivling remains submerged in the water throughout the year and visible only on the night of Pankoddhar EKADASHI (3-days before Shivratri). During this period water is cleared and devotees can see the Shivling.

As per belief, there is a stream on the head of the Shivling playing the role of the Ganges and the linga itself remains submerged under the water.

The flowers, sandal paste, 'Bilva-patra', etc. offered to Lord remain decomposed in the water emitting a special smell. People take it as Prasad to cure themselves from the diseases that they are suffering from.

The devotees also come here to pray Lord Loknath to cure themselves from any kind of disease.

Lot of devotees visit the temple during Shivratri. A meeting of Lord Siva and Lord Vishnu takes place on the day, known as" Hari-Hara BHETA". This union shows the co-existence of Hara and Hari culture at Puri. This is the main attraction of the visitors during Mahashivratri.

There are many festivals observed in the temple and 'Sankranti-Somobar-mela' is the most important one. On the last Monday of Baisakha Month, large number of devotees visit the Lord for worship.

Cooked rice (Anna Prasad) is offered to Lord as Prasad.

There are also many small temples inside the temple premises, like – Goddess Parvati and Lord Ganesh etc.

The holy pond in the temple complex is known as Parvati Sagar (ie. described earlier, under ponds of Puri). Visitors offer foods to fishes and turtles present in the tank.

Legend

Lord Ram on his way to Lanka to search Mata Sita had reached Srikeshtra. He meditated Lord Shiv at this place. Earlier, this area was the land of Shabars (ie. aboriginal tribes). During meditation of Lord Ram, he was presented with a Lau (Gourd – A type of vegetable) which was looking like a Shivling. Lord Ram established the same as the replica of a Shivling and worshipped the Lord for fulfilment of his desire. From that day, the Shivling which was established by Lord Ram was known as Laukanatha. With passage of time, it was known as LOKANATHA.

Lord Loknath is the guardian deity of Ratna Bhandar (Store house) of Jagannath Temple. He is also known as Bhandar Lokanath. The moving image of Lord LOKANATHA also accompanies the representative image of Lord Jagannath at the time of Chandan Yatra.

The representative deities of the above 5-Shiv temples (ie. PANCHA PANDAVs) accompany Madan Mohan and Ram Krishna during Chandan Yatra festival of Jagannath Temple. During this period Rama Krishna and PANCHA Pandav s sit in a Chap (boat) to perform water sports.

Alabukeswara Temple

This Shiv shrine is situated to the west of the Yameswara. As per Kapila Samhita, people pray the Lord for making barren women to get children.

It is located around 2-hundred meters distance from horse gate of Jagannath temple and at the starting of Manikarnika sahi.

Further, AGNESWAR, BATESWAR, KHETRAPALESWAR, CHAKRESWAR, BAIKUNTHESWAR, PATALESWAR, LOKESWAR are known as 8-Shivas of Srikeshtra.

Shakti Temples Of Puri (Srikeshtra)

Srikeshtra, Puri is famous as a Shaktipitha and it's importance is found in scriptures like – Devi Bhagabat, Skanda Purana and Kalika Purana etc.

As per many religious scriptures, it is identified as the Pada KSHETRA/ Pada Pitha (ie. where the feet of Devi had fallen).

As per Skanda Purana, Goddess Vimala resides in the 3rd circle of Shankha KSHETRA and 8-goddesses circumscribe the Mahavedi of Lord Jagannath, to protect Srikeshtra. As per Kalika Purana, Goddess Vimala is Vairabi and Lord Jagannath is Vairaba.

Many of such references prove that Puri was also a Shaktipitha.

The major Shakti Shrines of Srikeshtra, Puri are as under:

Bata Mangala

She is 4-handed Goddess and sits on lotus. She holds conch in the upper left hand and Trident in the upper left hand. The lower hands are of Abhaya and Barada mudra.

When devotees enter Srikeshtra, they offer their prayer first to the Goddess. Similarly while leaving the Srikeshtra, they keep her as witness of their visit to Lord Jagannath. They also pray for their safe and happy journey.

Legend

LORD BRAHMA, could not find the way when he was coming to Srikeshtra to consecrate the deities in the Srimandir. At that time, Bata Mangala had shown him the ways to Srikeshtra.

This temple is situated in Puri – Bhubhaneswar road and is around 3-kms from Puri, towards Bhubaneshwar.

Alama Chandi

The temple of the Goddess is situated at Atharanala gate of Srikeshtra. She is 4-handed Goddess Durga. As per Skanda Purana, this temple which is situated on the north side of Jagannath Temple used to protect the Ratna SIMHASANA.

At the time of Nabakalebara, the log of woods (DARU) collected from different parts of the state for construction of the chariot are placed here and entered in to Srikeshtra with a procession headed by the Gajapati king. The Saints, Mahantas of the Mathas and Sevayats etc. accompany the procession.

It is believed that, Maa Alamchandi who is seen standing on a corpse, shares the mystery behind holy wood with Lord Shiv, who is known as Krutibasa Mahadev, sitting to her side.

She is seen in Abhaya Mudra and blesses the Banajaga team in their endeavour and guides them back to Jagannath temple through the Debajana route (ie. northern door of Srimandir) for storing holy wood at Koili Baikuntha, also known as Mahasmasan.

The Saptapuri Puja of Jagannath temple is associated with the temple. On the day of Saptapuri puja during Saptapuri Amabasya (New moon day), Saptapuri is sent to this temple from the temple of Lord Jagannath as prasad / offering.

In the past, when the the kings and other guests used to visit Srikeshtra, they used to stay here and seek permission to enter Srikeshtra. After obtaining permission, they entered the Srikeshtra.

It is also known as ASTA CHANDI temple by many and presiding deity is the Goddess Alamchandi, one of the Astachandis of Puri.

The people worship the Goddess of the temple with the prayers of Astachandis of Puri. It is also known as Astachandi temple by many.

It is located at the entrance to the Puri town in Kumbharpada, near Atharanala bridge.

Charchika

This temple is situated near the office of the Jagannath temple. Every year, the chariots of Lord Jagannath, Balabhadra and Subhadra are constructed here. She is the superintending deity for the construction of Nandighosh Rath of Jagannath. The carpenters and the Sevayats involved in the construction of the chariot worship the Goddess at the time of Construction.

In the past and at the time of beginning of war, the Gajapati kings used to worship the Goddess.

Every year during return car festival, Goddess Mahalaxmi meets Lord Jagannath at this place, which is known as Laxmi Narayan Bheta.

Marichika

This temple is situated near Marichikot Chowk in grand road. The Goddess Marichika finds mention in Skanda Purana. The Goddess is stationed in the eastern side of the temple and protects the Ratna SIMHASANA of the Lord Jagannath.

Kanak Durga

The temple is situated in the premises of the present palace of the king (ie. Srinahar) and in front of the office of the Jagannath temple. She is the family deity of Gajapati king. The Jagannath temple administration provides some material for preparation of the prasad of the temple.

Narayani

The temple of the Goddess is situated in the Dolamandap Sahi and the street goes from the front of lion's gate. This is also known as Shakta Gundicha. During 16-days Durga Puja in the Ashwin Month, the images of Durga and Madhav sits here for 8-days after sitting 8-days in the Vimala temple.

Dakshin Kali Temple

The temple is situated towards the south-eastern side of the Lord Jagannath Temple in Balisahi, towards sea. It is believed that Daksinakalika is the guardian of the kitchen of the Lord Jagannath Temple. She protects the kitchen from any evils. The cooks

(Supakaras) enter the kitchen of Lord Jagannath with her vermilion (ie. Sundur) in their forehead.

The deity is enshrined in a modern temple at a higher raised platform. This east facing temple consists of a vimana and a Jaganmohan. The deity is four-armed and is seated on a corpse. She is shown with a dagger and holding severed head in two of her hands and drinking blood.

In Skanda Purana, she is described as Kalaratri, as she is black in colour. Sri Jagannath is regarded as Daksinakalika as per Tantra.

The Goddess protects the Ratna SIMHASANA of Lord Jagannath by sitting on the south side.

In the rituals of Saptapuri Amavasya (New moon day) the Goddess also plays an important role.

Shyamakali Temple

The shrine is situated in the old palace of the Gajapati Kings of Puri, which was present in Bali Sahi. This is in the southern side of Jagannath Temple.

She was the presiding deity in the old palace. The present palace is now situated in grand road, which is a new palace.

Harachandi Temple

This temple is in the south-western corner of Jagannath Temple at HARACHANDI sahi of puri.

As per Skanda Purana, she is one of the Shaktis (Goddess) among 8-Shaktis who protects the Ratna SIMHASANA of Lord Jagannath. She is described as Chandarupa in Skanda Purana.

The temple of seven mother Goddesses are worshipped in the SAPTA MATRUKA TEMPLE, located on the bank of Markandeya tank is also famous (described earlier).

The other famous Goddess temple of Srikeshtra are – Varahi (Gachakali in Bali sahi), Baseli (Baseli sahi), Vana Durga (Mani Karnika sahi), Ramachandi (in Ramachandi sahi, near railway station), Smasan Chandi (near SWARGADWAR), Jaduani (kundeibanta sahi), JHADESWARI (Station road), Uttarkali (Mati Mandap sahi), Mangala (Vimanbadu sahi) and Jayadurga temple of Bhitar kotha (near Narendra Tank) etc..

The eight Chandis--collectively called Astachandi, ie. Bata Mangala, Dakshinakalika, Harachandi, Vimala, Sarva Mangala, Ardhasani, Alamba and Alambika protect the Ratna SIMHASANA of Lord Jagannath.

From the kotha Bhoga of the temple administration, the Goddess Varahi, Baseli and HARACHANDI get the Khei (prasad).

The expanses for prasad and special Bhogas relating to Goddess Jaya Durga are borne by the Sri Jagannath temple administration.

Further DWARBASINI, MAHABAJRESWARI, SWANSBHAIRABI, BHADRAKALI, BEDHAKALI, BHUBANESHWARI, SITALA AND JAGNYESHWARI are known as 8-famous Goddesses of Srikeshtra.

As per some other views, Astachandis are – Vimala, Ramachandi, HARACHANDI, Baseli, Varahi, DAKSHIN kali, Jhadeswari and Alamchandi.

Nrushingh Temples Of Puri

Many researchers are of the view that Lord Nrushingh is the ancient/ earlier deity of Srikeshtra. As per Skanda Purana, when Lord Nilamadhav vanished, Lord Nrushingh appeared in Srikeshtra at the bottom of black sandalwood tree. Therefore, many Nrushingh temples are found in Srikeshtra, puri. Some of the important Nrushingh temples are as under.

Yagnya Nrushingh Temple

This temple is situated on the eastern side of Gundicha temple. This 4-armed image is sitting on a lotus and is holding conch and sphere in upper two hands and other two hands are in two laps. The height of the image is around 5-feet. Goddess Laxmi is in his left lap and carrier Garuda is sitting near the feet of the deity. This Nrushingh is connected with various rituals of Jagannath Temple. During different festivals, flower garlands are taken from Lord Jagannath and are kept here. During Ratha Yatra, the chariot of Lord Jagannath rests in front of the Nrushingh image.

Puranic Connection

As per Skanda Purana, king Indradyumna had performed the Yagnya at this place to seek the permission from Lord Nrushingh to establish Lord Jagannath, Balabhadra and Subhadra at this place. It is also understood that Acharya Sridhar Swami was blessed by Yagnya Nrushingh to write Bhabartha Dipika (ie. commentary on Srimad Bhagabat) at this place.

Pandu Nrushingh

This temple is situated in the Kandu hermit of Gurubada Sahi and the image is eight armed.

He is holding conch and sphere in two hands. Other 6-hands are engaged in tearing the body of the demon Hiranyakashyap.

While tearing the demon, it is placed on the head of his carrier Garuda, who is seating near the feet of the deity with folded hands.

As per Vishnu Purana, Sage Kandu could see Nrushingh at Srikeshtra on the full moon day of Margashir Month. Further, it is believed that Sage Kandu fell in love with Pumeca while meditating on the bank of the river Gomati.

As per locals, if a dead body passes through the side of the temple, the dead person goes directly to heaven.

Chakra Nrushingh

This temple is situated at CHAKRATIRTHA road, near Penthakata. This sea shore temple is situated on the eastern side of Puri and towards northern side of the temple of Sunar-Gouranga.

Here, three deities, ie. Chakra Narayan, Adi Narayan and Laxmi Narayan in the form of Nrushingh are worshipped. This temple is known as Chakra Nrushingh temple.

In the Chakra Narayan temple a large Chakra is worshipped which is made up of black granite with a statue of Lord Narayan at the centre.

As per local people, once Neelachakra (ie. top wheel of Jagannath temple) was flown away and fell at Chakratirtha to stop the cyclone at Puri.

Puranic Connection

On the 12th full moon day of Phalgun month (ie. Govinda Dwadashi), the wood was found at this place from which Jagannath, Balabhadra and Subhadra were made. While collecting wood from a BANKI MUHAN, king Indradyumna could see the image of Nrushingh inside the sphere mark in the log of wood. The deity was known as Chakra Nrushingh from that day(ie. as per Indra Nilamani Purana).

This day (ie. Govinda Dwadashi day) is observed as a holy festival and large number of devotees visit the place and take holy bath in the sea.

Some rituals of Jagannath Temple are having connections with this temple. On the birth day celebration of Lord Nrushingh, the flower garlands (Agnaya Mala) comes from the Jagannath temple and are placed in the Nrushingh temple.

Singhada Nrushingh

This temple is situated in the HARACHANDI sahi (ie. known as SINGHADA Tota). The Lord is worshipped by the Khuntia Nijogs (ie. sevayatas engaged in decorating Lord Jagannath). The temple was constructed by Anangabhima Dev in 13th century.

Chudanga Nrushingh /Sai Nrushingh

The temple is situated in CHUDANGA Sahi / Bira Surendra Sahi. Lord / Nrushingh image was installed by Chodaganga Dev around 12th century. Bira Surendra Sai had also worshipped the Lord. Hence, it is known as Sai Nrushingh by many.

Barabati Nrushingh

Ram Das, the Guru (Preceptor) of Chhatrapati Shivaji had got Siddhi at this place by worshiping Lord Nrushingh. The deity was established by him here (ie. Barabati jaga of Puri).

Dinanath Nrushingh

Dinanath, Swami of Dakshinaparva Math of Puri had established the Lord here.

Jejerama Nrushingh

The deity was installed by Nirankari Baba Jejeram of Punjab during the period of Raja Ranjit Singh. Initially, it was installed at Grand road near Dodovalla Dharmshala. As the place was destroyed, the image was shifted to Kundeibenta Sahi and near Jaduani library.

Arka Nrushingh

The Lord is the presiding deity of Mahiprakash Math of Puri. The deity was established by Mahipraksh Brahmachari of Mahiprakash Math.

Rendha Nrushingh

The temple is situated at RENDHA in Puri, Brahmagiri road. It was established by Gajapati king Kapilendra Dev (ie. around 14th century) as per advice of a Saint.

Hanuman Temples Of Puri

Some of the famous Hanuman temples of Puri are as under:

Daria Mahavir / Bedi Hanuman

Daria Mahabir Temple is situated at a distance of about 30 meters to the west of the Chakranarayan temple. It is a small temple dedicated to Hanuman and is on the sea shore. He is also known as Bedi Hanuman.

Legend

During ancient period, the sea was eroding the area. People of the area prayed to Lord Jagannath to protect them from the sea. Lord Jagannath ordered Lord Hanuman to protect the area from the advancing sea and he was stationed at this place. As Lord Hanuman was a great devotee of Lord Ram, once he had gone to Ayodhya to meet Lord Ram. The sea once again washed the area, in the absence of Lord Hanuman. From that day, Lord Jagannath tied up Lord Hanuman in a chain so that he can't leave the place. Since that period Lord Hanuman is watching the sea and protecting the area. The Hanuman, tied at this place is also known as Bedi (ie. tied with a chain) Hanuman.

This temple is connected with the pana Sankranti (13th /14th day of Baisakha and Odia new year) ritual of Jagannath Temple.

The idol has a laddoo in one hand and mace on the other hand. Other than Hanuman, the images of Anjana and Lord Ganesh are carved on the walls.

Siddha Mahavir Temple

Siddha Mahavir Temple is situated at a distance of about half a mile, to the west of Gundicha Temple. This is a small temple dedicated to Siddha Hanuman.

It is believed that Tulsidas resided at this place during his stay at Puri.

As per hearsay, Saint Tulshi Das meditated here to see Lord Ram in Srikeshtra.

Satisfied with his prayer Lord Ram had appeared and blessed him. It is also believed that Ram Charit Manas was a result of such blessings.

It is a beautiful spot.

Kanapata Hanuman

This is situated at the southern gate way of Jagannath Temple, puri. It is believed that the sound of sea is not audible inside the temple due to his presence. Lord absorbs the sound of sea.

Legend

Everyday, Lord Jagannath remains busy in listening large number of devotees and he does not find time for Mahalaxmi. Further, Goddess Laxmi could not come to the Jagannath temple, because of the presence of Lord Balabhadra, elder brother of Lord Jagannath. Only in the middle of the night Lord Jagannath gets out to meet Laxmi.

Goddess Laxmi is the daughter of Varuna (God of sea). As Shree Mandir is situated at the sea shore, the sound of sea always creates disturbances. As sea God is her father, She could not complain about it. Hence, Lord Jagannath ordered his dear devotee, Lord Hanuman to ensure that the sound of sea never enters the Maghanada boundary (ie. outer wall of the temple). Lord Hanuman made the entire boundary wall soundproof and always puts his ear on the wall to ensure that the sound of sea is never heard inside the temple.

As Lord Hanuman puts his ear near the boundary wall to make the temple sound proof from the sea, he is known as KANAPATA – HANUMAN.

As per another hearsay, it is said that as the sound of sea was disturbing the saints in meditation, they had requested Lord Jagannath in this regard. Lord ordered Hanuman to do the needful. Lord Hanuman absorbed the sound of the sea in his ear. As a result, the sound of waves of the sea are not heard inside the temple.

Bargi Hanuman

The Lord is the protector of Srikeshtra. The temple is situated in the gateway to Puri, near LOKANATHA temple (ie. on Srimandir – Lokanath road).

As per researchers, the Maratha soldiers, known as Bargis, used to oppress the people. However, they were worshippers of Lord Hanuman. They used to leave the place/ area, wherever Hanuman images / temples were found.

Hence, to protect Srikeshtra, Puri, this Hanuman image was established on the Jagannath-lokanath road and it was known as Bargi Hanuman.

LOKANATHA temple was also saved from the attacks of the Bargis.

Makaradhwaj Hanuman

This Hanuman temple is situated at Atharanala, which is another gateway to Puri. This temple was also established to protect Srikeshtra from the attack of Bargis from this side of the town.

Other Famous Temples Of Puri

There are also some other important temples of Puri, which are as under:

Siddha Bakula

This tree is situated near Bali Sahi. The Ashram of Javan Hadi Das was situated here and Hadi Das used to meditate Lord Jagannath at this place. It is believed that Chaitanya Mahaprabhu had planted a BAKULA Tooth brush to protect the Saint from the Sun during midday. The tree stands here and is having no trunk.

Tota Gopinath

This is situated in Goudabada Sahi in the backside of Jameswar Mahadev temple. It is a holy place for the Goudiya Vaishnavas. The beautiful image of Lord Krishna and Radha are worshipped here.

As per hearsay, Chaitanya Mahaprabhu had submerged with Lord Krishna at this place.

Sonar Gouranga

This temple is situated near Chakra Narayan temple in CHAKRATIRTHA road. The golden images of Lord Krishna and Chaitanya Mahaprabhu are worshipped here. This is a holy place for Vaishnav saints. As the temple is less crowded and in a peaceful surrounding, many people prefer this temple for prayer and meditation. There are also images of Lord Jagannath, Balabhadra, Subhadra and Sri Ram.

Dasavatara Temple

This is a ruined temple of the 'Dasavatara' of Vishnu near the Gundicha temple. Kabi Jayadeve – the author of Gitagovindam had stayed at this place.

He had written Dasavatara Strotra in his famous work Gita Govindam, being inspired with the ten incarnations of Lord Vishnu. The temple requires renovation. This temple plays an important role during Ratha Yatra and large number of devotees visit this ruined temple during this period.

The Temple Of Seven Mother Goddess (Sapta Matruka)

This temple is situated on the embankment of the sacred pond – Markandeya Soravara.

Brahmi, Maheswari, Aidri, Kaumari, Vaisnavi, Varahi and Chamanda are known as the seven mother Goddesses.Sometimes, Narasimha replaces Vaisnavi, a female form of the man-lion incarnation of the Lord Vishnu. The images of the said Goddesses are found here.

Further, this shrine of the seven mother goddess at the Markanda Pond proves that, once upon a time Puri was a Sakta Pitha and Goddess Vimala was the presiding deity of this pitha.

Gambhira

Chaitanya Mahaprabhu stayed here for 13-years and spent the final years of his life at this place. This was the house of Kashi Mishra. It was known as GAMBHIRA and the Radha kanta Matha.

One can look through a small barred window in to the room called "Sri GAMBHIRA", where Chaitanya Mahaprabhu lived. Here, a small lamp is lighted all the time and never goes out.

The original wooden sandals, quilt, water pot and bed of Chaitanya Mahaprabhu are found here. Holy mother Sarada Devi had also visited this place along with other devotees of Ramakrishna.

It is close to Siddha BAKULA and is around half km. from lion's gate on the road towards SWARGADWAR.

Temples like – Allapadma Thakurani (Pathuria sahi), Ashokeswar Shiv temple, Banambar Shiv temple, Batakali temple, Dhip Jaga Harachandi (Harachandi sahi), Gumani Mahavir temple, Hinjala Jagaghar Nrushingh temple, Kaliya Dalan Temple (Markendeswar Sahi), Kameshwar Shiv temple (Matimandap sahi), Krushna Kali temple (Gudabada sahi), Masani Mahavir temple, Narasimha temple (Harachandi sahi), Panchabati shiv temple (Marmao badi), Ramchandi temple (Ramchandi sahi), Sugriba Mahavir temple and jhadeswari temple (Station Bazar) etc. are also popular among the local devotees.

Swargadwar

This is the gateway to heaven. This is situated at the sea shore and it is south side of Jagannath Temple.

It is believed that, if any one is burnt at this place, he goes to heaven and all his sins are also burnt.

There are many legends/ PURANIC connections and hearsay about this place.

A. After wondering different holy places and as per God's advice, Sage Kandu came to this place which is near the sea shore of Srikeshtra. From this place he could see Baikuntha and the path from SWARGADWAR which leads to Baikuntha. He also meditated at this place and could hear the voice of Gods / Goddesses. He felt the uniqueness of the place which could not be compared with any other place. The place was named as SWARGADWAR by him and from that day it is known accordingly.

B. Lord Brahma had got down from heaven at this place to consecrate the images of Lord Jagannath, Balabhadra and Subhadra. He had come to earth at the invitation of king Indradyumna.

C. Pandavas had cremated the body of Lord Krishna at this place. During this period a voice was heard with the instructions not to engage themselves in such futile exercises as soul is immortal and it can neither be destroyed nor burnt.

To give it a new look, construction work is going on.

As this place is near sea, after cremation people take bath in the sea to get heavenly bliss.

The SWARGADWAR sea beach is also a beautiful beach and it remains crowded almost through out the day, especially during morning and evening hours.

Large number of devotees take bath in this beach during auspicious days and in the month of Kartik.

Apart from main temples as described above, there are many small temples in Puri. One can explore the same and each temple is having a history behind it.

Atharanala Heritage Bridge

This stone bridge over the extinct Musa river is located at the entrance of Puri town. It was constructed by Gangavamshi king Bhanu Deva in 13th century.

This is also known as Madhupur bridge and "Hulhuliya bridge". During ancient period, the pilgrims were facing difficulties to cross Musa river. The bridge was constructed to connect the town.

As the bridge has 18-arches (18-passages) it was known as Atharanala bridge.

Legend / Hearsay

King Indradyumna initiated to build the bridge on Musa river. As he failed to complete, he offered the heads of 18-Sons to this river.

As per the Almanac of Jagannath temple (Madala Panji), king Padmanabh Narendra of Ranapur kingdom built it, in memory of the sacrifice of his 18-Sons, in the war. It was built with laterite stones and is of medieval architecture.

The length of the bridge is 280-feet and height is 20.66 feet. It's breadth is 36-feet. As per Jagannath culture, it is an auspicious place.

From this place one can see the long distance view of Jagannath temple.

Due to high siltation and growth of vegetation, the bridge was closed to public. However, one can observe how the façade is decorated with images of deities, dancers, elephants, Navagrahas and floral decorations etc., although denuded.

Presently, the surrounding area is beautified and the 27-feet Statue of Garuda in red sand stone would attract any visitor. However, this area requires infrastructural development.

Pancha Tirtha

There are five TIRTHAs (sacred tanks) in Puri. They are Indradyumna near the Gundicha Temple, Manikarnika in the Marnikarnika Street, Markandeya towards the north of the Jagannath Temple and Swetaganga towards the south of the Jagannath Temple. These four sacred ponds together with the sea, make the Panchtirtha or five sacred waters in which pilgrims are used to take bath.

All these sacred TIRTHAs are found in 4-cardinal directions of Srikeshtra, Puri.

Each of these TIRTHAs were established by the sages and each TIRTHA is also having it's deity, ie. Indradyumna pond was established by king Indradyumna and Nilakantha Shiv is the deity, Markendaya Pond was established by Sage Markanda and Markandeswar Shiv is the presiding deity, Manikarnika pond was established by Kapalmochan Shiv and he is the presiding deity, SWETA Ganga was established by SWETA Madhav and the deities are SWETA Madhav, Matsya Madhav and Navagrahas. Similarly SWARGADWAR was established by Sage Kandu and Chakra Narayan is the presiding deity.

The details of these ponds are described in the following paragraphs/ pages. Besides, there are many religious shrines and sanctuaries found in each and every street of Puri.

Heritage Tour

Fifty three famous heritage locations like – temples, Mathas and Ashrams have been identified and divided in to 5-cycling and walking routes.

TEMPLES OUTSIDE PURI RELATED TO JAGANNATH TEMPLE

There some other temples outside Puri which are connected with some rituals with the Jagannath temple, Puri. Some of them are as under: –

Mangala Temple-kakatpur

During Nabakalebara, the Sevayats of Jagannath Temple implore the mercy of the Goddess to spot the trees for making the new images of the Lord.

Bali Harichandi – Near Brahmagiri

The temple has relation with the Jagannath temple in respect of Mahanavami ritual during Durga Puja in the Ashwin Month.

Mani Naga Thakurani (Ranapur Area)

Special puja is offered to the Goddess, before cutting the trees in the forests of Ranapur area, for construction of the Chariots of the Lord.

Bada Raulai Thakurani (Baramula – Gania – Nayagarh)

Special puja is offered to the Goddess before transportation of the timbers to Puri (ie. to construct the chariots) from the forests of Nayagarh.

Lingaraj Temple-Bhubaneshwar

For the ASHOKASTAMI car festival of Lord Lingaraj, the administration of Jagannath Temple spares some ropes for the chariot. The Rajaguru of Jagannath Temple also participate in the Astaprahari Puja in Lingaraj temple on the day of Shivratri.

Bharati Kotha Matha (Cuttack)

This Matha situated near the high court and is under the control of the Administration of Jagannath Temple.

Alarnath Temple (Brahmagiri)

During ANABASARA period of Lord Jagannath, the devotees visit the Lord.

Beleswar Mahadev Temple

It is situated near the sea shore towards east of Jagannath Temple. It is situated at the top of Sankha KSHETRA. As per religious scriptures, Lord Krishna had worshipped Lord Shiv at this place by putting a bel fruit (ie. wood Apple).

He had prayed Lord Shiv to protect the world from the demons of the patala Loka, who used to enter through this gateway to the world to destroy the mankind.

OTHER HERITAGE STRUCTURES OF PURI

Besides the temples as described above, there are other heritage structures like – Ponds, Mathas, Jaga gharas, Akhadas and Ashramas etc. which are having relationships with the temples and deities. They play an important role in various rituals / ceremonies and they are an integral part of Jagannath culture. One should visit them to know the golden heritage of the city. They are as under:

TANKS

The water tanks of Puri are important environmental and heritage resources. They are having great religious significance and are directly or indirectly linked with Sri Jagannatha temple, through a series of rituals and festivals which take place as part of the temple activity throughout the year.

The pilgrims used to follow a holy circuit known as PANCHA TIRTHA, covering the Mahodadhi tirtha (the sea), Rohini Kund (within the temple), Swetganga tank, Markandeshwar tank and Indradyumna tank.These ponds are protected and maintained through the ages.

In the past there were numerous tanks in Puri, which were the source of water for the inhabitants residing in different areas / sahis.

According to imperial gazetteer, these tanks were once connected with the river Musa and the quality of water was maintained by flushing it during monsoons.It is believed that due to silting, these connections have long since been closed.

The water tanks in Puri can be classified into two categories – artificial/ built and natural.

Almost all the tanks of Puri, which are of archaeological, historical, architectural, social, religious and cultural significance are man-made quadrangular tanks, with steps forming the periphery embankments which enables the devotees to reach the surface of water. The entrances to these tanks are marked by temples and smaller shrines.

The water level in these tanks are maintained mainly from rain water, supply from municipality and ground water.

Presently, there are five sacred tanks in Puri, which are – Markanda, Swetganga, Indradyumna, Narendra, and Parvati Sagar.

There was a holy tank in the Manikarnika temple. However, with passage of time, it has shrunk to a well.

There are also many smaller tanks and natural ponds which are located in various sahis (residential neighbourhoods) and with their associated temples, Jagagharas and akhadas.

Among these tanks, Pathar-pokhari, Bhatta jaga tank and Hinjala jagaghara tank are important.

The four sacred water tanks of primary significance, ie. – Swetganga, Markanda, Narendra and Indradyumna, are all owned by the Shri Jagannatha Temple Trust, though their maintenance is carried out by the municipality. Some of the most well known and historic tank of the city are as under:

Indradyumna Tank

This tank is situated on the north – western part of Gundicha Temple. It covers an area of 4.5 acres with length of 485-feet and width of 396-feet.

This tank is associated with king Indradyumna, who had constructed the Jagannath temple.

Sri Chaitanya Mahaprabhu is believed to have engaged in water sports (jala krida) with his associates in this tank. The tank has a small shrine dedicated to King Indradyumna. It is one of most sacred tanks in Odisha.

Legend

The origin of the tank goes to Mahabharat period. King Indradyumna had arranged the "Ashwamedha Yagnya" which was materialised by Lord Brahma. After end of the Yagnya, the Brahmins were gifted. This yagnya Kunda was known as Indradyumna tank.

The statue of Lord Jagannath, Balabhadra and Goddess Subhadra being constructed by Biswakarma was located near the Yagnya Kunda at Gundicha temple.

Puranic Connection

As per Skanda Purana, Lord Indradyumna had consecrated the Jagannath temple in the hands of Lord Brahma. He had donated millions of cows to the needy and Brahmins. A hole was created by the hooves of these countless cows which were brought by the king for offerings.

This hole was filled up with the sacred water poured to the hands of Brahmins by the king while donating the cows. Hence, the pond bears the name Indradyumna Sarovar and is considered as sacred.

There was a big old tortoise in this pond. It is believed that the labourers who carried stones for construction of Jagannath Temple were converted to tortoise because of hard work. They remained here ever since in the form of many tortoises.

The temple of Nilakantheswar is situated on the south-west bank of the tank. It is believed that devotees who worship Lord Nilakantheswar and offer pinda to their fore-fathers after taking holy bath in this pond on the 5th day of bright fortnight of Ashadha Month (ie. if it falls on Magha Nakshyatra), get the benefit of horse sacrifice. Devotees also performs SHRADHA ceremony on this day at the banks of this pond for liberation of their fore fathers.

There are several temples on it's bank.

The pond is located about 2.7 kilometres from the Puri Jagannath temple.

The approach road to the tank is through a narrow road branching out from the Konark road. OTDC has installed directional signage at the junction and at the edge of the tank but there is no interpretative signages with information on the cultural significance. The locals residing near the tank guide people about the significance and association of the tank

Markandeswar Tank / Markanda Tank

Markanda tank is one of the Pancha TIRTHAs of Puri and is situated at the end of Markandeya Road and towards north side of Jagannath Temple. It is around 1.5 kms from Jagannath temple.

It covers an area of 4-acres and is irregular in shape. It is 358-feet in north, 508-feet in east, 385-feet in south and 542 feet in the west. The sides are lined with stones.

As per legend Sage Markandeya meditated for a long time and Lord has saved Sage Markandeya from the danger of sea. He had arranged a Yagnya at this spot and a shiv temple was also constructed at this place by him.

As per Skanda Purana, Sage Markendaya stays near Kalpabata, after digging a hole, to worship Lord Jagannath.

This tank is also important as it is connected with a lot of rituals associated with Lord Jagannatha, the most important being KALIYA DALANA ceremony.

The temple of Markandeshawar is located on the South- western edge of the tank. It is having an ancient stone inscription pertaining to the Ganga dynasty.

The tank is located at Markendaya sahi.

Narendra Tank

This is the largest tank of Puri. It is also called the Chandana pushkarani / Pokhari after the famous Chandan yatra of Lord Jagannath.

It is surrounded by the Markandeswar sahi in the east, Bisoi Thakurani on the west, Brahmagiri road and Jatia Baba Matha on the north and Jagannath Ballabh Math on the south.

The tank was constructed around 14th / 15th centuries A.D., during the period of Gangavamshi kings. The tank covers an area of 14.757 acres. It is 834-feet by 873-feet in size. The approximate depth of the tank is 28-feet and water level is around 10-feet below the road level. The surrounding areas are picturesque.

The tank has an Island in its centre having a small temple known as Chandana Mandapa. It measures around 50" x 12". It is connected with the south bank with a bridge.

As per many researchers, the tank was previously a fine sheet of water, kept clean by flushing from the Musa river during the rains through a connecting channel in the western corner. Historically, silting has always been an issue in the tank and de-silting activities have taken place on 1866 AD, 1929 AD and 1972 AD.

Presently, both the inlet and the outlet of the tank are completely clogged and hence the traditional system is not in use. The water is stagnant.

A periphery road circumbulates the tank connecting the religious structures on the edge, which are, – Chara Ganesh Matha, Gopinath Ballabha Matha, Brahma Jaga and Jatia Baba Matha.

Chandan Yatra

The Tank is associated with the Chandan Yatra ritual. On the Akshya Trutiya day of each year, Madan Mohan (ie. representative of Lord

Jagannath) is taken to the tank, along with Shree Devi, Bhu Devi, Rama and Krishna and Mahadev. These are carried in a procession to the tank. The water sports are performed so that the Gods could evade the oppressive heat of Puri during summer months.

The images are cruised through the water body in colourful boats, while sandalwood paste is applied to their bodies. The boat ride on a decorated float is locally known as "chapa".

This festival can go up to 42 days and large number of devotees/ travellers visit the place.

There are sixteen ghats of the tank. Fourteen are named after the fourteen sons of Narendra Deva, one after the queen Kalandi Devi and one after Narendra Deva, which is the main Ghat. This is also known as Narendra Chakada Ghat, after Narendra Dev, brother of Gajapati king Kapilendra Deva. There are three ghats on the east, three on the north, six on the south and four on the west. The steps of the main Ghat are constructed with Khandolite stones.

Chara Ganesha is worshipped in the nearby temple.

Legend – 1

According to one legend, Narendra Deva, the brother of Gajapati Kapilendra Deva excavated this tank and it was named after him.

It is said that Veer Narendra Deva sacrificed his life for the sake of his motherland. After his death, his wife Kalandi Mahadevi took up sanyas and began to live in a garden. She was a devotee of Lord Shiva and Lord Krishna. Babaji Govinda Das was her Guru. One day the Guru gave a pumpkin seed to the queen. She planted the pumpkin seed in the area. The growth of the plant was so luxurious that it spread out over a large area. Hundreds of pumpkins were produced. These pumpkins were used for preparing the maha prasada at the temple. The news spread far and wide. Gajapati Kapilendra Deva heard about it and visited the garden accompanied by his Guru, Mahadev Brahma. At that time Babaji Govinda Das was engaged in the worship of Lord Gopinath.

Govinda Das blessed the king and requested him to excavate a tank named after late husband of Kalandi Mahadevi (ie. in the name of Veer Narendra Deva). He also requested him to name two ghats after Narendra Deva and his queen Kalandi Devi. Accordingly Gajapati king constructed this tank.

The king also constructed fourteen ghats and named these ghats after the fourteen sons of Narendra Dev. The Chandana bije ghat (Lamba chakada) was constructed for the purpose of conducting" Chandan bije" of Lord Jagannath. This chakada is named after Narendra Deva. He also constructed a temple of Kalandishvara Shiva and Gopinath on the bank of the holy tank. The Brahma jaga, named after the court poet Narahari Brahma, was also established. The famous Chandan yatra of Lord Jagannath is being observed with pomp and ceremony since those days.

Legend-2

There is also another legend which links the creation of the Narendra tank to a pumpkin seed. As per said legend King Narendra Deva of Ranapur was a great devotee of Lord Jagannath. Once he found a pumpkin seed in the courtyard of his palace. He gave the seed to his sarbarakara (Revenue Collector) to plant the seed in the name of Lord Jagannath and to offer all the pumpkins thus produced to the Lord. The sabarakara did as instructed. The pumpkin creeper grew to such an extent that it covered an area of fourteen acres. This creeper produced lakhs of pumpkins. The sabarakara sold the pumpkins and deposited the money to the king.

King Narendra Deva, in turn, offered the money to the Gajapati king of Puri. Subsequently, both the kings decided to construct a tank at Shrikshetra out of this fund. The tank was to cover an area of fourteen acres, the equivalent of the area covered by the pumpkin creeper. Thus the famous Narendra Tank came into existence.

Narendra tank is situated 1.5 kms north-east of Jagannath Temple. It is on the left side of grand road running from Jagannath temple to Gundicha temple and and one can reach it through an approach road from Grand road which passes through Dandimala Sahi.

Parvati Sagar

The Parvati Sagar is a small and rectangular pond. It is attached to the Loknath temple.

It is believed by locals that it is connected to the sea and it's water is holy which cures many diseases.

Lord Lokanath (in the form of a linga) always remains submerged in the water from the natural spring at Parbati sarovar.

The water of the tank is used extensively by devotees visiting the Loknath temple, especially the kawariyas during the month of Shravan.

The main access to the tank is through the temple. The eastern side of the tank has a small bathing ghat. The other 2 sides of the tank are bound by walls, and a peripheral road running around it.

The southern edge of the tank is provided with ghats and lined by small shrines.

Lord Lokanath is the guardian of the treasure house of Jagannath Temple and is known as Bhandar Lokanath.

The tank is situated on the western end of the Puri city and is around 3-kms from Jagannath temple, Puri.

Rohini Kunda

Rohini Kunda is located inside the temple of Lord Jagannath. It is one of the 'Pancha Tirthas' (five holy spots), the other four being Swethaganga, Indradyumna sarovar, Markandey sarovar and Tirtharaj Mahodadhi (Puri sea).

Puranic Connection

As per Skanda Purana, at the time destruction (pralaya / dissolution of the world) water flows from this place and engulfs the entire world. Similarly, at the time of new creation, the excess water is absorbed at this place.

Hence, the water of this Kunda is sacred.

Further, Lord Brahma when visited Srikeshtra had seen, how a crow sitting on the branch of a tree fell down on the water of Rohini Kunda and by virtue of this holy water, it took the form of 4-armed Vishnu.

Swetha Ganga

Swetha Ganga is a small and sacred tank situated towards west of the Jagannath temple, in the Manikarnika Sahi. It is situated between Lion's gate and SWARGADWAR.

According to the epic Mahabharata, Swethaganga was created from the nail of Lord Vishnu. It is believed that there is an internal connection between Sweta Ganga and river Ganga.

The tank also owes its name to the miraculous fact that, its water becomes milky white on the day of Magh Saptami.

On the banks of the tank, there are two small temples, one dedicated to Sweta Madhava and the other to Matsya Madhava, both incarnations of Lord Vishnu.

There are presence of many religious structures in close vicinity of this tank.

Puranic Connection

As per Skanda Purana, Sweta was a king of Treta era and was a devotee of Lord Jagannath. He meditated deeply to see the Lord. As a mark of his worship to Lord Jagannath, the tank is named Sweta Ganga.

It is also believed that after taking bath in the tank and seeing Sweta Madhav, if one dies, he is liberated.

Before visiting Lord Jagannath, the pilgrims bath in the sea and thereafter, they bath at Sweta Ganga and visit Lord Jagannath.

There is also a belief that, the devotees after visiting Sri Mandir, if they wash their feet in Sweta Ganga, they will be free from the sin of treading on the Mahaprasad.

Similar to the Ganga River, the Swetganga tank is also used for the immersion of remains and ashes of the dead and taking bath etc. after cremation.

The Gangamata matha is adjacent to southern periphery of the tank. There is a garden on the south edge of the tank. Here, Mogra and Tulsi are cultivated and are supplied to the Shri Jagannath Temple for the performance of rituals.

The tank is owned by the Shree Jagannath Temple Trust and is maintained by the Puri Municipality. Adjacent, Neel Madhab Binayak Samiti (also known as Ganesh Club) has taken the initiative for the maintenance of the tank and its edges. The tank has also got "Prakriti Mitra" award in the past.

All these heritage tanks which are important from the religious angle and for water management of the city require conservation. Various activities like bathing, washing, other house hold activities and drainage of water from the households which causes pollution should be stopped.

These water bodies which are of great cultural significance requires development through repairs, additions and facility improvements.

Through interpretative material or informative signage, there should be awareness campaign about their immense heritage significance.

MATHAS, ASHRAMS, AKHADAS AND JAGA GHARAS

The MATHAS, Akhadas and Jagaghars of Puri are of great heritage value and are continuing for generations. They are either directly or indirectly associated with serving the Lord. These institutions form the core of Jagannath culture and one may visit these places to know the Jagannath culture.

Mathas

As reported in the Puri Gazetter (1929) the "Mathas are monastic houses originally founded with the object of giving religious instructions to chelas or disciples and generally for encouraging a religious life." The heads of the Mathas are called Mahantas / Mathadharis / Mathadhisas.

In the past the sadhus / saints established these monasteries with the purpose of imparting education to chelas or disciples and feeding travellers, ascetics and beggars.

They were established on lands donated by the king and other wealthy people so as to provide ritual services in Shri Jagannatha temple.

Lands were also donated to the Mathas for 'Amritmanohi'-the proceeds thereof were spent in offering 'Bhoga' to Lord Jagannatha and the 'Mahaprasad' thus obtained, were distributed among the pilgrims, pupils, ascetics and all others.

There were large number of Mathas which are clustered around the temple. As the rituals of the temple and Ratha Yatra became more elaborate, more people started living in Puri.

The Matha complexes were / are having interconnected open courtyards as well as extensive area of garden and plantation. They were close proximity to Lord Jagannath temple complex.

Initially there were around 300 mathas in the city. As understood, there are close to 78 Mathas at present. This list has been derived based on the listing of Mathas prepared by INTACH, IGNCA and list of Mathas that received support for conservation under the 12th Finance Commiission.

Although these Mathas are spread in different parts of the city, however they are primarily located on important streets.They were situated mostly in the vicinity of the temple and few in the peripheries.

Out of the identified list of 78 Mathas only two Mathas are designated as protected monuments by Odisha State Archaeology which are Sidha Bakula Matha and Radha Kanta Matha.

Many of the Mathas are classified / are found on the basis of sects and sub-sects as under:

SAPTA MATRUKA Matha (Buddhism), GOBARDHAN Matha, Sivatirtha Matha, Gopal TIRTHA Matha, Mahiprakash Math (Saivisim), Markandeya Ashram, Languli Matha, Gangamata Matha, Ardhasini Matha (Shakti cult), Emar Math, Dakshina PARSWA Math, Uttar PARSWA Math, Trimali Math, Torani CHATA Math, Kaushalya das Math, Rebasa Math (Ramanuj sect of Vishnu cult), Bagha Akhada Math, Khaki Akhada Math, Nirbani Akhada Math, Nirmohi Akhada Math, Bada Akhada Matha, Sana Akhada Math (Ramananda sect of Vishnu cult), Radha Ballav Math (Nimbarka Math), Jagannath Ballav Math (Vishnu Swami cult), Salabeg Matha, Kabirchaura Math (Islam) and Mangu Matha and Baguli Matha (Sikhisim) etc.

Some Mathas have their kitchen in Jagannath temple. The Mathas related to Adi Shankaracharya, Ganapati Bhatta, Sridhar Swami, Ramanuj, Chaitanya Mahaprabhu and Vishnu Swami are associated with the rituals of Jagannath Temple.

There are consortium of 18-gaudiya organisations in Puri, which is known as Saraswat Gaudiya Vaishnava Sangha. There are also many Gaudiya Mathas in Puri, like – Sree Chaitanya Gaudiya Math, Sri Nilachal Gaudiya Math, Nitai Gaudiya Math, Sri Gopinath Gaudiya Math, Sree Madhav Goswami Gaudiya Math, Sri Saraswat Gaudiya Math, Purusottama audiya Math and Jaya Sri Damodar Gaudiya Matha etc.

Operation and maintenance of the building complex of some of these Mathas are undertaken by the sects associated with the Mathas. Some Mathas get support from Endowment Department of the Government of Odisha.

GOVARDHAN PITHA / GOVARDHAN MATHA

Puri is considered as one of the 4 pilgrimages that constitute the Chaar Dhaam quadrangle with Badrinath, Dwarka and Rameshwaram.

Shankaracharya had established 4 Mathas (chardham) to unite the different groups of sanyasis and also the people living in different parts of the country. The Govardhana Matha shares this honour with the Shringeri Matha in Shringeri, the Charade Matha in Dwaraka and Jyotir Matha in Badrinath. Govardhan Matha is one of the four cardinal institutions.

This monastery was founded by great Adi Sankaracharya who is believed as an incarnation of Lord Shiva. It was built more than 1000 (one thousand) years ago in the 9th century. The Govardhan Matha is commonly known as the Bhogo Vardhan Matha.

The person who is in charge of this Matha is given the title of Sankaracharya. This Matha is of special importance to the pilgrims who visit Puri.

Shankaracharya is the head of Mukti Mandap. He is also consulted by the authorities in all kinds of religious affairs and he is given certain privileges in the Jagannath temple at the time of his visit.

The Math provides Panti Bhoga service at the "22-pahacha / 22-Steps" on Ratha Yatra day.

As per Record of Rights, the Math performs number activities in temple rituals and the khei which is granted to this Math as a daily routine is unique and is rarely enjoyed by other Mathas of Puri.

Jagannath Ballav Matha

The Jagannath Ballav Matha is on the opposite side of the well known landmark of Municipal Market. It covers an area of 44-acres and is in the heart of city.

This is the pleasure garden of Lord Jagannath. It is said that Vishnuswami had established this Matha.

The representative images of the lords visit this Math on different festive occasions, like – Basanta Panchami, on the 1st, 4th, 5th and 12th days on the bright fortnight of Falguna (ie. during Holi).

This math supplies flower ornaments like – Tilak and Jhumpa for Badasinghara Besha and supplies "Kora"(ie. sweet food) for "Kaliya dalana" and "Pralambasura badha" Beshas. Dayana Chori, an important festival of the Lord is performed in this Math. During this period, the representative image of Lord Jagannath (Bije Pratima) visits this Math to steal Dayana leaves.

During Suna Besha of the Lord, the Matha provides Chula which is made of Tulshi, scented flowers and bamboo.

During Benta Parva, Lord DOLA Govinda visits the Math. In this occasion cocoanuts are assumed as deer and the Lenka shoots arrow on it as a representative of the Lord. During Heera Panchami and on some other occasions the Matha offers Panti BHOG.

As per Record of Rights, the Matha has to supply the Mashal (torch) during Abakasha rituals, Ballava BHOG and Khuamanda, Tilak, jhumpa (one type of flower ornaments) for Badasinghar Besha, Khatani BHOG (Arnna Mahaprasad) and to perform chamara services.

As understood, this monastery was established to pay homage to the famous personality of Ray Ramananda, who was one of the most renowned saints of the state in the 16th Century. This was the seat of Ray Ramananda. Chaitanya Mahaprabhu was taking rest in this Matha during Rath Yatra, when he was feeling tired after performing kirtan in front of the Rath.

Jatia Baba Matha

This is one of the preserved MATHAS of Puri near Narendra Pond. This Matha supplies the silken rope (Pattadori) for the Chandan Yatra.

Emar Math

It was established by Saint Ramanuj and is one of the biggest MATHAS. It is situated near southern gate of Jagannath Temple.

Chandrika and Chausar made of flowers (ie. flower ornaments) for Bada Singhar Besha of the Lord is supplied by this Matha. It offers / supplies "Pan Bhog" during Chandan Yatra, "Chakata Bhog" during Anasara period and "Bala Bhog" during Kartik month.

This Matha provides Tahia on Snana Purnima, Ratha Yatra, Bahuda and Niladri Bije days. It supplies part of Hathi Besha, Tuli for Pahandi and certain amount of sandlewood for Sarbanga Neeti on "Khalilagi EKADASHI", flower garlands for Nabanka Bedha and offers to "Adhar pana Bhog" and "Panti Bhog" on certain festive days. It also performs Upachar chamara and Allata services.

In the year 2011 AD, around 522 silver ingots of around hundred crore rupees were recovered form a walled up room. Recently another set of silver ingots were also found from the Matha.

Odiya Matha

This was set up by Atibadi Jagannath Das, a great poet and Saint of the state in early part of 16th century. *It supplies* "Trimundi chandua" and silk clothes for "Chaka Apasara", repairs "Kanaka mundi", supplies Til oil for "Phuluri Neeti", Oil and ghee etc. for "Deva Deepavali", "Chakata Bhoga" on Anasar, "Adharpana Bhog" and "Panti Bhog" on certain days. The Mahanta makes marjana of Ratnavedi on "Niladri Bije Day".

This Matha makes arrangement for the Pankti Bhog in the Jagmohan during Rukminiharan festival and supplies Black saree to Goddess Vimala. It also clears the Ratnavedi and supplies canopy and pillows for the Lord.

Bada Chata Matha

It is situated in front of the lion's gate of the temple. This Matha performs "kirtan" at the time of "Mangala Arati", "Pahuda Arati" and "Bala Dhupa". This Matha does the "Padma Besha" of the Lord and "Kshiri Bhog" is offered. However, the Matha was dismantled for security reasons. Only a small structure stands.

Mangu Matha

This is located on the side of EMAR Matha. It is associated with the memory of Guru Nanak. In the past, this math was suppling a Ram for sacrifice before the Goddess Vimala, each year on Maha Nabami night. This practice is stopped.

Baaul Math

This math is also associated with Guru Nanak. It is treated as a Gurudwara by the Sikhs. The Grantha Saheb is kept here and prayers offered to Guru Nanak.

It is said that Guru Nanak had rested at this place for some time, during his visit to Puri and had dug a well which is known as

Dedhasura Bhai Bohu kua. Devotees also visit this well and pray Guru Nanak.

Radhakanta Matha

Chaitanya Mahaprabhu visited Puri in 1510 AD and stayed in this Matha. Some of his personal belongings are preserved here. The Mahantas of this Matha are entitled to perform "Upachara Chamara Seva". Presently these are not done.

Chaulia Matha And Delhi Nablak Ram Das Matha

These two Mathas are near Gundicha temple which are under Jagannath temple managing committee.

Sata Lahadi Matha

This is situated in SWARGADWAR area. It was the burial place of Atibadi Jagannath Das. This Matha is being managed by a committee under the Chairmanship of Collector, Puri.

Kabir Chaura Matha

This Matha is in SWARGADWAR area. It is associated with Kabir sect. It is said that Kabir,. the mystic poet stayed here, during his visit to Puri.

Samadhi Matha

Saint Madhav Das used to stay here. He was away from the public and used to sit under an umbrella near the Swetaganga pond and meditate in the midst of Tulsi plants (Basil plants) staring at Nilachakra. The place was known as Uansadanda, from where Tulsi leaves were supplied for daily rituals of Lord Jagannath.

Earlier, he was visiting the temple daily. Subsequently he found that there is no difference between the Patitapabana flag and the Lord. He stopped going to the temple and started meditating at Uansadanda.

One day he never woke up after meditation. Days passed in the meantime. However, to everyone's surprise, he woke up one day.

As people came to know about his awakening, they rushed to the spot to have a glimpse of the Saint. He attained enlightenment by meditating and looking towards Nilachakra (ie. flag of the Jagannath temple).

Gajapati king with his commanders had gone to meet him. Madhav Das told them that the description contained in the Skanda Purana about origin of all incarnations from Lord Jagannath is true and Darubrahma is parambrahma.

His meditating place was given to the Saint and the servitors of Jagannath temple were instructed to serve Mahaprasad to him.

This was known as Samadhi Matha and Mahaprasad served in earthen pots was known as "Samadhi Handis".

Mata Matha (Shri Gour Bihar Ashram)

This is also known as Gupta Vrindavan of Puri. This is named after Gouranga Saint. As per the book "Chaitanya Charitamruta", it was the staying and meditation place of Chaitanya Mahaprabhu. His disciple Ram Dasi was also performing meditation and bhajan at this place. This is a beautiful place and famous for many statues of Gods/ Goddess like – Shree Jagannath, Laxmi, Radha-Krishna, Chaitanya Mahaprabhu and Lord Shiv etc. It is around 4-kms from SWARGADWAR.

Ramakrishna Matha

It is located at the sea shore near Chakratirtha. This property was donated by Sri Ramakrishna Basu, a devotee of Ramakrishna Paramhansha in 1916 AD. The Matha was started in 1932 AD. It is understood, the land and building was sanctified in the presence of Holy mother Sarada Devi and some other disciples of Ramakrishna.

There were some Mathas, who were connected with the rituals of the Jagannath temple, like – Chaitanya Gaudiya Matha, Purusottama Goudiya Matha and Punjabi Math etc.

Gopaltirtha Matha supplies a part of 'Hati besha' on the Snana Purnima day and ' makara chaula' on the Snana Purnima and Makara sankranti days and offers panti bhog at the temple of Lord Jagannath.

The Suna Goswami Matha is one of the most popular attractions for the visitors to the city. A couple of festivals associated with the religion of Hinduism are celebrated at the Suna Goswami Matha of Puri. Some of the most important festivals that are celebrated at this matha are the Banaklagi, the Chandan Yatra, the Agni Utsava and the Snana Purnima. The Mahanta who serves in this well known Matha of Puri is also the Mahanta for another renowned matha of the region; which is called the Darpa Narayana Matha. Record of Rights under Shri Jagannath temple (Administration) Act of 1952 enshrines in details about the rituals / Nitis to be performed by certain Maths, like – Odiya Math (supply of daily Ballav Bhoga, performance of upacha chamar and Alata services), Badachata Matha (daily recital of devotional songs with music during Mangala Arati and Badasinghar Pahuda rituals), Papudia Matha (to perform Sunabenta Chamar and Allata services), Chaulia Matha (Chamara seva),

Raghaba Das Matha (Chamara and Allata services, to supply Ballava and Khatani BHOG), Gangamata Matha (Sunabenta Chamar and Allata services), Radhakant Matha (daily sankirtan parikrama inside temple premises and upachara chamar services), Rebasa Matha (khatani BHOG and upachara chamara services), Radhaballav Matha (Upachar chamara and Allata services), Trimali Matha (chamara and Allata services, supply of dihudi(torch) at the time of ABAKASH and Gopal Ballav BHOG), Ramaji Matha and Mangu Matha (chamara service), Sanachata Matha and Balaramkot Matha, Chhauni Matha, Nua Matha and Venkatachari Matha(Chamar and Allata service), Jhanjapita Matha (Seba puja of Pada Padma),

Sriram Das Matha (Chamar and Allata services and supply of flower ornaments) and Rajguru Goswami Matha (chamara service during Abakash and Dhupa puja period) etc.

Some of the Mathas have the right to offer pankti and Khatani Bhog (cooked food offering) to the deities and there are 86-ovens in the Jagannath temple kitchen, allotted to several Mathas.

As understood from the temple priests, some of these Mathas have stopped performing the rituals and those who perform are doing this in a limited scale to continue the tradition.

Archeological Remains Of The Mathas

The Mathas in Puri are store house of archeological remains in the form of images and decorative motifs. These are found in these Maths and the temples, present inside them.

There are many mural paintings, deified images of saints built in stone, metal and wood etc. In some cases historical legends are also associated with these images. These requires proper documentation and study, before they fade away.

Further with the discovery of silver ingots from the Emaar Math, it appears there may be buried treasures in some Mathas which requires detailed Survey.

As per Anil kumar Dhir of INTACH, during great Odisha famine of 1866 AD, bullion was part of the payment made by the Britishers to various Mathas to purchase rice during famine years.

High scroll Warks and sculptural representations in Venkatachari Matha, the images of Goddess Laxmi and Saraswati in majestic artistic look in the doorways, Ornamental work at the temple door of Gangamata Matha,

Many stone images of Hanuman in various Mathas (ie. entrance of Ganga Mata Matha, three such images in Odiya Matha, one Hanuman in Kavir Chaura Matha etc) and many images are found in the Mathas. These were gifted / placed by the pilgrims who had found them in their native places.

A Vishnu image was placed in the Ramanuj Math by one Maharaja named Samarendra who found the image in Baghawada (Tripura).

Each Matha has their presiding deities belonging to various cults. The Nrushingh image of Pandu Ashram is 8-armed and is of rare design. Various parts of the body of Hiranya Kashyup and the weapons of Vishnu are found in different hands. The image of Ugrasen in Bhrigu Ashram is a rare image. The four armed Gopaldev image in Jagannath Ballava Matha is an image of Krishna-Vishnu.

Many images related to Jagannath cult, other deities and of preceptors and Saints made of wood are found in various Mathas.

One will find wooden images of Jagannath cult, either as Patita Pavana or Trimurti or Chaturdha Murti.

The wooden motifs are found in the doors and windows of these monasteries. The artistic representation of Navagunjar, ornamental art work and many geometric diagrams are found in nicely carved windows.

The Vidur Matha is unique, where the image of Vidur is worshipped in the monastery as the presiding deity besides one set of Trimurti and Chaturdha Murti of Lord Jagannath. After the metal image was stolen, the new image of Bhubaneswari, the presiding deity of Gopal TIRTHA Matha is worshipped.

Burial Temple (Gurvayatana)

These shrines were constructed in the memory of the departed gurus of some particular sects. These were found within the complex of Mathas.

Presently due to urbanisation and selling of the Matha land, these burial temples have been disconnected from the Matha precinct and can be found scattered in the sahis or along street edges. In the absence of information in the form of signages, it is difficult to recognise their significance. At many places and around these temples, garbages are thrown around them which implies lack of awareness amongst people.

Presently, under the recent road widening scheme around Shri Jagannatha Temple, some of the architecturally significant and historic Mathas like – Uttar Parsva Matha, Dakshin Parsva Matha and Emar Matha were impacted. Proper documentation and preservation of artefacts are required for posterity.

ASHRAMAS

There are many Ashramas in Puri. Four Ashramas, ie. Angira Ashram, Kandu Ashram, Markendaya Ashram and Bhrigu Ashram, in the name of 4-ancient sages are important which are connected with certain rituals of Lord Jagannath.

These Ashramas are believed to be as old as Puri and they are situated in 4-directions.

Angira Ashrama which is named after Sage Angira is at Dolamandap Sahi and in the eastern side of Jagannath Temple.

The Bhrigu Ashram which is named in the name of sage Bhrigu is at Bali sahi and in the south side of Jagannath Temple.

Kandu Ashram which is named in the name of Sage Kandu is in the south-west side of the temple and is in HARACHANDI sahi.

Markandeya Ashram which is named after Sage Markandeya is situated at Markandeswar sahi in the north-west side of the temple.

The sages Angira and Bhrigu related to Vedic period. The sages Kandu and Markandeya belong to PURANIC period.

Tradition assigns some Mathas/ Ashrams like the Vrugu Ashram and the Angira Ashram even to an earlier date.

On the ninth day of the bright fortnight of Shravan, the Nrushingh deity of Lord Jagannath temple visits these 4-ashramas in a ceremonial manner and this is known as "Badi Nrushingh Bije".

"Sital Bhog" is offered to the deity in each Ashram. On the full moon day of Margashir, Nrushingh again visits to all these Ashrama.

Lord Sudarshan visits to all these Ashrams except Kandu Ashram on the full moon day of Shravan (Gamha Purnima) and on kumar Purnima (ie. full moon day of Ashwin). Sudarshan visits Kandu Ashram on the day of Radhastami.

Goddess Mahalaxmi visits Kandu Ashram on the 5th day of the dark fortnight of Bhadraba to observe Rishi Panchami Brata.

The construction period of these 4-ashramas are not known and it is believed that these are as old as Vedic and PURANIC period. There are some important Ashramas like – Maa Anandamayi Ashram (near SWARGADWAR road), Abhiram Paramhansha Ashram (Marichikote lane), Bhagabata Ashram (near Bus stand), Haridas Ashram (Sarbodaya Nagar), Pranabananda Ashram (near CHAKRATIRTHA), Neelachala Ashram (SWARGADWAR area), Bharat Sevashrama (SWARGADWAR area), Satsangha Ashram (near CHAKRATIRTHA road) and Nigamananda Ashram (lokanath road).

Goshalas

The listing provided by INTACH has identified one goshala which is located in Markandeshwar sahi. Historically, this goshala rendered services to the disabled cows.

Bada Danda / Grand Road

Bada Danda is a very wide road and is the main road of the town. This wide road used for the journey of the Lords during the famous Car Festival.

It extends from the Gundicha temple to the eastern gate (Simhadwara) of Jagannath temple, the exact distance being 2688.0696 meters (8,326 ft.).

This wide road spreads out somewhat in the shape of a fan through various SAHIS with Badadanda as its handle.

King's palace is on the Bada Danda and it has only a few residential quarters /Government offices/ public buildings. It is crowded mostly by shops, lodging houses, Dharmasalas and Mathas.

Seven Important Streets (Other Heritage Streets) / Linked to Sahis Of Puri

Besides Bada Danda (Grand road) there are seven important streets/linked to SAHIS in Puri where most of the temples and Mathas are found. These streets represent the respective SAHIS. They are: –

Harachandi Street/ Harachandi Sahi –

This street is famous for KAPAL MOCHAN temple, Basuli Devi and some Mathas like – Odiya Matha, Naga Matha, Maha Prakash Matha and Surangi Matha etc.

Bali Street / Bali Sahi

This street is famous for – Sweta Madhav, Sweta Ganga, Sidha BAKULA, ASTA Sambhu, Barahi, old palace of Gajapati king, Puri, Bata Lokanath, Shyama Kali and Mathas like – Siva TIRTHA Matha, Kabir Chaura, Vidur Ashram, Venkatachari Matha, Radhakanta Matha, Gangamata Matha, Jhadu Matha, Bhrigu Ashram and Veda Vidyalaya etc.

Gauda Bada Street / Gauda Bada Sahi

Major shrines found in this street are – YAMESWAR temple, Tota Gopinath and Mathas like – Hari Das Samadhi Matha, Suna Goswami Matha, Sata Lahari Matha and Purusottama Matha etc.

Kalika Devi Street / Kalika Devi Sahi

Main temples on this street are – Maha Kaleswar, DAKSHIN kali, Gacha kali and Mathas like – Emaar Matha, Mangu Matha and Avadhuta Matha etc.

Dola Mandap Street / Dola Mandap Sahi

This is important for – Jhanjapita Matha, Siddha Matha, Angira Ashram and Radha Ballav Matha etc..

Markandeya Street / Markandeya Sahi

This is famous for – Markandeswar Mahadev temple, Bada CHATA and Sana CHATA Matha, Papudia Matha, Languli Matha, Ramjee Matha and Trimali Matha etc.

Kundhaibenta Street / Kundhaibenta Sahi

The main shrines in this street are – Neelkanth temple, Ramachandi temple, Maushima temple, Hatajodi THAKURANI, Jhadeswari, Sunara Gauranga and Mathas like – Bharati Matha, Rajaguru Matha, Chaulia Matha, Balagandi Matha, Mahabir Matha, Jagannath Matha, Dasabatar Matha etc..

Sahis

During earlier times, the population of the town were mostly the priests and people attached to various activities of the temples in the city. These town colonies are called SAHIS and these are situated in different streets around the Grand road (Bada Danda).

These are, ie: Harachandi Sahi (with Baseli Sahi) on the west, Goudabada Sahi on the south-west, Bali Sahi on the south, Matimandapa Sahi with Kalikadevi Sahi on the south-east, Dolomandapa Sahi and Mochi Sahi on the east, Kundhei-benta Sahi, Hara – Gouri Sahi on the north-east and Markandeswar Sahi and Chudanga Sahi on the north. These sahis are crowded with houses. These are clustered thickly around Jagannath/ other Temples. The Mathas belonging to different sects of Hinduism with vast estates are also found in these Sahis / nearby to these Sahis.

AKHADAS AND JAGA GHARAS

Puri was initially divided in to seven SAHIS and each sahi had one Akhada and many jagagharas. These are the traditional social infrastructure located in each sahi, where the youth learn martial arts and dance forms like Odissi or Gotipua etc.

It is believed by many that these institutions were created during 11th century under the patronage of king Chodogandadeva to safeguard the city and Jagannath Temple from invaders as the outer wall i.e. Meghanada Prachir, to protect the temple was not built during that period.

To safeguard the temple, there were certain clubs or Jagas near entrances and at some strategic points were established in the city. They got the patronage form the kings and a jaga culture was developed.

Akhadas are the apex institutions in each sahi, which are supported by several subsidiary jagagharas. There are total 8 akhadas and 62 jagagharas in Puri. The akhadas were traditionally headed by a sahinayak, the chief administrator of akhada who worked under the guidance of Naiksardars (appointed by the Gajapati Maharaj of Puri).

Traditionally, akhadas were the centres, where various social issues related to law and order, bilateral issues were resolved and literary and cultural aspects of sahis were promoted.

Similarly jagagharas were the centre for promoting martial arts, wrestling, Odissi and Gotipua dance. The akhadas were serviced by men and skill provided by the jagagharas.

Each jagaghara comprised a temple, khela jaga i.e. wrestling arena, pond and various trees such as coconut, mangoes etc. In the temple, Lord Mahavir (Hanuman) is generally worshipped who is the symbol of physical strength and celibacy. The tank is used as a bathing place.

Traditional equipments such as wood of different sizes like Mudgara, a bed for wrestling known as Phulka, a tank and an open space and some musical instruments like Mardala are found in Jagagharas. These traditional equipment are in the process of being replaced with the modern gym equipment in the recent times.

The jagas were having their own flower garden and orchards etc. and they manage their affairs from the income derived from these sources.

Members of the Jagas are called Sangas (friends). They take part in the Ratha Yatra and Chandan Yatra of Lord Jagannatha, while displaying various forms of martial arts, acrobatics with knives, swords and fireballs etc. for the entertainment of deities and general public.

During Chandan Yatra they perform during entire period of Bahara Chandana yatra i.e. for 21 days.

During Ramanavami, they enact folk dramas in Sahi Yatra (street plays) where the procession starts from the Jagagharas to the competitor sahi or badisahi. For example: Balisahi is the badisahi of Harchandi sahi. At present these are the centre for training for wrestlers at local level as well as district level. District level competitions are also held at these jagahgaras.

Although most of the jaga gharas and Akhadas have lost their importance, some of them, like – Barabati, Tapanga, Gandamala, Khuntia, Hinjala, Gadajaga, luhagada, Champagada, kadambagada, Bajragada, Jadu Tiadi, Nagakota, Khakikota, Mali, Brahma, Gopali, Sundara, Satabakhara, Panda, Jamai Khuntia, Sankha Kota and Nrushingh Ballav are still existing.

Due to development in the technique of modern warfare and development of modern musical system, instruments and patterns etc., the jaga and Akhada culture are almost declined.

However, both Public and Government should come forward to upkeep and revive this ancient and traditional jaga and Akhada culture.

RAGHU NANDAN LIBRARY

The Raghunandan Library, was established in 1921 AD. It is one of the oldest libraries of the State. It is located in front of the Simhadwara and is maintained by the Emar Matha.

One will find many old copper-plate inscriptions and rare palm-leaf manuscripts. Some of these are carved with fine writings and intricate drawings. From the terrace of the 4th floors of the library, one can have a good view of the temple and the town.

Yoga Ashram And Veda Bhawan

At Puri there is a Yoga institute called -Karar (ie. for Kriya Yoga teaching) Ashram near Swargadwara, and a Veda Bhawan where discourses on the Vedas are conducted.

Similarly Harihareananda Gurukulam, near Balighai with magnificent Guru Mandir, beautiful gardens, forests and large number of cows is a nice place for meditation. It is a major international centre for Kriya Yoga.

This living tradition continues and is extremely important as part of India's rich religious cultural traditions.

Hundi In Shree Mandir

The HUNDI is installed at the Nata Mandap of the temple. The amount received is deposited in a Bank. The collection of donation is also circulated in various newspapers. This is installed for a noble purpose. The funds are utilised mostly for welfare of the servitors, day to day management of the temple and celebration of different festivals and performance of rituals.

Ratna Bhandar

The treasury of the Temple is known as the Ratna Bhandar. It has been enriched by the devotees of all over the country and by donation of the past kings. According to the rules and practices of the Temple, whatever jewels, gold or silk etc. are offered to the deities by the pilgrims are to be stored in Ratna Bhandar.

As understood, it consists of 7- rooms and 3- rooms are used for various ritual of the deities. The ornaments/ jewelleries and other valuables which are used in Suna Besha are stored in these 3- rooms.

The precious ornaments and jewlaries are stored in other rooms. There are various views about these ornaments and valuables.

As per Madalapanji, King Anangabhima Deva, in addition to his numerous grants of land, had donated 2, 50,000 mahanas (one Mahan is equivalent to 40-kgs) gold for preparing the ornaments of Lords.

Similarly, the Suryavanshi kings who were great devotees of Lord had enriched the Ratna Bhandar with their liberal gifts of gold and other jewels.

In the walls of Jagannath Temple, there is inscription about donation of utensils and ornaments etc. on his 41st Anka (ie. in 1466 A.D.) by Gajapati king Kapilendra Deva.

As per Odisha Gazetteer, "The fabulous riches of the Temple of Jagannath had induced the Muslim invaders to raid and plunder the Temple from time to time, the worst being that of Kalapahad in 1668. During the time of Raja Purusottam Deva of Khurda, even a Rajput General named Kesodas Maru was induced by the Mugul Subedar of Cuttack to plunder the Temple of Jagannath. On the pretext of coming on a pilgrimage to Jagannath Puri during the car festival, Kesodas occupied the sacred temple by force and looted it and stopped the daily puja, ceremonies, etc., of Lord jagannath. Raja Purushottama Dev came with a mighty force to rescue the temple from the hands of Kesodas but was defeated.

In spite of several raids and plunder, the Ratna Bhandar of Jagannath still remains a valuable asset of the temple. In 1893 AD, Manmohan Chakravarti had noted that many of the ornaments given to the God in 1466 A.D. were still in use.

A detailed list of the valuable jewels of Lord Jagannath which includes gold ornaments, pearls, diamonds, coral, etc. are found in the Record-Of- Rights (Part-IV) prepared under Puri Shree jagannath Temple Act, 1952.

There are 150 items of gold ornaments in Bahar Bhandar (outer treasury) which includes three gold necklaces (Haridakanthi Mali) weighing 818 and 710 tolas respectively ; and various other gold ornaments some of which are set with precious stones. The Bhitar Bhandar (inner treasury) has 180 items of jewellery which include 74 items of pure gold ornaments some of which weigh more than 100 tolas, plates of gold, pearls, diamonds, coral, etc., and 146 items of silver articles, some weighing more than 500 tolas each.

The Raja of Puri who was the Superintendent of the temple was in charge of the Bahar Bhandar with three locks and Bhitar Bhandar with double locks. One key was remaining with the Raja, one with the Bhandar Nayak and the third key of the Bahar Bhandar with the Bhandar Mekap. In accordance with the provisions of Sri Jagannath Temple Act, 1954 (section 15) safe custody of the Ratna Bhandar is now vested with the Sri Jagannath Temple Managing Committee".

As per news reports (Indian express dated – 26/4/2018) the Ratna Bhandar had 120-kilograms of Gold and 221-kilograms of silver 40-years back. However, there is no information about the value of the items in the store house.

As understood, earlier the Ratna Bhandar was opened in 1978 AD. There is a belief that opening of the mysterious Ratna Bhandar is vice, although there is not any scientific evidence about the same.

However, as per various reports both the outer and inner Bhandar are in a perilous state with several cracks in the walls and it requires urgent attention.

Important Festivals Of Puri Town

Besides the main festivals in the Jagannath temple as described above, some other important festivals/ Yatras / Upayatras of the town are as under:

Sahi Yatra

This is a fortnight-long festival which begins on Ram Navami day and it celebrates the birth of Lord Rama. It is one of the oldest and popular festivals of Puri and is believed to have begun in 1230 AD.

During this Yatra which is a street play, traditional weapons of Jagagharas are taken out to the street in grand procession and the wrestlers get an opportunity to display their strength and skill.

The procession starts from the narrow lane of each Sahi and finally comes to the Grand road of Puri. The procession is accompanied by decorated elephants, horses, flag bearers, flame torches and music bands playing drums, trumpets and conch shells.

Main Sahis like -Harachandi Sahi, Baseli Sahi, Markandeswara Sahi, Dolomandapa Sahi, Matimandapa Sahi, Bali Sahi and Gaudabada Sahi are responsible to carry out the grand event.

Each sahi is having its own flag and each sahi is assigned a different event to play, like- birth of Lord Rama, killing of demon by goddess Durga, Ravana lifting Kailash Mountain, capture of Sita by Ravana, battle between Parasuram and Lord Rama, war between Rama and Ravana etc. The actors of each sahi wear huge and elaborate masks of ten headed Ravana, five faced Ganesh, Nursingha and of various deities and demons.

The Naga decoration during the Yatra is unique and is indigenous to Puri and not seen anywhere. Although the theme of the Yatra is religious, it is also partly martial.

Pankodhar Ekadashi

This is celebrated in the month of Phalgun (ie. February-march). The moving image of Lord Lokenath who is the treasurer of Shri Jagannath Temple (ie. Bhandar Lokanath) is brought to the Lokanath temple in a procession and is worshipped. This is celebrated with festivities at this temple.The inner sanctum of Lokanath temple is cleaned during this period.

Maha Shivratri

This is celebrated on the 14th day of the dark fortnight of Phalgun month (February-march) in various Shiv temples of the city. However, the Shivratri festival at Lokanath temple is very famous.

This Shivling which is believed to be established by Lord Ram and remains under water through out the year is cleaned and the water is pumped out before the festival.

The devotees worship Lord Shiv after taking bath in the adjacent holy tank, known as Parvati Sagar. The water of this tank is believed to cure various diseases.

Amavashya Yatra

This is celebrated every month during new moon day. The moving image of Lord Jagannath, in his Narayan Utsav image visits SWARGADWAR.

As believed, SWARGADWAR is the gateway to heaven for mortals after their cremation. Also through this path, the Gods and Goddesses descend upon the earth to pay their respects to Lord Jagannath. To welcome them the representative image of Lord Jagannath is taken in a procession to SWARGADWAR on each new moon day.

During his onward journey, the Narayan image stops briefly at the Ugrasena Ashram in the Bali Sahi, so that the Lord can bestow darshana to one of his most devoted followers of all times, Ugrasena Muni. Similarly, during return journey, the procession comes via the Hara Chandi Sahi after blessing the servitors of the temple residing in the area.

Sudarshan Yatra

One of the murtis of existence of the Lord is the Sudarshan Murti, charged with protection and inspection of the entire city and its accounts. In order to scrutinise the various parts of the city, the Sudarshan Murti is taken regularly on procession via Dolmandap Sahi, Markandeshwar Tank, Bali Sahi and Jambeshwar Mahadeva.

Krushna Janmashtami

This is celebrated on the 8th day of the dark fortnight of Bhadraba Month (August-September). Madanmohan, the representative deity of Lord Jagannath is worshipped as Srikrishna. Madanmohan, Rama and Krishna are placed in the swing.

Various other festivals like – Nandostav, Banavhoji Besha, KALIYA DALAN Besha, Pralambasura Badha Besha, Krishna Balaram Besha, Vastraharan, Dabangi Lila and Nikunj Lila etc follows on subsequent days. Krishna Janmashtami is also celebrated in different Mathas.

Durga Puja /Dussahara/ Gosani Yatra

During this festival, unique clay images of the Goddess are worshipped at many places of the city with grand traditional decorations. On immersion day, they are taken out in colourful procession through various streets of the city. The images are lined before the Lions gate of Lord Jagannath temple on their way to the sea.

This is one of the most important celebrations in Puri, which is also known as 'Gosani Yatra'.

Kumar Purnima /Rasa Purnima

Kumar Purnima is dedicated to unmarried girls, who wear new clothes. In the evening the girls offer "Chanda Chakata"(ie. a sweetmeat made of cheese, Lia / Khai) besisdes flowers to the moon. The unmarried women also keep fast for getting suitable grooms.

This is observed on the full moon day of Ashwin Month and signifies arrival of winter.

Gambling on this day is considered as auspicious and locals indulge in this practice till late night. Kauri khela (dice game) a form of gambling is performed in Jagannath temple beteween Lord Jagannath and his consort Mahalaxmi.

Kartika Purnima And Panchkua

This is celebrated in the holy Month of Kartik (ie. October-November). It is the favourite Month of Lord Jagannath. It is believed that during this Month Lord Shiv and Lord Vishnu visit the earth. The devotees who undertake this Brata are known as "Habisiali".

They take predawn bath at sea and visit Lord Jagannath temple in early morning during the period of Mangal Arati. They take food only once either "Maha prasad" or prepare their own "Habisha" food with allowed vegetables and pulses. Those who can't come to Puri, they worship holy Tulshi tree (Basil plant) treating it as the image of Lord Jagannath.

The last 5-days of Kartik Month are known as "Panchuka" and are considered as highly auspicious. Large number of devotees including widows visit Puri during this period.

The Jagannath temple administration also reschedules the daily rituals of Lord Jagannath to facilitate the "Habisialis" to have darshan of the Lord.

On the Kartik Purnima day (ie. full moon day of Kartik Month) Lord is worshipped with special pujas / rituals. This is the most important day of the Month. Lord Jagannath, Balabhadra and

Subhadra are adorned with gold ornaments and flowers (ie. known as – Raja Rajeshwari Besha). Devotees take bath in the sea and offer prayers to Lord Jagannath and in other temples of Puri.

Prathamastami

This is celebrated on the 8th day of the dark fortnight of Margashir (November – December) This day is celebrated for the long life and happiness of the first born child of the family.

Jhulan Yatra

This festival is celebrated for 7-days from the 10th day of the bright fortnight in the month of Shravan (August-September) and full moon day marks the end of the festival.

Madanmohan (representative image of Lord Jagannath), Goddess Laxmi and Saraswati are placed in decorated swings in Jhulan Mandap of Jagannath Temple. It is also observed in different Mathas of the city.

Madala Panji

The Madala Panji is the official chronicle of the Jagannath Temple at Puri.

It is believed that the writing of the Madala Panji was started in the later part of the 16th Century A.D. i.e. during the Bhoi dynasty of Khurda.

The Madala Panji was written in four volumes namely (a) Raj Madala, (b) Niti Madala, (c) Khei Madala and (d) Karmangi.

It is the property of the Jagannath temple of Puri, and the volumes are kept in the custody of (a) the Raja of Puri (b) Deul Karan, (c) Tadhu Karan, (d) Patajoshi Mohapatra (Chhatisha Nijog Nayak) respectively.

The scribes of these volumes were Sithakaran, Behera Karan, Dandi Karan and Panjia Karan. It was being written on palm leaves with a stylus or Lekhani and presented in annual bundles (from Sunia to Sunia, the Odia New Year's Day).

It is not known when Madala Panji stopped being written. As per researcher, the raid of the Jagannath temple at Puri by the followers of the Mahima Dharma on 1st March, 1881 does not find mention in the Panji. It proves that it must have stopped before that date.

Uniqueness Of Jagannath Temple

The Jagannath temple at Puri is one of the CHAR – DHAM pilgrimages where the idols are believed to be made from log of wood during the time of king Indradyumna of Mahabharat period. Millions of people throughout the world visit this mighty historical structure to seek the blessings of the Lord. The Temple, the half – carved wooden idols in the inner sanctum and it's Rath Yatra are unique. The English word "Juggernaut" shares its origin from this annual parade/ Ratha Yatra of the Lord.

Many of the following mysteries and specialities of the temple have caught the imagination of the traveler.

Defying The Law Of Nature

The flag which is mounted on the top of the Jagannath Temple flows in the opposite direction to the wind's course without any scientific background to back it up.

Climbing The Temple

Every day a priest climbs on the walls of the temple (ie. whose height is equivalent to that of a 45 storey building) to change the flag, atop the temple dome. This ritual is continuing since the time of construction of the temple. This is performed with bare hands without any protective wear. It is believed that, if the ritual is skipped one day from the calendar, the temple will be shut down for a long 18 years.

No Shadow

The shadow of the main tower temple is not seen during any part of the day and in any direction. It is believed that the construction style of the temple is an architectural marvel.

Riddle Of Sudarshan Chakra

This Chakra is around 20-feet high and weighs more than a ton which is fitted at the top of the temple. One can see the Chakra from any corner of the city and irrespective of the position, one can always feel that the Chakra is facing towards you.

Placing such hard metal weighing about a tonne at the top of the temple without any machinery just with human force is a marvel during the then period.

As the chakra looks same from every direction the architectural technique is a mystery.

No Fly Zone

No bird is seen flying above the Jagannath temple. This area is a no flying zone for the planes which is rare in any other temple in India.

Temple Food / Prashad / Offerings

The temple is famous for it's kitchen where 56-varieties of food are prepared. This is considered as one of the largest kitchen in the world which is under the direct monitoring of the Goddess Mahalaxmi, as believed.

As per various religious scriptures, wasting of food is considered as a bad sign. Although large number of people visit the temple, the Prasad prepared every day is never wasted. This is a miracle.

As per hearsay, if there is any fault in preparing the food, a shadow dog appears in the temple kitchen. All the prepared food is wasted and all the 56-varieties of food are prepared again.

Sound Of Sea Inside The Temple

The temple has four doors. Before entering the temple through the lion's gate one can hear the sound of the waves of the sea.

But once, one has crossed the Sihma DWAR (lion's gate) one will no longer hear the sound of the waves. As long as one is inside the temple, one will not hear the sound of the waves. When one leaves the temple, one can hear the sound of the waves.

As per hearsay, it was the desire of the Goddess Subhadra, the sister of Lord Jagannath and Balabhadra who wished for silence within the temple premises. Other legends about the silence of sound of waves inside the temple are described in earlier paragraphs.

Reverse Directions Of The Breeze

Usually in coastal areas the breeze flows from sea to land during the day and vice versa in the evening. However, this is different in Puri coast.

Magical Methods For Cooking

The traditional way to cook the Parsadam is preserved by the priests here. Exactly seven pots are used as vessels mounted over one another and are cooked using firewood. Enchantingly, the top most pot is cooked first, and the rest follows the same order.

Disintegration Of The Deities / Naba Kalebara

The deities are buried from every 12/14 / 18 years, one above another, replaced by new ones. These deities are made up of neem wood and are believed to be disintegrated on their own.

Rath Yatra

The Rath Yatra is an annual festival in which the deities are carried outside the main temple on 3-chariots to Gundicha temple.

The chariots are pulled by thousands of devotees from the Lion's gate of the Jagannath temple to Sri Gundicha temple through the 3 kms long 'Grand Road', locally known as 'Bada Danda'. The three chariots along with the deities return to the main temple during Bahuda Yatra.

Irrespective of caste, creed, sect, religion and sex distinctions, general public is allowed to pull the chariots. This Yatra displays the divine values of love, compassion, equality and fraternity.

The festival symbolises the desire of the" benevolent deities "to come down to the level of the common man to share the joys and suffering of all humanity. Rath Yatra indicates that the deity is equal for every person on earth and grants equal opportunity to all, which is unique.

ANNEXURE

It would be in volumes, if one tries to describe the historical, religious and cultural importance of Lord Jagannath and Puri. However, the author has tried to describe in brief about the origin of Lord Jagannath, cult of Lord Jagannath, famous devotees of Lord, Devadasi system, Gajapati king and celebration of all the festivals at Jagannath temple for the information of any visitor and for a general reader.

Jagannath – Lord Of The Universe

Jagannath is the supreme God from whom the Avataras incarnate. He is eternal but he changes his body to teach us that one is not the body and is the soul. If one fills Sat-Chit – Ananda, then one will feel and enjoy eternal bliss.

A) Origin Of Lord Jagannath

The origin of Lord Jagannath, Balabhadra and Subhadra is shrouded in mystery. Some researchers are of the view that, worship of wood (DARU worship) at Purusottama on the eastern sea shore is found in Rigveda.

As per "Utkal Itihas" of Pandit Krupasindhu Mishra, Jagannath temple was constructed during 100-200 century BC.

As per Ramayana, the family deity of the Ikshyakus was called Jagannath. The name of Jagannath is also found in Mahabharata with Vishnu Sahasranama.

In the Vana Parba of Mahabharata there is mention of Vedi in the sea shore of Kalinga and any one who climbed the platform was becoming strong and powerful. This Vedi of Mahabharata was identified with the raised platform of the temple / place of worship of Lord Jagannath.

Puri is known as NILADRI / Nilachal (blue mountain) and as per some it was a wooded hill /a high sand dune. The Shabara tribes used to worship their tribal deity, might be a log of wood / some wooden images.

Krishna is addressed both as Purusottama and Jagannath in Vishnu Purana. Vishnu is worshipped by Aditi as Jagannath in the Vamana Purana.

The name of Jagannath and Purusottama finds mention in different Puranas/ scriptures like – Brahma Purana, Brahmanda Purana, Narada Purana, Tantra Yamala, Skanda Purana, Matsya Purana, Padma Purana, Kapila Samhita and NILADRI Mahodaya etc.

God Purusottama finds mention in the Anargharghava Natakam of Murari Mishra during the period of 9th century AD and Prabodha Chandradaya Natakam of Krushna Mishra in 11th century AD. Mention of Purusottama of Odra (ie. earlier name of Odisha) is found in the 10th century inscriptions in Sarada Devi temple (in Maihar of Satana, MP), Brahmadeo temple inscriptions of Kalachuri era of 9th to 11th century AD and Nagpur stone inscriptions of the rulers of Malwa in early part of 12th century AD.

From the above, it is proved that the glory of the Lord and importance of Purusottama KSHETRA was existing, before the construction of the present Jagannath Temple by Chodaganga Dev.

Tribal Origin

Most of the researchers are of the view that Lord Jagannath was the deity of the aboriginals and was worshipped at the eastern coast of Odisha around 1200-BC. Initially it was worshipped in the form of tree, then in the form of wooden pole and with passage of time it was converted to a Brahminical deity.

Tree / Khamba (pillar / post) worship was in practice and while trying to give it a human shape, it might have formed a strange shape. Perhaps, that might have originated the shape of Lord Jagannath.

Some are of the opinion that when the Aryans came in to contact with the Sabaras / aboriginal tribes and in order to bring them in to their fold, the word Darubrahma might have come in to vogue.

The story/ hearsay of finding Lord Jagannath among the aboriginals / Shabaras are heard in different forms in Odia folk-lore in different parts of the state / medieval Odia literature/ the Puranas. Some of the versions of the story/ hearsay in different parts of the state are briefly described as under: –

Kantilo (Nayagarh District) – Nilamadhab

Kantilo is famous for the NILAMADHAB TEMPLE/ NEELAMADHAB. As per legend, the origin of Jagannath culture, started from this place/ Lord Jagannath owes origin from this place.

The temple is on the twin hills on the right banks of the river Mahanadi. The twin hills are known as Brahmadri and Niladri.

It is surrounded by green forests. The hill ranges are at the left of the temple. The temple is very old and is a famous Vaishnav temple.

The temple structure is like Jagannath temple of Puri. Similar rites and rituals like Puri are observed here.

One will also find Lord Nilamadhab temple on the right side of Lakshmi temple in Puri – JAGGANNATH TEMPLE COMPLEX.

Lord Nilamadhab is the main deity among the followers of Lord Jagannath.

This is a east facing Pancharath type temple. The Viman, Jagmohan, and Garuda Mandap are squarish and frontal Mandap is rectangular.

The niches of the temple houses images like Trivikram, Varaha and Narasimha etc. as Parshwa Devatas (ie. Side Gods and Goddesses).

The temple was built by Gandhamardan Dev, the last king of Boudha royal family.

There is constant flow of holy water from the feet of Lord Nilamadhab, which is the main attractions of the temple. Some believe that, the narrow spring connects the feet of the Lord with river Ganga.

Legend

As per mythology, after the death of Krishna, his spirit took the shape of a small stone. BISWABASU found the stone and felt the divinity and worshipped it as Lord Nilamadhab.

Hence, the original form of Lord Jagannath is Nilamadhab, an ancient God worshipped by Sabaras, a pre-aryan tribe.

Biswabasu, the local Sabar chief was worshipping "Kitung" (ie. the God known in the Sabara dialect), in a small cave in the Brahmadri hills, near Mahanadi. In Puranas, the earlier figure of the Lord was in the form of "BLUE SAPPHIRE (ie. Indranila) "and accordingly, it was a "blue tongue image", known as Nilamadhab.

The wooden image (ie. Daru murti) came/ introduced with the passage of time and a temple was built at the place near the confluence of the rivers.

In some places of Odisha, especially Palalhara, Shabars worship a blue rock in the Groove of Sal trees. They call it Nilamadhab.

There is also some indirect reference of this place /God in Rigveda.From the palm leaf inscriptions, it is found that before establishment of Lord Jagannath, at Puri, King Indradyumna traveled near the banks of River Mahanadi to find Lord Nilamadhab and went to Puri after visiting Goddess Charchika of Banki.

As per myth, Lord Nilamadhab, appeared in the dream of King Indradyumna.

When the king enquired about the details of Nilamadhab from his priests, it was told that the God is worshipped somewhere in the forests of Utkal near Mahanadi. The king instructed Bidyapati to find out God Nilamadhab.

Vidyapati traveled many parts of Utkal in deep forests and hills and at last came to KALIPALI, near Mahanadi river, where Biswabasu, the Sabara chief was staying. The Sabara chief treated Bidyapati well and he stayed there for some period as a guest. During that period he fell in love with Lalita, daughter of Biswabasu. Both were got married with the blessings of Biswabasu. As Biswabasu was going everyday to the cave to worship Lord Nilamadhab, Bidyapati came to know about Lord Nilamadhab from Lalita. Bidyapati requested Lalita, to take her to that place for which she agreed with the condition that, he had to go there blind folded.

When Bidyapati was going blind folded, he was carrying mustered seeds which he was dropping at some intervals.

When the monsoons came, the seeds grew to plants and Vidyapati was able to locate the cave of Lord Nilamadhab.

Bidyapati went to king Indradyumna and told the incident. Both of them started to reach the place of Nilamadhav.

In the dream, the king heard that Lord Nilamadhab had disappeared from the cave and floating in the sea.

As they were ignorant about God, king Indradyumna, requested Biswabasu to forgive them and to come to Puri. Biswabasu forgave Bidyapati and came to Puri, where all of them saw that the floating divine image behaved like a log of wood and came to shore.

The idols of Lord Jagannath, Balabhadra and Subhadra were made out of that log and placed in a small temple for worship. The present temple was constructed subsequently during 12th century.

In Kantilo, Shabars are found in Kalia Pali, who claim themselves as descendants of Biswabasu. According to their version, Biswabasu was worshipping. "Kalia Madhab".

Dhan Changada Village/ Dhangda Hills And Lalit Madhav Temple – Nayagarh District

This area is linked with Biswabasu, Bidyapati, Lalita and tribal SABARAS (ie. a primitive tribe).

DHAN Changda village and Dhangdi hills are nearby and the AKHADAPADA VILLAGE is in between.

The remains of a fort and many images of Lord Vishnu were found in this area by the historians.

As per legend, Biswabasu was worshipping Lord Nilamadhab in a dense forest and he used to cross a river to reach the place. The river KAMEI is near the village.

There are places with names, like – DEUL PADA, GADA MALA /GADA MANA and CHADURI TAILA etc.

As per some historians, GADA MALA/GADA MANA was the fort of Biswabasu, as some remains of the fort is found in the area.

In Odiya, CHADURI means deserted wife (ie. wife, whose husband has deserted her). From the legend, it is known that Lalita, Daughter of Biswabasu, was punished as she had betrayed her father, by disclosing the place of worship of Nilamadhab. She was left in a nearby forest. Hence, CHADURI TAILA is the forest, where she was left.

Dhangdi is a type of tribal dance. Dhangdi is the hill, where Lalita used to roam and dance. Similarly, the name of Dhanchangda village is derived, from the area where the tribals used to dance.

Many copper plates with inscriptions which describes like, "certain area was given as a gift as a memory of their parents and if anybody occupies the same unauthorisedly, he would go to hell". The remains appear to be of 8th century. These(ie. seven number of copper plates) are found in Nayagarh treasury. There are also many areas earmarked in different names, nearby this village. (ie. like – BALLAV LAND, DWARPAL JAGIRI, BADHEI HATA etc). The land was given to the people who were engaged in different works relating to worship of GOD – NILAMADHAB.

This area is important from archeological point of view. The Dhangdi hills is situated at the confluence of KUSUMI, KAMEI and KUANRIA RIVER.

LALIT MADHAV TEMPLE is on the top of this hill, which was constructed by Debraj Jena, a local teacher. A small image of Lord Vishnu is also found near the main image. It is told that, the small image was found in the same area.

The area is scenic. It will be liked by any tourist.

A major festival is held during DHANU SHANKRANTI (Nov-Dec) at this place.

To reach the place one has to drive 2-kms on the BHUBANESWAR-KANTILO ROAD and has to cross the KAMEI RIVER. From that place one has to move 3-kms on the road near river Bandha / embankment to reach DHAN CHANGDI VILLAGE and DHANGDI hill. One has to arrange one's own vehicles to reach the hill and the village, from the main road.

Koraput

The Jagannath temple of Koraput is the main temple of the town and is surrounded by 9- beautiful and small temples.

It is known as Sabara Khetra as it was discovered and worshipped by the Sabaras, a primitive tribe of the area. It was built around 12th century in ancient Kalinga architectural style.

All these temples are in tranquil surroundings encircled by the beautiful green hills. The whole Koraput town can be seen from this place. The view is panoramic.

One can reach the temple by climbing around 100-Steps from the bottom. One can also take the vehicles to reach there. The hill top on which, the temple stands is known as "Sabara Srikhestra".

Besides the presiding deity of Lord Jagannath, Balabhadra and Mata Subhadra, various idols of Hindu Gods /Goddess are there. There is a museum in the temple complex, where lord Jagannath is seen in many colourful decorated statues / with many decorations.

The temple allows access to all castes and religions without any distinction, which is a speciality. As one tourist observed, "free access of everybody to the shrine demonstrates the concept of Jagannath culture and it's tribal origin".

It signifies oneness of mankind. It is against untouchability and any kind of discrimination against people.

Hearsay

It is believed that Savar king Biswavasu worshipped Sri Jagannath in the cave Khillamunda of Jagamunda hills which was a part of undivided Koraput district. Biswabasu was a SAURA tribal chief and he worshipped the lord in the form of Daru (ie. Wooden form). The wooden form of the Lord is found in all the temples of Koraput district.

RATH YATRA – KORAPUT

Rath Yatra is the most famous festival of the Jagannath temple of Koraput, where the local tribes participate in large numbers.

The tribal women make sweets to offer the same as "prasad"(ie. offering) everyday. pineapple and Jack Fruits are offered to the Lord during Rath Yatra.

The sweeping ceremony (ie. Chhera Panhanra) is performed by a tribal chief of parija community. (ie. DASI NAYAK). For tribal devotees of Koraput, Lord Jagannath is of much religious significance.

Further during 15-days ANASAR (ie. confinement due to fever), before Rath Yatra, only descendants of Biswabasu (ie. People having tribal connections) are allowed to attend.

During Rath Yatra special invitations are sent by the management committee to the tribal leaders of various villages, by sending betel nut (ie. supari). The tribal people reach in advance before Rath Yatra and take various responsibilities to perform the festival. During Rath Yatra tribal chiefs of different villages are felicitated by presenting headgear (ie. Siropa – ritual turban).

This shows how Jagannath culture is originated from tribal culture.

One will find different kind of dance forms and various tribal art forms which are displayed during the festival. Their traditional Dhemsa dance will enchant any visitor.

The modern Management education system, should learn a lot from this festival as to how different duties are performed without any force and voluntarily by the tribals, who were away from the modern education system in the past.

Jagannath Temple of Koraput is situated in a quiet place. Arati / prayer of lord especially, during evening time will be liked by any visitor.

From the vegetarian eatery one can take the Maha prasad, which is similar to Lord Jagannath temple of Puri. The sweet dish of this temple, especially Malpua is unique.

There is provision of comfortable lodging at affordable rates in the temple complex. In the temple complex one will also find religious shops.

Gajapati District

SAORA /SAURA /SAVARA are one of the primitive tribes of the country and are found mostly in the Paralakhemundi area of GAJAPATI District and Gunupur area of Rayagada district which is known as the "SAURA COUNTRY".

Depending upon occupation, dress, habits, food and social customs, there are 25-Sub-divisions amongst SAURAs. However, they are divided mainly in to Lanjia – SAURA (ie. live in hills and practice their old customs /practices) and Sudha-SAURA (ie. who live in plains and have adopted many customs of the locals). 5-Sub -

group of SAURAs, ie. Lanjia, Jara, Arsi, Bhima and Sudha are found in GAJAPATI District. They strictly follow their cultural identities.

The Raika Soras are found in Raigarh mutha and they do not take animal flesh. The Bhim Saoras are living in Jiranga area and they link themselves to Bhim, one of the five Pandavas.

The Jara Saoras are famous throughout the country and it is believed that one of their ancestors had killed Lord Krishna with his arrow, as depicted in scriptures.

JARA SAVARS

As per Odisha Gazetteer on GAJAPATI District, "More interesting is the story of Baragharia Jhara who are the 12-families. On no occasion the 12-families will become -13 families, otherwise the 13th will be destroyed. The Jara Savaras are a branch of primitive Savara tribe, commemorating the legendary Jara of Mahabharata. They are the worshipper of the deities enshrined in MAHENDRAGIRI. They are important from ethnic and mythological point of view".

Lord Jagannath

As per legend, Lord Jagannath was originally worshipped by the Sabara tribes.

As per some historians, the original deity "Kitung"(ie. God of wood) was worshipped by the Sabara tribes of MAHENDRAGIRI hills. Later it was known as "Jagunta" and with passage of time it was known as Jagannath. Earlier, Paralakhemundi which was part of Ganjam had more than 30-gadajats and king of each Gadajat had direct relation with GAJAPATI kings and they have accepted Jagannath culture and Vaishnavism.

Further as per locals, one will find "Daru Brahma" at the top point of Mahendragiri. Some believe that, the initial wood for making the idol of Lord Jagannath was from this place.

It is also believed that the sacred tree, ie. Brahmadaru, fell from this peak and the river Mahendratanaya swept it to Bay of Bengal. The oceanic Current swept it to Bankimuhan at Puri.

As per Odisha Gazetteer, Dr. Benimadhav Padhi in his book "Daru Devata" has traced the origin of Jagannath to the Daru worship by the Savaras in the pre-historic times.

Tree worship is a very ancient cult. The protoaustroloids worshiped the ficus tree and their religion was known as the "Cult of Ficus Tree". Gradually tree worship had spread into other religions.

Till today, the Savaras or Sauras of Ganjam and Korapurt district worship tree as their "Kitung" which in Saura language means god. They believe that their "Kitung" dwells in a tree outside their village.

They never cut the tree which they call Jagant (a special name of Kitung), nor cut any other tree in the area where it stands. They also believe that their Kitung has ten incarnations which is exactly similar to the concept of ten incarnation of Vishnu. The word Jagannath is never a Sanskrit word, nor a Pali word; presumably it is the sanskritised form of austric word "Jaganta".

Sundargarh District-jangha Dev

The temple of JANGHA Dev is found in many places of Sundargarh district, like – Sadhubahal, Khuntagaon, Baunsen and Bhoipali village in Baragaon Block.

The lower part of the body is worshipped by the devotees in these temples, which is believed as the lower part of body of Lord Jagannath (ie. from thigh to knee, which is known as – JANGHA in Odia language). JANGHA BADA DEV is believed as a part of Lord Krishna by many.

There are many hear-says about origin of Lord JANGHA Dev. It is said that Pandavas after completing funeral rights of Lord Krishna, had thrown the remnants ie. Navi Brahma in to the ocean. The inhabitants of the forest collected the lower parts of the Lord. They started worshiping it and later identified themselves as Gonds.

As per hearsay, JANGHA BADA DEV was brought from Phuljhar of MP to the dense forest of Sundargarh during Mughal invasion. The king of Gangapur was in doubt about his divinity and he threw the Lord in Safei river. However, the Lord appeared outside through a fish. Lord is worshipped in Baunsen village / other places of the district since that period.

Every year on Shamb Dasami day (ie. December/ January) JANGHA Dev is brought outside the temple and is kept in an open pavilion for worship by the devotees.

Before bringing JANGHA Dev to an open place, the devotees start the procession of Kalash Yatra (ie. earthen pots on the head). The Ganda devotees carry the wooden lower part of Lord Krishna, symbolising JANGHA DEV on shoulders and take out the procession.

Large number of devotees from Odisha, Jharkhand and Chhattisgarh, especially from the Gond communities, assemble here to offer puja.

Lord Jangha Bada Dev

Athamallik (Anugul District)

As understood from the locals of this area, before arrival of king Pratap Deb, the area was ruled by Sabara / Shavaras /Tribal chief. The indigenous tribes used to worship Lord Jagannath in a cave. It was of wooden statue with wide eyes and limbless.

The Hindu priests kidnapped the Lord and left the place in a boat through the river Mahanadi. Lord Jagannath was installed at the main temple at Puri, where his worship is continuing.

As per hearsay, Kohi-I-Noor, the largest diamond was adorning the Lord. However, there is no authenticity about it.

As per some historians, Maharaja Ranjit Singh during his last illness in 1838 AD had offered to donate the famous Kohinoor diamond to the Temple of Jagannath. But the Diamond could not find its way to the temple of Jagannath as the royal custodian had not performed the royal wish after his death.

Sheorinarayan

Many scholars like Hiralal and J P Singhdeo etc. are of the opinion that the original place of Lord Jagannath was Savarinarayan / Sheorinarayan of Chhatishgarh, around 40-kms from Bilaspur. This is a tribal area and was inhabited by the Shavars, Gaudas and other aboriginal tribes. There are many legends associated with this place.

As per some legend, this place was a forest in which an old shavar was worshipping Lord Jagannath. Later on, the deity was removed and sent to Puri. As per wish of the Lord, the place was named as Sheorinarayan which contains the name of the worshipper and the worshipped.

Daitapatis

The Daitapatis are the hereditary servitors in the temple of Jagannath at Puri. During the Snana Yatra and the Car festival, they take care of the deities.

They consider the Lord as their family member. At the time of Nabakalebara (when the deities, being made of wood, change their body in every 12-19 years) they mourn for ten days and perform Suddhikriya on the eleventh day as one would normally do for a family member. They also claim their descent from the Savaras.

Other Legends

As per Skanda Purana, in Satya era (age of truth) king Indradyumna of Abanti heard about the glory of Purusottama KSHETRA from the pilgrims. He was amazed after listening the descriptions of the KSHETRA, where God Himself was being worshiped as Purusottama on the Blue Hill situated in Odra Desa(ie. earlier name of Odisha).

The king ordered his family preceptor to send somebody to trace it and Vidyapati was sent for the purpose. Vidyapati came to Utkala and settled in a Savara village situated to the west of the Blue Hill. He was acquainted with Viswabasu (ie. Sabar king) who used to worship the Lord. Vidyapati with folded hands requested him to show him the Lord and also revealed to him the secrets of his mission. He had told Viswabasu that his royal master would not touch food until his return.

Viswabasu was in a dilemma and thought if he would show the Lord, the place would be accessible to all. After much persuasion and out of compassion for the king, Viswabasu took Vidyapati through a narrow track and showed him the Lord. Vidyapati was overwhelmed with joy. He returned to Avanti and described his experience to the king.

The king prepared for the pilgrimage and sage Narada had also accompanied the king in his pilgrimage to Nilachal.

In the mean time, in order to fulfil his pledge given to Yama (ie. God of death), Lord Vishnu made the shrine of Nilamadhava invisible under the sand.

When Indrdyumna accompanied by Narada reached the borders and was informed about the disappearance of Lord Nilamadhav, he was completely disheartened.

As per advice of Sage Narada, he offered a thousand Aswamedha (horse) sacrifices. He saw the Lord in the form of Nrushingh in the dream.

On the closing day of the Aswamedha sacrifice and during his bath, his attendants came and informed him about the floating of a Daru with four branches, on the sea at BANKI MUHANA. After performing the rituals, the king brought the Daru (floating wood) and placed it on the Yagnya Vedi (sacrificial alter) in Gundicha temple.

While king was discussing with sage Narada about fashioning the log into an image, he heard a voice from the heaven saying, "God Himself will make His own image. The aged carpenter standing with his tools should be shut up in a room for fifteen days and utmost secrecy should be maintained about the construction of the image".

King Indradyumna carried out the instructions and at the end of the allotted time Jagannath, Balabhadra, Subhadra and Sudarsana appeared on the Mahavedi. Being directed by a voice from heaven the king adorned the images with silken cloth and painted them with their respective colours. He also built a temple to install the image.

As per some other legend, Vishwakarma in the guise of an old carpenter was engaged to construct the images. He took a time period of 15-days to construct the image and king could here the sound of construction. After end of the 14th day (ie.at the beginning of 15th day) he could not heard the sound and opened the door. He saw the Lord in half built position and the carpenter was also missing. The king blamed himself. In the meantime he heard the voice from the heaven and came to know that Lord himself had taken the form as per his own desire.

King Indradyumna went to heaven to invite Lord Brahma for the consecration ceremony of the Lord. Substantial time passed in the meantime.

During this period, another king Galamadhava took possession of the temple.

He was worshipping an image of Madhab in it.

At last Brahma came. Indradyumna and Gala were reconciled to each other and the image of Madhab was shifted to a smaller temple. Brahma consecrated the temple and the images of Lord. After leaving the temple in charge of Gala, Indradyumna proceeded to Brahmaloka/ heaven.

As per Odisha Gazetteer,

"A slightly different version of the story is found in Musali Parva of the Mahabharata written by the great 15th century Odia poet Sarala Das. According to him Narayan or Savarinarayana was being worshiped by the Savaras in the forest and being informed about it, King Galamadhava of Kanchi proceeded to the Savara village to take possession of the deity.

In the meantime, the deity had disappeared. King Galamadhab was angry with the Savaras thinking that they had hidden the deity. He waged war against them and killed all the Savaras, excepting one, when the voice of Vishnu from heaven advised him to desist from the holocaust, as the Savaras were His great devotees. Lord Vishnu also cursed Galamadhava for extinction of his entire line of succession.

The story of Indradyumna begins after this. Lord Krishna was killed by the arrow of Jara, a fowler. Arjun consigned the body of Krishna to flames, but the flames could not consume it. Being directed by a voice from heaven, Arjun threw the body of Lord Krishna in to the sea. It floated in the form of a Daru(ie. wood) on the shores of the sea. Jara had followed the body of Krishna along the sea coast. King Indradyumna, knowing that Vishnu will appear at Nilagiri (the Blue Hill), had constructed a temple there.

Krishna informed Jara in a dream that, he would appear in Rohini Kunda in the shape of Daru (log of wood). Indradyumna got the information from Jara and sent his men to lift the Daru from Rohini Kunda. But all his efforts failed. Then as directed by Lord, king Indradyumna employed the service of Jara (ie. the fowler) and Vasu (ie. the Bramhin) who jointly lifted the Daru from Rohini Kunda. Jara and Viswakarma together fashioned the log in to three images of Balabhadra, Subhadra and Jagannath who, according to poet Sarala's version, stood for Shiv, Brahma and Vishnu respectively. The incomplete images are ascribed to the opening of the door before the allotted time".

In some other legends, it is connected to the epic Mahabharata. When funeral fires failed to consume Krishna's dead body, then directed by the heavens, Arjuna placed the body on sea. Floating in the form of a log, the body travelled for thousands of years from Dwarka on the Western Coast to the Eastern shores of the country, where it was found by Indradyumna, King of Malav. While the temple has been demolished and rebuilt several times since then, it is from that same log that the deities of Puri are claimed to have been created.

W.J. Wilkins also traced the origin of Jagannath worship to tribal sources and had described, "The Probability being that He (Jagannath) was the local divinity of some, now unknown tribe, whose worship was engrafted into Hinduism and the God when admitted into the pantheon, was regarded as another manifestation of Vishnu".

Hunter remarks, "The very origin of Jagannath proclaims him not less the god of the Brahmanas than the low-caste aboriginal races".

After narrating the story of Indradyumna in his "Orissa" Hunter further adds, "In the foregoing legend we find the aboriginal people worshiping a blue stone in the depths of the forest. But the deity has grown tired of the Jungle offerings of the primitive people, and longs for the cooked food of the more civilised Aryan race. When the Aryan element at length comes on the scene, the rude blue stone disappears, and gives place to a carved image. At the present hour, in every hamlet of Odisha, this two-fold worship co-exists. The common people have their shapeless stone or block, which they adore with simple rites in the open air, while side by side with it is a temple to one of the Aryan gods, with its carved image and elaborate rites".

The Sabaras / Tribals in some parts of Odisha still worship wooden poles with face and eyes. They call their God as "Jagaboi" / Jaganaelo / Jaganta. It is believed the word Jagannath is derived from "Jagant" (ie. means the Lord of the universe).

Jain Origin

As per many researchers and eminent historians, Jagannath culture is having relations with Jainism. Pandit Nilakantha Das was of the view that, the image of "Kalinga Jeena" which was taken away by Mahapadma Nanda of Magadh and was recovered by King Kharavela is actually that of Lord Jagannath. The word Jagannath is derived from "Jeenanath".

As per Odisha Gazetteer, "Late Pandit Nilakantha Das is the chief exponent of the Jain orign of Jagannath. According to him Jagannath is primarily a Jaina institution. He has tried to identify the Nilamadhava of the legends with the famous Kalinga jina of history." This Jagannath, it appears, was there in the coast of Kalinga (present Orissa) as a piece of black stone which was called Kalinga Jina or symbol of Jina in Kalinga. Later on, it was somehow analysed and the analytic name Nilamadhava was given to it". Pandit Das believes that under the stress of the Sunya or nihilistic theory which developed out of the Mahayanic system of Buddhism, "The Jain symbol, i.e., the stone called Kalinga Jina, came to be explained as Nila (black, nothingness) Ma (mother, creative energy) and Dhava (white, i.e., the phenomenal universe)'. Thus the image of Jagannath (of black colour representing Sunya), Suvadra (the creative energy) and Balabhadra (of white colour representing the phenomenal universe) has evolved from Nilamadhava or the old Kalinga Jina. Pandit Das further adds," Nilamadhava, therefore, represents a philosophy which means from a noumenal nothingness produced a full phenomenal appearance, and this was on account of Ma (Mother element or producing principle)".

Sudarshana, according to him, is the Hindu name given to the old Jaina symbol 'Dharmachakra', and Kaivalya (liberation) a term so exclusively common in Jagannath, has been derived from Jaina sources.

Kedarnath Mohapatra, the distinguished historian, and Pandit Binayak Mishra are among the other advocates of the Jain view/ origin of Jagannath. These two scholars have even tried to identify Indradyumna, the legendary founder of the Jagannath worship at Puri, with Kharavela, the great Jaina emperor of Kalinga".

Some jain philosophers/Jain scholars have linked the Jain Trinity of Samyak Gyana, Samyak Charita and Samyak Dristi (ie. Tri Ratna of Jainism) with Sri Jagannath, Balabhadra and Subhadra.

Some other scholars have also opined that there is a great similarity between images of Nilamadhav and Tri Ratna of jain religion. As per inscriptions in Hathi Gumpha cave, there was worship of "Adijina" in Kalinga and worship was done at "Pithunda", which is identified with Puri. Similarly Mahaprasad of Lord Jagannath is known as "Kaivalya" and this is a derivative of "Kaivalya" or concept of salvation of Jains.

Buddhist Origin

As per Mahayana Buddhists, the image of Lord Jagannath was that of Buddha.

Scholars like – Prof. Wilson, James Fergusson and Gen. Cunningham are of the view that, the figures of Jagannath, Balabhadra and Subhadra are the three devotional representations of the Buddhist symbol of Triratna, "Buddha", Dharma and "Sangha".

Some researchers opine that, Hueintsang had mentioned places like – Puspagiri, Parimalagiri and Charitra Puri. Present Puri is believed to be the Charitra Puri of Chinese traveler and there were 5-Budhist Stupas nearby. One of the Stupas may be of Lord Jagannath and other Stupas were around it, which might be PANCHA MAHADEV. However, it requires further research.

As the Buddhists believe in worship of physical relics after death, the "Brahma" (ie. that is placed at the naval of Lord Jagannath) is nothing but the Buddhist tooth relic, that was brought from Kushinagar to Kalinga.

The term Jagannath was applied to Adi Buddha by Raja Indrabhuti of Sambal. Adi Buddha is even now called Jagannath in Nepalese Buddhism.

As per Odisha Gazetteer, Indrabhuti used to propitiate Jagannath in the beginning of his esoteric work.

"Snana Yatra" and car festival are Buddhist practices. Ratha Yatra of Lord Jagannath resembles the procession of Buddhists image, as written by Fa-Hian. Buddhism also does not believe in caste or class distinction and during Ratha Yatra and some other celebrations, caste distinction is not found in Jagannath culture.

The assimilation of Buddhism in to Hindu religion took place after Buddha was considered as the 9th incarnation of Lord Vishnu.

The ten incarnations of Lord Vishnu is found in the panel, inside the Jagannath temple of Puri. Some opine that after decline of

Buddhism, Jagannath might have become new Buddha and Jagannath cult does not belong to any particular sect.

As per Odisha Gazetteer, "According to Rajendra Lal Mitra, during the four centuries preceding the Christian era, Odisha generally and the district of Puri in particular were under the domination of the Buddhists. After the conquest of Kalinga by Ashoka in 261 B.C., Buddhism got an extra impetus under royal patronage. It is also evident from the accounts of the famous Chinese traveller Hiuen Tsang that Mahayana form of Buddhism flourished in Odisha in the 7th century A.D. The advocates of the Buddhist origin of Jagannath believe that Puri was an ancient seat of Buddhism and the worship of Jagannath is a relic of some Buddhist cult. The story of Buddha's tooth-relic, as it is found in the 12th century Sinhalese work Dathavamsa, written by one Dhammakitti Thera, was once in wide circulation. It is mentioned in this story that the sacred tooth of Buddha remained for centuries at Dantapura in Kalinga. This Dantapura was identified by some with Puri. King Guhasiva of Kalinga worshipped the sacred tooth in a temple, but a king who ruled at Pataliputra forcibly took it away from him. Subsequently the sacred relic was restored to Guhasiva, but while fighting with a powerful neighbouring king he fell in the battle. In order to fulfil the wishes of her deceased father, princess Hemamala surreptitiously conveyed the sacred relic in her hair to Ceylon in about 300 A.D. where it is worshipped to this day. Basing on this legend, Fergusson writes there can be little doubt but that the Temple (of Jgannath at Puri) now occupies the site where formerly stood the Dagoba containing the celebrated tooth-relic. Sir Alexander Cunningham in his works 'The Stupa of Barhut' and 'The Bhilsa Topes", advocates the view that the figures of Jagannath, Subhadra and Balabhadra had been derived from the Buddhist Tri-Ratna or Triple-Gem symbol signifying Buddha, Dharma, and Sangha, set up together in one of the Sanchi sculptures.

In the "Ancient geography of India", Sir Alexander Cunnigham has stated, "The three shapeless figures of Jagannath, and his brother and sister, are simple copies of the symbolical figures of the Buddhist Triad, Buddha, Dharma and Sangha, of which the second is always represented as a female. The Buddhist origin of the Jagannath figures is proved beyond all doubt by their adoption as the representative of the Brahminical avatara of Buddha in the annual almanacs of Mathura and Benares". The Indian scholars like N.K

Bose, Rajendra Lala Mitra, Dr. Harekrushna Mahatab and others have also supported the Buddhist view of Jagannath. By referring to a stone of Ashokan polish with the symbols of Buddha, Dharma and Sangha at the top recently discovered at Bhubaneswar and now preserved in Ashutosh Museum of Calcutta, Dr. Mahatab observes, The symbols are a little different from those found out at Sanchi and other places but the Bhubaneswar symbols are almost exactly like the images of Jagannath, Balabhadra and Subhadra.

The Bhubaneswar discovery proves that, in Odisha the worship of the symbols was prevalent since the Asokan period.

According to Dr. Mahatab, the Savaras of Odisha were converted to Buddhism during the reign of Ashoka and worshipped the Tri-Ratna symbol placed in a Buddhist Stupa at Puri. Later in the 7th or 8th century when Buddha was considered as an Avatara of Vishnu, Jagannath was also considered to be an Avatara of Vishnu. Gradually Buddhism lost itself in Vaishnavism".

For the half built image, Skanda Purana describes that, God himself wanted to take this form of image in the era of Kali (Kali Yuga) for fulfilment of the wishes of the devotees. Lord appeared in disguised form at Purusottama KSHETRA by the prayer of Lord Brahma. Further as per Bamadeva Samhita, God wanted to be in this form.

Although there are many arguments and counter arguments put forth by the scholars regarding origin of Lord Jagannath, but no one is able to ascertain the same. However, many scholars subscribe to the view about the association of the Savaras / aboriginals with Jagannath worship from its very inception.

B) Jagannath Cult

The cult of Jagannath is a synthesis of divergent religious creeds and schools of philosophy that prevailed at different periods of time. It is both one and many.

As per Pandit Nilakantha Das, "all the gods and goddesses attacking and appealing have found a place in the compound of the Jagannath temple of Puri. Jagannath has welcomed and embraced all, but been overwhelmed by none and has lost Himself in none". He is the master of all the universe and in Vedas, he is described as "Virat Purusha". Various religious scriptures have described Jagannath as

"Parambrahma" (supreme soul), omnipotent (Sarbashaktiman) and omnipresent (Sarvavidyaman).

As per Odisha Gazetteer, "The crude figure of the Jaganath triad do not approximate to any anthropomorphic concept of the known gods and goddesses of the Hindu pantheon. In the daily rituals, practices and festivals of the temple Jaina, Buddhist, Saivite, Tantric and Vaisnavite influences are clearly discernible. Jagannath is both Sankara's Advaita Brahman and Mahayanic Sunya. Acyutananda Das, the famous 16th century saint-poet of Odisha, in his Sunya Samhita has conceived both Krishna and Jagannath as Sunya Purusa, or void personified. Frequent mention of Jagannath as Buddha is found in Mahavarat of Sarala Das (Adi Parva, Musali Parva etc.) and in the Daru Brahmagita of Jagannath Das. The absence of caste distinction in the temple of Jagannath, especially in partaking of the Mahaprasda; the car festival, and the bathing festival of the lord are ascribed to Buddhist influences. For Sakta Tantrics, Jagannath is Bhairava and Vimala is Bhairabi ('Vimala sa Mahadevi Jagannathstu Bhairava'). In the month Asvina, during the Durga Puja, animal sacrifice is made before goddess Vimala which is singular of its kind as otherwise bloodless rituals are performed in the temple. "

The five principal sects of Hinduism (ie. Vaishnavism, Saivite, Shakti, Ganapati and Saura/ Surya) are found in the Jagannath temple complex, Puri.

The Shiva temples (ie. Kashi Vishwanath, SIDDHESWAR, RAMESWAR, Bedha loknath, Parasunatha, Dhabaleswar and PATALESWAR etc), Shakti temples(ie. Sarbamangala, Vimala, Bedhakali, Uttar Durga, Mahalaxmi, Sitala and Bhubaneshwari etc), Ganapati temples (Siddha Vinayak and Nritya Ganapati etc.), Surya temple (ie. near Mukti Mandap and Mahalaxmi temple) and different temples of Vishnu (ie. Radhakrishna, Khirachora Gopinath, Nrushingh and Ram etc) are surrounding the Jagannath temple.

He is also worshipped as the synthesis principal deities of Hindu religion, Ie. Jagannath (Vishnu), Balabhadra (Shiv), Subhadra (shakti) and Sudarshan (Surya) etc.

Jagannath is also worshipped as Lord Ram. On Ramanavami day Jagannatha is dressed as Sri Rama. On Snana Yatra or bathing festival Jagannath is worshiped as Ganesh and is decorated accordingly.

One will also find the temple of Satyanarayan in the inner boundary. He is worshipped by the Muslims as Satya Pira and the

Hindus as Satyanarayan. Further the prayers to Lord Satyanarayan is a mixture of Odia, Bengali and Urdu.

Some scholars also opine that Jesus Christ had spent 12-years at Puri. As the whereabouts of the preacher was not found during this period and it was assumed that he might have come to Puri during that period to complete his pilgrimage. However, it requires further study/ research.

As per Dr. Ramachandra Mishra, author of various books on Lord Jagannath, –

- Jagannath triad are interpreted as Pranaba of Veda, Devi of Tantra, Siddhi of yoga, Hare Ram Krishna of Mahamantra.
- Reciting the name of Jagannath, one can recite Pranaba (ie. OM / AUM), Gayatri Mantra and Mahamantra.
- Jagannath is the Sadhana as well as Siddhi of a Sadhaka.
- He is the supreme, from which world is created. He is the creator, preserver and destroyer of the world.
- The temple of Jagannath is identified Gokul of Krishna, Sahasrara of Yoga, Trokona and Satakona of Tantra.
- He is the Purushottama and combines the aspects of Trailokyamohan, Sridhara, Krishna and Kama.
- He takes the form of Nrusingha to protect the devotees, the form of Trailokyamohan to cherish them.

The food offered to Lord is Mahaprasad, which is unique and it is shared by all irrespective of any caste.

The colour of the deities represent the human beings in different parts of the world, ie. Jagannath (Black colour – people of India and Africa etc), Balabhadra (white colour-european/ westerners), Subhadra (yellow colour – Chinese/ Mangoloids) and Sudarshan (red colour- Red Indians / West Indies etc.).

Although Hindus are allowed inside the temple, but duri Car festival any one can see him irrespective of any caste and religion.

Besides the Vaishnava and Saiva saints, many devotees of other faiths, like – Nanak (founder of Sikh religion), Tulsidas (composer of Sri Ram Charit Manas), Salabega (Muslim Saint and poet), Jaban Haridas (Muslim devotee), Captain Bitto (Christian), Shankar Dev of Assam and Dasia Bauri(a low caste Hindu) etc. were the great devotees of Lord.

As per Dr. Ramachandra Mishra, Author, "The cult of Jagannath is all comprehensive and it's composition has become so curious that it become very much difficult to comprehend him in one only form. Every one from any religion, caste, creed or colour can take shelter at the lotus feet of the Lord and make him the representative object of worship of his own cult or creed".

Jagannath is never a sectarian deity. Even the Pancha Sakhas of Odisha(ie. Jagannath Das, Balaram Das, Achyutananda Das, Yashovanta Das and Sisu Ananta Das) inspite of their individual views with Sunya, Yoga, or the cult of Bhakti, all of them sing the glory of Jagannath in one voice and they were mainly responsible in making the cult of Jagannath as the mass religion of Odisha.

Lord Jagannath represents the "religion of Man" and one will find assimilation of many contradictions and traditions within it's fold that is most amazing. He transcends all forms and is beyond the limit of an icon.

As per W.H Hunter, "The true source of Jagannath's undying hold consists in the fact that He is the God of the people. As long long his tower rises upon the puri sands, so long there will be in India a perpetual and visible protest of equality of man before God".

As per researchers on Jagannath cult, the institution of Lord Jagannath influences every sphere of life – cultural, social and religious and He bridges the gap between the ruler and the ruled.

C) Famous Devotees Of Lord Jagannath

Jagannath culture teaches us that religion is not different from one another and true religion without sectarian beliefs would unite the whole world.

Lord Jagannath accepts the devotees irrespective of caste, creed and colour.

As a result Jagannath culture is an assimilation of all religious beliefs.

Due to diversity and rich cultural heritage, many Saints and seers from all parts of the country irrespective of their religion and different beliefs had visited this holy city. They had contributed a lot for enriching the Jagannath culture.

Some of the famous devotees from different sects associated with the place and with Lord Jagannath are as under:

Adi Shankaracharya

Shankar was born around 8th century at Kalady village in Kerala. As he was born with the blessings of Lord Shiv, he was named as Shankar. He completed his education from the Gurukul at the age of eight and embraced himself as a Sanyasi against the will of his parents. He had mastered all religious scriptures and yogic techniques from his Guru and great Saint Sri Govindapada Acharya of Onkarnath situated in Madhya Pradesh.

He had propounded the doctrine, "Brahma, the ultimate All is the reality. The only means to lead us to the goal of realisation is to overcome all sense – attractions". Learned priests, Pundits and many persons listened to his discourse. He was conferred the title of "Acharya" and he became Shankaracharya. He is believed as the path finder of Hindu religion.

He had visited different parts of the country with his followers explaining vedantic texts and various religious scriptures.

For the spiritual welfare, he had established 4-mathas in four corners of the country. He had established these Mathas in four directions so that the great wisdom of the Saints contained in Vedas and Upanishads etc. could be preserved.

During the course of his journey, he had visited Puri and found that the deities were not in the temple. The deities were removed 144-years back.

With his efforts, the deities were brought back to Sri KSHETRA and were placed on the Ratna SIMHASANA on the new moon day of Shravana Month by Padmapadacharya in his presence. That day a diamond Chita was placed on the forehead of the deities. The same tradition is continuing till today.

The system of rice offerings to the Lord was also started by him. He had established the "Bhogavardhana Pitha"/ Govardhan Pitha with Padmapada as the Acharya.

The king had given the power to the Matha to test the Puja pandas for their eligibility. The Acharya of the Matha is the chairman of the Muktimandap Pandit Sabha. In case of dispute regarding rituals, he has to guide. He is permitted to enter the temple with his "Danda".

As per some researchers, his image was below the Ratna SIMHASANA of Lord Jagannath and was removed from the main temple subsequently and was placed in the Jagmohan of Laxmi temple. It is also believed that he had made reunification of different sects at Puri and one will find co-existence of Saivsim, Shakti cult and Vaishnavism at Puri.

Adi Shankaracharya had number of contributions for the Jagannath temple of Puri.

Ramanujacharya

During the period of king Chodaganga Dev, Acharya Ramanuj had visited Puri. At that time, Lord was worshipped in Tantric ways. He advised the king to perform the rituals as per Vedic rites. However, he could not succeed. Emaar math of Puri is also associated with him. Many legends like-garuda, the carrier of Lord, flying him to the bank of Bhargavi river and throwing way of Ramanuj several miles away while he was in sleep, are heard.

Ramanuja was a great Vaisnavite teacher from the south and the philosopher of the Visistadvaita School. He visited Puri in the early part of the 12th century A.D. and his visit gave a fresh impetus to Vaisnavism in Odisha.

The contemporary Ganga monarch of Odisha Chodaganga Deva seems to have come under the influence of Ramanuja.

Chodaganga was a devotee of Lord Shiv and was called 'Parama-Mahesvara' in his earlier records, but in later records he has been described both as Parama-Mahesvara and Parama Vaisnava, and also as a devotee of Vishnu alone. Though Ramanuja did not succeed in his attempt to introduce certain modes of his own sect of Vaishnavism into the worship of Jagannath, still Vaisnavism flourished in Odisha under royal patronage.

The existence of famous Emara Matha and the Ramanuja Matha at Puri and the Alvarnath Temple at Brahmagiri in Puri district are reminiscent of the visit of Ramanuja, the last of the Alvar saints, to Puri.

Chaitanya Mahaprabhu

Chaitanya Mahaprabhu who was the 10th child was born on 4th February (ie. which was a lunar eclipse day and also DOLA Purnima / Holi) at Navadwip, West Bengal. His forefathers are hailed from Jajpur area of Odisha. His family name was Viswambhar and he was called as Nimai by his mother. He had taken Sanyasa at an early stage of his life by renouncing all material connections.

Initially he visited Puri, passing through and worshiping – Khirachora Gopinath of Remuna (Balasore), Varaha of Jajpur, Sakhigopal of Barabati fort and Bhubaneshwar. Nityananda broke sacred stick (Danda) of Chaitanya in to three parts and threw it in to the river, when he reached the river Bhargavi, 8-kms from Puri.

He fell in to ecstasy, when he saw the flag of Jagannath Temple from that place and he moved slowly with dancing and chanting hymns. Thousands of his supporters joined with him in the 8-kms route to reach Jagannath temple. When he reached the Jagannath temple premises, he rushed towards the Ratna SIMHASANA to embrace the Lord and he fell down. However, Vasudev Sarvabhauma, a Brahmin Pundit took him to his house in the unconscious state. He stayed at Puri for a short period and thereafter he went to south after taking permission from Lord Jagannath. He returned to Puri in 1512 AD during the time of Bath festival of the Lord (Debasnaa Purnima).

During the ANABASARA period as Lord could not be seen he went to Alarnath of Brahmagiri, with the permission and advice of Lord Jagannath. Whenever, he was in Puri he used to spend his time in singing and dancing before Jagannath. He had settled down at Puri in 1455AD, at the age of 30. He had advised his followers for Sankirtan of Lord Krishn's name which enables the purity of the soul and respect to all.

He believed that the manifestation of supreme Lord Krishna is Lord Jagannath.

It is believed by many that he fell down during the Rath Yatra while dancing and told his attendants about his impending departure on the 8th day. Chaitanya's spirit went to the abode of the Lord and it took place in the temple of Tota Gopinath, as believed by some.

It is believed that the climax of Vaishnavism in Odisha was reached in the 16th century with the coming of Sri Chaitanya whose long sojourn at Puri until his death brought a miraculous change in the religious life of the people. Under Chaitanya's influence, Vaisnavism became the dominant faith of the people of Odisha and Jagannath came to be regarded primarily as a Vaisnavite deity.

Ballavacharya

He was born in a Brahmin family of South India in 1479 AD and his earlier name was Ballava Bhatta. He is the founder of Pusti-Marga which is based on the salvation of soul through Bhakti. His centre was at Varanashi. He came to Puri in the 10th year of life with his parents. He was greatly influenced by Chaitanya Mahaprabhu.

Jayadeva

He is the 12th century poet from Kenduli village of Puri district and composer of Gitagobinda.

As per Madalapanji, king Narasingha Dev had given him the permission for the recitation of Gitagobinda for the first time in the temple of Lord Jagannath. He was a great devotee of Lord Jagannath and was worshiping the Lord at Sri KSHETRA staying under a banyan tree.

Not only Gitagobinda is connected to Lord but also Gitagobinda Khandua (silk clothes) is worn by the Lord at night when he goes to sleep as a mark of love to Jayadeva. His Gitagobinda still echoes in the temple premises at the time of Badasimhar Besha of the Lord.

Sridhar Swami

Sridhara Swami was born in Marei village, near khirachora Gopinath of Remuna, Balasore. He was the disciple of Saint Ramakrushnananda Swami, in charge of Chandrasekhar Mahadev of Kapilash and head of Shankarananda Math of Puri. He learnt the Nrushingh Mantra from him and worshipped him in the form of Laxmi Nrushingh. He was head of Shankarananda Math, Puri and had written commentary on Srimad Bhagabatgita and Srimad Bhagbat Mahapurana.

As per hearsay, his book Bhabartha Dipika was on the lap of the Lord in the morning, although it was kept in front of him in the night.

His writings are accepted by the followers of both the dual and non-dual school of Vaishnavism. He was a great follower of Lord Jagannath.

Tulasi Das

Tulasi Das, who was a great devotee of Lord Ram came to know that Lord Ram had instructed Bibhisana to worship Lord Jagannath in the era of KALI. He came to Puri and prostrated before Lord Jagannath and he could not find Lord Ram. With distress and anguish he went away and took shelter at a distant place of Puri.

As per hearsay, Lord Ram appeared in the dream and reminded him his own writings in Ramacharita Manasa, ie.

"Binupada Kalai Sunai Binu Kana
Kara Binu Karai Karama Bidhi Nana
Anana Rahit Sakal Rasa Bhogi
Binu Bakata So Bada Hi Yogi"

In English, "He works sans hands, walks without legs, he chats without tongues, he consumes without mouth, he consumes all and perceives everything without eyes".

Tulasi Das wake up and went to the temple. He saw Lord Ram, Laxman and Mata Sita.

He saw the Lord on the 11th day of the bright fortnight which was a Thursday. If any EKADASHI falls on Thursday, on that day "Danda Katra Niti" is performed. Bhitarachu Mahapatra holds the Danda (stick) and the deities are dressed as Ram, Laxman and Sita.

Further Jagannath is known as Jagadish in Hindi speaking areas.

The place of staying, where he returned after seeing Lord Jagannath as Lord Ram, was known as Tulasi Chaura. This place is famous as he had slept here and dreamt about the Lord. Pilgrims used to see the flag of the temple from this place, which is treated as holy.

Balaram Dasa

He was born in the village Erabanga in GOP of Puri district. His father was a minister in the court of king Prataprudra Dev. From his early childhood he learnt about – Vedas, Puranas and various philosophical writings. He came in contact with Chaitanya Mahaprabhu and was a great devotee of Lord Jagannath.

He followed a separate school of thought known as" Gyana Misra Bhakti Tatwa". His philosophy was based on Kundalini yoga.

He had written Odia Ramayan which is known as" Jagamohan Ramayan"/ Dandi Ramayana. He had also written several other books.

There are many legends and hearsay about his link with Lord Jagannath.

He had breathed his last by hearing the sweet voice of the Lord and seeing him. It was known as "Gupta Sri KSHETRA" and the samadhi of the great devotee is also present here.

Jagannatha Dasa

He was born in Kapileswarpur village of Puri. His father was a Purana panda in Jagannath temple. He was conversant with Veda, Puranas and Upanishads etc. from the early childhood.

He had translated Bhagabat Maha purana in Odia to please her mother. He used to recite his Odia Bhagabat under the Kalpabata of Jagannath Temple.

Chaitanya Mahaprabhu was so much pleased with his recitation and the translation of Bhagabat that he honoured him with the epithet "Atibadi" for his poetry and had put his uttariya on his head.

He was a great devotee of the Lord and in his Bhagabat Mahapurana, he has repeatedly used the name Lord Jagannath in place of Srikrishna.

There is a Samadhi Mandir near the sea, where he breathed his last.

Achutananda Dasa

He was born in Talakana village near Nemal of Cuttack district. It is believed that he was born with the blessings of Lord Jagannath. He got the blessings of Chaitanya Mahaprabhu on the day of Ratha Yatra, when he came to Puri at the age of five.

He had written many books and translated Harivamsha Purana. As per hearsay, he could show his practice of Yoga before the king, by raising his body two feet above the ground by meditating on the name of Lord Jagannath.

He had visited all the important religious places of the country and after his return he sought the blessings of Chaitanya Mahaprabhu. He blessed him by giving cymbal and advised him to preach the name of Hari and he started preaching Hari name from Puri.

With the blessings of the Lord Jagannath, he stayed in Nemal and continued the worship of Lord till his death.

He was not only a devotee of Lord Jagannath but also a fortune teller. His palm leaf manuscripts are found in many places of the state and the devotees get answers of their personal questions.

Ganapati Bhatta

He was born at Kaniari village of Karnataka in a Brahmin family. He was a pious, learned and a great devotee of Lord Ganesh.

From Brahma Purana he came to know that Lord Jagannath, in the subtle form of Brahma, is worshipped at Nilagiri (Puri) and devotees are liberated by seeing him in the naked eye.

He reached Nilachala (Puri) by crossing many rivers and mountains. When he reached Puri, he saw the devotees are leaving Puri with the Mahaprasad. He could not believe the presence of Brahma in a subtle form at Puri. He wanted to return without seeing the Lord.

Legend

Lord Jagannath could realise the pain of the devotee Ganapati Bhatta and appeared in his dream. He realised his mistake and proceeded towards the temple which was the day of Snana Purnima and three deities were in the bathing platform. However, he could not believe it as Brahma and he wanted to see Ganapati, who was subtle form of Brahma for him. He was not convinced and wanted to return.

Lord Jagannath could realise the wish of the devotee and instructed Mudiratha in a dream to search Ganapati Bhatta and to tell him that God can take any form to fulfil the desire of the devotees. After much persuasion, he came near the Bathing platform. He was astonished to see a trunk from the mouth of the Lord. He was repentant and prayed Lord for forgiveness. He prostrated before the Lord and meditating on the Brahma, he passed away.

Accordingly, every year during the Snana Yatra and after end of bathing ceremony, Lord is decorated in the form of Lord Ganesh.

From this incident, it is assumed that Brahma is all pervading and Lord cherish the desire which the devotee has in mind.

Rasikananda

He was a disciple of Shyamananda, whose earlier Gurus were disciples of Chaitanya Mahaprabhu. He had popularised Radha

Krushna cult in Odisha. He was conversant with Veda, Upanishads and Tantra Shastra etc. at an early age.

He was a great devotee of Lord Jagannath. As per legend, RASIKANANDA had started a long pilgrimage to see the Lord in the chariot. He and his disciples were tired and fell asleep under a banyan tree at Tulsi Chaura, near Malati Patapur.

In the meantime Lord Jagannath, Balabhadra and Subhadra were placed in the car and were driven to Gundicha temple by thousands of the devotees. However, the chariots could not move beyond Balagandi despite several attempts. In the night Lord Jagannath appeared in the dream of Mudiratha and advised him to invite RASIKANANDA, who was sleeping near the Tulsi Chaura. With the instruction of the king, RASIKANANDA was brought in a procession and was greeted by the king at Atharanala. He came to Balagandi and prostrated before the Lord and could realise the blessings of Lord for him.

This incident happened during the period of king Narasingha Deva (1621 AD to 1647 AD).

The king had provided him land in Bali Sahi near Goddess Gachha Kali. He established the Monastry, which was known as Kunja Matha.

Shankara Dev

He was born in the auspicious day of Vijaya Dashami in the Baradua village of Assam in 1449 AD. His father was a feudatory king of Bhuyan.

As per hearsay, Jagadish Mishra one Vedanta Pundit from Varanashi taught him Bhagabat as per instruction of Lord Jagannath. From him he came to know that Lord Jagannath is Brahma and is identified with Krishna.

He visited Puri with his followers at the age of thirty two. He was attracted by the place and the people and stayed for a period of three and half years. He also learnt Odia Language and written a book known as "Oresa Bamana" which is very popular and a base book for Vaishnavism in Assam. The book is based on the glories of the Lord and contain 21-kirtan songs in Assami language.

He returned to Assam from Puri and preached Vaishnavism in his own style with emphasis on Satsanga, Nama Sankirtan and recitation of Bhagabat. His teaching were accepted by many despite criticism from his enemies. He had proved the merits of his teaching in the court of king Nara Narayan. Ultimately the king became his disciple.

His philosophy is based on Eksharan Naam Dharma, where God can be realised by extreme devotion and faith in one God and the way to find God is by uttering his name, ie. "NAAM".

He also came to Puri for the second time and met Jagannath Dasa, a great devotee of Lord Jagannath and author of Odia Bhagabat. The translations of both of them were based on the commentary of Sridhar Swami. Both of them popularised moral teachings of Bhagabat in the rural villages by establishing Bhagabat Tungi (Bhagabat Ghara) and Nama Ghara. Both of them considered Lord Jagannath as part of Shaguna and Nirguna Brahma. Jagannath Dasa had also influenced Sankara Dev in writing Bhagabat in Assam.

Although Shankara Dev was against idol worship and taking prasad after Puja, however, he used to visit Jagannath temple and used to take Mahaprasad during his stay at Puri.

Legend

When Shankara Dev was at Puri, a kirtan was performed. During the kirtan, Balabhoga was offered by covering it with a plantain leaf.

When the kirtan was continuing, three cats in different colours entered the hall to take the prasad, placed in the pot. However, the devotees did not allow them to take the prasad, as the prasad is offered to the deities after end of the Kirtan. The cats tried 3-times to take the prasad, but they were not allowed. At the end of the kirtan, the Prasad was distributed among the devotees.

In the night Lord Jagannath appeared before Sankara Dev in the dream and told him that they had gone to Kirtan Hall and they were not allowed to touch the Prasad.

Shankar Dev could realise the mistake and came to know that Maha Prasad is acceptable even if it is touched by a dog and can be taken without hesitation and which is above the considerations of touchable or untouchable.

From that day Shankar Dev did not refuse to take the prasad.

Shankar Dev And Rath Yatra

He was too fond of Lord Jagannath that he introduced Ratha Yatra in Satrusala, an Assam village in the boarder of Bangala Desh. Rath

Yatra is performed every year and the height of the chariot is around 20 to 25-feet which is built in Pancharatha style. It is constructed in Assam style of architecture. However, Lord Krishna and Balaram sit in the Rath. The songs from "Oresa Bamana" and "Gundicha Kirtan" of Sridhar Swami are recited.

Shankar Dev was a great devotee of Lord Jagannath and popularised the cultural heritage of Odisha in Assam.

Srimanta Shankardev Namghar / Assamese Namghar – Puri

It is situated at Loknath road around 15-kms away from Jagannath temple. It was established in 1984 AD with the efforts of Assam NAMGHAR samiti.

Here, Naam Prasanga is practiced twice daily, ie. in the morning and evening. There is a guest house attached to it.

Javana Haridasa

He was born at village Budhan (now in Bangaladesh) in the year 1449 AD. He lost his parents in the childhood and was brought up by a Muslim, named Malaya.

He was reciting the name of Hari from his childhood and was a great devotee of Lord Krishna. He later came to Phulia, on the bank of the river Ganga and was famous for his Bhajans. However, the Kazi of the area pressurised him to leave the name of Hari and utter the name of "Kalama". However, he told that for a devotee both Allah and Hari are the same. The Jaban king was not satisfied and he was beaten mercilessly. He sat in meditation and fell down after some time. He was thrown to the river Ganga, treating him as dead.

However, he became conscious and started chanting the name of "Hari". He left the place and went to the forest, where he used to utter 3-lakh names of Krishna every day. He came in contact with Adwaitacharya and later came in contact with Chaitanya Mahaprabhu.

He came to Puri with Sri Chaitanya and stayed at Siddha BAKULA Matha. He used to participate in all the activities of Sri Chaitanya, at Puri.

He used to meditate on Hari Nama in the open. One day Sri Chaitanya took one stick used by Lord Jagannath for cleaning his teeth and planted on the spot where Hari Dasa was reciting Hari Nama. This stick took the form of a tree and provided shade to Hari Dasa.

Everyday, he used to recite 3-lakh names of Krishna and Mahaprasad was taken after that. One day Sri Chaitanya sent Mahaprasad to him, but he only touched the same and had taken a little bit. When Chaitanya arrived and enquired about not taking the Mahaprasad, it was informed by him that he had not completed the recitation of 3-lakh names.

At last with the blessings of Chaitanya and hearing the kirtan of Hari Nama, he fainted and his soul passed away with the chanting of Hari Nama.

His body was taken in a chariot to Mahodadhi (ie. sea side) and subsequently to the lion's gate of Jagannath Temple. Chaitanya Mahaprabhu dug the grave and distributed Mahaprasad in his own hands.

As per Sri Chaitanya, Jaban Hari Dasa was the greatest devotee of Lord Krishna and Jagannath. His Samadhi is known as Hari Dasa Thakura Samadhi Matha. It is also proved that Lord Jagannath accepts the devotees irrespective of caste, creed and colour.

Salabega

Salabega was born on 16th September, 1592 AD (ie. on the day of Radhastami as opined by some researchers). His father Lalbeg was a Mogul warrior under general Man Singh. They were fighting to defeat the Afghans, who were given asylum by the king of Khurda.

During journey of Lalbeg to Puri, he was attracted by Lalita, a Brahmin widow of Danda Mukundapur. He lifted her forcibly and proposed to marry her and Salabega was born from them.

Lalbeg went to Delhi after staying for some days at Cuttack. Salabega was brought up by his mother who was leading a Hindu way of life.

Lalbeg was appointed as the Subedar of Bengal by Jahangir, after death of Akbar. When Odisha became a new Suba in 1607AD, Lalbeg came to Odisha to handover the charge to a new Subedar. During this period he met his wife and son Salabega. He was not happy with his wife, as she was leading a Hindu way of life. Lalbeg took them with him to Bengal. His son Salabega used to assist his father in fighting with the Afghans. During one fight, Lalbeg was killed and Salabega was brought to his mother in a critical condition. Despite best efforts Salabega could not be cured. His mother surrendered him to almighty Krishna and advised his son to utter the Hare Krishna Mahamantra.

After a period of 21-days Lord Krishna appeared in his dream and smeared the sacred powder in his wounds. He was completely cured and from that day he was a devotee of Lord Krishna. He had heard from his mother that Lord Krishna is Lord Jagannath in the era of Kali to bless the downtrodden.

Although, he became a great devotee of Lord Jagannath, but he was not allowed to enter the Temple, being a Muslim. However, he used to see Lord Jagannath on the day of Ratha Yatra.

As per Madalapanji, Mirza Ahmed Beg (ie. brother of Noor Jahan) was the Governor of Odisha and he attacked Jagannath temple during his first tenure (1621AD to 1624 AD). The Sevayats shifted the deities to hide it.

Salabega was disturbed and he was able to convince Mirza Ahmed Beg about the futility of attacking Jagannath temple. Thereafter, he did not attack the temple during his second stint of Governorship between 1625 AD to 1628 AD.

Even he visited the place where Salabega used to sing Bhajans.

Gajapati king Narasingha Dev was also pleased with him and he was listening his songs with devotion. The king had allotted a piece of land in a place near the Maushima temple, where Salabega established the Chatamatha.

Everyday, large number of people used to visit the place where Salabega used to sing Bhajans in honour of Lord Krishna and Lord Jagannath.

Unfortunately his mother breathed her last, when she came to see him.

Thereafter, he went to Brindavan. But he tried to come to Puri during the period of Ratha Yatra. He was ill during his journey and he could not reach Puri during scheduled time of the Ratha Yatra.

As per hearsay, the chariots of the Lord could not move for one month due to heavy rains. A month passed and Salabega could reach Puri to see the Lord. The Gajapati king was able to understand as to why the chariot did not move. After seeing Salabega in Grand road, Gajapati king descended from the elephant and embraced Salabega.

To commemorate the incident, the Nandighosh Chariot of the Lord halts for a while in front of the Chhata Matha, where the Samadhi of the devotee is situated.

From that day Salabega stayed in Puri till his death. He had composed more than 150-Songs / Bhajans about Radhakrishna, lord Jagannath and Lord Shiv etc.

As per hearsay, when he died in the year 1646 AD, his followers wanted to cremate his dead body in their own way, but suddenly the dead body of the great devotee was transformed to a bunch of flowers. As per orders of Gajapati king, his mortal remains were buried and a Samadhi was erected where Salabega used to sit and sing / compose songs of devotion.

Kabir Dasa

He was born at Lahartalao near Varanashi in 1389 AD. Anangabhima Dev was the king of Utkal / Odisha during that period. Sometimes the sea used to cross the shore and flowed near the lion's gate.

King prayed Lord Jagannath to contain the sea. In a dream the king was instructed by the Lord to invite Kabir Dasa from Varanashi to check the flow of sea.

The king sent his minister to bring Kabir Dasa to Puri. He came to Puri and after prayer to Lord Jagannath he sat on a meditation.

As per hearsay, from next day the sea left the place and flowed at a distance from the temple.

At the place, where he meditated for shifting the sea, an Ashram was constructed by the king. This was known as Kabir Chaura.

"Tank Torani" (ie. water mixed rice Mahaprasad) is the specialty of the Matha and it is believed that it cures many diseases. The rice Mahaprasad is provided by the temple administration.

Another legend linked to the Saint, is the wearing of cap while entering the temple.

He was obstructed when he tried to enter the temple wearing a cap on his head. Lord Jagannath was displeased.

As a miracle on that day, it was seen that every devotee was putting a cap in his head while praying the Lord. The matter was informed to the king.

Bada panda (ie. head priest) of the temple had a dream, where Lord told him that Kabir was his prime devotee and he should not be debarred to enter the temple. Kabir came to the temple next day and prayed to Lord with folded hands.

Captain Bitto

He was the captain of a French ship which was sailing from Balasore to Pondicherry. In the ship, besides other materials, there was a special bell and some jewels for a newly built church at Pondicherry. While the ship was passing near Puri, it was observed by him that a severe cyclone was approaching the ship. He rang the danger bell to inform the crew. There was hue and cry and everyone was worried, as to how to save oneself.

During this period, Captain observed that a man was praying in front of a Photograph for safety. On enquiry by the captain, it was informed by him that he was praying to Lord Jagannath to save all from the danger and only he can save his devotees from any danger. The captain was moved by the strong faith of the man and he also prayed the lord out of despair.

When he opened his eyes, he saw that the cyclone had already changed it's direction. The people were happy and danced in joy and captain declared that they were saved due to blessings of Lord Jagannath.

Captain also enquired from the passenger about the whereabouts of Lord Jagannath and intended to offer the jewels and the bell as a token of gratitude to Lord Jagannath. Further, Caption commanded to drive his ship towards Puri. When the ship reached Puri, he went to the temple gate and donated the jewels and bell to utilise the same for the services of the Lord.

This bell (ie. with French words inscribed in it) is found in the NILADRI VIHAR of the Jagannath temple, Puri. Although French Government had requested for return of the bell, the same was not accepted by the Mukti Mandap, as it was a donation made by a devotee.

Dasia Bauri

Baligaon village (DASIA BAURI PITHA) holds an important place in the state of Odisha and in the Jagannath cult. This ancestral place of legendary Bhakta DASIA and his reference in the devotional songs of the state, is a part and parcel in the life of the people of the state.

The village is the testimony, which proved how a simple and poor weaver can communicate with the Lord directly and how Lord accepts the offering.

DASIA, a great devotee of Lord Jagannath, was born around 500-years ago, at Baligaon to a poor, untouchable weaver family. He used to weave and sale clothes in the nearby Praharajpur village, dominated by Brahmins. He and his wife Malati were living in a hut with abject poverty.

As he was untouchable, he was not allowed to the prayer hall of the village. He used to listen, the recitation of Bhagavat of Jagannath Das, at a distance. During his visit to Rath Yatra (ie. Car festival) at Puri, he was deeply attracted towards Lord Jagannath. He could see God every were. He could even see, the Lord in the cooked food offered by his wife in a banana leaf and he used to dance in joy. He became a great devotee of the Lord. It is told that, after coming from the car festival, he had seen the Lord in his dream and he had requested the Lord to accept his offerings.

Legend–1

DASIA came to know that the villagers of Praharajpur were going to Puri, in their bullock-cart filled with coconut, to worship and to offer those coconuts to Lord Jagannath. As he was having the desire to send a coconut, as offering to Lord, he therefore requested, one of the villagers of Praharajpur to give him one coconut, so that he can send it to the Lord.

However, the villager asked for a new towel in exchange for giving the coconut. He received the coconut by giving the new towel to a villager. He had also approached the villagers to take the same coconut from him to offer it to Lord Jagannath. However, he had requested to offer this coconut only to the Lord and to bring back the same, if the Lord did not accept. The rich villagers were surprised and had frowned on him. At last with fervent appeal of DASIA, they took the coconut with them.

When the villagers reached the temple and as they were having a cart load of coconut to offer, they were preoccupied with their offerings. They forgot to offer the coconut of DASIA to Lord.

When they were returning from the temple, on the Grand road they remembered about the offering of the coconut of DASIA to

Lord. Instead of going inside the temple, they offered the single coconut to the Lord at the entrance gate of the temple.

To their surprise, the coconut disappeared from their hand, when everyone was present. This story spread throughout the area and the villagers of Baligaon and Praharajpur were greatly surprised.

Legend – 2

His wife Malati, could not walk such a long distance to Puri, to see the Lord during Ratha Yatra. She requested her husband to describe about the Lord and how the Gods look during the Ratha Yatra. He took her to the GOTHAGADIA POND which was situated at the backside of his hot and asked her to go deep in to the water of the pond.

His wife was able to see the decorated chariots in the reflection of water in the pond along with the image of Lord Jagannath /trinity, in the water.

The pond bounded by banana and Amla trees still exists. No one baths, cleans the clothes /washes the utensils in this pond. Even no one catches fish in the pond.

It is told that, once a villager tried to catch the fishes for cooking. To his surprise, the cauldron was filled with blood. Since then, no body has tried to pollute the pond or catch fish.

Legend-3

It is told that, the Panchasakhas came to DASIA and wanted to see the glimpse of Lord in person, as he was able to show the image of Lord Jagannath to his wife. They were amazed to see the images of the lord through Dasia.

Legend – 4

DASIA was very poor. It was difficult on his part to meet the daily needs. One night, they had nothing to eat. Lord Jagannath, appeared in disguise in his house and asked for food. His wife Malati could not find anything to offer, excepting a small grain of left over food, in the pot. She offered the same to the guest, as no guest is returned hungry as per tradition. The guest left the place being satiated.

That night, the king of Puri came to know in the dream that DASIA had nothing to eat and he is hungry. Thereafter, king arranged food everyday to the house of DASIA. Further, as per tradition, after prasad/Bhog is offered to the deities in the Jagannath temple, Puri, the first offering is sent to DASIA BAURI.

Legend – 5

Every year DASIA, used to send a basket full of Mangoes to Lord Jagannath. It is told that, the priests would find the kernels at the altar, as the Gods had eaten the fruits.

DASIA was known throughout the area and people started respecting him, as the great devotee of Lord Jagannath. There are also many other legends/ hearsay s about him in the area.

Presently, there is a East facing Jagannath temple, which was constructed with the initiative of local people.

It consists of main temple and the mukhashala with 22-Steps. Lord Jagannath, Lord Balabhadra and Maa Subhadra and Sudarshan are the presiding deities. The height of the main temple is 55-feet and width is 25-feet.

Nrushingha, Varaha and Vaman are the side Gods. Madan mohan, Bhudevi, Sri Devi along with Goddess laxmi and Bimala are present inside the main shrine.

A life size Bronze statue of DASIA has been set up on a pedestal in front of the temple. Any one will feel the divinity, when one will observe the statue in kneeling position, in front of Jagannath temple, with flowing hair, well built body and holding a sacred coconut in his folded hands for the Lord.

One will find a good library in his memory, with rare holy books, in this place.

The samadhi (tomb) of DASIA BAURI is conical shape with two eyes drawn on the body. The Basil garden of the Samadhi Peetha is nice to visit.

There is a monastery built during 16th century in this place. Here, images of Radhakrishna, Chaitanya and other monks are worshipped.

One will find a wheel is worshipped at this place. It is believed that it was gifted by Lord himself to his devotee DASIA. Palm leaf manuscripts are also being worshipped in the monastery.

It is told and as per hearsay, some scholars from Bhubaneswar had taken the manuscripts to study the same. To their surprise, the writing on the palm leaf was vanished. They returned the same to the monastery.

The priests of the monastery were sad, as writings on the palm leaves had vanished. But when the same was kept in the monastery, after some days, the scripts started appearing on the palm leaves, which was a miracle. Once again, the significance, of the these pothis (ie. manuscripts) and the divinity was established.

His birth anniversary on Bada Ekadasahi of Kartik(ie. Shukla Ekadashi) month and death anniversary on Bada Ekadashi of Magha month(ie. 11th day of the bright fortnight of Magha Month), are celebrated as a major functions of the area. Jhulan parva and annual day of the temple are other major celebrations.

Tulshi leaves from the nearby garden(Basil garden) and lotus flower from the nearby pond(pink and white) of this place, is sent to Lord Jagannath temple, Puri which is the favourite of the Lord, till date.

For the tourists, there is a two room guest house of OTDC nearby.

This beautiful lush green village with coconut trees and banana plantations is a must visit place for any visitor. The small river Ratnachira (ie. a branch river of Bhargavi) meandering in patches adds to the scenic beauty. Filled with Malati creepers, lotus flowers and Basil garden, this will be a sacred place for any tourist.

One has to move 30-kms on Bhubaneswar-Puri Road. Near Nirmala, one will find a Board of OTDC. It is 15-kms from PIPILI. From that place, one has to move 2-kms in a narrow road to reach BALIGAON VILLAGE, the birth place of the great devotee of Lord Jagannath.

Guru Nanak

Guru Nanak, founder of Sikhism was a great devotee of the Lord. During his life time, he had undertaken Udasis (long journeys) in different directions.

His arrival in Jagannath Puri (which was one of the four Dhams established by Adi Shankracharya) in 1508 AD was one of the longest journey.

As per one legend, when he sent Mardanana, one of his prime Muslim follower/ devotee, to collect Mahaprasad from the Jagannath temple for him and his followers, he was not allowed to enter inside the temple. He returned in grief from the temple to the sea shore, where Guru Nanak was sitting with the followers. He narrated the entire incident.

Guru Nanak prayed Lord Jagannath and a miracle happened. At the time of evening Arati and in the presence of the king, a golden pot filled with Mahaprasad flew from the temple to the sea shore, where Nanak was sitting. King followed the pot and came to Nanak and prayed him.

Nanak had advised the king that Lord Jagannath is not confined to the temple and he is not only the Master of Hindu religion but also the Master of all religions and is in the heart of all devotees. Guru Nanak also showed his palm to the king and he was astonished to see the images of Lord Jagannath, Balabhadra and Subhadra in it.

In another incident, he requested a black man sitting in his side to take a form and to grace the devotees by showing his original form.

When he was speaking a man and woman sitting by his side slipped away. Once again Nanak requested the black man to show his form and immediately the form was changed. Everyone could see Lord Jagannath.

Guru Nanak informed that the man and woman who disappeared near a well were Lord Balabhadra and Subhadra. This well is known as "Dedhasura Bhaibohu Kua) which is near the sea shore. The place where Lord Jagannath appeared is known as Bauli Matha, which is linked to Guru Nanak in Puri.

Similarly, once Nanak was sitting in the Jagmohan at the time of evening Arati of Lord Jagannath. As per custom every devotee has to pay their homage to the Lord by standing at the time of Arati. Hence, the temple priest objected to his sitting during that period. However, Guru Nanak quoted from Padma Purana stating that in Sri KSHETRA one can pay homage to the Lord by sitting, crying and murmuring, as homage / Arati is offered from the inner heart of the devotee which is the real Arati.

Guru Nanak's visit to Puri is found in his Janam Sakhi (biography).

He stayed in Puri for around one and half month. Some of the important Aratis (shabads) like, "Gagan Mein Thal........ Bhav Khandana Teri Aarti Hoai." which are part of Guru Granth Sahib are recited by the Sikhs everywhere during Akhand Path.

Similarly Jaidev's hymns found in the well known composition of Gita Govinda are also incorporated in the Guru Granth Sahib.

Historical Connection Of Puri With Sikhs

As stated above Guru Nanak visited Puri in 1508 AD. After Guru Nanak, no Sikh Guru except Guru Tegh Bahadur had visited Puri. The second Sikh Guru, Guru Angad Dev had tried to consolidate Guru Nanak's teachings and to propagate the same. For that purpose, Janam Sakhis (ie. biography) of Guru Nanak's life and his visit to various places were got written in details.

In the Janam Sakhi of Bhai Bala, Guru Nanak's visit to Jagannath Puri is mentioned in great detail. Two places, Mangu Math and Bauli Math also find mention in the Janam Sakhi, as these Mathas were connected with Guru Nanak.

As understood, the Udasi followers, ie. Baba Shri Chand, who undertook propagation of the tenets of Sikhism during 4th and 5th Sikh Gurus are presently managing Bauli Math and Mangu Math in Puri. They became Sanyasi and did not marry.

Baba Sri Chand had adopted Baba Gurditta, the eldest son of he Guru Hargobind, the sixth Guru of the Sikhs and entrusted him the missionary work of Sikhism in various parts of India. The chief missionary appointed for Jagannath Puri was Almast, who had done impressive missionary work in the areas of the present Uttar Pradesh during the life time of Baba Shri Chand.

Almast had built many Dharmshalas in many places connected with the visit of Guru Nanak including the buildings at Bauli Math and Mangu Math at Puri. As he was deeply religious, he was liked by many. Due to his good work, Guru Tegh Bahadur chose to visit Puri in 1670 AD.

Guru Tegh Bahadur stayed at Bauli Math, which was said to be dug by Guru Nanak for about a fortnight and got the same repaired. Guru Tegh Bahadur opened a free kitchen i.e., Langar for the pilgrims of all faiths and further explained to the people the principles of Guru Nanak's mission and philosophy. The ordinary people as well as the learned Pandits were impressed by Guruji's way of life and exposition of the philosophy of Sikhism.

The people of the area who had great respect for Guru Nanak and other Sikh Gurus was further deepened by his visit.

Bhai Himmat Singh of Jagannath, Puri, in the same traditions, came and offered his head to Guru Gobind Singh at Anandpur Sahib in 1699 AD, at the time of creation of Khalsa Panth as one of the Panj Piaras. The thread of historical connection of Puri from Guru Nanak's first visit to the creation of Khalsa Panth is continuous in one way or the other.

Due to religious persecution of the Sikhs by Aurangzeb and other Mughal Emperors, the Sikhs had to leave their religious places and had to go into hiding. As a result Puri lost connection with the Sikhs for some period.

It was only in 1838 AD, when Maharaja Ranjit Singh during his last illness offered to donate the famous Kohinoor diamond to the Temple of Jagannath at the suggestion of his astrologer, that the place finds mention in the Sikh history again. The royal custodian Beli Ram refused to accede to the royal wish of Maharaja Ranjit Singh, and Kohinoor Diamond could not find its way to the temple of Jagannath, Puri. Beli Ram and his family suffered a tragic death and the Sikhs lost their kingdom in a short time.

Although, Kabir and Chaitanaya who had visited the place have impressive Maths constructed by their followers, but Guru Nanak and his philosophy is unrepresented at such a great historical and religious place.

These days, many people do not know anything about Guru Nanak's visit to Puri and the historical places connected with Guru Nanak's name.

It is understood that, in 1993, Guru Nanak Universal Brotherhood Society had taken initiative to construct Guru Nanak's Memorial at the sea shore of Puri to commemorate Guru Nanak's great historical visit to Puri, and to project his philosophy at a place where other religions of India stand represented in one form or the other.

Puri, therefore, is an important place in the mind of the Sikhs and it's long historical connection with the Sikhs should be popularised as it contributed to Sikh history till the time of Guru Gobind Singh.

Despite various religious traditions and practices, Jagannath culture treats the humanity as one family.

Honb. President and First Lady along with Honb Governor, Minister and Saints

President Ram Nath Kovind, while inguarating the world Vaishnav conference(ie. which was organised by Gaudiya Mission and Srikeshtra Gaudiya Vaishnava Sangha) to mark the 150th birth anniversary of Srila Bhakti -Siddhanta Saraswati Goswami Prabhupada, the founder of Goudiya Math and Mission in Puri, had said, “ God is worshipped in all it’s forms. But the tradition of worshiping in Bhakti -Bhav(devotion) has been significant. Sri Chaitanya Mahaprabhu used to say with humble attitude considering themselves to be smaller than grass. One must be more tolerant than a tree, devoid of any sense of ego and must give respect to others. Sri Chaitanya Mahaprabhu’s constant love for God and his drive to connect the society with the thread of equality gives him a unique reputation in Indian culture and history “. This is also the essence of Jagannath culture, which strengthens the unity in the cultural diversity and keeping it’s objective of human welfare as the most important aspect.

D) Devadasis

The deities were entertained by presenting the dance and musical performances by the dancing girls who were known as Devadasis or Maharies. This was considered as a part of temple service. The earliest inscription in this regard is found during the period of Udyot Keshari (ie. around 9th century). During the period of Gangavamshi and Gajapati kings, it was a part of daily service and regular feature in the Jagannath temple.

The Devadasis / Maharis were generally initiated to the order after compulsory marriage with lord Jagannath and they were one of the nijogas of Lord Jagannath.

As per the Mukhalingam epigraph, Chodaganga Dev is credited to have introduced Devadasi service in the temple of Lord Jagannath. As per Madalapanji, recitation of Gita Govinda of Jayadeva in the Jagannath temple was introduced by king Narasingha Deva. The wife of Jayadeva was a Devadasi and was offered to Lord Jagannath by her father. As per wish of the Lord in the dream, her father offered her to Jayadeva, who was a great devotee of the Lord. The Gajapati kings had made provisions for maintenance of the Devadasis in the holy shrine of Jagannath Temple for singing Gita Govinda and performance of dance (ie. they were getting Khei (Remuneration) from the Temple daily).

They were divided as – Nachuni Mahari (dancers) and Gayani (singers). The Gayanis were further divided as – Bhitar Gayani (ie. singing inside the temple) and Bahar Gayani (ie. singing outside the temple).

However, with the invasion of the Muslims on the Jagannath temple, these activities were affected. They were employed to provide entertainment in royal courts by the subsequent rulers and stigma was attached to their activities. In course of time and due to various court orders, the system was discontinued. There is no Devadasi system at present.

E) Gajapati Maharaja (King)

As per record of rights of the Jagannath Temple, Gajapati Maharaja is the principal and foremost servitor of Jagannath Temple and his service is the hereditary service of the royal dynasty of Puri. Despite abolition of the monarchy, Gajapati king of Puri holds the dynastic importance as main servitor of Lord Jagannath and a symbolic personality of the culture of Odisha. Even today, the Almanacs and the horoscopes of the new born carry the name of one reining year of the Gajapati king.

From the period of Gangavamshi kings till the present kings of Bhoi dynasty, all the Gajapati kings had not only propitiated Lord Jagannath as the principal deity but also had taken steps for development of the temple and Jagannath cult. Although many of them had functioned from different places like – Jajpur, Cuttack, Khurda and Puri but the ancestors of Ramachandra Deva, the founder of Bhoi Dynasty have been swearing in as the Gajapati Maharaja of Puri, since 16th century (ie. from 1568 AD of Ramachandra Deva) till date.

After the images of the Lord were burnt by Kalapahad, the new images of the deities were made and installed in the Ratna SIMHASANA of present Jagannath temple, by Ramachandra Deva (1), who was known as Abhinaba Indradyumna / 2nd Indradyumna. He had also established the Neela Chakra(blue wheel) on the crest of the temple.

The present Gajapati king (Gajapati Divyasingha Deva – since 8th July 1970 AD) is of 19th generation. As they are staying at Puri, they are known as Puri Gajapati.

Till today, Gajapati king of Puri is addressed as, "Shree Shree Shree Veerashree Gajapati Goudeswar Nabakotikarnatotkala Kalabarageswar Viradhiviravar Bhuta Vairaba Sadhu Sasnotirna Routraja Atula Balaparakrama Sahasra Bahu Kshetriyakula Dhumaketu Maharaja Adhiraja ------(name of the king).

He is worshipped as an incarnation of Vishnu and numero uno servitor of Lord Jagannath. Similarly, queen is treated as Laxmi and is not supposed to directly face Lord Balabhadra. During her visit, the palanquin enters the inner portion of the temple and is parked near kalpabata (banyan tree).

The temple is evacuated of all other visitors. Only Mudiratha accompanies the queen. This is known as "Gahana BIJE".

The name of the Gajapati kings appear in cyclical order and generation wise as – Divyasingha Deva, Mukunda Deva, Ramachandra Deva and Birakeshari Deva.

Similarly the names of the queens appear as – Leelavati Patamahadevi, Padmavati Patamahadevi, Chandramani Patamahadevi and Suryamani Patamahadevi.

They are named chronologically one after another and is continuing for around 3-hundred years.

The Gajapati king scavenges the chariots to consecrate them for the Ratha Yatra and BAHUDA Yatra (Return car festival).

During Rath Yatra, before coming to the temple, he offers worship inside the Palace to Kanak Durga and wears the sacred thread. Thereafter, he comes to the temple in a Mehena / Tamjana (ie. palanquin made of wood, ivory and silver) with traditional attire welding sword and accompanied by temple commander / security employees. The procession is led by the servitor Behera Khuntia holding a cane and accompanied with trumpet blowers and drum beaters. He is hailed with "Hari Bola", when he is carried through the crowd. He offers Arati before the Lord and scavenges the platform with golden broom and consecrates the chariot by sprinkling sandalwood water. In the absence of Gajapati, the ritual is performed by the Mudiratha.

Gajapati also performs Chherapanhara during DOLA Purnima (Holi) and Chandan Yatra etc. He has the privilege to perform services during several Beshas of the Lord.

The second day of the bright fortnight of Bhadraba Month is celebrated as "SUNIA"(ie, beginning of the new year as per tradition). As per legend this was the birthday of mythical king Indradyumna, hence the past kings were celebrating this day as the new year day to begin the collection of the revenue.

Some of the daily offered items of the Lord are also sent to him. During their birthdays, special prasad is provided to the palace.

The seat of Gajapati never remains vacant. The ritual of the dead king is performed only after the successor is coronated.

He acts as the Chairman of the Shree Jagannath Temple Managing Committee.

F) Nomadic Life Of The Lord (Ie. Attack On Jagannath Temple, Shifting Of Lord And Non Performance Of Ratha Yatra)

There were several external attacks on the Jagannath temple to seize the treasures of the temple. As the Gajapati kings of Puri / Khurda were having autonomous/ semi autonomous status, there were attempts from several Muslim invaders to deprive them of the same. As Lord Jagannath represents the state, there was struggle for dominance over Jagannath temple.

As per Asit Mohanty, a reputed scholar on culture, Jagannath temple in Puri was plundered 17-times from 1340 AD, when Illias Saha, was the Sultan of Bengal to Mohammed Taqui khan's attack of the temple in 1733 AD.

Ratha Yatra was also suspended several times during these periods. As per Bhaskar Mishra, former Deputy administrator of Shree Jagannath Temple Administration, Rath Yatra was not held on 32- occasions between 1568 AD to 1735 AD.

Due to attack of the temple on several occasions, the idols were shifted to various parts of the state through bullock carts and boats etc. There were two special category of Sevayats, known as "Chapa Dalai" and "Aria Sevakas" who were assigned duties to transfer Lord from the temple to interior Chilika.

As per hearsay, the idols (Trinity) were hidden for 144-years when Raktabahu, a jaban king was involved in attacking the temple.

Heritage expert Surendra kumar Mishra is of the view that, Sri Mandir was attacked 18-times (ie. including the attack of Raktabahu) in the past and presiding deities were taken out of the temple 22-times during the period of aggression. They were kept outside the temple for 164-years and 4-months. Ratha Yatra of the deities were organised outside Puri for 8-times and once inside the Jagannath temple.

- During the period 670-AD to 675-AD when Raktabahu attacked the temple, the deities were taken to Sonepur. They were worshipped near Chhalia hills for 45-years.

  Later they were shifted to a cave opposite Chhalia hills, where the deities were kept hidden for 99-years. During this period Rath Yatra was not observed.

  As per legend, when Raktabahu with a group of Yavanas tried to attack the temple to plunder it, the priests of the temple could know it in advance and escaped with the image of Lord and the wealth. When Raktabahu had attempted to punish the sea, it receded. When the army of Raktabahu marched towards the area, the sea surged up abruptly and swallowed them. The area was flooded and Chilika lake was formed. Many times Chilika lake had given shelter to Lord Jagannath.
- Kalapahad, general of Bengal Goernor – Sulaiman Kirrani had attacked the temple in 1568AD and the deities were shifted by the servitors to Chhapali, near Chilika. He sent the army to Chilika acting on a tip off and took away the deities to the bank of the river Ganga. The deities were set on fire. However, Bishar Mohanty, a Vaishnavite was able to recover

the Brahma / soul of the Lord and consecrated it at Gada Kujanga of Jagatsinghpur district. Gajapati king Ramachandra Deva brought the Brahma to Puri and installed it in the newly carved idols. There was no Ratha Yatra between 1568 AD to 1577 AD.

- Mirza Khuram, a commander of the Nawab of Bengal had attacked the temple in 1601AD. The idols were taken secretly by the temple servitors to Panchamukhi Gosain temple at Kapileswar, around 14-kms away from Puri. Rath Yatra could not be held during this period.
- During the period of king Purusottama Deva of Bhoi dynasty, the temple was attacked in 1607 AD by Hashim Khan, the Mughal Sebedar of Odisha. The idols were hidden in the Gopal Jew temple near Khurda fort. Ratha Yatra could not be performed and the deities were installed at the Jagannath temple during return car festival (ie. Bahuda).
- In 1610 AD, Keshu Das, had attacked the temple and had burnt the 3-chariots of the Lord.
- When Kalyan Mall, the son of Todar Mall (a famous courtier of Akbar) became subedar of Odisha, he had attacked the temple in 1611 AD. During the then period, the images were shifted by the servitors to Mahisanashi in Chilika lake.

  Kalyan Mall again attacked the temple in 1617 AD and the idols were shifted to Gurubai of Chilika lake. Rathayatra could not be performed during the above periods.
- Muslim Subedar Ahmed Bag had attacked the temple in 1621 AD. The idols were shifted to Andharigarh at Banapur area and subsequently to Gadamanitri village in Khurda district. There was no Ratha Yatra during 1621AD and 1622 AD.
- The temple was continuously attacked by Ekram Khan, the Mughal commander of Odisha from 1692AD to 1707 AD. The idols were shifted from the temple to places like – near Khurda, subsequently Bada Hantuada village in Banapur. During these periods there was no Ratha Yatra for around 13-years. Some are of the view that the idols were kept from 1692 to 1699AD at Bada Hantuada village, while some others claim that the idols were kept up to 1707 AD in the said village.

As per records of Madalapanji, during the period of Gajapati king Narasingha Deva, Ratha Yatra was once held inside the Bhoga Mandap (ie. Hall of offerings) to save the idols from the attack of Ekram khan.

- Mohammed Taqi khan, Deputy Governer of Odisha had attacked Shri Mandir in 1731 AD. The idols were taken to Kankanasikhari Kuda in Chilika lake.

  Later the idols were shifted to Harishwar Mandap at NAIRI village of Chilika Tehsil of Khurda district and finally to Chikili village near the foothills of Chakadimbiri at Khallikote.

- Mohammed Taqi khan again attacked the temple in 1733 AD. During 1733 AD to 1735 AD, the images were shifted to Harishwar Temple and than to Marda temple near Hatibari hill in Polosara of Ganjam. The idols were brought back to Puri in May – 1736AD. During 1733AD to 1735 AD, the Ratha Yatra of the Lord were not performed.

As per some other researchers the temple was invaded several times as under:

1st invasion was by Raktabahu, second invasion by Illias Shah, Sultan of Bengal, 3rd invasion by Feroze Shah Tughlaq in 1360 AD, 4th invasion by Ismail Ghazi (commander of Allauddin Hussain Shah of Bengal Sultan) in 1509AD, 5th invasion by Kalapahada in 1568AD, 6th invasion by Suleman and Osman, 7th invasion by Mirza Khurram in 1601 AD, 8th invasion by Hasim khan in 1608AD, 9th invasion by Kesodasmaru, 10th invasion by Kalyan Mall in 1611AD, eleventh invasion again by Kalyan Mall in 1612 AD, 12th invasion by Mukkram khan in 1617 AD, 13th invasion by Mirza Ahmed Beg, 14th by Amir Mutaquad khan in 1641AD, 15th invasion by Amir Fateh khan in 1647 AD, 16th invasion by Ekram Khan in 1699 AD, 17th invasion by Muhammad Taqi khan in 1731AD and 18th attack was done mostly by some devotees due to dispute with the temple administration in 1881AD.

During these periods the deities were transferred to various places to save them.

G) Festivals Of Lord Jagannath

Different festivals are celebrated in honour of Lord Jagannath, Balabhadra and Subhadra. These festivals are mentioned in different Puranas and Almanacs of the state.

The festivals of the town / temple are divided in to 4 primary categories, ie. the 12 primary rituals observed at the Jagannath Temple as prescribed by tradition in Skanda Purana and 78 other small festivals of Jagannath culture known as yatras or upayatras. In the metaphysical system, the festivals are known as 'Yatra'. Many festivals of Puri are related to Lord Jagannath and the Jagannath temple.

The 12-main festivals, ie. Chandan Yatra, Snana Yatra, Rath Yatra, Sayana, Dakshinayana, UTTARAYANA, Parswaparivartan, Uthapana, PRAVARANA, Pushyapuja, DOLA, Damanaka Chaturdashi are covered in earlier paragraphs (ie. major festivals of Jagannath temple). These are being observed in Puri since time immemorial and survive to this day in the exact same form as described in the Skanda Purana.

The most significant of all the festivals is the Nabakalebara, which is observed once in every 8- 19 years.

The important festivals/Yatras of the Temple are described in brief as under:

Chandan Yatra

The festival begins from Akshya Trutiya (i. e., the 3rd day of the bright fortnight of Baisakh) and lasts for forty-two days. 'Chandan Yatra' means, Sandalwood festival (ie. worshiping of the deities with sandalwood mixed water). It is divided into two periods of 21 days each, ie. Bahar chandan or outer chandan (21 days) and Bhitar chandan or inner chandan (21 days).

During outer Chandan, the images of – Madanmohan, Rama, Krishna, Lakshmi and Saraswati are taken outside in a procession to Narendra tank.

The five shivas known as Pancha Pandavas, ie. Lokanath, Yameswar, Markandaya, Kapal Mochan and Nilakantha, also accompany Madan Mohan (the representative of Lord Jagannath) to the Narendra tank.

Every day the procession starts from lion's gate to Narendra Tank amid hymn, bhajan, kirtana, mridanga, ghanta etc. The traditionally decorated royal elephant takes the lead followed by two gigantic decorated palanquins carrying the deities to their destination. The sacred vimanas (ie. palanquins) are carried on the shoulders of the professionally earmarked viman badus. Thousands of devotees assemble to have a glimpse of the yatra, to offer puja & pankti bhoga to the deities throughout the journey. Conventional huge wooden sheds (ie. chamundiya) are erected in the route of their journey which enables resting of the deities. On the way, the deities are worshipped by different Mathas (ie. by offering Panti Bhoga).

The boats are well decorated and the deities enjoy the evening cruise.

In one boat, Madan Mohan, Laxmi and Saraswati are placed. Rama, Krishna and the Pancha Pandavas (five shivas) are placed in another boat.

Various rituals are performed in the picturesque Narendra tank with the accompaniment of music and dance. On the last day of the festival 'Bhaunri Yatra' is performed(ie. the deities move in a circle in each corner of the tank for 21-times).

During this procession, devotees carry the umbrellas(ie. Chatris) made by the skilled artisans of Pipli displaying the rich art and craft of the area. Thousands of people are seen taking a dip in the holy Narendra Tank, which is considered to be auspicious during this part of the year.

After the completion of the outer chandan yatra, the inner chandan yatra starts inside the temple and lasts for 21 days. Various rites are performed inside the temple which are out of view of the public.

This auspicious day also marks the beginning of the construction of the Rathas/ chariots for the ceremonial sojourn of Jagannath, Balabhadra and Subhadra to the Gundicha temple on the day of car festival.

Snana Yatra

This is observed on the day of Purnima or full moon day, in the month of Jyestha (May-june). This is the bathing festival of the deities and is also known as 'Devasnan Purnima' / 'Snana Yatra' (Bathing Festival).

The images of Jagannath, Balabhadra and Subhadra along with Sudarsana and Madanmohan are brought in a procession to Snana Vedi (ie. known as Pahandi) which is situated on the north-east corner of the outer enclosure of the temple (ie. Meghanada Prachir).

The deities are bathed with one hundred and eight pitchers of water taken from Suna Kua (golden wall) near Sitala temple, which is used only once in the year. Then the deities are dressed in Ganesh Besha / Hathi Besha and are worshipped.

The length and breadth of this bathing platform (Snana Vedi) is 76 feet. It is at such a height that visitors standing outside the temple also get a clear view of the deities.

According to Skanda Purana when King Indradyumna installed the wooden deities he arranged this bathing ceremony.

Large number of devotees visit this Yatra, as it is believed that the devotees wash away all sins, if one sees the Lord on this day.

The deities are taken in a procession to the main temple at night.

Anabasara / Anasar

After the end of Snana Yatra day / bathing ceremony, the deities are supposed to fall ill (fever) and do not return to the Ratna SIMHASANA. They are concealed from the public view for a period of 15 days (ie. a fortnight from Snana Purnima to Asadha Amabasya / New moon day of Ashadha).

This period is known as 'Anabasara' or 'Anasara'. They are removed to a side room in the porch and are placed in Anasara pindi (ie. three circular stone pedestals for the deities). For proxy worship of the deities, a bamboo stick wall bearing the paintings of the deities (ie. known as Dasabatar Pati) are placed. During this period the "Daitas Patis" attend to the deities and special Anasara rituals are performed.After the ceremonial bath, the paint on the idols are badly damaged and the deities are given fresh coat of paints for renovation.

As understood, "Anasara" is a tribal dialect of the "Saura's", which means "to dry up". During this period the paints given to the deities are dried up.

Maha Anasara / Naba Kalebara

When there are two months of Asadha which usually comes in a cycle of 11to 18 years, Maha Anasara during Navakalebara is performed.

Naba Yauban And Netrotsava

As stated earlier, the deities are renovated during Anasara period. They become fit for public view. They are dressed in their finest robes and ornaments.

This festival of the re-appearance of Lord Jagannath to the devotees after anasara is called Navayauvana (ie. which means fresh youth).

As the devotees could not see the Lord for 15-days, there is a great rush of pilgrims on this occasion.

Netrotsava

On the next day of NABA YAUVAN the finishing touches are given to the eyes of the deities and the ceremony is known as Netrotshaba.

The repainted deities are brought to the main platform for the devotees to see and to pay homage which is called ' Nava Yauvana Darshan'. The devotees get the first glimpse of the deities on this day before Rath Yatra.

Ratha Yatra

As per Skanda Purana, Rath Yatra is performed as per the wish of Lord Jagannath to see his birth place (Yagnya Vedi, Gundicha temple). This is also known as Maha Vedi Yatra.

As per many poets and from various literature of Odisha, the origin of this Yatra goes to Gundicha, ie. queen of king Indradyumna.

Some historians and researchers link the Rath Yatra with the influence of Buddhism and some opine that Ratha Yatra was started by Gangavamshi kings.

The concept of Rath is also found in Upanishad, where the body is considered as Chariot and soul is the master of chariot, intellect is the charioteer and mind is the rein.

As per Skanda Purana, Lord Brahma had seen the deities in Rath, when he came to Puri for consecration of the deities.

Hence, it is difficult to ascertain the time from which Rath Yatra was started. It is as old as the consecration of Lord Jagannath.

This World famous Ratha Yatra or Shri Gundicha Yatra or Maha Vedi Yatra of Lord Jagannath takes place on the second day of the bright fortnight in the month of Asadha (June-July).

The deities are brought from the temple to the newly built and massive chariots in a swinging manner known as Pahandi. The deities are brought from the Ratna SIMHASANA in a procession one after another in the order, ie. Sudarshan, Balabhadra, Subhadra and Jagannath.

The sound of bells, trumpets and drums (Telengi Baja) reverberates the air. At the northern exit of Natamandap and at the last seven stairs, the deities are decorated with Tahia (ie. a large head gear made of Sola). The deities proceed to the respective chariots after passing through Ananda Bazar, Baishipahach (ie. 22-Steps), lion's gate.

Sudarshan is placed in Devadalana Rath of Subhadra, Sri Balabhadra in Taladhwaj, Subhadra in Devadalana and Lord Jagannath in Nandighosa Rath.

Chariot

On the auspicious day of Akshya Trutiya, the construction work of the chariots commence. The priests observe the fire sacrifice (Homa) near the palace, where the palanquin carrying the images of Rama Krishna and Madan Mohan are placed. After the fire sacrifice, the sarees are tied by the Padia karana on the head of carpenters, after which the construction work of the chariots start. The carpenters, painters, blacksmiths, sculptures, tailors involved in making the chariot are traditionally associated with it for generations. Some of them are also servitors.

Each chariot is a 3-tier structure, ie. lower part including wheels, wheels to pedestal (2nd part) and pedestal to top (3rd part). At the top of each chariot a triangular flag is fixed on a metal wheel.

There are 34-components in a chariot and around 125-carpenters work for 58-days (ie. from 3rd day of the bright fortnight of Baisakh to 15th day of dark fortnight/ new moon day of Ashadha Month) in the Ratha Khala (ie. in front of the palace of the king) to construct the chariots. The chariots are constructed in the Pancharatha style of the temple and the parts of the Rath can be compared with different parts of the body of a human being.

2188 pieces of wood are used for construction of the chariots and 1072 pieces of logs of Phasi, Dharua, Mai and Simili etc. are brought from the forests of Daspalla, Ranapur and different forests of mainly from Nayagarh district. The static and dynamic stability of the chariots are technical marvels due it's techno – engineering details. Each chariot is covered with new clothes for it's canopy like roofing and nearly 1090 meters of cloth are used for the purposes. The chariots are fastened with four long sturdy ropes so as to facilitate the devotees to pull them. These ropes are around 8- inches in diameter and around 250-feet long.

On the day following the new moon day of Ashadha Month (ie. first day of the bright fortnight of Ashadha), the completed chariots are placed in front of the temple gate (lion's gate). The chariots are consecrated and get ready for the Rath Yatra.

The chariot of Lord Jagannath is known as Nandighosh/ Garudadhwaj / Kapidhwaj. The height of the chariot is 13.5 meters. It is having 16-wheels and it uses 832 pieces of wood. It is guarded by Garuda and Daruka is the charioteer. The red and yellow colour clothes are used in the canopy and the rope used for pulling is known as Sankhachuda. It's flag is known as Trailokyamohini and it's horses are known as Shankha, Balahaka, Sweta and Haridashwa. The nine presiding deities of the chariot are – Varaha, GOBARDHAN, Krishna, Nrushingh, Rama, Narayan, Trivikram, Hanuman and Rudra.

The chariot of Lord Balabhadra is known as Taladhwaj. The height of the chariot is 13.2 meters. It is having 14-wheels and it uses 763 pieces of wood. It is guarded by Basudeva and Matali is the charioteer. The red and green colour clothes are used in the canopy and the rope used for pulling is known as Basuki. It's flag is known as Unnani and it's horses are known as Tribra, Ghora, Dirghasharma and Swornanava.

The nine presiding deities of the chariot are – Ganesh, Kartikeya, Sarvamangala, Pralambari, Hatayudha, Mrityunjay, Natambra, Mukteswar and Seshadeva.

The chariot of Lord Subhadra is known as Darpadalan / Padmadhwaj / Debadalana. The height of the chariot is 12.9 meters. It is having 12-wheels and it uses 593-pieces of wood. It is guarded by Jayadurga and Arjuna is the charioteer. The red and black colour clothes are used in the canopy and the rope used for pulling is known as Swarnachuda. It's flag is known as Nadambika and it's horses are known as Rochika, Mochika, Jita and Aparajita.

The nine presiding deities of the chariot are – Chandi, Chamunda, Ugratara, Vanadurga, Shulidurga, Varahi, Shyamakali, Mangala and Vimala.

Rituals

On the day of Rath Yatra, various activities like – completion of morning Arati, Avakash (brushing of teeth and bath), wearing of dresses, fire sacrifice in the kitchen, performance of puja for Sun God and Dwarapalas, offerings as per 16- Upacharas, offering of 12-pots of special cooked rice(khechudi), cakes and Takua and other rituals like – Manglapama, Doralagi and Tuli etc., are performed first.

Thereafter, the Daitapati hands over mailam to Changada Mekap, Palia khuntia shouts "Mahima "Mahima"(ie. Oh Lord) and Daitapati unfastens the deities.

After performance of the above activities, the Pahandi (ie. known as Dadhi Pahandi) starts with the sounds of GHANTA (gong), Kahali (trumpet) and Telenga Baja (South Indian drum). The umbrella bearers unfurl the umbrellas and Sudarshan leads the way.

When Sudarshan reaches the 7-Stairs near the exit of Nata Mandap, Lord Balabhadra is unfastened first followed by Subhadra and Lord Jagannath. The three deities are given Tahiya offered by Raghav Das Math. Thereafter, the deities are placed in the respective Rathas. The Changada Mekaup caries chakapasara (circular cushion) and puts them in the back of the 3-deities. The deities are fastened.

The images of Madan Mohan and Rama Krishna are brought in planquain by Vimanabadu. Madan Mohan is kept in Nandighosh and Rama – Krishna are placed in the chariot of Balabhadra. Two big chests are brought by Kotha Suasias containing the daily and ceremonial robes, ornaments which would be used by the deities during Rath Yatra (ie.for their stay outside).

This is kept behind the chariot of Lord Jagannath. They also keep the dresses, ornaments, puja material, plates and pitchers etc. in two other chariots.

Then the Lenka and Pailas proceed to blacksmith to obtain special head ornaments (ie. Chita) which are made of Sola and are studded with gold ornaments and gems. The deities are also adorned with garlands.

Cherapahara (Sweeping Ceremony)

After the garlands are offered to the deities, the Gajapati king of Puri comes to the chariots in a swing palanquin (ie. known as Mehena) for mopping. A festive band also accompanies him.

He first visits the chariot of Balabhadra and Daitapatis welcome him with bouquet. King offers reverential salute to the deity (Danda Pranam) and obtains the pitcher filled with water (ie. Hatuani) from the Gadabadu (ie. Sevayat). He humbly supplicates the same (ie. known as neuchali) and then offers flowers to the deity. The Bhandara Mekap hands over the incense gold container with camphor to the king. Arati is performed and the deities are whisked with gold Chamar by the king. The royal preceptor (Rajguru) consecrates the golden broomstick and hands it over to the king. The Bhandar Mekap circumbulates the deities of the chariot and sprinkle white flowers. King follows him and moves round the deity by cleansing the circumbulated passage. The king sprinkles holy water in the cleaned passage and sprinkling of sandal powder follows.

After the end of Cherapahra ceremony, the Bhois fasten the charioteers in three Rathas.

The wooden stairs are unfastened and wooden horses are yoked. Thereafter, ropes are fastened, the Rathas are handed over to the police for pulling by the devotees.

The Rath of Lord Balabhadra is pulled first, followed by the Rath of Subhadra and then Lord Jagannath on the grand road. On the way, various Mathas make offerings to the deity. The cars are taken to Gundicha Ghar one after another.

After reaching Gundicha Ghar, the deities undergo ceremonial bath / MAHASNANA by the Puja Panda and are dressed with Bairani/ Boirani cloth. It is followed by holy launch and other ritualistic offerings. Uncooked food is offered during the journey by the car and Puja panda offers food in 16- ritualistic offerings. In the evening, the lamps are lighted, incense sticks are burnt, sandal paste is offered and followed by Badasinghar Dhupa.

The Palia Pasupalakas offer the Arati during bed time and the deities are covered with Srimukha Khandua (PATA cloth). The frontage of the deities on the Rath is sealed with screen.

Next day various a rituals are performed from morning to evening. Goti Pahandi is performed one after another (ie. Sudarshan,

Balabhadra, Subhadra and Jagannath) and the deities retire to Gundicha palace. The trumpet of victory (Vija Kapali / Vije Kahali) leads the procession, Modiratha festenes the rope (doralagi) and offers the flowers. The images of Madanmohan and Rama Krishna are carried by the Mahajans and place it in the Bhandar Ghar of Gundicha palace. After change of dress (mailama), the Daitas unfasten the deities from their respective seats and bring them to the flight of stairs. The salutations "Manima Manima" are uttered by the Chau Khuntia.

The Tahias given by the Raghav Das Math are presented to the deities. Sandle paste and Dayana Mala are offered to the deities by Pati Mahapatra.

The deities are greeted with incense, camphor, 7-lamps, holy grass, raw rice and sweet betel. The deities enter the Gundicha Ghar ceremonially and on the way sacred food (Pankti BHOG) is offered.

Gundicha Ghar Navadin Yatra

During their stay at Gundicha Ghar, the deities take Maha Snana, dressed in new dresses and other rituals are performed, as is conducted in Sri Mandir.

The rituals performed during the stay of the deities at Gundicha Ghar is known as Gundicha Ghar Navadina Yatra.

Heera Panchami

Goddess Lakshmi goes to meet Lord Jagannath in Shri Gundicha Ghar on fifth day starting from and including Shri Gundicha Yatra. As Goddess Laxmi is not brought with Lord Jagannath during Ratha Yatra to Gundicha Ghar, she goes there secretly and breaks a piece of wood of the chariot out of anger. It is performed at the night and she returns to Jagannath temple through Heragohira sahi, instead of Grand road.

Dakshina Murti

The chariots are placed facing the south – west direction on the 8th day, which is known as Dakshina Murti.

Sandhaya Darshan

On the evening of 9th day large number of devotees visit Gundicha Ghar to have the last DARSHAN of the deities at that place. It is believed that if one sees the Lord at Gundicha temple, he will not have rebirth.

Bahuda Yatra

The return journey of the deities are performed on the 10th day of the bright fortnight of Ashadha Month, which is known as 'Bahuda Yatra'. After offering Puja, the deities are dressed and come to the chariot in Dadhi Pahandi. The Chera Pahanra (sweeping ceremony) is performed by the GAJAPATI king.

The chariots start their return journey and they halt at Maushima temple on their way back to receive cake from their aunt. Then the chariots move and the chariots of Balabhadra and Subhadra reach the Lion's gate first. The chariot of Lord Jagannath stays back in front of the palace of the king.

Suna Besha

This Besha is performed on the 11th day. They are dressed in gold ornaments.

Return To Niladri

On the 12th day and after evening rituals, the deities return to the temple with the blowing of the trumpets and in a procession. Lord Balabhadra and Goddess Subhadra are taken to the SIMHASANA in Goti Pahandi.

Lord Jagannath is left behind. As per the instruction of Goddess Laxmi, the lion's gate is closed. After a heated quarrel between Daitas and Devadashis, Lord Jagannath offers Rasagola (sweets) to Goddess Laxmi. His return to Sri Mandir is known as NILADRI BIJE and end of the famous Rath Yatra of the Lord.

The Ratha Yatra is the grand finale of a series of festivals spread over the summer and the monsoon month starting from Snana Yatra (ie. bathing festival, which is the beginning of the festival) to Niladri Bije as described above and is one of the longest festivals of the world.

Legend Of Cherapanhara

The sweeping ceremony of Lord Jagannath, Balabhadra and Subhadra during Rath Yatra is linked with the legend of conquest of Kanchi (ie. Kanchi Abhiyana). As per legend Gajapati king

Purusottama Dev had wanted to marry the daughter (Padmavati) of the king of Kanchi.

But when Kanchi king saw that Gajapati king was sweeping the area of the Lord during Rath Yatra, he felt it as an unworthy act of a king. He declined to give the hand of his daughter to the Gajapati king. Gajapati king Purusottama Dev felt insulted and attacked the kingdom of Kanchi, but he was defeated.

However, Gajapati king prayed to Lord. Pleased with king's prayer, Lord Jagannath mounted on a white horse and Lord Balabhadra mounted on a black horse, left their abode and started in an expedition to Kanchi to help the king.

On their way, they felt thirsty and met a milkmaid Manika, who offered them the butter milk to quench their thirst. As they were not having any money, they offered her a ring to pay the price. They also advised her to return the ring to the king in lieu of the price of the butter milk.

When the Gajapati king and his army passed the area, the milkmaid obstructed them and asked for the price and produced the ring as evidence of transaction. King identified the ring as that of Lord Jagannath and knew about the Devine support of the Lord in the war. Gajapati king led the expedition and was victorious. He brought the Kanchi princes with him to Puri.

He instructed his minister to get the princes Padmavati married to a sweeper.

When Gajapati king was performing the sweeping ceremony of the Lord, the minister tactfully offered the hand of the Princes to Gajapati king Purusottama Dev.

Sayana Ekadashi

Sayana Utsava / Sleeping Ceremony is performed on the 11th day of the bright fortnight of Asadha. The representative images Sri Narayan, Vasudeva and Bhubaneswari representing Jagannath, Balabhadra and Subhadra respectively are brought to the well-decorated sleeping chamber and placed on the cots, at night. They are offered Bhogas. After camphor Arati, the deities are put on their respective beds and the door is closed. They sleep for four months for the welfare of the universe.

Garuda Sayana Dwadashi

This ceremony is observed on the 12th day of the bright fortnight of Asadha, ie. a day after Hari SAYAN EKADASHI. Garuda, the carrier of the Lord is prayed to sleep.

Dakshinayan Yatra / Karkata Sankranti

As the sun begins to move to the autumnal equinox, this festival is observed on the day of Karkata Sankranti. The deities wear Boirani cloth and decorated with sandal paste. Cooked rice is offered to Digpalas (ie. presiding deities of different directions). Rice is offered instead of cooked rice, if the deities are in the Rath.

Chitlagi Amabasya

This is observed on the new moon day in the month of Shravan. The gold and stone set Chitas (ie. ornaments of the forehead) which were removed during Bathing festival of the Lord (Snana Yatra) are again put on them.

Badi Nrushingh Bije

This is performed on the 9th day of the bright fortnight of Shravan Month. Lord Nrushingh moves around 4-ashrams (ie. Markanda, Angira, Kandu and Bhrigu) to protect the people from Cholera.

Jhulana Yatra

It is celebrated in the temple of Jagannath usually from the 10th day of the bright fortnight of Shravan Month up to Pratipada (ie.for 7-days). Madanmohan, the representative deity of Jagannath; Saraswati, and Lakshmi are placed on decorated swings in Jhulan Mandap. Different Mathas of Puri also celebrate this festival with festivity.

Birthday Of Balabhadra (Gamha Purnima/ Balabhadra Janma)

The birth day of Lord Balabhadra is celebrated on the full-moon day in the month of Shravan. The idol of Balabhadra is made in Sola and life is given to the idol. The idol is immersed in water after the puja is over.

Sasti, Markandeya, Varuna along with Ganesh, Navagrahas, Indra, Dasa Digapalas and village Gods/Goddess are also worshipped.

The deities wear gold and silken Rakhis.

Rakshya Panchami / Rahu Rekha Lagi

This is celebrated on the 5th day of the dark fortnight of Bhadraba Month.

Rahurekha (a type of ornament on the fore head) is taken from store house. These ornaments are offered to Lord Jagannath, Balabhadra and Subhadra.

Janmashtami

It is celebrated in the temple on the 8th day of the dark fortnight of Bhadraba for the birth of Lord Krishna. Madanmohan, the representative deity is worshipped as Srikrishna. Madanmohan, Ram and Krishna are placed on the swing.

On the next day Nandotsaba is observed and rituals are performed indicating the celebrations made by Nanda for the birth of his son. Subsequent to Nandotsaba, various festivals relating to Krishna Lila like Banabhoji Besha, Koli Bika, Kaliya Dalana, Pralambasura Badha etc. are performed.

Satpuri Amabasya / Saptapuri Amabasya

This is performed on the new moon day of Bhadrab. On this day huge quantities of sweets known as Satpuri Tada are offered to the deities.

Ganesh Chaturthi

This festival is observed on the 4th day of the bright fortnight in the-month of Bhadrab. Panji Puja is done in Saraswati temple and various Pujas are performed in the temple of Ganesh.

Rekha Panchami / Rishi Panchami

This festival is celebrated on the 5th day of the bright fortnight in the month of Bhadrav.

Radhastami

The festival is celebrated on the 8th day of the bright fortnight in the month of Bhadrab. On this day rituals are performed by taking out Shri Sudarsan to the four Ashramas.

Parswaparibartan

The Parsvaparibartan (turning of sides) festival is performed, on Haribasara day or the 11th day of the bright fortnight in the month of Bhadrav.

At the evening of this day, after the usual rituals are over, the deities are made to sleep on the other side (ie. opposite to which they were laid previously). Earlier, they were facing north and during this celebration their side is turned to opposite side (ie. South). After offerings are over, the door is closed.

Sunia / Bamana Janma

This is celebrated on the 12th day of the bright fortnight of Bhadraba. Various rituals are performed to celebrate the birth day of Bamana, incarnation of Lord. Odiya New year in the name of Gajapati king starts from this day.

Ananta Chaturdashi

On the 14th day of the bright fortnight in the month of Bhadraba, the ceremony is performed in Shri Ananta Basudev temple.

Indra Govinda Puja

This is performed on the full moon day of Bhadraba Month. On this day Indra offers puja to Lord.

Sahasra Kumbha Abhishek / Shakta Gundicha

Abhisek of goddess Durga is done at Marjana Mandap on the 8th day of the dark fortnight of Aswina. From this day Shola-Puja is performed for 16-days in the temple of Shri Bimala and other goddesses.

Lord Madhav is taken from the temple and is allowed to sit with Goddess Vimala in the outer gate of Vimala temple for 8-days. After sitting for 8-days, they both are carried to Narayani temple of Dolamandap Sahi for worship for 8-days. This is known as Shakta Gundicha.

Dwitiya Osha

It is performed in the temple of goddess Lakshmi.

Dussehra And Ayudha Puja

This is celebrated on the 10th day of the bright fortnight of Ashwin Month. Lord Jagannath is dressed in golden ornaments. Ayudha puja is performed.

Vijay Yatra is observed with Ram-Krishna in planquain, Durga-madhav in chariot and Madan-Mohan in Viman.

Kumar Purnima

This is celebrated on the full moon day of Ashwin Month.

On this day the Sevakas representing Shri Jagannath/ Madhav and Shri Lakshmi play dice/ Kauri khela. Being defeated in play, Lord Madhav is captivated in the Mahalaxmi temple for seven days.

Earlier, the servitors escorted Mahalaxmi to the sanctum and sanctorum of Jagannath temple where "Kauri Khela"(conventional small coins in conch cells) was played atop the Ratna SIMHASANA. The game is played by servitors on behalf of Lord Jagannath and Mahalaxmi. As per tradition Lord Jagannath concedes defeat.

Gambling on this day is considered auspicious and locals indulge in this practice till midnight.

Hari Utthapana Ekadashi/ Prabodhan Yatra / Rising Ceremony

This is observed on the 11th day of the bright fortnight in the month of Kartik. From the Devine slumber, the deities are awakened. The festival is also called 'Probadhana Yatra' or rising ceremony.The sleeping house(SAYAN Ghar) is opened and with Arati and puspanjali the deities are prayed to awake. After MAHASNANA (royal bath), the deities are placed in Ratna SIMHASANA and they are decorated with sandal paste. Clothes and ornaments are offered. After Arati and prayer, the SAYAN deities are placed in the Bhandar Ghar. At the end, the rituals relating to sleeping (ie. Pahuda) is performed.

Garuda Utthapana Dwadashi

It is celebrated on the 12th day of the bright fortnight of Kartik.Garuda, the charioteer of the Lord is prayed to rise from sleep.

Navanna / Offering Of New Rice

Various extra Bhogas are offered on this occasion. There is no fixed day for this festival but it is fixed by the temple astrologer according to the stars of Shri Jagannath.

Prathamastami

This is performed on the 8th day of the dark fortnight in the month of Margasira. Parents observe/ worship during this day for the welfare of their first born child. The deities are worshipped with Camphor Arati and puspanjali.

Radha Damodar Puja /Besha

This puja is performed during Kartik month.

Prabarana / Odhan Sasthi

This is celebrated on the 6th day of the bright fortnight in the month of Margasira. From this day ghodalagi begins, i.e., the deities are dressed in winter garments/ warm clothes up to Basanta Panchami.

Deva Deepavali

Lord Jagannath offers lamp to his forefathers from the 13th day of the dark fortnight of Margashir Month up to 15th day of dark fortnight of the month.

This festival teaches people to pay due regards to their parents.

Bakula Amabasya

This is observed on the new moon day of Pousha Month. The deities are offered Gaintha pitha (ie. a special cake) with Mango flower (ie. BAKULA) inside.

Pusyabhiseka / Ramabhiseka

This Abhiseka is performed for the representative deities, like- Rama, Sita and Lakhamana for which it is also known as Ramabhiseka.

This is observed on the full-moon day in the month of Pousa. Pots filled with perfumed water are taken from Bhoga Mandap to the Ratna Vedi.

During this festival the same rituals such as Adhivasa, etc., are performed as in Snana Yatra / Bathing ceremony.

The royal aspect of Lord Ram along with his coronation at Ayodhya is highlighted. The deities are armed with floral bows and arrows.

Uttarayana Yatra / Makara Sankranti

It is performed on the Makar Sankranti day (around 14th January) when the Sun moves towards vernal equinox. On this day, Makar chaula, ie. plain rice with jaggery, coconut and cheese etc. are offered to the Lord. Generally new rice is harvested just before the festival.

Basanta Panchami

This is celebrated on the 5th day of the bright fortnight of Magha Month. Panti Puja is done in the Saraswati temple, and there is some modification in Ghodalagi i.e., in the winter garments worn by the deities.

Magha Purnima

This is observed on the full moon day of Magha Month. GAJAUDDHARANA Besha takes place on this day.

Shiv Ratri

The birthday of Lord Shiv is performed in the Lokanath temple. Hari (Lord Vishnu) Hara (Lord Shiv) Veta takes place at Shri Lokanath temple on this day. This shows the co-existence of Saivsim and Vaishnavism.

Benta / Shikar (Haunting)

This festival is performed on the 1st, 4th, 8th and the 12th day of the bright fortnight of Falguna Month.

On these days the image of Dolagobinda is taken to Jagannatha Ballava Matha which is known as the pleasure garden of Lord Jagannath. Here, Coconuts are struck with arrows by some Sevakas symbolising/ mrugaya or hunting of the Lord.

Dola Yatra

It is celebrated from the 10th day of the bright fortnight of Falguna Month up to the full-moon day. The representative deities of Lord Jagannath are taken to the Dola Vedi and various rituals are performed. This is also known as Vasantotsav. Fagu or red powder is sprinkled on the deities and on this day the deities are decorated with golden ornaments (Raja Besha).

Chaitra Gundicha

This festival is observed on the 6th day of the bright fortnight of Chaitra in the Sun temple inside the temple enclosure.

Ashokastami

It is celebrated on the 8th day of the bright fortnight of Chaitra.

Shri Bhandar Lokanath is taken in a procession to Isaneswar Mahadev where certain ceremonies are performed. The deity returns to the temple after attending to some rituals at Jagannathaballava Matha.

Sri Rama Navami

This festival begins with the celebration of the birth of Shri Rama on the 9th day of the bright fortnight of Chaitra and continues for some days. Rama Lila depicting different aspects of Lord Ram's life is performed through different functions by different sahis of the town.

Damanaka Chaturdashi

This festival is celebrated on the 12th, 13th and the 14th day of the bright fortnight of Chaitra. The representative deities of Rama and Krishna are taken in a procession to Jagannath Ballava Matha from where a scented plant called Dayana is stealthily brought by them. On the next day this is offered to the deities by observing elaborate rites.

Pana Sankranti / Mahavishuba Sankranti

Special rituals are performed in the temple on this day. Birthday of Lord Hanuman is also performed on this day. The day marks the beginning of the Odia new Year.

Niladri Mohodaya

This is observed in the temple on the 8th day of the bright fortnight of Baisakh month. This is considered as the day on which the deities are placed in the Jagannath temple after coming from Gundicha temple in a Chariot.

Birthday Of Nrushingh

This is observed on the 14th day of bright fortnight of Baisakh. The birth day of Nrusingha is performed in the temple.

Rukmuni Bibaha

This is observed on the first day of the bright fortnight of Jyestha Month. It relates to marriage of Rukmini to Lord Krushna.

Sitala Sasthi

On the 6th day of the bright fortnight of Jyestha Month, Lord Shiv and Goddess Parvati comes to the temple after marriage. They are greeted by DOLA Govinda and Maha Laxmi in Mahalaxmi temple. They are also worshipped. This shows the co-existence of Sivaism and Vaishnavism in the Jagannath temple.

Rajendrabhiseka

Abhishek of Lord Jagannath is performed in the temple on the 10th day of the bright fortnight of Jyestha Month. On this day the marriage proposal of RUKMUNI is given to the Lord.

Rukmuni Harana

On the 11th day of the bright fortnight of Jyestha Month, Madanmohan(representative deity of Lord Jagannath) elopes Rukmini from the temple of Sri Vimala, while she performs the worship. The marriage is performed thereafter.

Besides the 12-important festivals, all the other festivals as described above show the amalgamation of different cultures in Jagannath cult. The festivals relating to Lord Jagannath are occasions of great religious experience and devotional fervour.

H) Nabakalebara

The word "Nabakalebar" is a combination of two words and signifies, ie. "naba" means "new" and "kalebar" meaning" body". So, literally, Nabakalebar means the assumption of a new body. It is an ancient ritual connected with Sri Mandir, Puri, when the idols of Jagannth, Balabhadra, Subhadra and Sudarshan – unitedly referred to as the Chaturddhamurati (ie. holy quartet) are replaced by new set of idols.

This ceremony is performed in a year in which there are two months of Ashadha (ie. a leap Month falls in the Month of Ashadha). The extra month is known as Mala Masa / Purusottama Month.

The lunar year being 354 days and 9-hours and solar year being 365 days and 6-hours, a difference of around 11 days occur and after around 32 / 33 months the difference become equivalent to a lunar month (ie. leap year).

Although, leap month may come in all the lunar months, however Navakalevar ceremony is conducted only in the leap month of Ashadha, as the deities are put in ANABASARA (ie. Anasar hut) for repair and painting, just after the full moon day of Jyestha. As Nabakalebara requires the change of old body and more time is needed for the purpose, the deities are placed under Mahaanabasara only at the time of leap year in Ashadha Month. As per religious scriptures, king Indradyumna had installed the carved image in the month of Ashadha.

The astrologers sometimes prescribe 2-months of Ashadha instead of one and this usually occurs in every 8 to 19 years.

Concept

Some scholars are of the view that Lord Jagannath owes it's origin and was worshipped by the tribals in the form of wooden images.

As per Skanda Purana Lord Jagannath performs "Manava Lila" (ie. acts like a human) by taking a DARU form (ie. wooden image). As the man borns and dies, so also the DARU form of God (ie. Lord Jagannath and others) dies and borns like a man.

Further as per Shreemad Bhagavat Gita -

"Vasansi Jirnani yatha vihaya -
Navani grhnati naro 'parani -
Tatha sarirani vihaya jirnany –
Nyanyani sanyati navani dehi" (ie. 22nd verse of the Second Chapter)

The age-old tradition of Nabakalebar is based upon the philosophical conceptual background like one wears a new garment upon discarding the old one. Similarly the immortal soul accepts new material bodies and gives up the old one.

From the practical angle it is believed that most of the deities are made up of stones / metals / jewels. As Lord Jagannath is made up of wood, it is perishable in nature. Hence, these are replaced from time to time.

As Neem wood is strong, resistant to pests and insects, durable and is treated as auspicious by all, it is selected for the images of Lord, who is the God of the Universe.

From some Hindu scriptures and Silpa Sastras, it is observed that people pray for four objects – longevity, strength, victory and wealth. The deities made from metals / others can only bestow some, whereas deities made of wood can bestow all.

History

There is not any definite source regarding the history of Nabakalebar. However, the earliest performance of this ceremony are ascertained using the semi-historic records of Madalapanji of Jagannath Temple, folklore, mythology and hearsay. Some researchers have identified around 27 Nabakalebaras and the history of 25 out of the 27 Nabakalebars leading up to Nabakalebar 2015 have been described in some publications.

Identifying Daru / Wood

The God/ Lord at Jagannath Puri is referred to as Daru Bramha, with "Daru" literally translating as "wood". This wood, that is changed at every Nabakalebar is of utmost significance and the selection procedure for the same follows a number of rituals under extremely detailed prescription.

The tree from which the "Daru" for Jagannath is gathered has to be taken from a tree marked with the shankha (conch) and chakra (wheel), having four main branches.

The neighbourhood of the tree should have a cremation ground, a temple dedicated to Lord Shiva and another heritage component.

The Daru of Balabhadra should have 7 branches, a bark of light brown or white color, and the sign of plough and pestle on it. It is mandatory that there should be a cremation ground and heritage structure in the vicinity of the tree.

The Daru of Subhadra should have 5 branches, a yellowish bark and the marking of a lotus.

The Daru of Sudarshan should have 3 branches, reddish bark, and the mark of a chakra with a depression in the middle.

Ritual Procedure

Number of rituals are performed for searching and making the new images.

Generally there are four distinct stages involved in the process, ie. Searching out the DARU, carving out the wooden structure, consecration of the images and insertion of life substance and finally giving the final shape through repeated coverings by paints and clothes etc.

The ritual starts at the Jagannath Temple on the tenth day of the bright fortnight of Chaitra Month (ie. more than 2-months before Bathing festival).

During the mid day rituals of this day, a garland measuring 12 - feet is used to worship the Gods.

After completion of the worship, this garland which is named Agyamala – a token of the Lord's permission, is given to the leader of the procession who has to set out on the search for the Daru / wood. Mahapatra carries this garland along with four Daitapatis to the ANABASARA Pindi. As per temple tradition the Daitas are assigned the task of finding the Neem tree.

The Gajapati king also issues a proclamation to Vidyapati, Daitas and Brahmins well versed in the Vedas to form a core group and to go for the search of the trees that would provide logs for making the images. Although their number is predetermined, this is the minimum number and has scope for addition of extra members. The Daitas are assisted by Pati Mahapatra, Brahmin priests, 4-vishwakarmas (carpenters), Lenka (temple guards), Deulakaran (temple accountant), Kahalia, Taduakaran and others.

The entire party (ie. dressed in new garments) sets forth on their mission from the Gajapati's palace after receiving the official command from the King to find the Daru. This has to be carried without respite till the tree is found and the garland is placed on it.

After send off from the palace with rituals, the party moves to Jagannath Ballav Matha and on to the Mangala Temple at Kakatapur, a village situated 45-kms away from Puri.

After reaching Goddess Mangala of Kakatpur, they perform sacred Bath (Maha Snana) of the Goddess, offer Maha prasad and recite Swapnabati Mantra in the night to obtain permission/ direction from the Goddess in the dream to find the Neem tree. It is also understood that there are large number of Neem trees in Kakatpur area.

Here, the group may stay for 15 to 30 days till the oldest Daitapati is visited in his dream by Goddess Mangala who directs him towards the exact location of the trees.

The search party is divided in to 4-batches and go to search the Neem wood in different directions, as per directions given by the Goddess in the dream.

IDENTIFYING DARU / WOOD

For each deity – Jagannath, Balabhadra, Subhadra and Sudarshan, the wood has to have different qualities, but all the wood should be from a Neem tree.

There are strict rules for selecting the trees. Darus (wood) having the symbols like – ant hill on the ground of the tree, tree must not be affected by lightening, ponds / river / funeral ground/ Hermitage/ temple nearby, not bear any branch from it's foot up to 10/12 feet, taste of these trees should be slightly sweetish, should not have cut marks and have snakes below the tree etc.

The bark should have a dark coloration and the foot of the tree should have an anthill with a snake hole. The tree should not have any birds' nests and there should be no perched bird on it. It should also be free from parasitic plants and creepers. Other trees surrounding this tree should include the Varuna, Sahada and the Bela trees etc.

The tree for Sudarshan 's DARU should have 2- branches, 7-branches for Balabhadra's, 5-ranches for Subhadra's and 4- branches for Jagannath's.

The colour of Sudarshan DARU is generally yellow and should bear the symbol of Naval posture.

The colour of DARU for Balabhadra should be generally white and should bear the mark of Hala and Langala.

The colour of the DARU of Subhadra should be red and bear the mark of lotus.

The colour of the DARU of Jagannath should be black and should bear the mark of conch, wheel, mace and lotus.

The wood (DARU) is selected taking various specifications as stated above.

On finding the tree, the Daitapati places the Agyamala upon the tree. The surroundings of the tree are then cleansed, perfumed water sprinkled and a platform erected at the foot of the tree for the Vana Joga (fire sacrifice) ceremony). A temporary hutment is also set up near the tree, known as Sabar Palli, where the group would reside for some time.

The Brahmins conduct the rituals. The Daitapatis sit in meditation for 3-days.

During this period, a ritual known as "Ankuraropana"(ie. sowing of some seeds for germination) is performed. After Ankuraropana is over, the sacrificial fire is offered for 3-days and thereafter the trees are cut. Lord Nrushingh is worshipped as the presiding deity during the entire ceremony.

The tree is touched by a golden axe by the Vidyapati, a silver axe by the Daitapati and finally with an iron axe by the carpenters (Maharana). Only the middle portion of the DARU remains after cutting the sides.During tree cutting, 108 names of God are chanted continuously.

The holy DARU is covered with PATA Bastra and are carried in four wheeled carts newly built for the purpose from the trees like – kendu, vata and tamarind etc.

After the tree has been felled, it is transported – with all branches intact, to Puri on a newly made, four wheeled, wooden cart pulled by Daitas, people and other Sevakas. From the Sakhigopal side, the cart is taken to Alamchandi temple and from Konark side to Yagnya Nrushingh temple.

When the sacred woods reach the Alamchandi temple, which is near Atharanala (ie. gate of Puri), the Gajapati king is informed.

Maa Alamchandi

She is guarding the Srikeshtra at Atharanala gate. She scans the holy wood for Nabakalebara, in her third eye to free it from evil powers, before the deities are carved out.

After arrival of holy wood in her temple, a special ritual is performed before the Goddess on behalf of the Gajapati king. It is believed that she scans the the holy wood in her third eye in the midnight after the secret ritual.

There after, Gajapati king gives directions to bring the DARU in a procession to the temple. The woods are taken inside the temple through North gate.

Before the holy wood enters the workshop in Koili Baikuntha, Maa Sitala guards the first step to remove all obstacles through her cooling effect. The holy wood enters the workshop in Koili Baikuntha and as believed all the deities keep a watch on the transition of the trinity to newer idols.

On Snana Purnima day the holy logs are bathed along with the old deities. Then the woods are taken to DARU Ghar (stacking room of sacred logs).

The work that proceeds is executed under strictest confidentiality. Even the head priest of the temple is not allowed to visit the special enclosure where the carving of the idol is being done.

At this place, after prescribed rituals have been performed by 108 Brahmins, the three most experienced wood carvers begin to work on the idol of Lord Jagannath. Two more groups, each with three carvers simultaneously start carving the idols of Balabhadra and Subhadra. More than 50 people assist them. The carving has to be completed within 21 days. During this period the carvers are not allowed to leave the temple premises and are provided with only Mahaprasad for food.

These 21 days are marked with incessant chanting of Vedas and devotional songs being sung outside the Koili Baikuntha – a process known as Akhanda Bhajan.

Also during this period, Abhishek of Lord Shiv, recital of thousand names of Lord Vishnu and Chanting of Mantras for Chandi are performed in the Jagmohan of the main temple. Fire sacrifice which continues for 15-days during this period, the Mantra of Nrushingh is recited. On the 10th day of fire sacrifice, the new images circumscribe the main temple for 3-times. On the 13th day, sacrifice is offered and on the 14th day Nrushingh is worshipped. Thereafter Gajapati king of Puri performs the closing ceremony (purnahuti) of the Yagna.

Once the idols have been made and the rituals as stated above are performed, the images are brought from Koili Baikuntha to the Anasarapindi chamber of the temple for transformation of Brahma from old to the new forms (ie. This is the most auspicious ritual of Nabakalebar, which is known as Ghata Paribarttana).

Three senior most Daitapatis (ie. one each for Jagannath, Balabhadra and Subhadra) are involved in the process. After a day of fasting and meditation, the Daitapatis, with their eyes blindfolded and hands wrapped in silk, perform the ritual of Ghata Parivartan that involves the transfer of the Bramha, or the soul of God from the old idol to the new. The content of the Brahma or the Ghata is unknown as are the details of the rituals, which is performed under strict secrecy.

It is performed In the dark night of Krishna Chaturdashi in the month of Ashadha.

Even the CCTV Cameras and Electricity of the entire area in and around the Shree Jagannath Temple is turned off to respect the darkness and silence that is required for this ritual.

Different sects have different interpretations of Brahma (ie. what is actually the Brahma). While Buddhists think, it is a tooth of Gautam Buddha, Vaishnavites are of the opinion that it is a live Shalgram Shila fallen from heaven and tribals think it to be the unburnt navel portion of Shree Krishna that floated to Puri from Dwarka after his death, as a log of wood.

Once the Ghata Paribarttana is complete, the old idols are considered dead and are buried, along with their subsidiary deities, beds and chariots into a well of Koili Baikuntha. The deities are carried on the shoulders of the Daitapatis through Beherana DWAR for burial.

Though the same well is used for each burial, the remnants from the past Nabakalebar are never found there.

As the Daitapatis consider the Lord as their family member, they mourn for ten days and perform Suddhikriya (ie. rituals related to death) on the eleventh day as one would normally do for a family member. On 10th day they proceed to Markandeya tank to cut their hair, nail and to take purifying baths.

During this period of one month the public could not see the new deities. The Daitas prepare the deities, necessary paste is administered and they are wrapped in silk clothes. They are painted by the painters. The whole process is performed during Mahaanabasara. On the first day of the bright fortnight of Ashadha Month, the deities appear in Ratna SIMHASANA, known as Navayauvan Besha (fresh youth).

Thereafter the finishing touches are given to the eyes of the deities, known as NETROTSAVA. Rath Yatra, the most important celebration of the Lord is performed on the following day.

This concludes the Nabakalebar. Rath Yatra is celebrated subsequently with the new deities.

There is a general belief that the devotee washes away all his sins, if he gets a vision of the Lord on this day. Therefore, it attracts lakhs of pilgrims from all over the world.

Sriangaphita

Sometimes during emergencies, the circumstances do not allow for Nabakalebara. At that time the "SRIANGAPHITA" ritual is observed in Jagannath temple. During this period, the new idols of the Chaturdhamurti are neither carved out from DARU (wood) nor the transformation/ transfer of the Brahma takes place.

However, a secret ritual known as "SRIANGAPHITA" is performed by the Daitapatis and Vidyapatis. During this period, all the coverings from the deities are removed and they are wrapped up in new coverings and painters (chitrakaras) paint the images.

This is performed generally during attack of the temple and due to financial crunch etc. As understood, this was performed last in 1893 AD due to financial problems, when Queen Suryamani Patamahadei was the administrator of the temple.

For performance of Nabakalebara, some researchers are of the view that it was a necessity as the the idols were prime targets of sacrilege by the invaders from time to time.

The Jagannath Temple was a symbol of prestige and power of the respective kings. During ancient period, there was inter-kingdom strife and continuous struggle to gain power by annexing other kingdoms. The seat of the Lord and the idols were often the prime targets of the invaders.

Many iconoclasts and invaders, like – Raktabahu – a Yavan invader, Kalapahad – a Muslim general and Kesodasmaru – a Rajput Chief, Mughal Emepror Aurungzeb and Taki Khan etc. had attempted to raid the Jagannath temple for temple treasures and destruction of deities. The deities were shifted to different places from time to time and Nabakalebara might have been performed, when they were again returned to the temple/ installed.

Even believers of other faiths other than Vaishnavism had attempted for religious supremacy.

Hence, some researchers have opined that, initially, Nabakalebar can be said to have been a circumstantial necessity rather than ritual. With passage of time, it was observed with elaborate arrangements and rituals in a regular manner.

SANKHA SREE KSHETRA

SANKHA SREE KSHETRA

1. Balabhadra,Jagannatha, Subhadra & Sudarsan
2. Khetreswari Vimala
3 Mahalaxmi
4. Uttar Durga
5. Bata Mangala
6. Garuda Stamva
7. Bhoga Mandap
8. Kalpabrukhya
9. Rohini Kunda
10. Bata Ganesh
11. Uchsta Ganapati
12. Sri Saraswati Devi
13. Nabagraha
14. Konark Suryadev
15. Padapadma
16. Yagnyabata
17. Angeswar
18. Indranidevi
19. Khetrapala
20. Swana Vairabi
21. Mukteswari
22. Chstrakali
23. Batamarkandeya
24. Katyayani
25. Gopeewara
26. Beda Kali
27. Pataleswara
28. Bhubaneswari
29. Vaikuntheswara
30. Yagnyaswari
31. Isaneswar
32. Sitaia Devi
33. Pakasala
34. Dakhineswara
35. Kundaleswara
36. Ram Chaitanya Temple
37. Baravai Hanuman
38. Nirmalya Hanuman
39. Alaka Batika
40. Chakra Narayan
41. Rameswar
42. Chaturdhama
43. Kanapata Hanuman
44. Niladri Vihari
45. Bavabyeswara
46. Sialilata
47. Koili Vaikuntha
48. Tapaswi Hanuman
49. Survarnakupa
50. Ananda Bazar
51. Devasnana Mandapa
52. Meghanada Prachira
53. Singhadwara (E.gate)
54. Aruna Sthamva
55. Badachhata Math
56. Chhauni Math
57. Pejanala
58. Prahari Hanuman
59. Dakhinadwar (S. gate)
60. Durgamadhava
61. Mangaleswari
62. Paschimadwar(W. gate)
63. Uttardwar (N. gate)
64. Sri Lokanath
65. Rameswara
66. Kandunursingha
67. Kandu Asrama
68. Nikumvilabata
69. Harachandi
70. Chamundeswari
71. Banadurga
72. Basheli
73. Kapalmochana
74. Manikarnika Teertha
75. Ghatamangala
76. Vagabati
77. Markandeswara
78. Markandeya Teertha
79. Saptamatruka
80. Alamba Devi
81. Atharnala
82. Makardhwaj Hanuman
83. Vargavi River
84. Mukteswara
85. Bata Mangala
86. Kapoteswara
87. Vilweswara
88. Siddha Hanuman
89. Indradyumna Teertha
90. Nilakantheswara
91. Adinrusingha
92. Gundicha Mandapa
93. Mausima
94. Marchika Devi
95. Charchika Devi
96. Sodasha Putri
97. Narayani
98. Angirasrama
99. Angirabata
100. Dakhina Kali
101. Ugreswarashrama
102. Swetaganga
103. Muktisila
104. Adisankara Pitha
105. Swargadwara
106. Varahi Devi
107. Shyama Kali
108. Bedi Hanuman
109. Chakra Teertha
110. Chakra Narayan
111. Mahodadhi Tirtha
112. Jagannatha Ballava
113. Kashi Biswanatha
114. Visweswari
115. Narendra Sarovar

Lord Jagannath, the temple complex and the holy city of Puri are having large number of attractions for any visitor. It's religious sanctity, architectural grandeur, sea-scape beauty and moderate climate would take one on a journey down the memory lane.

CHAPTER 3

Konark

The name Konark signifies, kona (means-corner) and arka (means - Sun / Surya). It may be due to it's position where the Sun appears to be rising at an angle. It is also known as 'Arka Kshetra'. As per legend this temple stands as a testimony to the sacrifice of Dharmapada, a young boy.

Europeans called it "Black Pagoda" due to it's pagoda like structure and colour / dark façade. It was helping the ship in navigation. It is said that, there was huge 52-ton magnet in this temple and the ships were drawn to the shore due to it's magnetic power.

It is a UNESCO WORLD HERITAGE SITE and famous for it's unique Kalinga architecture which is a monumental representation of the Sun God. It is designed like his chariot with elaborately carved stone wheels, pillars and walls. The Sun God is standing in chariot which is being pulled by 7-horses. He is seen holding with a lotus in both his hands and is flanked by two dawn Goddesses, Usha and Pratyusha, shooting arrows to dispel the darkness.

Konark Sun temple is the third link of the state's golden Triangle with Lord Jagannath Puri and Bhubaneshwar.

Noble laureate Rabindra Nath Tagore had described this magnificent and massive Sun temple, "as the place where the language of stone surpasses the language of man".

The temple is an enigma and no historians, archeologists and researchers can claim with certainty, the real story behind Konark.

Although, there are Sun temples at Martand in Kashmir, Modhera in Gujarat, Ranakpur and Osian in Rajasthan, Lonar in Maharashtra and Kumbakonam in Tamilnadu, Wooden Konark at Buguda in Ganjam district of Odisha, Biranchinarayan temple at Palia in Bhadrak district of Odisha and in many other sites with different styles of architecture, however the magnificent Konark temple is admired for centuries for it's majesty and grandeur.

Chaitanya Mahaprabhu and Abul Fazal, the court historian of Akbar had visited the temple.

Abul Fazal had wrote about the temple, "Even those, whose judgement is critical and who are difficult to please stand astonished at it's sight".

The temple is a blend of science with architecture. From construction to collapse and discovery at a later stage, there are many theories and legends as described below but there is no unanimity as yet. It is one of the wonders of Incredible India.

History And Legend

Konark is an ancient and important place for worship of Sun God. It's reference is found in mythological texts like-Shiv Purana, Skanda Purana, Bhavishpurana, Varahapuran, Brahmapuran and Samba Purana etc. It is known as Maitreyavana in Kapila Samhita.

Legend – A

As per Samba Purana, Samba (son of Lord Krishna and Jambavati) was proud of his handsome appearance and once ridiculed sage Narada and who to avenge himself, led Samba to a secret bathing place of his step mothers. They were struck with the personal charm of Samba and wanted to enjoy his company.

In the meantime, Narada led Lord Krishna to this spot. Lord was furious at his son's apparent lack of propriety and cursed him to be smitten with leprosy, which would affect his beauty.

Samba pleaded for his innocence, but as the curse could not be withdrawn, he was advised to practice penance in the Mitra vana near Chandrabhaga to propitiate Sun God to cure him of the diseases.

Samba had performed severe penance for 12-years at Mitravana, near the confluence of Chandrabhaga river with the sea. He was succeeded in pleasing the Sun God and he was cured from leprosy. In gratitude, he had decided to erect a temple in honour of Sun God.

One day, while Samba was bathing in Chandrabhaga, he discovered an image of Sun God standing on a lotus pedestal holding two fully bloomed lotuses in both the hands. The image was believed to be constructed by Vishwakarma. Samba installed the image in a temple built by him at Mitravana. Since then it is a sacred place.

As per Bhavishya Purana, the local Brahmins did not agree to worship the image. Samba brought eighteen Maga / Magha families (ie. Sun worshippers) from Shakadwipa (Iran) to perform the rituals. They popularised Sun worship in this part of the country.

Legend-B

Some legends say that rays of sunlight cure skin diseases / leprosy at this place. Mayur, poet and ambassador of king Harshvardhan was cured from leprosy at this place.

The place is also linked with Multan, ie. a place in present day Pakistan. Multan was a major center for Sun worship and Chenab river flowing nearby was also known as Chandrabhaga.

Some say Konark's earlier name was Kainapara / Konagar / Kona-Kona and was an ancient port city of Odisha.

There was a smaller temple of Sun God at the same location may be of 9th century during the period of Somavamshi kings. As per live historyindia, "As per Madalapanji-----king Purander Keshari built a Sun temple at Konark in 870AD. It is said that the remains of this temple can be seen behind the existing Sun temple compound and it is known as Chhaya Devi / Maya Devi temple".

It had gone through many collapses and reconstructions and there are also many other legends about construction of this temple.

Legend-1

Anangabhima Dev-lll (1211-1238 AD) had worshipped Sun God (Surya) to get a son in the family as some Saint had suggested them to pray the Sun God.

With the blessings of Sun God (Surya), he was having a son, whom he named as Narasingha Dev. He was born after continuous prayer of 12-years. Hence, number 12- was lucky for Narasingha Dev.

The queen mother of Narasingha Dev had advised him to build the temple.

The temple was built as a gratitude to surya. He had also declared that the temple must be completed in 12-years with 1200-artisans.

Legend – 2

This temple was built by Narasingha Dev-1 in 1295AD to fulfil the the promise of his father (Anangabhima Dev lll) to expand the Jagannath temple in Puri, which was built by Chodaganga Dev.

Legend – 3

Some say, the king built the temple in the memory of his lady love, Mayadevi.

Legend – 4

The king had a deformed spinal cord. To get rid of his deformity and to have a healthy offspring, he had prayed Sun God and built the temple as a token of worship.

Legend-5

The Muslims have conquered major portion of the Northern India towards end of 13th century excepting Odisha. There was a Great War between Tughan Khan (ie. General of Nasiruddin Muhammad) and Narasingha Dev, where the Muslim army was defeated.

The temple was built to commemorate military success against Muslim invaders.

From various records and studies, it is believed that the temple was constructed in the 13th century (ie. between 1253 AD to 1260

AD) by Narasingha Dev – 1 from the Eastern Ganga dynasty. Shivai Samantara Mahapatra was the incharge of the construction.

As per Times of India (article dated 15/1/2015), "The Sun temple has left many awed and curious. If the beauty and grandeur of the place has been spellbinding, the missing links in it's life cycle have remained a jigsaw puzzle few have been able to unravel. This is the enigma of the monument, whose history raises more questions than answers".

Konark Temple

CONSTRUCTION

The book "New Light on Sun Temple of Konark" published in 1972 AD by Alice Boner, S R Sharma and R P Das, describes in details about the entire temple building.

As per the researchers, "This is like a modern day ITES (Information Technology Enabled Services) project manual comprising details such as – type of artisans, milestones, frequent review and inspection by the royal family, bottlenecks, hunger strikes etc.. It was one of the first temples to be completed on target date, ie. 11th day of Magha Shukla Paksha, February of 1258 AD. The first puja began on Sun God's birthday as "Padmakeshra DEULA". (ie.

The image of Surya was installed on Sunday, the 7th day of Magha Sukla pakshya – Magha SAPTMI – 1258AD).

As per researchers, the palm leaf manuscript called "Baya Cakada" / BAYA CHAKADA written in Karani script in old Odia language was collated in full set of 73-leaves.

It gives in details and chronological events regarding construction period for 12-years(ie. 1246AD to 1258AD).

To construct the temple 1200 workers/ artisans were engaged for 12-years.

The king had spent an amount equivalent to the state's revenue receipt for around 12-years. It is also believed that his father-in-law, who was a Pandya king, had also sent a team of sculptures.

As per madaras courire.com, Around the time of temple's construction, there was a mighty solar eclipse – represented in the area by a depiction of "Rahu", the demon that eats the Sun during such eclipses.

There is a beautiful and inspirational story about the construction of this temple.

HEARSAY/STORY

A. The main architect was Bisu Moharana, who had left his birthplace to devote himself completely to the work. At that time his wife was pregnant.After some time, his wife gave birth to a boy who was having inborn talent of construction of temples/ buildings. Other children used to make fun of him, as he was having no father at his home. When he was a 12-year child, he decided to meet his father.

   In the meantime, the construction work of the temple was in full swing.

   Despite the creative talent, energy and commitment of the artisans, the completion of construction remained impossible to predict. The king issued the instructions to complete the work by a set date. The team of architects, led by chief architect, Bisu Moharana lost hope of completion.

   However Dharmapada, the 12-year Son of the Chief Architect arrived as a visiting onlooker. He became aware of the despair and became a part of the construction work. He studied the theories of temple architecture and constructed the most important part of the temple, ie. cupola (ie. last coping stone at the top of the temple) which his father/ other artisans could not complete. At last he immolated himself by jumping in to the sea to save the honour of his fellow workers.

As per hearsay, Dharmapad had completed the final construction of the temple in a single night to save 1200-craftsmen from execution and then sacrificed himself to prevent the story from spreading.

This is the inspirational story of renunciation, where a young boy sacrificed his life to save the lives of others after achieving the ultimate glory.

B. King Narasimha Deva had given deadline to the sculptures to finish the temple. If they would fail to finish the top (ie. Dadhi Nauti) within the deadline, they all were supposed to be killed.

Hence all the sculptures and workers were under pressure. Before the deadline, Dharmapada, a 12-years old by and son of Bisu Maharana, had finished it.

Some believe Dharmapada was the incarnation of Sun God. He had demolished the ego of the king. As he gave his life by jumping from the temple top to the river Chandrabhaga, which was flowing just beside the temple, the temple became unholy and by circumstances Lord could not be worshipped long, inside the temple.

C. The temple was constructed with Chlorite stones from Nilagiri hills, soft sand stone from Siddhadurga (some believe as – Sindhudurga) which were transported in big barges to the mouth of Chandrabhaga river, near Konark. The temple was built using scaffolding, cranes and pulleys along with rollers for hoisting heavy stones.

There was casting of iron beams and this was interspersed with stone beams and were bolted to bear the load. Some of the beams are not rusted as yet, which proves that there was an advanced smelting foundry.

Chlorite, laterite and greenish khondolite stones were used to construct the temple. The stones were fully finished, polished and fitted together using iron cramps and dowels so that the joinery was almost invisible. Two magnets held together the entire structure. Some of the stones were weathered ferruginous and oxidised sandstone.

As there is more enduring power of the Chlorite stone, it was used for more important construction works, like doorways, the idols in the shrine and for making sculptures of musicians etc.

The core of the foundation and platform are made up of the laterite stones. The main structure is made of Khandolite. None of the stones are available in the area and might have been brought over long distance by rafts on the river and seas.

As stated in earlier paragraph, during construction of the main tower of the temple, the artisans had placed iron plate between every two stone pieces. There was a load stone at the top of the temple which is believed to have been a massive 52-ton magnet. According to legend, the main statue of Sun God was built of a material with iron content. It is said that, the image of Sun God was floating in the air in the middle of the temple without any physical support due to unique arrangements of the top magnet, the bottom magnet and reinforced magnets around the temple wall. This was held in balance by the magnetic forces.

It was built in such a way that, the Sun rays would cross the Nata Mandap and would fall and reflect from the diamond placed at the crown of Sun God.

The first rays of the Sun fell on the forehead of the main deity giving an impression of rising Sun.

D. A ship with crew whose captain was James Stewart was on it's way to Rangoon. The ship was carried away by a strong tornado. The crew knew that they were well away from their route. They had lost all hope. However, suddenly one of the crew came running and informed the captain that a huge black geometric figure was visible in the horizon. Through the binoculars, he could see the legendary Sun temple, known as Black Pagoda. The temple had saved not only the ship and crew but also had guided thousands of sailors on safe track in the Bay of Bengal.

   As per UNSECSO, "It is one of the outstanding examples of temple architecture and art as revealed in it's conception and in the sublime narrative strength of it's sculptural embellishment. The Sun temple is the culmination of Kalingan temple architecture, with all it's defining elements in complete and perfect form. A masterpiece of creative genius in both conception and realisation ".

It was originally built on the sea shore which was also used as a landmark for the sailors of Bay of Bengal. However, now it is at a considerable distance from the sea.

The palm script manual "Padma Kesara DEULA karmangi" written in karani script details the rituals performed in the temple.

TEMPLE

The temple is in the form of a heavily decorated chariot of Surya drawn by 7-Spirited horses on 12-pairs of elaborately decorated wheels. It symbolises the movement of Sun God in the sky. The temple compound is 857-feet by 540-feet (ie. 261.21 meters from east to west and 164.59 meters from south to north).

The temple is standing on a sprawling 12-acres patch and is aligned in an east-west direction. It is surrounded by casuarina plantation and other trees on sandy soil.

There are 2-gates, ie. one on the eastern side facing the Nata Mandir and other on the southern side facing the porch of the Sun temple.

There are 6-temples in the Sun temple complex and 2- big wells. It comprised of Nata Mandap/ Nrutya Mandir (dance hall), Jagmohan (frontal porch) and Rekha DEULA (main temple/ inner sanctum) arranged along the east-west axis. The Rekha – DEULA – Jagmohan complex forms the chariot, while the common plinth or pista forms the matrix on which the wheels and horses of the chariot are carved. The Nata Mandap stands apart.

It is a Pancharatha temple, as at is broken by 5-projections.

Within the complex, there are two minor temples of Mayadevi and Narayan and a Bhogamandap for common meals.

The present day surviving structures are the – Entrance, Nata Mandir (Dancing hall), Jagmohan and Bhoga Mandap (Dining hall). There is an elevated walkway around the temple.

The temple as seen today shows it's glory even in the ruins of what it is now.

Entrance To The Temple

The entrance leads to the shrine of the deity of Sun God (Surya) which was made up of Chlorite stones. As one enters the temple complex, one will find two massive lions, crushing the elephants (ie. Gaja-Singha) at the main entrance of the temple. The elephants are having two ivory tusks.

Some opine that, it symbolises the supremacy of Hinduism (ie. represented by lion) over the Buddhism (ie. represented by elephant). Each elephant lies on the top of a human body. This is lying at the eastern staircase of the Nata Mandap.

Gaja-Simha

As per many, these two massive structures as described above are the royal guards of the temple. The man is at the bottom, elephant(represents Laxmi, ie. prosperity) is in the middle and the lion(ie. represents Goddess Durga, ie. power) is at the top. These sculptures signify that a man has to overcome them to attain spiritual progress and to approach God.

Nata Mandir/ Nata Mandap (Hall Of Dance)

A flight of stairs through the main gate would take one to the magnificently pillared / finely carved platform called Nata Mandir (ie. hall for dance and theatre). The pillared platform was designed for dance performance.

This is in front of the Jagmohan. It was for offering Arati and also dance Performance by the Devadashis during worship. It's style is that of Jagmohan.

A small portion of the dancing hall is survived. It is built over a square shaped separate platform. It has access stairs from all the four sides. As on date only pillars are left with sculptures carved in it.

The pillars, plinths and staircases are intricately carved with reliefs of dancers, their dance performance along with their emotions.

At the entrance of the Nata Mandir, there is a pair of war elephants. There are 3- openings at the top platform which were designed to allow the Sun rays to fall strait in to it. They were designed keeping in view the different position of Sun in different seasons. There is no roof and it appears that the roof has collapsed.

As per some views, the Nata Mandir (dancing hall) in it's original form was in existence for many years. The then kings broke the structure intentionally as it was considered as unnecessary.

As per scriptures surya has to be welcomed with the accompaniment of musical instruments like cymbals, drums and flutes etc. From the surviving sculptures, it is observed that the beautiful musicians are heralding the passage of surya across the sky. The limbs of the musicians are poised in rhythmic movement. The faces are finely sculptured from Chlorite stone which is suitable for finer carvings.

The tribhanga postures of the body, the mudras, the costume and jewellery worn by the dancers would capture anybody's imagination. The dancers are also carrying Chamaras, incense burners and lamps in their hands.

The sculptures of dance poses and displaying/ playing of musical instruments are linked with celebration of different festivals.

However, the carvings of apsaras, male-female dancers in various poses from different dance forms, musicians playing different instruments and many carvings of audience enjoying the show are it's attractions which exists only on stone.

After observing the sculptures of the Nata Mandir, one can compare the then dance style of 13th century Odisha, with the Odissi dance styles of today.

Climbing down from the elevated area of the Nata Mandap, one will see the Jagmohan and the main temple.

Jagmohan (Audience Chamber/ Hall In Front Of The Main Sanctum/ Porch/ Mukhasala)

Jagmohan (gathering hall) is the principal structure of the surviving ruins. It is around 128-feet high. It's outer width is 28-meters and plinth height is around 7-meters.

This is the frontal porch / assembly hall facing 3-Successively receding tiers, the terraces between each containing statutory groups of musicians. The 3-Sides are punctuated by ornately carved doorways and 3-flights of carved staircases, all with monumental images of horses and or / elephants. Set in to the plinth are 24-heavily ornamented wheels, 12- on each side while along the principal staircases are the horses (Ie. eastern side).

3-Sun Gods stand at 3-outside corners of the Jagmohan depicting different positions of Sun, at dawn, noon and dusk.

The roof of the Jagmohan is stepped pyramidal form. some of the finest forms are on the terraces of the different levels of the roof. At higher level on pyramidal roof there are sculptures of musicians. The edge of the Gandi (ie. roof tiers) are having scenes of processions which are intricately carved.

The upper portion of the walls of the Jagmohan contain large sculptures.

It stands on the same platform as the main temple (ie. Viman). The main temple which is crumbled is behind it.

It has 4-doorways on it's four sides. The western door leads to inner sanctum (ie. Antaral). The other doors lead to outside the porch. It is adorned with exquisite stone carvings all over.

The door-jambs are green coloured with intricate carvings in Chlorite stone.

The rest of the structures are in Khandolite and laterite stones.

There are wide steps to reach the Jagmohan. These are flanked by horses which are carved in stone. It is having elaborate architectural decorations. There is practically no access to Jagmohan. The interior of the hall was bricked up and all the doors are closed.

A hole was created in the top portion of Jagmohan and sand was poured in to it. It is filled with sand and stone packing materials to prevent falling of stones and to prevent it's collapse.

Alignment Of Doors

The doors were aligned with the movement of the Sun. The front and back doors get the sun rays on equinox days and the two side doors get the first rays of the Sun during northern and southern movement of the Sun.

Main Temple

Major portion of the main temple including temple complex is destroyed. The Chariot of the temple is 100-feet high. Next to the chariot was once a 230-feet high Shikara/ sanctum which no longer exits.

As per researchers, the Sun temple was used for prayer only for a short period. It was one of the tallest temples in India and was taller than the Bruhadeswar temple, Tanjavur.

The presiding deity which was in the main sanctum has fallen off. There is a 5-feet wide ornamental Chlorite block on the sides and top of the doorway of the inner sanctum.

This is the largest structure of the temple complex. Along the 3-Sides are the subsidiary shrines with life sized Chlorite structures of surya, reached by 3-flights of stairs. The Dikpalas or guardians of 8-directions are recessed in to niches on the upper registers. In the interior, a flight of steps leads down to the sanctum, which contains a single pedestal in the center bereft of the presiding deity. The floor of the room is paved with Chlorite slabs.

Simhasana (Ie. Throne /Seat/ Pedestal)Of The Presiding Deity

The seat of the presiding deity (ie. deity is missing) is made of Chlorite stone. It's base and sides are decorated with beaded boarders. The king and Queen are sitting in the front. The sides of the seat are decorated with beaded boarders and are enclosed with rows of the elephants. Various scenes from day to day life, like – women carrying offerings, standing in groups with folded hands and musical instruments are also found.

As per researcher, Sun God was actually occupying the pedestal otherwise this pedestal, smaller one above it and semi-circular channel in the pedestal for easy flow of water etc., would not have existed.

There are beautiful carvings on the wall of the main temple, which is the speciality.

The main temple, Jagmohan and hall of dance in eastern gate was constructed in such a way that the first ray of Sun would fall on the head of the idol of the Sun God placed in the main temple, passing through the doors of all temples.

The giant wheels of the chariot are against the sides of the platform. The Main temple, Jagmohan and Bhog Mandap are built on a line. But Nata Mandap is on the second line.

Lord Shiv in his wrathful form ie. Bhairav, guard the temple from evil forces.

Three large Chlorite sculptures of Sun God still exist on the lower section of the shikara. On the south and west portion, the Sun God is bejewelled wearing long boats and standing in a chariot pulled by seven horses.

Bhoga Mandap (Hall Of Offering)

From the side lawns of the temple, a series of drains are leading to a platform. This was the kitchen-cum-dining area which was known as Bhoga Mandap. A small portion of the dining hall has survived.

It is square in shape and the height is around 30-meters. It has a pyramid top. It has access from 3-sides, ie. north, south and east with flight of stairs. There are demarcated areas for grinding grains and spices.

The outer face of this raised platform are decorated with numerous sculptures like – farmer working in field, king in the battle field and ladies doing make up and playing with their kids.

There are two nearby wells around it. When the well was emptied, a Chlorite image of Ganesh was found which is displayed in the ASI museum.

The well no-1 which is located north of kitchen might have been constructed to supply water to the community kitchen and Bhoga Mandap.

The well no-2 was located in front of the main temple's northern stairwell. It had foot-rests, a washing platform and a drainage system, for wash water. It might have been built for the pilgrims to wash their hands and feet etc. on their way to the temple.

The life size sculpture of the war horse is near the east side of the stair.

War Horses

Two gorgeously carved war horses crushing down the warrior are found at the southern side. They display the strength, energy and former martial glory of the state. The height is around 7-feet and length is around 10-feet. This is also the symbol of Odisha Government, whose replica is also found in the interpretation center.

Emblem Of Odisha Government

The horse of the temple has been accepted as the emblem of Odisha Government. This is a circular seal depicting a representation of the warrior and horse statue found at the Konark sun temple. The crest of the emblem is the lion capitol of Ashok.

Colossal Elephant

Two richly decorated elephants situated on masonry platforms are found at the northern side. Earlier these elephants were in the side walls of the steps at the northern and southern sides of the Jaganmohan and were found in the mass of debris. The elephant is the symbol of wealth. Besides the above two elephants, there are large number of elephants in the temple, may be these sculptures represent the protector of the temple.

These amazing elephant sculpture was the proud mascot and brand icon of Indian Tourism for several years.

Giraffe Sculpture

Giraffe sculpture is found in the temple which is not found in the country. It indicates trade links with Africa.

Sculptures Of Foreigners

It is observed that there are sculptures of Persians with long caps. There are sculptures of Chinese travellers / traders with their characteristic features. Eating noodles with chop sticks on a folding table shows the Chinese people. Temple with sculptures of global people and food shows the unique characteristics of the temple.

Architecture

The temple is an example of glorious and magnificent Kalinga architecture. It consists of Shikara (crown), Jagmohan (audience hall), Natamandir (dance hall) and Viman (tower). The mighty Simha-Gaja (lion-elephant) welcome the visitor at the entrance.

The temple complex covers an area of around 261 by 164 meters. Every inch from top to bottom of the exterior has depiction of historical, social, mythological, psychological, Kama sutra and religious stories. The concept of Dharma, Artha, Kama and Mokshya are reflected in various sculptures of the temple.

As per some studies, the construction of the temple was so accurate and intricate that, the first rays of the rising Sun used to fall in the image of the Sun which was in the inner sanctum. It would illuminate the sanctum and the presiding deity.

The temple is built in the form of a chariot where Surya God rode across the sky. It is a 100-feet high chariot being pulled by horses and wheels carved out of a single stone. It is built of Khandolite rocks / weathered ferruginous and oxidised sand stone.

There are 3-main statues of Surya (ie. South, West and North walls) and 2-images of Bhairava.

The southern side Sun is known as "Mitra" (ie. represent childhood and rising Sun. The height is around 8.3 feet).

The western side Sun is known as "Pusan" (ie. represents youth and mid day Sun. The height is around 9.5 feet).

The northern side Sun is known as "Haritaswa" (ie. represents old age and evening sun. The height is around 10-feet.)

Horses

The chariot is pulled by 7-horses. 4-horses are on the left side and 3-horses are on the right side. The name of the seven horses are – Gayatri, Brihati, Ushnih, Jagati, Trishtubha, Anushtubha and Pankti which possibly stand for the rhythmic representation of the sacred verses of the Vedas.

Some opine that 7-horses represent the 7-days while others say that 7-represents, 7-components of colours in a rainbow (ie. VIBGYOR). The magical Number 7- is having spiritual, historical and materialistic significance. In Hindu weddings, the bride and groom take 7- rounds around the fire God (ie. Agni Devata). The periodic table has elements in the group of -7. An Octave has 7-musical notes. Hence, the 7-horses represent the magical number which surrounds us.

Konark Wheels

The Konark wheels are the brand ambassador of the Konark temple. These are found in mementos, post cards, travel books and magazines. The very sight of these wheels would make any one awestruck.

The platform of Konark temple is engraved with 24-intricately designed wheels of the chariot (ie. two rows of 12-wheels on each side taking together both the sanctum sanctorum and the entrance hall). The wheels are 9-feet, 9-inches in diameters. There are 8-major spokes and 8-minor spokes in the wheel which symbolises the day cycles. The wheels are detailed and realistic and even have axles and pins to hold them in place.

The wheels of the chariot are exquisitely decorated around their axles and peripheries. Every inch is carved and made in great details.

Major spokes are thick, elaborately carved and much wider than the thin spokes. Each part represents modern day equivalent to 3-hours.

These 8-parts are divided in to halves creating a section of 1.5 hours.

There are 30-beads between each major and minor spokes, which means 1.5 hours (ie. 90-minutes) are further divided in to 30-parts (ie. each bead represents 3-minutes). These beads are slightly elongated at the sides. This shape creates 3-sections. The shadow can fall at the centre of the beads or on either sides of it. This indication helps to divide 3-minutes of of the beads further in to single minutes.

It is understood that there are 2-wheels that tells time accurately which are located on east and west side of the temple, when the Sun passes from one side to other. Some say 4-wheels are used as Sun - dials.

However, the mystery of other 22-wheels are not known as yet. Some believes that when it turns night, certain wheels might act like moon dials and continue to tell time even at night.

The carvings on the spokes differ from wheel to wheel and they have some hidden meaning, which are yet to be deciphered. One can see carvings containing foliage, birds and animals etc.

Some of the plants carved on these stones appear during certain season only. Some of the carvings related to mating of animals, which happen only during certain time of the year.

The axles of the wheels project by around one feet from the surface. On the face of the axles there are various sculptures, like – images of Krishna playing on a flute amidst cowherd, people seeking mercy and king seated on elephant facing a group. The carvings behind and around the wheel are so much varied that as one walks around the platform more and more, one will spot something new and different.

It is believed that with more research / study, one can know about the linkage of the seasons, animal behaviour, different fruits in different seasons and movement of the migratory birds etc. from the sculptures of other wheels. Some say, these wheels are emblematic and represents "wheel of life", ie. pattern of creation.

As there are 24-wheels, the number 24-represents the 24-fortnights in a year and also 24-hours of the day.

Further 12-wheels on each side symbolises 12-months of year (12- Zodiacs).

The whole depiction conveys that the time is controlled by the Sun God who travels from east to west in his chariot escorted by his charioteer Aruna.

Three Chlorite structures of Sun God as stated above depict the Sun God at varying stages of his journey, ie. youthful in the morning, at full strength around mid-day and tired but satisfied at Sunset.

Magnets

The Sun idol was in a floating condition just above the high raised pedestal inside the inner sanctum, due to use of large pieces of magnet in the temple construction. Further the loadstone magnet installed on the top of the sanctum was capable of dragging the ships sailing in the area towards the coast and there were ship wrecks.

As per some other researchers, during the construction of the main tower of the temple, the artisans had put an iron plate between every two stone pieces and a massive 52-ton magnet was placed at the top of the temple. Further, the statue of Sun God was also built with the material having iron content. Due to this unique arrangement, the statue of Sun God inside the temple was floating in the air.

This requires further research.

Sculpture Of Sun God Wearing Boat

In the southern niche of the temple there is a large idol of Sun God wearing boots. This is a very rare idol found in the country which shows a God wearing the boat. As per researchers this is attributed to the Central Asian influence on the sculpture. He is wearing a short lower garment in the drawer style and many ornaments. He hold lotus stalks in both hands. He is surrounded by celestial dancers and the king offering obeisance along with the family priest.

The entire sculpture stands on a Chlorite pedestal and is made from a single piece. It's height is 3.38 meters, width is 1.8 meters and thickness of 71-CMs.

Latitude Of The Temple

As per researcher Sun God at Konark is situated at 19-degree 53'27"N (east coast near Bay of Bengal), Sun God at Karnak in Egypt (Mediterranean coast) is situated at 25-degree 43'7"N and Modhera Sun temple in Gujarat is situated at 23.5 degree north. These temples are situated in nearby latitudes (ie. latitudinal differences are not much). There may be reason behind it.

Erotic Sculptures

The temple has large number of erotic (ie. Maithun) sculptures in it's Shikaras.

As per some estimation, 40% of all the carvings consist of erotic and amorous scenes.

It depicts love making by the couples including oral sex and same -sex ones. The couples pose in a variety of amorous poses. These are explicit representations of sexual indulgence and the temple has the highest concentration of erotic sculptures in the country.

Not only famous Kama Sutra is portrayed on the temple walls but also what are the effects of engaging in so much sex, after delivery of baby how the ladies make themselves clean, what the ladies use at the time of their periods and so many daily life routines are designed as sculptures on the outside wall. Even the practice followed by Bonda women after childbirth are reflected in the temple wall.

They are found more in the second level of the porch structure (ie. middle layers) and in outer walls.

There is not any definite explanation/ evidence regarding presence of such sculptures on the outer walls. However, they represent fertility which ensures the continuance of life.

There are various views /opinions about these sculptures which are as under:

- These sculptures were built after Kalinga war / other major wars to promote love making due to huge loss of lives. This was for more child births and for more warriors for Kalinga.
- As the artisans were away from home for a long time and were missing their wives, they have made these sculptures.

  However, the logic for both the above points are not acceptable to many.

- Some are of the view that the sculptures adorning the temple have been inspired by Kamasutra, the world's original guide to sex. It is understood that all the 64-type of "ratikrida" mentioned in Vatsayan's Kama sutra are found here, as sex is an essential part for wholesale living. For the architects the love making is a symbol of the union of individual soul with universal spirit.
- Some say, this imagery was influenced by Tantric beliefs. Further, the erotic figures were meant to test the self-restraint of visitors before God.
- Some others are of the view that these depictions are believed to lead people to spirituality. Various activities outside the temple represent worldly activities and beyond that and within the temple, there is the image of God. The devotees/ visitors must overcome the worldly pleasure to feel God.

  As per the blogger Jitu Mishra, "the erotica depicted in Konark offers -------how life needs to be celebrated to attain "Mokshya" through "Kama", two essential pillars of Indian wisdom. Unfortunately, today discussing sex in open forum is seen as a taboo. Work pressure, alternative lifestyles and stress especially in urban India has kept people distant from Kama. Perhaps a visit to Konark and appreciating how our ancestors celebrated life may inspire us for a deeper retrospection to tune our lifestyle in sync with ancient wisdom and practices.
- This erotic art symbolises the merging of the human soul with the divine, achieved through sexual ecstasy and bliss.
- It is also understood that the temple was constructed following the rise of Buddhism in Odisha. People were becoming monks and were practicing abstinence. The erotic sculptures were used by rulers to create interest in sex and procreation.

  These erotic sculptures in Konark represent a society where the artist had the freedom to sculpt where love scenes in the temple did not evoke disgust in public perception. These sculptures reflect people who took delight in the pursuit of all kinds of pleasure.

All these sculptures show the thorough knowledge of human anatomy of the artisans and a proof of technical experience of centuries.

OTHER SCULPTURES

The temple is famous for it's intricacy and profusion of sculptural work. The exquisite stone carvings cover the entire structure. As per Indiatales, "the temple was built like Titans but finished like jewellers". The carvings are found in minute details.

Between Chariot wheels and the plinth of the temple, it is decorated with detailed reliefs of animals, scenes of royal life and military crusades, mythical and semi-human figures, Demi-Gods and Gods/ Goddesses etc.

Around two thousand elephants small and big march round the base of the main temple. It is felt, as if, they are bearing the entire structure upon their backs.

Thousands of images adorn the exterior walls of the temple and most of the sculptural reliefs are arranged in bands, friezes and panels around the plinth and walls. The surface ornamentation is found around the doorways and roof recesses. The large sculptures are found predominantly along the stairways.

There are 3-impressive carvings of Sun God at 3-Strategic locations to catch the Sun at dawn, at noon and at sunset, as described in earlier paragraph.

As per some other interpretation, the morning sun is identified with Brahma (ie. the creator), the mid day Sun is identified with Maheswar (ie. the destroyer) and evening Sun is identified with Vishnu (ie. preserver).

On the walls there are also carvings of the daily life of the human cycle. Man and woman are seen in their daily activities, like – girls are seen wringing their wet hair, standing by a tree, looking from a window, playing with pets, putting on makeup while looking in to the mirror, chasing a monkey, managing family belongings, dealing with workers, preparing for bed, hanging out with her partner, blessing of a son by the mother, students with teacher, yogi in Yogasana, mother with the child, old woman in walking stick, girls playing musical instrument etc. Every sculpture teaches something about different stages of life.

There are soldiers, hunters, village folk and nobleman. There are many type of images of Gods, Goddesses, Kinnar, Gandharva, male musicians, festivals and rural life, war and haunting, animals and birds, mythical creatures.

The interconnectedness of all beings are expressed in composite creatures, ie. part human and part animal. Nagas represent the benign protection of nature.

Men and women are engaged in activities of everyday life. There are scenes where man is carrying his goods, like street venders of today, travellers preparing a meal along the road side, there are festive processions, warrior being greeted with Namaste and an old woman is taking leave of her family may be for a pilgrimage etc.

Scene of the royals being greeted by a group and military procession are popular themes in many sculptures.

Some are having foreign type of clothing and are having Giraffe, with them which is not an Indian animal.

It is believed that the two lions at the entrance, pair of war horses and pair of elephants were guarding the 3-Staircases that led to the main temple porch. They were covered with plaster and painted dark red. The visual impact of the original temple with different colour combinations would have been quite different to the eye, than what is seen today.

Collapse/ Destruction Of The Temple

There are many opinions on how the temple fell in to decay within three hundred years of it's construction.

Mythological Version

Sun God was attracted by the beauty of a girl who was playing in Chandrabhaga beach. When he made sexual advances towards her, the temple was collapsed.

Other Versions

As per hearsay, there was a massive magnet at the centre of the temple. This was interfering with the compasses of travelling ship and was causing ship wrecks.

The load-stone / magnet was removed during Portuguese period. As a result, the other stones and beams held in alignment by the magnetic forces were crashed and brought the temple to destruction.

From Madalapanji, the Almanac of Jagannath temple, the temple was destroyed by the invasion of Kalapahad. He had removed the structural support of the temple and damaged the idols. The invaders had also taken away the Kalasha (ie. arch stone/ crowning stone) on the top and the lotus flag (ie. Padma Dhwaj) of the temple. He had broken most of the idols as well as the side temple of Konark. Due to displacement of arch stone (ie. DADHINAUTI – in Odiya), the temple gradually collapsed and the Mukhsala / porch suffered damage due to falling down of stones from the temple top, on it.

As per a later entry of Madalapanji, the big lion (Gaja Singha) which was on the eastern side of the temple fell down towards east and there was collapse of the eastern temple wall. At that time, the hands of the image, which was worshipped was broken. The Chalanti Pratima (ie. portable image) was shifted to Jagannath temple, Puri. As per this version, it was an engineering failure that led to fall of the temple.

Besides the above points, some opine that there was improper maintenance of the temple. The upper half of Viman was exposed to severe storms and rains, which could have loosened the walls.

This led to falling of the Gaja-Singha on the temple. It caused an imbalance of the temple structure leading to gradual collapse.

Some say it was devastated due to natural calamities like – cyclone, earthquake or lightening etc.

As per views of some researchers, the foundation of the temple in a weak soil might be the other reason for it's collapse.

The biological analysis of moss layers estimate the abandonment of the temple might be around 1573AD, which is almost equivalent to the accounts of Madalapanji.

With the removal of the sacred image from the temple and as the activities of the port was closed due to attack of sea pirates from time to time, Konark became deserted. The temple area was enveloped by dense forests and sand over the years.

STATUS OF PRESIDING DEITY

Disappearance of the presiding deity is shrouded in mystery and there are many views about the same.

Due to Muslim invasion from time to time and as Odisha came under Muslim control in 1568-aD, the priests of the temple removed the presiding deity, which was lying in the inner sanctum of Konark Sun temple, for safety of the deity and to save the sanctity. They buried the image under sand for years. Later, it was removed and kept in the temple of Indra in the temple complex of Jagannath temple, Puri.

Some also opine that the image which was worshipped in the temple is yet to be discovered.

As per some other opinion, the Sun image now kept in the National museum of Delhi, is the presiding deity of Konark Sun temple.

The load-stone / magnet of the temple was removed during Portuguese period and as a result, the main image along with the main temple was crashed.

While others opine that Kalapahad had removed the structural support of the temple and damaged the idols.

After disappearance of the main image of Sun God, the temple was deserted and it was lying in the dense forests for years. It lost it's glory and was the abode of sea pirates.

Arun Pillar (Sun Pillar) /Arun Stambha

The pillar is made of monolithic Chlorite and the height is around 33. 8 feet. It is dedicated to Arun, the charioteer of Sun God.

Some say, it was a victory tower (ie. victory against Muslim invasion) which was erected as a symbol of prestige in addition to the construction of Sun temple, Konark.

This Arun pillar from Konark was shifted from the entrance of Konark temple during Maratha rule by a Maratha Brahmachari named Gosain and was put in front of the lion's gate of Puri.

Discovery Of The Temple

Abul Fazal had described about this temple in Ain-I-Akabari around 1580 AD.

Chaitanya Mahaprabhu had visited this temple.

As per Madala-Panji, Baba Brahmachari had found this temple in a damaged condition in the midst of sand mounds and creepers. There was heavy damage in the northern and eastern sides of the main temple.

He brought the Aruna Stambha (pillar) to Puri which is now present at the Lion's gate of the Jagannath Temple. The image of Raja Narasingha Dev-l is at Mukhashala of Laxmi temple and Navagraha stone from the southern side is now in Gundicha temple.

In an early painting of Fergussion in the year 1838AD, the south – West portion of the temple was still visible. It is understood that this portion was collapsed in 1848 AD.

During early part of 1900 AD (ie. between 1900 AD to 1903 AD), on the order of the then lieutenant Governor of Bengal-j A Baurdilion, the sand and stones were cleared around the temple. The chariot wheels, horses and sculptures in the walls were found during clearances. The Jagmohan was filled with sand after sealing the four entrance gates to avoid collapse. It's interior was partitioned with 15-feet wide stone wall. It took around 3-years to fill it.

The excavations continued up to 1939 AD and other portions of the temple complex was found.

Three reliefs were found on the south face of the beam of the main temple, ie. worship of Mahishamardini, Jagannath and a Shivling (ie. broken). These sculptures prove the co-existence of different cults and also about royal patronage.

One will find a Nataraja and idols of Surya with Vishnu, Vayu and Agni etc.

The Temple was taken over by ASI and was declared as a world heritage site by UNESCO in 1984 AD.

OTHER TEMPLES

The Sun temple has ruins of other two smaller temples known as Mayadevi Temple and Vishnu temple besides the Navagraha temple.

Mayadevi Temple

The temple is situated towards West of the main temple. It is dedicated to Maya Devi, wife of Sun God. Some are of the view that this temple was built around 11th century. Some say, it is the temple of Chhaya Devi, wife of Lord Surya/ Sun God.

There are many views about this temple. Some say it was made to worship Sun God. It was an ancient Sun temple, when present temple was built.

Others believe that it was dedicated to one of the wives of Surya.

There are many beautiful carvings in this temple. The carving, which depicts a lady waiting for her husband to come back home, is a major attraction. The sculpture of crocodile holding a fish in it's mouth is unique.

This temple was discovered in 1909 AD during excavations. It has a compound wall, porch and sanctuary.

As per hearsay, the image of Ramchandi was removed from this temple when Muslim overrun the temple complex.

Vishnu Temple

This small temple was discovered in 1956 AD. It is located on the south-west corner of the temple complex. The height of the temple is around 7-feet (2.13meters). This east facing temple is made of bricks. It is Pancharatha in plan having a sanctuary and a porch. The super structure is missing. At the time of excavations, the long pedestal in the Viman was empty. It appears there might be more than one image. During clearance of the debris around the temple during 1906-07, an image of Vishnu was found. The other image was most probably Balaram which was found in 1906-07 and is preserved in the museum of Konark. There were sculptures of of Varaha, Vaman and Trivikrama etc in the sanctum.

From these discoveries, the temple was believed to be a Vishnu temple / temple having vishnu affiliation.

Some also believe that it was a Vaishnavite pilgrimage site and Chaitanya Mahaprabhu had visited Konark and also prayed here.

Nava Graha Temple

The Navagrahas(ie. nine planets) with impressive doorways are located just outside the Sun temple at the North-East corner. It contains a huge coloured stone slab with images of 9-planets made up of black Chlorite stone. The slab was initially kept above the entrance of main doorway. A part of it is still worshipped. The Chlorite stone is richly carved and measures around 6-meters long, 1.2 meter high and 2-meter deep.

One has to walk a small distance from the exit of Sun temple to this Navagraha temple, which is a living temple.

HISTORY

The original Navagraha slab was lying intact in debris near Jagmohan. It was later discovered by the Asiatic society of Bengal. They wanted to move it to Kolkata museum. In 1893-aD, it was cut in to 2-pieces longitudinally for easy removal. However, due to heavy weight and sandy soil, this slabs could not be removed. It remained discarded for around 60-years at a distance of around 400-meters away from the main temple. It was installed in this area in a separate shade by Government of India at a later date. Now this is known as Navagraha Temple (ie. Temple of nine planets).

It is engraved in a single stone and is placed in iron beam and located in the North-eastern part.

CONSERVATION

As per many conservationists, huge volume of sand in the Jagmohan is posing threat to the structure. There are cracks and seepage of water. Big stone blocks have also reportedly fallen off.

The central building and research institute, at Rorkee had conducted a scientific study in to the temple's structural stability.

There are many opinions varying from scientific to local solutions. Some favour getting rid of sand while others want the status quo. Some are proposing to support the temple with steel rods.

There are frequent news regarding removal of scaffolding that has encased the temple. There are also news about removal of sand from inside the Jagmohan.

However, the salty sea air and heavy seasonal rainfall affects the carvings.

Although the monument requires urgent conservation measures, the conservation plans remain unclear to the conservationists/ environmentalists for the decay.

Many steps are taken up to mitigate the impact of saline action, water logging, erosion and vegetative intrusions.

ASI has introduced plain stones only where original stones are missing or to fill up gapes for structural stability.

About conservation measures, the renowned Indologist Prof AL Basham had said, "if the world wishes Konark to be preserved for posterity, action and expensive action such as a developing country cannot afford alone must be taken quite soon".

UNIQUENESS

The temple which is built in the form of an ornamented chariot is the finest example of temple architecture anywhere in the country/ world. The present temple is only half of the original height, that we see today. The uniqueness of the temple is as under:

- The architectural beauty of the temple testify the boundless creativity of the artists of odisha.
- It is the latest and last version of Kalinga style.
- This is one of the most important temples in the country, whose planning and construction records are preserved in the form of palm-leaf manuscripts.
- The stones used were not available nearby and sea route was used to bring the stones. Even some stones might have been brought from outside India.

As per some researchers, as there was no Khandolite stones nearby, such huge amount of rocks might have been brought to the temple from far off areas through rafts made with huge timbers and through Prachi river / Kadua river/ Chandrabhaga river which are dead now. The stone blocks were lifted may be with the help of pulleys, wooden wheels or rollers.

- Some of the sculptures are finished in jewellery details. As per front line dated 20/6/2008, the temple celebrates all of life and divinity that pervades it all.
- Interlocking and first time use of iron as the building material was used in temple construction. Massive iron beams are used to construct higher floors.

The iron clamps and joints used in beams etc. show their usage in the temple.

The fittings and finishing were so flawless that, the joints are not visible.

This displays the metallurgical heritage of India in general and odisha in particular. The iron ore and it' metallurgical treatment is apparent more than 800-years back.

- It is believed a 52-ton magnet was used to create peak/ load stone of the temple. Due to attraction of the magnet the main idol of the temple remained suspended in the air. There are various theories about the removal of magnet and about missing idol as described in earlier paragraphs.

- Giant elephants at the entrance and on the platforms are depicting, as if, they are at war. In a rage, some of the elephants are crushing the hunter. It appears, they might have participated in some war.
- The sculptor of giant lion crushing the elephant is found at the stairs near the entrance. It is interpreted as a symbol of a successful military campaign. Some opine that it is symbolic and conveys that one will be crushed who gets too much of wealth and power. The entire structure is made of one piece of stone.

  This also awakens within one the attitude of fearlessness, with which one has to face the demons of ignorance that block the path towards knowledge. The devotees enter in to the temple inspired by these fearless creatures.
- The sculptures of the lion crushing the elephant and elephant crushing the man is a speciality. Lion represents power and elephant represents wealth. It illustrates that major problem faced by the human beings are unbridled money and power and they should be kept under control. This imparts the value of education.
- Each wheel has miniature sculptures. These are not only ornate wheels but they are Sun-dials. With the help of protruding middle knob, one can calculate the local time.
- There are large number of erotic images including love making by same -sex. As per experts, the sculptures in this temple depict all the 9- Rasas (ie. emotions found in Indian scripture). The emotion of love and romance are depicted more, which catches one's eye.
- The Giraffe, which is not found in India, is an important sculpture of the temple. It indicates the trade link with Africa and awareness about the animal, that is not native to India. King Narasingha Dev and his queen Sita Devi (ie. builder of this temple) are found next to the Giraffe structure.
- In the southern portion of the temple, a larger than life size surya stands majestically on his chariot with Aruna. Surya is depicted wearing boats which is not an indigenous tradition.

This shows constant interaction of the people of the area on the north -west of the sub -continent. The king and family priests can be seen kneeling before the deity.

- There are 3- images of Sun at three directions/ three different sides to catch the rays of the Sun at sunrise, noon and Sunset. The sculptures of Surya in Chlorite stone that makes them stand out in green stone on the walls, are seen at the top of Mandap. The high boots are worn by these figures.
- As one moves around the temple in a clock wise pattern, one will observe a lot of Naga – Nagini sculptures at the level of human eye. These sculptures are half human and half serpent. Women engaged in martial art or riding horses are found around them.
- The wheel number 6- was adorning the red coloured Rs20/- currency note and now this is found in many Rs10/-currency notes (ie. issued by RBI in - 2018 AD). In this wheel one will find the life of a hunter sculpted on it.
- The global nature of Indian kingdoms especially Kalinga (ie. the then Odisha) is reflected in the sculptures of Konark. The Chinese travellers/ traders with their features like – eating noodles on a folding table with chopsticks, are a speciality. The Persians with long caps are also found here. Some researchers interpret these sculptures with trade links of Odisha, both with the West and the east.
- When one will see the temple from the outside during sunrise, one will notice that the chariot shaped temple appears to be emerging from the depths of blue sea carrying the sun.
- The temple is well lit with halogen lights. In the night it is an amazing experience.

Archeological Museum

There is a dedicated archeological museum near the temple complex, which is another attraction at Konark. There are around 260- antiquities, various sculptures, images of Gods and crocodiles etc. The carvings related to the ruins of the Sun temple are found in the museum. Some of the structures and parts fallen from the temple can be found here.

There are four galleries where various antiquities are displayed. Around 62-antiquities, like – fragmented wheel made of crushed stone, statue of Sun God of sand stone and different incarnations of Lord Vishnu are found in the first gallery. Second gallery is having around 108-antiquities, like – parts of main temple wall, heavenly nymphs, stone-crocodile head and stone carved vegetation etc.

The third gallery is having 45-items like – statue of Surya Narayan and king with his army etc. Huge sculptures like – some part of Sun's statue, idol of a man tied to an elephant's trunk and dancing figure with couple's statue are housed in the fourth gallery.

It is one of the most prominent places for tourists.

Light And Sound Show

The light and sound show held in the evening is one of the major attractions. It is also one of the best light and sound shows in India. High definition projectors are used with state- of – the – art 3-dprojection mapping technology to project images in to the monument.

From the light show one can know the religious and historical significance of the temple in a visually appealing manner. Wireless headphones are provided during the show, whose duration is around 40-minutes. One can choose the narration like – Odia, English or Hindi.

The voice of Kabir Bedi is used in the English version, voice of Bijaya Mohanty in Odia version and voice of Sekhar Suman in Hindi.

Interpretation Center/ Site Museum

The state – of-the-art Konark interpretation center is developed by The Indian Oil Foundation. The interpretation center which is spread over 8-acres of land has 5-galleries with interactive exhibits/ touch - screen kiosks and multimedia displays. It was inaugurated by the then Union Minister of Petroleum and Natural Gas, skill development and entrepreneurship, Dharmendra Pradhan on Utkal Divas day on 1st April, 2018 AD. The galleries also display the history, culture and architecture of Odisha and Sun temples across the world.

It tries to recreate the temple, as it would have been built. It explains the concept of Sun worship. The sculptures of the temple with individual details are recreated by famous sculpture late Padma Vibhushan Raghunath Mohapatra and Sh Bijay Nayak. The medieval engineering concepts of the Sun temple of Konark and various other Sun temples of Odisha and India with historical interpretation are found. The scale model of original Sun temple of Konark and it's current state would charm any visitor.

The replica of the horse is the original sculpture, which was earlier in the Sun temple premises. This sculpture has been accepted as the emblem of Odisha Government.

The handicrafts and artefacts of Odisha are other attractions.

A 15-minute animation film about mythology and history of Konark Sun temple is also screened in a specially designed air – conditioned auditorium having good acoustics systems.

DANCE FESTIVAL

The Konark dance festival is organised in the first week of December every year in the backdrop of Sun temple. It is held around 5-days (ie. around 1st December to 5th December) and attended by many celebrated dancers.

A series of popular classical dances such as Odissi, Kathak, Bharatnatyam and Manipuri etc. can be witnessed in this amazing dance festival. The temple is transformed in to a stage during the Konark dance festival. It attracts a lot of foreign and Indian tourists.

This has helped to revive the unique dance tradition of the state. When the sun sets in the horizon and stars appear in the sky, the open – air Auditorium reverberates with the beats of Raga and Tala to fill the air is an experience difficult to forget.

KONARK DANCE AND MUSIC FESTIVAL

This is another classical music and dance festival in Konark which is held in February.

This dance festival is held at the Konark amphitheater with the façade of Sun temple showing from the magnificent backdrop and in the midst of cashew and casuarina trees.

This was started by Guru Gangadhar pradhan in 1986 with an intention to revive the classical dance forms.

It is held around 3-days in February. Some of the classical dances like – Odissi, Kathak, Kuchipudi, Kathakali, Bharatnatyam and Manipuri and tribal dances from various states are displayed during this festival.

The craft bazar outside the amphitheater selling handicrafts, Patta paintings, jewellery from sea shells and embroidered clothes are other attractions.

One can explore different Odia cuisines in several food stalls.

INTERNATIONAL SAND ART FESTIVAL

The international sand art festival takes place at Chandrabhaga beach near the temple, at the time of Konark dance festival (ie. 1st December to 5th December). Several domestic and international artists participate in the event. Each of these artists using beach sand come up with beautiful art works/ sculptures. The theme of the competition changes every day.

The beach is dotted with various stalls from food to handicrafts. The panel of judges decide the winner of "Sand art festival".

Shopping

The locals shops sell handicrafts, paintings, various stone and decorative materials. The souvenirs and sea shells are plenty. The "Chandua", appliqué work of Pipili in all it's varieties are available.

Near the ticket counter at the entrance of the temple there are also souvenir shops on both sides. The miniature version of Sun temple are the Best Buy at this place.

The Urban Haat of Konark is a new shopping complex, just behind the Panthanivash. It covers an area of around 2-acres with a rural ambience.

There are also other Local shops selling shells, conches, cowries, handicraft items made from coconut, palms and local goods.

One should purchase some items to keep as a memento.

KONARK SEA BEACH / CHANDRABHAGA BEACH

Konark sea beach is named after Chandrabhaga river, which was joining the sea here. Chandrabhaga is also known as the place of rising Sun.

It is one of the most beautiful and pollution free beaches of the country.

Leisurely stroll over the sands at this enchanting sea beach would be a lovely experience. One can enjoy the beach activities like – Sun bathing, surfing and many more.

The lengthy stretch of sands, blue and undulating waves of the sea make this beach as one of the sought after destination.

The Chandrabhaga Beach Became One Of The Asia's First Beaches To Get Blue Flag Certification Due To High Standards Maintained For Water, Safety, Information And Environmental Education Etc.

This blue flag certification was awarded by the "foundation of environmental education" (FEE) in 2018AD.

The beach is known as "lovers paradise".

The sight of various fishermen in the midst of sands and sea - water is amazing.

Watching the sunrise and sunset in blue waters over a clear sky is astonishing.

There are many restaurants/ food stalls nearby. Beautiful seashell handicrafts are another attraction of this beach.

It is around 3-kms from the Konark Sun temple.

LIGHT HOUSE

As per historians, Konark temple was a reference point for ships in the sea during the maritime trade between Odisha and South-East Asian Islands like BALI, JAVA AND SUMATRA etc..

The light house was constructed at Chandrabhaga beach on 1st March 1968 AD to guide the ships. It is a round masonry tower with height of around 30-meters.

Visiting this lighthouse area of the beach has a feeling of old world charm.

CHANDRABHAGA TANK AND MAGHA SAPTMI

Chandrabhaga river used to meet the sea at this place. The river no longer exists/ flows near the temple. Now, it is represented by a small tank / shallow pool of water, having the same name.

The ritual dip in this tank on Magha Shukla SAPTMI day(ie. seventh day of the bright fortnight of Magha Month) is treated as holy. It is celebrated as the birthday of Sun God. This is also known as Ratha SAPTAMI.

Large number of devotees/ pilgrims bath in the tank / sea before sunrise. They watch the sunrise in the sea, pray Sun God and seek his blessings. This is followed by worship of Navagraha. This place is very close to the sea and the Ramachandi temple.

Legend

Sun God was attracted by Chandrabhaga, who was a beautiful daughter of a sage. She was so beautiful that, Sun God had come down to earth to ask for her hand in marriage. As Chandrabhaga refused, he chased her to the river. To save her honour, she jumped in to the river and sacrificed herself.

Sun God blessed the river with medicinal properties in repentance and named it as Chandrabhaga.

Since that period, the devotees take a dip in the holy river as a tribute to Chandrabhaga. This is celebrated on the 7th day of the full - moon fortnight of Magha month. They also pray to rising Sun God at the this place in the morning.

Chandrabhaga was considered as a place for natural cure for lepers. It is believed that a dip in the pond / sea can cure skin diseases/ leprosy.

A fair is organised on this occasion which is known as Chandrabhaga Mela.

Samba dasami is also celebrated on the 10th day of dark fortnight (ie. waxing phase of moon) in poush month at this place.

VISIT

As the temple is dedicated to Sun God, the best time to visit the temple is the morning and evening hours.

To know the intricacies of the carvings and chariots etc. one has to spend more time.

September to March is the best time to visit the temple, as the weather is pleasant during that period. The climate remains hot and humid during the summer months. Official guides are available in different languages to explain the visitors.

TICKETS

One has to purchase entry tickets to go inside the temple premises. The tickets for Light and Sound show can be brought at the venue. One can also book the tickets through online.

STAY

There are plenty of hotels at Konark, Puri and Bhubaneshwar etc. for the visitors to stay and tour the place.

As Konark is less crowded and more serene, it is better to stay in the hotels / resorts at Konark. Also Konark will be liked by any sea food lover.

Konark Sun Temple is around 60-kms from Bhubaneswar and 35-kms from Puri by a marine drive road along the sea beach.

There are various buses run by OSRTC, private operators from Bhubaneswar, Puri, Cuttack and from different parts of the state. The Konark Bus Stand is near the Sun temple. The nearest Railway station is Puri. One can hire a taxi from Puri / Bhubaneshwar to visit Konark. There are plenty of taxis and one can easily get taxis on hire.

Biju Pattanyak International Airport is around 65-kms and takes around 1-hour drive to reach the Sun temple.

RAMCHANDI TEMPLE

RAMCHANDI temple is situated in a scenic surrounding and the Goddess is believed as more ancient than Konark sun temple.

For the religious tourists, Ramachandi temple, which is a famous Shaktipeetha is worth visiting. The temple is surrounded by Casuarina plantation. The image of Goddess Chandi is seated on the lotus. The temple is half hidden by sand mounds and is near the confluence of Kushabhadra river.

Ramachadi Temple

In the temple complex one will find the inner sanctum (Viman) and Jagmohan. It is an open and flat roofed structure. This north facing temple is constructed with sandstones, bricks and laterite stones. An open flat roofed temple is built at a later date. The height of the main temple is around 30-feet and the Jagmohan is 12-feet.

Ten armed Goddess Ramchandi (ie. in the form of Dasabhuja Durga) made of black Chlorite is the presiding deity of the temple. She is having a silver crown on her head. The Goddess is piercing Mahishasura, (the demon) by trident. Her carrier, lion is carved in the pedestal.

The side Gods found in three sides of the central niche are – headless Buddha, a four armed Devi and Biranchi Narayan. It is believed the Buddha image was broken by Kalapahada. As per researchers a broken image of Marichi of Buddhist pantheon is found in the wall

On the floor of the Jagmohan, there is a lion installed on the octagonal pillar. Two images of Varaha and Trivikram are found in the niches of the Jagmohan.

Legend

The legend regarding the Goddess is very popular.

The following adage/song had immortalised the place.

"Bhala Ramachandi Bhalare
Kala Pahada Ku Duare Basai
Bhala Pani Ani Galare"

(ie. The song describes, how the Muslim invader Kalapahad was kept waiting, when the Goddess went to fetch water")

KALAPAHAD, a Brahmin turned Muslim had vowed to destroy all the temples of Odisha, during 16th century. After destroying Konark temple, he proceeded to destroy the Jagannath temple, at Puri.

As RAMCHANDI temple was on his way, he also wanted to destroy this temple. When he reached at the temple, Kalapahad was feeling thirsty. A maid servant requested Kalapahad to wait at the door, till she brings water from the river. Actually, the maid servant was the Goddess. She was dressed / disguised as a maid-servant (Maluni) and went out to bring water from the river, keeping Kalapahad, waiting at the temple gate.

After long wait, Kalapahad became anxious and became more thirsty.

As the maid -servant did not return, he entered inside the temple. To his surprise, he found the throne of the Goddess was empty. Kalapahad thought, the Maluni might have taken the deity with her. He followed Maluni with anger. When he reached at the bank of the river, he saw the floating Goddess in the middle of the river. As the river was deep and full, he came back without destroying the Goddess.

In the process, destruction of Jagannath Temple, Puri was delayed and the priests were able to shift the Trinity/ Idols of Jagannath Temple, Puri.

A priest saw the Goddess in the dream and he was instructed to build a temple near the river and to keep the Goddess in that place. The place was known as RAMCHANDI, as per the name of the Goddess.

As per local legend, she had guided Lord Ram to defeat demon king Ravana.

She is the wish fulfilling and the most benevolent Goddess of the area. The image is gracious. It is believed that, she is the presiding deity of Arka Kshetra and she was worshipped in a small shrine in the Sun temple complex.

There are panel of Dash Mahavidyas in the inner walls of Jagmohan / temple premises.

The ten Goddess, ie. Laxmi, Vairabhi, Bagala, Dhumabati, Chhinnamasta, Matangi, Bhubaneshwari, Sodasi, Tara and Kali are depicted in their traditional Patta style painting of the state. It is also linked to Tantric practices.

East facing Rameshwar Shiv temple is in the north-west corner of the temple complex.

Kankeswar temple is also nearby.There are some small temples in the complex and all the temples are overlooking the sea.

The entire temple complex is surrounded by a brick – built boundary walls and measures around 80-feet by 40-feet.

The temple complex is having a partial skeleton of a whale that was found in the Bay of Bengal near the temple in 1994. Sometimes the skull is draped in garlands and treated as if it is a deity.

VISHNU TEMPLE

A broken brick temple said to be the temple of Lord Vishnu is located behind Ramachandi temple. The pillar in front of the temple is said to be as Garuda pillar. The images of Laxmi and Saraswati are found in the walls of the temple.

There is no deity inside the temple.

KONARK MATH

The monastery is situated towards the south of the Sun temple. The Matha belongs to the cult of Nirakar Brahma / contemplation of the eternal void.

It is known as Samba Ashram by the local people. In the DHUNI Kunda, the fire is burning continuously, since the beginning of the Matha.

Some also believe that, it was the Ashram of Chandrabhaga's father, who was a sage.

The Matha was founded by Hari Mahanti alias Ananta Abadhuta. The Abadhuts used to collect offerings for their livelihood.

There are also 3- other MATHAS nearby, ie. Chandrabhaga Matha, Biranchinarayan Matha and Mahabir Tungi.

As per Odisha Gazetteer, near the Hindu Matha, a Muslim priest named Saidu Shah lives in a hut. He offers regular prayer at a particular spot near by believing that to be the abode of the Muslim Saint Jahania Jahangast Pir Mukadam.

BHAGABATI TEMPLE

This is a small but beautiful temple of Goddess BHAGABATI, situated in a scenic surrounding. The roaring sound of the waves and big oak trees are other attractions.

Raja festival is the famous festival of this place.

It is around 200-meters away from the main Bhubaneshwar-konark road, opposite side of Konark college.

RAMCHANDI BEACH

The beach is named after the presiding deity Ramchandi, which is just behind the temple. This is a peaceful beach and good place to relax near Konark. The confluence of the river Kushbhadra and the Bay of Bengal at this Beach is scenic.

The beach is known for it's silvery sand on the shore and for it's spectacular sun rise. One can watch the sunrise / sunset and have a morning/evening walk on the silvery sand with blue water, nearby.

This is one of the most picturesque and unexplored beaches in Odisha. Line of tall palm trees add to it's attractions.

The poem, "Ramachadira Sandhya", ie. An evening in Ramachandi, written by great poet / A member of Panchasakhs, Pandit Nilakantha Dash describes about the scenic beauty of this place.

As the beach is the merging point of the river and Bay, there are not any high waves. The scenic beauty of the confluence would charm the visitor.

It is popular for sailing, swimming and sun-bathing etc. One, having a good swimming skill, can venture on a traditional boat to explore the nearby coast.

One can take a boat ride to enjoy the confluence of the river with sea, where Bay of Bengal is at the back and river is at the front.

Some tourists observe,

"Untouched sandy heaven explored only by a few. A God like appeal of the beach – A spiritual experience rare to find in the tangible world."

It is a nice place for spending some quality time with friends and family.

Ramchandi temple and beach is around 7-kms from Konark on the Puri-Konark marine drive. It is around 70-kms from Bhubaneswar.

KONARK SURF FESTIVAL / RAMCHANDI SURFING FESTIVAL

Konark is a destination both for the National and global travellers. Sun temple, golden sands, blue sea and the Balukhand sanctuary famous for deer, are visitors delight. It is the epicentre of festivals like dance, art, sand art and surfing.

The beaches of Konark especially Chandrabhaga beach and Ramchandi beach are some of the best beaches in the country. The long sea coast of these two beaches offers fun water activities and water sports for the visitors.

Ramchandi beach is situated at the merging point of Kushabhadra river and Bay of Bengal. It is named after Goddess Ramchandi.

These two beaches are covered with golden sands, cashew plants and huge palm trees, nearby. These are ideal beaches for long walks and collecting shells etc. The beaches are good for activities like – sailing, boating, swimming and sun bathing.

Konark has been hosting one of the largest and prettiest festivals of surf since – 2012 AD.

For last many years India Surfing festival is held at the Ramchandi beach on Puri-Konark marine drive. The beach becomes a place of excitement as surfers from across the world reach the place to ride the waves. One will find many tourists and adventurists during this period.

The sport of riding through the water waves is liked by the adventurous tourists.

The SUP cup, which is India's biggest Stand up Paddle (SUP) competition is held in this beach.

The competitions like walk on water, yoga on water events, long boarding, kite surfing and skateboarding competitions are the attractions.

Due to ideal coastal conditions, more and more people are now attracted to this sport in this beach. It is considered as one of the best place for the surfers.

To avoid any casualties, rescue boats and medical facilities are provided.

The art, dance, photography, film making, sunbathing, solar clay therapy and the music festival in the evening, along with the fun cum adventure event in the sandy beach will be a life time experience for any visitor during this period.

This is generally held /performed during November to February. The festival begins with different themes every year to inspire and keep people/ participants to display their new styles / innovative ideas.

As observed by many, "Ramchandi beach have brought the surfers across the globe. Large participation in the surf festival shows that Odisha is in the process of transformation in to a hub of surf tourism and Ramchandi beach being the heart of all".

GENERAL

The area around Konark has many ancient monuments, temples and beaches.

For tourists who are visiting Konark can visit the nearby places like – Astaranga beach, famous Shakti Pitha Kakatpur – Mangala, archeological sites – Kuruma, Gangeswar Temple-GOP, Varahi temple, PIR JAHANIA SHRINE and Balukhanda sanctuary etc. This is covered by the Author in another book under "Puri District ".

There are a number of smaller shrines situated in the nearby places of Konark. Some of them are – RAMESWAR, Chitreswar, Triveniswar and Utpaleswar (All Shivlings), Rudrani, Khileswari, Charchika and Chiteswari (ie. various forms of Goddess Durga).

There are references about Konark in Kapila Samhita, Madalapanji, Prachi – Mahatmya, Bhabisya Purana, Brahma Purana and Samba Purana etc. and these are mythical references about the place.

Konark finds mention in numerous stories, poems and novels. Mohanjit's book of poems "Kona Da Suraj" which revolves around Konark, won the Kendriya Sahitya Academy Award for Punjabi language.

The works of Sachidananda Routray – Jnanpith award winner (-Bhanga Mandir, Konark), Gopabandhu Das (Dharmapada), Mayadhar Mansingh (Konark, Konarkara Lashya Lila, Mumurshu Konark), Manoj Das (Dharmapada- Nirbhul Thikana, Konark Sandhane, Kalapahadara Trushna-Ramachandi, Bruntahina phulara stapathi – Sibei Santara), Pratibha Ray (Shilapadma) and Sun temple is the setting of the "Interpreter of maladies", a short story in Jhumpa Lahiri's Pulitzer Prize winning collection of the same etc., describe Konark along with the mystery and legends associated with it.

As per Times of India, "the only thing about Konark where unanimity exits is it's undisputed beauty, the heightened level of creativity, the intricate carvings, the erotic scenes telling tales of creation and procreation and simply, the architectural magnificence".

As per Sir John Marshall, "I think there is no monument in Hindustan that is at once so stupendous and proportionate at the same time like the Black pagoda of Konark". The Sun temple at

Konark has an abundance of sculptures that depict Kama, Artha, Dharma and Moksha.

One should visit Konark temple at least once, which is unparalleled anywhere in the world and even in partially ruined state, it reflects the genius of the builders. This temple is a scientific marvel of medieval India. The pristine beaches, monastery, nearby ancient temples and other beautiful monuments of Konark area as stated above will also be loved by the travellers which are added attractions.

CHAPTER 4

Chilika Lake

Chilika lake, the queen of natural scenery, known as Swiss lake in the continent and encircled by picturesque Eastern Ghats, is a place with the serenity of it's own. As per geologists and from a fossil found near the south-western edge indicates the formation of the lake about 3 to 4-thousand years ago.

Chilika means soil inundated by water. It is the finest wetland in the sub-continent.

This wander creation of nature has attracted many poets, nature lovers, bird watchers, the tourists and visitors throughout the year.

In the words of great poet Radhanath Ray,

"Utkal Kamala Vilas Dirghika
Maral Malini Nilambu Chilika
Utkalr Tuhi Charu Alankara
Utkala Bhubane Sobhar Bhandar"

In English

"Oh ! Goddess Laxmi of Utkal, with long magnificent shore line,
Whose blue waters are filled with flocks of swan,
You are the best jewel of Utkal (odisha),
In Utkal area, you are the store house of scenic beauty."

The lake also finds mention in "Bandir Atmakatha" written by great freedom fighter Gopabandhu Das, when he was traveling as a prisoner in the train and the lake was viewed from the train (ie. in 1920AD).

This shallow bar – built estuary pear shaped lake, covers an area of 1165 – square kms. (approx) in the monsoon season and 906-square kms. in the dry season. This is the largest Brackish water lake in India and second largest coastal lagoon in the world. The lake is spread over KHORDHA, puri and Ganjam districts of Odisha. It extends from Bhusandpur in puri district to Ramba-Malud in Ganjam district.

The channels connect the lake with Bay of Bengal. The lake is connected with the sea at the old mouth at Arakhakuda and at new mouth at SATPADA.

It was designated as the Ramsar wetland in October-1981.

52-streams including Daya, Bhargavi and many small rivulets drain in to the lake.

Archeological Excavations at Golabai which is near the lake, in KHORDHA district, provide the evidence of culture, boat-building centre and maritime activities of the area as far as 2300-BC. This was a developed place during Neolithic, Chalcolithic and iron ages.

It was a major harbour during the emperor Kharavela, the king of Kalinga, who was also known as the "lord of the sea".

Ptolemy, the Greek geographer had referred, Palur which is near southern tip of the lake at Kantigarh.

The Chinese pilgrims Fa-Hien and Hiuen-Tsang had also mentioned about the famous port "Che li talo". Some historians believe, it may be near Chilika.

During ancient period the king of Kalinga was known as Lord of the sea.

There are also legends of 4th century, which describes about origin of Chilika linked to Pirate king Raktabahu.

Legend

The pirate king Raktabahu had decided to raid Puri with his navy. To avoid any detection and for a surprise attack on Puri, the pirates anchored their ship at on offshore place(ie. out of sight). However, the inhabitants of Puri came to know about it and fled away. The abandoned city was left to the pirates. Raktabahu became angry and thought that this was due to the trick played by the sea. He tried to punish the sea for the betrayal. However, the sea parted to let the pirates to march in. As the pirates marched and entered in to the area, the sea surged back. Everyone was drowned and this large lake was formed in the process.

The seventh century ship anchors and stone memoirs at Village Kanas, near Chilika show evidence of naval engagements near the lake.

Marine archeological studies show that Chilika was once a safe harbour for ships bound for SE Asia and other parts of the world.

As per some researchers, some rocks in the southern sector are marked by a band of white formed by remains of coral. This band is at 8-meter height above the current water level. It indicates, the area was once used for marine activities and the water was much deeper.

The 10th century BRAHMAND PURAN also mentions about trade and commercial activities with Java and Malaya etc. through Chilika.

In the words of the poet,

"Atitar Tuhi Sakhi Puratan
Dekhilu Narar Utthan Pattan
Kete Rajadhani To Tire Utthita
Hoithanti Puni Astamita"

In English,

"you are the witness of the past,
You have seen the rise and fall of men.
many empires had rose in your shores
You have also seen the fall of them."

The lake has influenced the spiritual, Religious and scenic aspects of the state over the years.

This is home to 800 species of fauna with some rare and threatened species like green sea turtles, Dugong and black-bucks etc.

Out of around 2900 species of flowering plants found in the state, 726 species are found here. As per CDA(Chilika Development Authority), 323 aquatic species, which Includes 261-fish, 28-prawns, and 34-crabs are found here.

For centuries, fishing is the main activities in the Island.It provides livelihood to more than 2-lacs fishermen. The lake is home to Irrawaddy dolphins in the country. A small population of BOTTLRNOSE DOLPHINS migrated from sea, are also found here.

This lake is the largest wintering ground for migratory birds in the sub-continent. Some threatened species listed in IUCN RED list are found here. Around 9-lac birds visit the lake during winter months.

When one visits the lake, It looks as if never ending spread of water which is broken, only by small Islands. Rich bio-diversity, it's socio-economic importance and spectacular display of colourful avian charm will enchant any visitor. The sighting of large number of boats in the blue waters show the rural life at it's best.

The lake is best described by some authors as: – "Chilika lake seems like a vision crafted by some imaginative artists in the mists of pre –history".

Further in the words of the great poet Radha Nath Ray,

"Sundar Truptir Absad Nanhi
Jete Dekhuthile Nua Dishuthai"

In English,

"A thing of beauty is joy for ever"

Hence, any visit to state will remain incomplete without a visit to this lake. For a tourist/visitor, the lake can be visited / divided in to four parts: – Northern, Central, southern and Outer channel.

However, the spit of Chilika is changing constantly. The sand bar and mouth are shifting. It is also being silted up by the rivers running in to it and making the lake shallow.

The lake can be enjoyed from Balugaon, Barkul, Rambha, SATPADA and MANGALAJODI. One can also enjoy the scenic beauty of lake while passing through the road (NH-16) and in train (ie. Howrah – Chenai route). A boat ride amidst blue water, scenic beauty of the lake and green hills around will be a life time experience for any visitor. The lake is the best site for Bird watching, Dolphin watching, boating, fishing, wetland viewing and camping.

Getting around and across the lake to visit different places / parts would require time, as this is the largest lake in Asia with rich diversity.

The major tourist spots / important places of the lake are as under:

MANGALAJODI-THE PLACE WHICH EVOKES THE ORNITHOLOGIST INSIDE YOU

This is the northern portion of Chilika lake which is the largest brackish water lake in Asia. This is a vast wet land and is one of the offbeat places not only in the state but also in the country for any visitor and naturalist.

This village is filled with mango trees and bamboos.

This is a wet land with shallow waters and is a favourite destination for many migratory birds. The area is large, around 10 square kms. This is an attractive and amazing place of outing, for a day.

The flat area looks endless, a feeling being at the end of the world.

It was an ancient fishing village. This is a reclaimed place for the waterbirds. This is a place where the local people have become bird watching experts/guides, who were once poaching the birds. They are a changed man who are protecting and promoting the tourism of the area.

Thousands of migratory birds from different places of the world are attracted to this wetland habitat. One will find so many migrant and local birds here. This place is worth visit even for a non-bird watcher.In this pristine paradise the birds come in an annual journey year after year.

For the boating facilities with a small sail boat/bamboo-pole controlled country boat, one has to pay around Rs1000/-for a duration of 1.5-hours to 2-hours.

Here no motor boats are used, to avoid disturbances and so that the visitors can see maximum birds from a short distance.

The trip starts from the watch tower which is around 2-kms away. When one will visit inside, it will be observed that the freshwater swampy land had been branched out to a net work of water lanes/ channels and surrounded by flock of birds. it is told that there are 30 channels. The main channel runs north-south for about 3-kms and a nature trail running parallel to it is around 2-kms, which ends at the watch tower. The boatman and a guide who are quite friendly will accompany the visitor. One will be touched by their stories about the birds and the passion in them. The chirping/ murmuring sound of the birds and gurgling sound of water as the boatman rips the oar, is a life time experience for any one.

With sightings of flocks of geese over the head, one cannot forget the folk song of the boatman from the Odia film – "MATIR MANISH",

"Udi Gala Gendalia Jhadi Dei Para,
Raja Jhia Bahuduchi Dekhi Budha Bara"

In English translation: –

"The geese flew, flapping their wings,
the princess returned/ returning, after meeting her old husband".

The boatman/guide will unravel many more magical moments, than one can imagine.

BIRDS – AT – MANGALAJODI

It is told, in the peak season this area hosts more than 3-lac birds. It is declared as an "International Bird conservation Area" and a significant waterfowl habitat. This is also designated as a Ramsar Site. There are around 200 species of birds in the peak season, out of which 80-are migratory birds. MANGALAJODI supports over 2-lacs waterfowl in winter with population of 15-species exceeding 1% of their bio-geographical population.

During visit one will find large number/ lakhs of black – tailed GODWITS, LARGE EGRET, LITTLE CORMORANT, GREY WAIGTAIL, COMMON SNIPE, GREY HERON, BLACK WINGED STILT, GLOSSY IBIS, CHILIKA CHIKEN (PURPLE MOORHENS), WHISKERED TERNS, ASIAN PIED STARLING, BRONZE WINGED JACANA in colourful coat, OPEN BILLED STORKS and NORTHERN PINTAIL. The reflection of the birds in the water looks beautiful.

BRAHMINY SHELDUCK who are from colder climate of Ladakh area will charm any visitor. They along with black tailed Godwits are the stars of visit. It is told that, they are found in couples/stay in pairs, who can been seen together in the night and seen separately in the day time.

One cannot but stare in awe at the amazing beauty of the birds, as the boat passes through the shallow water in it's own speed. It is sheer nature's magic that every year they come all the way from their homelands despite innumerable hardships.

These birds arrive in the middle of October and remain up to February-March. The reeds(ie. mostly Khagra reed) and the vegetation in this marshy land provide them food and shelter. One will also find large number of lily flowers in this wetland which gives an amazing view.

However for any enthusiast, one has to visit for long hours in the morning and evening time, to have a view over the larger area of the wet land.

Taking photos of the birds, watching their flights, their bath, feeding and listening their sounds during the boat ride will be an amazing experience.

The local villagers /Guide will help in locating various birds. They provide binoculars and books to locate the birds. The guides are patient and will show different birds with their names.

One can also watch the birds on some watch towers and the standing on the long embankments during sunset and sunrise.Flock of birds circle the skies over the area. The anchored Boats, Crimson sky and Flocks of birds in the background of the rising /setting sun will mesmerise any visitor. At the peak of migration and during night, the bird murmurs of the day becomes "bird roar".

One will be astonished to see how so many species of birds visit this place year after year without forgetting the route, to make it their winter home which is secure and a safe place for them. Some birds from as far as Caspian Sea, Mongolia, central and south east Asia, travel around 12-thousand kms to reach the place.

As per the views of some visitors, "MANGLAJODI is far ahead of other wet lands in terms of richness of the habitat, number of birds and the proximity at which one can see the birds". "It has the potential to become one of the sought after destination for bird watchers".

The birds from Russia /Siberia, Mongolia and Ladakh can be seen in this place during winter.

CHILIKA BUFFALOES

One will find CHILIKA BUFFALOES in MANGALAJODI and Bhusandpur area, who enters deep in to the water. They are known as "Night Queen of Odisha".

They feed on the vegetation that is grown there. They remain in the lake for several days together. They are raised in the open under hot sun and heavy rains. Their influx clears the shoreline and key to lake's sustainability. They are also crucial for the eco-system of the lake. They benefit the migratory birds. Some birds can be seen riding on their backs. They help in checking the growth of weeds and plants which may clog the lake. It is a zero investment income source. The milk from them is tasty and remain fresh for a week without refrigeration, may be due to high salt content.

Steps should be taken to preserve the CHILIKA BUFFALOES.

Photo Exhibition In Mangalajodi – Mangalajodi – National Chilika Bird Festival:-

The Odisha Wild Life Lounge, Birds of Odisha, The Bhubaneswar Bird Walks and MANGALAJODI Eco-tourism organises photo – Exhibition on MANGALAJODI. Photographers from different parts of the country contribute their images on MANGALAJODI which are displayed and sold. The proceeds are used for community development.

It aims to place MANGALAJODI, in the global tourist map, by hosting workshops and promotional stalls.

Stories About Manglajodi

One will listen stories about a Ghost in the area, from the local people. They believe that, there was a Ghost in a nearby tree where many people were killed and no one likes to go to that area, in the night.

On enquiry it is revealed that, there are no trees in that area at present, but the felled tree still evokes panic. it is understood that 7 - people have died.

However, it is rumoured that, a murderer soul lives in that area/tree in the past and who goes near, suffers from various diseases. Because of death of some people in mysterious circumstances, nobody goes to the nearby area.

However, social activists blame the same and claim that lack of basic health care, are the reason for the widespread superstition.

No Change Impossible-Mangalajodi

MANGALAJODI was known as a poachers' village in the past. It is said that on some days 4000 ducks were poached by using nets, traps and pesticides. They were supplied to markets nearby. Even there were people known as "Veerappan of Chilika" who used to kill the birds in large numbers. The villagers used to carry a duck as a gift to their friend / relatives or to get the work done from others.

In this place one will be amazed to see, how a visionary-NANDA KISHORE BHUJBAL, of Tangi area, had attempted to bring an end to poaching by taking the villagers in to confidence. His true living story, is a story of struggle, sacrifice and achievement.

It is understood that, the transformation in him began with his repentance, when he was overcome with guilt, -the first time he shot an Egret with an Air-gun. He renounced poaching and stood -up against the most notorious poachers.

He along with Madhu Behera of WILD ODISHA, had given the villagers, the idea of alternative livelihood. Over a decade of persuasion and continuous support from different agencies helped a lot. He is known as the one man army of the area.

By taking them/ villagers in to fold of MAHAVIR PAKSHI SURAKSHA SAMITI (which also got PAKSHI BANDHU AWARD FOR THE YEAR -2001), they partnered with the forest department, Royal Bank of Scotland and Indian Grameen service and initiated community development schemes. The villagers were provided training about migratory birds, to become tourist guides. This was a challenge for them, for not only changing the mind set of the people but also offering alternative livelihood.

This is an exemplary story where the poachers have become protectors of Migratory avifauna. Even some members of the community work along with the forest guards throughout the night to ensure safety of the birds.

If this area can be developed further with the help of local people, they will get more opportunities for livelihood and income. The concept of eco-tourism was facilitated.

It is an example of a sustainable eco -system which is community owned. Here people participated successfully for development of Eco-tourism.

If one wishes to enjoy the area, one can stay in one of the Eco Tourism -lodges/ Godwit Eco Cottages of Mangalajodi. Although it is rustic, one will have an idea about the area, village life and nature trails. There are cottages and dormitories. They also offer packages which include stay, meals and guided boating.

A non-vegetarian, can satiate the taste buds by mouth watering local small prawns, boiled with little salt and dipped in Mayonnaise besides the prawns of Chilika.

These lodges are run to help the local people to act as guides and to help in the conservation work. The Mahavir PAKSHI Surakhya Samiti, tourism department and several wild life organisations are taking steps with the help of local people to protect the birds of the area.

For some research scholars it is an important place to study the eco -system in the wetlands, local livelihood and it's impact on climate change. The business model can be replicated in other parts of the state and country which is economically viable and environmentally sustainable.

Culture And Spirituality Of Mangaljodi Area

For a religious tourist, there is an old Raghunath temple, more than 250 years old, which is the centre of religious activities. This temple is owned by Mahapatra Community, but any one can worship in this temple.

There are other temples and religious places in the area like PATITA PABAN TEMPLE, GUPTESWAR TEMPLE, NILKANTHESWAR DEV TEMPLE, MAA MANGALA TEMPLE, MAA BRAHMINI TEMPLE, MAA BALIMAJHI DEVI TEMPLE.

PATITA PABAN temple is the oldest and biggest temple of the area. The temple of MAA BALIMAJHI is a picnic spot. The scenic beauty and lonely atmosphere will attract any tourist.

It is also believed that NILAKANTHESWAR TEMPLE was built in 7-days and ancient name was Jhuntikeswar.

One can enjoy DANDA YATRA in the month of Chaitra (March -April) and PAIKA AKHADA which are performed by some villagers in style.SHREE RAM LEELA FOLK THEATRE performs Sri Ram Leela during Ram Navami, which is nice to watch.

MYTHS

The name MANGALAJODI is linked with many myths. The village has twin temples. This is the reason for calling this place as MANGALAJODI.

It is also believed that in the past it was a harbour, where the boat and ship used to halt, when the state was a maritime power.

The place is well connected. This is in KHORDHA district. It is around 70-kms. from Bhubaneswar and 75 kms. from Puri, The roads are good. It is around 5 kms from the NH -16 from Chandpur, Tangi. It takes around 1.5 hours from Bhubaneswar.

Muktheswar and Kalupada Ghat are the nearest rail heads, which are on the Howrah -Chenai route. The nearest bus stop is Tangi.

Best time to visit the area is November to February/March. Large number of birds can be seen between mid December to mid January. However, resident birds can be seen through out the year. Although winter months are the best time to visit the area, this place also carries distinct beauties in summer and rains.

However with the help of local community, this area requires further development with suitable infrastructure and fishing boats are to be prohibited in this wetland.

SATPADA-CHILIKA LAKE

SATPADA is in the eastern side of Chilika. It is the place where Chilika lake meets the Bay of Bengal. The name is derived from the group of seven villages. (sat-means seven, pada -means village). This is surrounded by lagoons from three sides. This is near the village Panaspada. It is a popular tourist spot.

It is around 120-kms from Bhubaneshwar and 50-kms from Puri.

After crossing Brahmagiri, one will find the lake water in the fields, where tiger prawns are grown.

This place is the best for sighting Chilika Dolphins-known as Irrawaddy Dolphins (Orcaella brevirostris). This place will be liked by any nature lover.

The place has also opportunities for any visitor for canoeing, kayaking and boating.

One may book an OTDC tour, in a boat to experience the lake and the lagoon. There are also many private boats/ different types of Boats are available, which can be hired. One family or group is allowed in one boat. The group may consists of 6-adults and 2-children. The dolphin motor boat association also provides the boats on hire.

As the boat enters the dolphin point, the boatman switches off the engine to maintain silence. If one is lucky, one will be able to see a number of dolphins, may be close to the boat or at a distance frisking in the water. These beautiful dolphins jumping in water, in front of any one, will give an ecstatic experience, as if, never seen before.

Dolphins -At Satpada

As these dolphins are greyish in colour and very shy in nature, they are difficult to spot.

There are certain points where one will find dolphins and local boatman knows these areas. The boats are required to maintain 50-meters distance from the dolphins and not more than 5-boats are allowed at a time near the dolphins. The best time as told by the boatman is around early morning hours, before crowds came in.

In SATPADA, one will enjoy frequent sights of dolphins in it's blue water.

The dolphins in this area are lightly coloured all over and slightly white on the underside. The mature dolphins weigh around 130 -kg and length is around 7-ft. Highest number of Irrawaddy dolphins in the world are seen in this place. The environment of the area is suitable for stay of the dolphins.

They are now endangered species and they face noise pollution from the mechanised boats. Their reproduction period is from July to January.

The govt and environmentalists should come forward to safeguard these species from extinction.

SEA MOUTH ISLAND

One should visit this place /spot, where the lake meets the Bay of Bengal. It is amazing and memorable. Cruising, to reach the place is an unforgettable experience which is around 15-kms from SATPADA. If one wants to see, only the meeting point of the lake with sea, boats are available from Gabakund, Mirajpur, Arakhakuda and Sipakuda.

One could see the meeting point very close to RAJHANS Island on the sandy strip. However, one should not swim at this area, as the beach is sloping and it is deep within few steps.

The sea mouth is the place /piece of land which remain submerged during high tide. At low tide it gets accessible.

It is an unexplored stretch of beautiful beach of around 30-kms, across the sand bar. The dolphins also prefer this area. It is almost a virginal white sand beach.

The sound of the waves of Bay of Bengal breaks it's strides on the silent beach front. One will feel oneself, as if Robinson Crusoe in this silent and virgin sand, spreading miles after miles together. One can take a leisurely stroll for hours across the sandbar, on the unexplored beach. It is a good destination for relaxation and rejuvenation.

A non -vegetarian, can also enjoy under the palms and casuarinas, the freshly netted fried fish, prawn and crabs of the lake, cooked before the visitor. Local people come with tables, chairs and other utensils to cook and give the fried items. One will find many make shift food stalls.

One may also find some pearls sold from the oyster shells. However, one should not be tempted to by the pearls. It appears, they are brought from Hyderabad and sold as natural pearls.

RAJHANS ISLAND

There are trips to Rajhansa (royal swan) Island, where the sand bar separates calm Chilika lake from the turbulent Bay of Bengal, close to sea-mouth.

It is one of the many Islands in the lake mouth of SATPADA.

It takes around 1.5-hours of boat journey, which is around 18 - kms. The boat will pass through many fishing villages located in the Islands of the lagoon.

One will experience un-spoiled sand bar on one side and the Bay of Bengal on the other side, with forests and small mountain in between.

It will be a life time experience to see and feel, the amazing sight of sun, sand, crystal clear water of the lake in one side, turbulent sea in another side and the music of swaying casuarina trees.

During clear days the sun rise and sun set are the major tourist attractions of the area.

Along the outer channel, one will find the cashew plantation and layer of plantations to save the area from erosion and also from high wind speed during cyclones. This is coastal area management practice to fight sea erosion. There are sand dunes on one side and forest on the other.

There is a forest rest house on the sand bar, which separates the two landscapes.

One may bask in sun and take a sea bath in this Island.

Rajhans Island is also famous for red crabs which are big in size. They are scared of humans and run in to their holes, as one approaches them.

From Satpada, one can visit a number of Islands like heavens Island, little bird Island, mini Kali jai temple Island, little Island which are worth visiting.

There are also Islands nearby for red crabs, which attracts the tourists.

Boats are available from SATPADA to carry the tourists. Boating facilities are also available for exploring Bay of Bengal through the channels.

There is a vessel service from SATPADA to JANHIKUDA. The distance is 5-kms. It reduces the journey time between Puri and Berhempur.

MUSEUM

One's visit will not be complete without visiting the museum/Fish aquarium and Dolphin watch tower. From the museum one will get an idea about the bio-diversity, wetland and the famous dolphins. One will also know the fishing types, fishing community and birds of the area. There are different models and displays that explains the various aspects of the lake. The video show of Chilika development Authority is worth watching. From the hall one can see the scenic beauty of the lake.

Tourists can visit this place throughout the year. In monsoons the lake has a separate charm with dark and miles after miles of clouds enveloping the lake. However, the best time to visit the place is in winters.

If one likes to stay, OTDC Yatri Nivas is more popular which is located, near the shores.

Government is also developing an Eco -park on 4.5 acres of land. The dolphin lights are also designed to be installed over a stretch of 400-metres.

OUTER CHANNEL

Outer channel is the lifeline of the Chilika lake. There are many beautiful places near the outer channel, which would be liked by any visitor.

Manikpatna /Manikapatna

This is an historical site. Some historians had identified this area as the old port Chelitalo, found in the books of Hiuen Tsang. Some say the port may be near Konark /Puri.

This is also an important archeological site. Some archeological remains, like -porcelain ware linked to China, knobbed wire to Roman Empire and a Ceylonese coin of $11/12^{th}$ century etc -were found in this area. This indicates, the existence of a port and it's trade link with many countries.

ASI findings reveal that, this area was playing an active part in trade and business with China, Burma, Shri Lanka, Thailand and many Arab countries up to $11/12^{th}$ century.

It is on the northern end of the lake and on the left bank of Kushbhadra river.

The name is derived from the nearby village of Manikpatna. The village is near the archeological site. It is on the outer channel of Chilika lake.

It is believed that, the village was named after Manik, a milk-maid who had sold curd to Lord Jagannath and Lord Balabhadra, when they passed by.

The milk-maid Manik is an important historical character in Jagannath culture and the place bears the living history of GAJAPATI king's victory over Kanchi.

This is the holy place in the area, where the feet of Lord Jagannath and Balabhadra had touched.

Legend

After defeat in the Kanchi expedition, the GAJAPATI King, Purushottam Dev prayed lord Jagannath for the blessings, so that he can conquer the said kingdom again.

With the blessings of the Lord, the king moved with his expedition to Kanchi.

Moved with the prayers of the king, Lord Jagannath and his elder brother Balabhadra had also started their expedition to Kanchi by sitting on the back of the black and white horse in the disguise of soldiers. In the way, they felt thirsty and drank the curd from the milk-maid-MANIK.

Manik asked for the payment from them for the curd. As they had no money, they gave their ring to Manik and told her to collect the payment from the king and return the ring to the king.

GAJAPATI king won the battle. When the king was returning, Manik obstructed the king and asked for the payment. She also produced the ring as an evidence. King was astonished to see the ring, as it was the ring of Lord Jagannath. The king came to know the divine support and his subsequent victory in the war.

The king was also delighted and granted the village to Manika, which was known as Manikapatana.

This story has been described in the Odiya film Manika, released in-1986.

BHABUKUNDALESWAR / BHABAKUNDALESWAR TEMPLE OF LORD SHIV

This Shiv temple is at Manikpatna. It is close to the new sea – mouth.It is decorated with many images and carvings. The huge Shivling is in black chlorite stone.

This temple is the blessings site of GAJAPATI king's Kanchi - Kaveri expedition. The legendary Manik, believed to offer curd to lord Jagannath and Balabhadra at this temple site.

There is also a mosque in this area.

The speciality of the religious shrine of this place is the entrance door, which is in the shape of a open jaws of a whale.

For generations, the people of this locality live in harmony, which shows co-existence of both the religions.

The other speciality of the region is the curd, which is prepared in bamboo baskets. SATPADA is the nearest bus station to connect the village.

Barunakuda

It is a small Island famous for it's scenic beauty. There is a temple of Lord Varun (ie. God of sea). This tiny Island is near Magarmukh. It is between the sea and the lake. This is a place of solitude. As it is not known to many people and a quiet place, one can enjoy it.

Berhempura

It is a small Island village near SATPADA. Natural beauty and green surroundings make this Island a visitor's paradise. One can relax in the Clean and dust free atmosphere of the Island.

The Eco -cottage of Chilika Island resort is an ideal place to explore and experience the Island.

Dolphins can be seen at the surrounded water body of BERHEMPURA and Mahisa Island near SATPADA.

The name of the place is derived from DARU BRAHMA OF LORD JAGANNATH, as the Lord was shifted through this route to inner portion of Chilika to protect from the Muslim invaders.

One may visit the ancient deities-Nabgraha (nine planets) which is near the outer channel. One can watch the small dear, BALI HARINA at BRAHMAPURA. It is a place of scenic beauty between the lake and the sea.

Chourbar / Choubar Shiv Temple

There is an old and dilapidated Shiv temple at Choubar near SATPADA. It is an artistic temple and close to Alupatna village along outer channel. There are many stories linked with this temple.

VILLAGE -MOTTO

Near this village, a 32-kms long and narrow outer channel connects the lagoon to the Bay of Bengal. The shifting of the mouth opening has led to the development of 32-km long barrier Island with width ranging from 100 meters to 1500 meters, with by Bay of Bengal towards east and narrow outer channel towards west.

The SAND BAR AND MOUTH OF THE LAKE is an unexplored stretch of about 32-kms of empty beach, which separates lake and sea.

MAGARMUKH

The mouth of the old channel to the sea is known as MAGARMUKH (mouth of crocodile). It is about 300 feet. The Dolphins prefer this area.

An artificial new mouth has been opened by Chilika development authority at this place. The mouth was opened during the year 2000AD.

It is around 32 kms. This connects the lake with Bay of Bengal at Arakhuda village.

By utilising some mathematical data and based on recommendations of central water and power research station, pune and National institute of oceanography (Goa) and ocean Engg centre of IIT, Chenai, they have opened the new mouth near Magarmukh of SATPADA, at a distance of – 18-kms, south -west of the old mouth, to enable sea water to enter the lake, by a shorter route.

Before the opening of the new sea mouth, the distance of sea mouth from Berhempur was 20-kms, but now it is 5-kms.

Chilika Lake is connected with the sea by a series of tidal inlets. The inlets are maintained by the discharge of inflowing streams during monsoon and by tides and ebbs during non-monsoon seasons.

Imbalances in the ingress and egress of sediments due to continuous exchanges between lagoon and sea, causes sedimentation of the mouth and it's shifting. Some are closed and some are opened at various locations.

It is understood that, during -1914, the opening mouth of the channel was near Arkhakuda

The barrier Island that separates the outer channel from the sea is now progressively degraded due to closure and opening of other mouths.

However, it is a nice place for any tourist, which is the north-eastern end of lagoon.

BARKUL

Barkul is the base for visiting this part of the lake. The place is between beautiful hills and Chilika lake. It offers a lively atmosphere, far from the maddening crowd and one can cherish the peace and tranquility of the area.

Here, there is a water sports complex. The facilities for canoeing, kayaking, boating and water scooters are available. For a joy ride with family, one can try a paddle boat ride. Adventurists can enjoy the water scooter, speed boats and other adventurous drives.

This is located at the edge of the lake and is the hub to visit places like KALIJAI temple /Island, NALABANA bird sanctuary, Parikud and Malud Islands etc.

There are also private boats available here, for boating to different places in the lake.

The Panthanivas of OTDC is a nice place for food, stay, parking space and for booking Govt boats. There is plenty of space here. One can enjoy the seafood from Panthnivas and various eateries nearby. There is an inspection bungalow of PWD, where one can also stay.

One will find many restaurants near the main road.

The grand lagoon and the scenic surroundings will charm any visitor.

Here, boating during sunsets are memorable in the background of the lake, fishing boats and the hills of Eastern Ghats. It is a lovely place for any visitor to spend quality time.

It is 145-kms from Bhubaneshwar on NH-16 and 70-kms from Berhempur. It is a small town on the northern side of Chilika lake.

NALABANA ISLAND

This is a small Island of 16 -square kms (around 1500-acers). It is the core area of Chilika lake. It was declared a bird sanctuary in – 1973, for it's varied flora and fauna, which is also a Ramsar designated wetland. It is a must visit place for any bird lover. One will be amazed to see this bird sanctuary, which is a gift of nature. It is also known as the Island of reeds.

During monsoons, this area is submerged. In winter, with the decrease of water levels, the Island is exposed.

Large number of birds fly from different regions to feed on it's vast mud flats and supportive Eco system. Small places, which appear like Islands, are filled with birds. It is a paradise for bird watchers.

This sanctuary is covered with water reeds, hence the name NALABANA (ie. weed covered Island – forest/ Reed forest).

The sanctuary is a dense habitat of diverse resident and migratory birds. Many rarest migratory birds found in the sanctuary are Asiatic Dowitchers, spoon -billed Sandpiper, Pallas's fish-eagles, spot -billed pelican and Dalmatian pelican etc.

Many types of Flamingos, Siberian cranes, herons, Egrets, Storks, white ibis, BRAHMINY ducks, pintails, falcon, river terns, sea eagles, kites and Pochards can be seen during visit.

Long -legged species like flamingoes, herons and storks etc. can be seen in shallow waters and mud flats. The birds with short height can be seen on twigs etc. Moorhens, coots can be seen in higher vegetated areas. Longer legged avocets, stilts and godwits can be seen in deep water, where they get their feed.

Gull -billed and river terns can be seen in their nesting colonies. It is believed that, the nesting colony of Indian river terns in this bird sanctuary is the largest nesting colony in south east Asia.

One will be astonished to see flamingoes from Rann of Kutch and Iran.

World's most widespread bird of prey, ie. peregrine falcon, are seen here.

One should have binoculars to have a close watch and to see their flying patterns.

The chirping birds in the creeks of the marshy area and their flying formations will charm any visitor.

One can experience as to how the birds collect their food and make nests in the sanctuary.

It is told that the core area of NALABANA Island which is 6-square kms attracts around 3 to 3.5-lac waterfowls of different species.

Birds from as far as Aral Sea, Mongolia, Central Asia visit the area to escape the cold and they start their homeward journey with the onset of summer, ie. from March.

Best time to visit the sanctuary is between October and March. Maximum number of migratory birds are found during this period.

Barkul is near the centre of the lake. The sanctuary is one and half hour's boat ride from Barkul and around 2 hours journey from Balugaon.

As one approaches towards NALABANA, the reflections of sunshine enhances the beauty of the lake. One will find more and more migratory birds in the way during the journey. If one is lucky, one may spot some rare Irrawaddy dolphins on the way to NALABANA.

Visitors are prohibited from alighting on the Island/ entry is restricted. Forest department permission is required to visit the core area. However, boatman can take the visitor very near to the Island (ie. sanctuary boundary)/ outer periphery, where he can anchor the boat for a longtime so that visitors can watch more and more number of birds from the sanctuary boundary.

Here, one will find many boats with visitors who are witnessing these beautiful birds.

Though the Island can be visited throughout the day, however in morning hours (ie. especially during period of sun rise) the view is amazing to see the birds in their morning action.

KALIJAI

It is a small Island in Chilika. The main attractions of this Island is a small temple of Maa KALIJAI, which is a major holy shrine of the area.It is a beautiful destination both for the tourists and pilgrims. It is told that the temple was built by Jagannath Mansingh, king of Banpur in the year -1717. This hillock is around 29-acres. This is the abode of Goddess KALIJAI- one form of Maa Kali. The temple becomes KALIJAI because of Maa Kali and Maa Jai. Jai was a village girl of that area.

Earlier, it was under the Zamindar of Parikud Island.

One can reach the place either from Balugaon or Barkul through a pleasant boat ride. One can observe an excellent view of the never ending lake from the top of this hillock Island. It will be an awesome journey.

The distance from Barkul is 8-Kms and from Balugaon, it is 12 - Kms. It is situated near the Naval base -INS CHILIKA. The firing range and training camp is nearby.

It will take around 2-hours for the entire round trip. The boats can be hired from the OTDC counter. Private boats(ie. motor boats and country boats) are also available from both Barkul and Balugaon.

During journey in the boat, one can see a small Island of large stone, turned white/grey due to defecation of birds, as many birds rest during their journey to NALABANA. This small hill is known as Chadheihaga.

The temple is famous for the worship of Goddess Kali and the girl Jai. The Goddess is famous in the folk lore and legends and she is the reigning deity of the lake and family deity of all fishermen.

During boat ride, one can listen the Odiya song /poem of Pandit Godavarish Mishra, from the boatman:

"Bhala Kari Naa Buhare Nauri
Jhia Ku Maduchi Dar.
Gade Gada Loka Chanhi Bashithibe
Jhia Jiba Sashughar"

In English –

"Oh Boatman ! please drive the boat cautiously, as there is fear in the mind of the girl.
The people of the area are waiting for her, as she is going to her mother-in -laws house"

As it was Jai's first ride, seeing her plight, the father of Jai had advised the boatman to move the boat cautiously.

One will find a small temple in this rocky Island. A bright, colourful sculpture of horse facing the lake, is standing erect at the entrance of the Island.

Red threads in the form of wishes of the pilgrims, encircle the neck of the horse.

In the temple besides Goddess KALIJAI one will see other images of Malajai and Kanak-Durga. There are two lions in front of the temple, which is filled with vermilion.

No one lives in this area in the night excepting the temple staff. One will find large number of hens in the Island. It is told that, earlier, there was animal sacrifice and now it is stopped. The people leave the birds in the Island as a token of their sacrifice before the Goddess.

People believe that a visit to KALIJAI will fulfil their wishes.After worship, when one will return in the boat, the glimpse of the birds encircling the boat, mostly sea -gulls is worth watching.

Legend-1

There was a girl, named Jaai, who was already married as a child, to a boy in Parikud of Chilika. During that period child Marriage was rampant and the girl generally stays with her parents till she comes of her age. When JAAI came of her age, she was sent to her in-laws house. On that eventful day, the married girl was going with her father, to her mother-in-laws house. As her in-law's house was in Parikud Island in Chilika, they took a boat to ferry them across the lake. During journey, their boat was capsized in the gorge of the lake due to severe cyclones. The boatman and his father survived, except the girl. Despite searching, they could not locate her.

After the accidental death, the people of the area believed that, she had attained some spirituality.She had reincarnated as Goddess Kali and (JAAI/JAI) became the Goddess of the nearby people and was worshipped as Goddess KALIJAI. It is also believed that many boatmen had listened her voice in that area in the evening time.

The stone where the boat dashed, was named as KALIJAI mountain / hillock and a temple was built in her memory.

The Goddess, this area and mountain are revered as the saviour of many lives.

It is believed that Banpur was the village of the father of the Goddess Kalijai and Parikud was her in-law's house.

It is still believed by some boatman that there is a whirlpool in that area, where the accident took place, and they take a semi circular path to avoid the whirlpool.

The boatmen of the area also believe that she protects them /their ferry from any mishap. No boatman and fisherman enters the lake /sea of the area without praying the Goddess for a safe journey.

Legend -2

As per "The history of Parikud" by Radha Charan Panda, it is stated that the king of Banpur Harisevak Mansingh, was defeated by the king of KHORDHA and he came to Parikud in -1779. Again his son Bhagirathi Mansingh was attacked by the king of KHORDHA. Fearing defeat, the king preyed before the Goddess.

By the grace of Goddess, large number of Flamingoes in the Chilika lake marched forward, as it was winter time. The army of KHORDHA saw them from a distance and they thought that a large army of the king of Parikud was marching towards them in Chilika. Out of fear, the army of KHORDHA king left the place.

The people of area thought that king had won the battle (ie. JAYI / JAI-in Odia) due to the blessings of Goddess Kali. Hence the Goddess was known as KALIJAI.

Some people believe that, the real name of KALIJAI is, KALA(means -time) and JAI (means -victory), which signifies victory over the time /era. She was the presiding deity of Parikud palace. This temple was built to protect the inhabitants of the area, from the enemy, who may come from sea-route.

As the temple remains in-accessible during rainy season, the rulers of PARIKUD had built another temple at Parikud for her Puja during that period.

Fair

On the occasion of Makar Sankranti (ie. Jan -14), a big fair is held here. Lakhs of devotees visit the place for celebrating the festival and to worship the Goddess.

It is told that, there are 132 villages having fishermen population of around 50-thousand. They visit the temple on this day to offer the puja.

The ancestors of king of Parikud were also worshipping the Goddess as their protector.

They used to come from their fort with a procession of boats to this temple to offer special puja and to offer new clothes. They perform the coronation ceremony of the Goddess, on that day.

The festival is enjoyed with music and dance. The area becomes full with motorised and country boats.

The grandeur of the festival will attract any visitor.

Rambha

Rambha is the southern part of Chilika. This is a beautiful place in natural surroundings. It is a small town. It is around 1-km from Chilika lake.

For a food lover one can enjoy Chilika prawns, crabs and Khainga fish etc. at this place.

OTDC Panthanivas is the best option for visiting this part of Chilika area. One can see the lake from some of the cottages. The chirping sound of the birds and watching the lake from the verandah is a rare experience.

Here, there are 5 -seater /-10-seater boats and both the speed boat and motor boats are available. Private boats are also available. However, it is better to book the boats from OTDC COUNTER AT PANTHANIVAS.

There are many Islands and beautiful landscape near by Rambha /RAMBHA BAY. The surroundings of Rambha bay will add charm to one's visit.

Rambha Palace-Rambha-ganjam District

This palace was built in the middle of 19th century by the Khallikote king and was the residence of Khallikote queen. The building was constructed with sand stone, laterite stone, bricks, marble, wood and terracotta tiles etc.

It is a double storied building with portico, terrace and front staircase. The upper story roof is supported by the beams. Durbar hall, drawing room and 20-rooms are part of the palace.

This is being renovated into 24-room facilities. There would be an exclusive bird library, so that many tourists can watch the birds of Chilika lake from here. This would contain reference book for birds.

A dolphinarium will be developed to educate people on conservation aspects of the endangered marine animal which is seen in Satpada region.

In some of the rooms and it's interiors the original painting will be kept to retain the original grandeur of the palace.

The old fittings would not be altered to maintain the aesthetics of the place.

This palace is famous for holding the first session of Utkal Sammilani in 1902AD had played an important role for formation of Odisha state. It is around 130-kms from Bhubaneswar.

Besides the palace, scenic beauty of the nearby places like – Breakfast Island, Honeymoon Island, birds Island and Ghantasila hills etc. would charm the visitor.

Breakfast Island /Lighthouse Island

It is around 3-kms boat ride from Rambha. The Britishers used this place as their breakfast point, hence the name. There is a lighthouse. One can see this place from the train. This is between Badakuda Island and Somolo Island.

The king of Khallikote constructed a bungalow in this Island which is now in dilapidated condition. Here the water is dark blue.

Ghantasala Hills

From the Breakfast Island, one side of the hill is known as Ghantasila / GHANTASALA hill. The hill is having a cave and temple of Bholanath(ie. cave temple). The stones are very big and looks like fantastic nature of art in the midst of the blue water of Chilika. Going to this place is also adventurous. There are many legends about this hill. As understood from the fishermen ringing bells are heard from the hill top. It is around 3-kms from Rambha and takes around 40-minutes by boat to reach here.

Dinosaur Park /Birds Island

From Ghantasila hills, one will reach Dinosaur Park. It is in near to east Ghantasila hills. This is a small Island having a statue of the Dinosaur. It was damaged due to cyclone. People also call it as the Bird's Island. It is in the southern sector of Chilika.

Dinosaurs Island -Rambha

One can climb to the top of a small hill of the Island which is filled with trees, rare herbs and shrubs etc. Large number of birds visit this place. The bird watchers will find the opportunity to see variety of bird – nests in their natural habitat. The rocks have become white due to droppings from the birds,as they halt in the Island. The enchanting view of Chilika can be seen from the top of the hill. While returning, the view of sunset in the background of vast lake is mesmerising. It is around 4-kms. from Rambha.

HONEYMOON ISLAND /BARKUDA ISLAND

It is also known as Barkuda Island. One will find various plants around the Island. The place is famous for the aquatic limbless lizard, found specially at this place, beside other species. The view of the red and green algae on the bed of the dark blue water of the sea -bed is amazing.

It is 8-kms from Rambha. It is surrounded by clear water with natural habitat. It is adjacent to SANKUDA Island.

SOMOLO ISLAND AND DUMKUDI ISLANDS

This place was famous in the past, for the honeymoon house of the king of Khallikote. Now, it is in dilapidated condition. One will find a small pond, a well and the bathing place of the queen near the pond.

It is the central and southern sectors of the lake and situated in the background of Khallikote range of mountains.

If one is lucky, one can find Irrawaddy dolphins in this area. The remnants of Eastern Ghats are found in this portion of the lake.

SANKUDA ISLAND

This is a Eco tourism spot. It is 7-kms from Rambha. Here, one can stay in the tented accommodation. This is a nice picnic spot. It is one of the popular Island in the region. As it is pear shaped, it is also known as Shank Island. There is an ancient bungalow of the king of Khallikote. One will find many floral species in this Island.

BEACON ISLAND

It is a beautiful location in the midst of a scenic water spread and surrounded by Eastern ghats. It is a conical pillar built by Mr. Thomas Snodgrass, the then Tax collector of Ganjam (during British period) to put light on the top.

The room was the camp office of the collector. In -1790 AD, there was severe famine in Ganjam district, known as PANCHAMANIA KANTARA, when the price of rice /paddy had gone up to 5-mana (15-kgs) for one rupee and which was very expensive at that time. To give wages to the people during famine, the collector had asked them to built the room with a light post at this place, in -1792. He used to take records relating to relief work, to the Island for his office work and used to spend several nights at this place.

STORY OF SNODGRASS

He was a tax collector of Ganjam District between 1791- 97 AD. He progressively spent more time in this Island. The revenue of the district fell and news of his lavish lifestyle reached East India company's office at Madras. SNODGRASS ignored their letters. They sent Mr Brown to releive him from the office but SNODGRASS threatened to shoot him. He utilised the remoteness of the area and as the place was cut off during monsoons, to his advantage.

At last the Governor sent a small body of soldiers to bring him back. While carrying the records, SNODGRASS sank all the tax records in the middle of the lake, claiming it as an accident. He was removed from the job and was denied pension. He fought back in London by becoming a street sweeper in front of the office of the East India Company. He used to confront the wealthy directors everyday. To escape from the public ridicule, at last SNODGRASS was given pension. From a distance, this conical pillar looks like a floating boat with a mast during the day. It is in Rambha Bay in Ghatsila hills which is surrounded by Eastern Ghats.

It is a tiny Island formed by submerged mass rock in the lake. Beacon and Honeymoon Islands are close by.

PARIKUD

This is an important Island inside Chilika lake. It is surrounded by the lake on three sides and the Bay of Bengal in one side.

It is spread over 96 Mouzas which consists of 120 revenue - villages and some hamlets of Krishnaprasad Panchayat Samiti. This comes under Brahmagiri constituency. This is a group of composite Islands in Garh krishnaprasad block.

The area is famous for the great poet and writer -Mayadahar Mansingh, Lalit Mansingh (former foreign secretary of India) and Chilika Gandhi -Udaynath Jena.

PARIKUD is confined to the block area of Krishnaprasad Panchayat Samiti.

The old palace of the king, built at Krishnaprasad is beautiful. One can visit this Island to understand their culture, temples and to ascertain as to how the lake -Island is now a transformed place, from a punishment area during past. During winter season, the boat journey to the Island is an avian spectacle. One can visit the place in the early hours and enjoy the beautiful area throughout the day. Malud and Charichak are the important market places in Parikud.

From Malud market one can buy all kind if Chilika products like prawn, crab and variety of fishes.

The boat journey is enjoyable in the midst of the dolphins and birds.

HISTORY

Earlier this area was under Banpur king. When the King of Banpur Harisevak Mansingh was defeated, he shifted his base to Parikud in -1774 AD. His kingdom was known as Parikud Gurubai and the capital was Nrushinghgarh at Gurubai. Subsequently, the king Bhagirathi Mansingh shifted his capital to Krishnaprasad in -1798. Due to locational advantage, the Britishers and other Kings could not attack Parikud.

Legend

It is told that a milk -man of the area informed the king of Parikud, (BHGIRATHI MANSINGH) about killing of an Eagle by a crane in the Krishnaprasad area. The king was charmed and thought, if a crane can kill an Eagle, there is something speciality in that area. He shifted his capital to that area and built his palace at Krishnaprasad.

Due to it's location, this area could not be attacked and it was independent for a long time. However, when the Britishers invaded Odisha from south in -1803 AD, FATEH MUHAMMED, a boatman from Kandakhai of Malud who was in charge of the ferry of the area, met them and had shown them the Eastern route to Puri. The Britishers reached Puri. As return gift, Britishers had given the free hold areas of Parikud and Malud to Fateh Muhammed, which is presently the Krishnaprasad block.

All types of festivals are celebrated here and there are around 25 - temples of Various Gods and Goddesses in the area.

The main occupation of the people of the area is mostly fishing and some farming.

PARIKUD PALACE -PARIKUD (KRUSHNAPRASAD)

It is a magnificent palace situated in an Island surrounded by Chilika lake on 3 sides and Bay of Bengal on the other side. It was built in the early part of 17th century.

It is also known as Krushna prasad palace and was established by king Bhagirathi Mansingh in 1798 AD.

This is being developed as a tourist site and the palace is renovated in to heritage homestay.

It has 5- royal antique rooms with attached bathroom, Darbar Hall and lions gate. Every room designed with high ceilings, high windows, corridors and antique furniture. Little bit of history is displayed in each corner. The dining room has a beautiful old world charm.

Part of the palace is used as a museum.

Parikud Palace

One will see large number of birds nesting in Chilika and nearby bushes. One can enjoy the local sweet Mathapuli (ie. made out of

Urad dal and sugar syrup. This is famous in BANAPUR / Khordha / Chandanpur etc.).

As per Odisha Tourism, "Beautiful in disposition and mystical in it's folk lore, the Parikud palace nestled between the Bay of Bengal and Chilika on the Krushna Prasad Island opens one window to history of the lagoon and other to breathtaking views". There are two ways to reach by the road and the waterway. It is around 175-kms from Bhubaneshwar.

OTHERS

Gurubai Island

As per Puri district Gazetteer, in -1615 AD, the Sevayats of Lord Jagannath temple had anticipated the attack of the temple by Kalyan Mall, for second time. Accordingly, they had hidden Lord Jagannath in the GURUBAI Island of Parikud. Lord Jagannath was transferred from Chakanasi Sipanasi of Parikud.

There is a legend that the the sage of Chaubarsadhu Ashram had come to Chakasani to pray Lord. Many clay pots and coins were found from this place, which proved that Mahaprasad was offered to Lord.

In -1617 AD, Makram khan had attacked Puri temple again and Lord Jagannath was kept at Gurubai Island.

When Muhammed Takkikhan, Naib of Odisha attacked the temple at Puri, the Sevayats kept the Lord in a hill.

Ramchandra Dev- II of Bhoi dynasty had embraced Islam to protect the lord from the attack of Takkikhan. He is known as second Indradyumna, as he was the keeper of National cult of Odisha (ie. Jagannath cult).

The Island of Gurubai was the safest place, as it is situated in the middle of Parikud. A sacred alter of stone under the banyan tree is found here.

It is a big village mainly inhabited by fishermen community.

There is a Jagannath temple and a Charchika temple, which are built by the residents of nearby 5-villages.

The pujas/ rituals are performed as per Jagannath temple, Puri. However, Ratha Yatra is not observed here. Parikuda royal family looks after the temple.

MALUD ISLAND AND BEACH

It is one of the main Islands inside Chilika lake. It is 22-kms from NH -16 and is connected by road to Berhempur. Tourists coming from south can reach SATPADA and Puri through this route.

Tourists can reach the Island by boat from Barkul. Sun rise and sunset are memorable experiences here. It is nearby Rambha.

This Island inside Chilika is in the eastern sea shore towards the sea.

During winter, many birds used to come here from Siberia and Man Sarovar of the Himalayas

Malud Beach

It is a small Island. The beach that faces Bay of Bengal is pristine with calm water. The white sands of the beach is having a silky and clean look. Watching the sun set and sun rise in this place is mesmerising. One can enjoy the swimming, boat ride and water sports of the area.

The Dadhibamana temple nearby, can be visited to worship the Lord. One will find the idol of Garuda along with the deity of Jagannath.

CHILIKA AND LORD JAGANNATH

As per Madala Panji (ie. Official Almanac of Jagannath Temple), Jaggannath Temple was vandalised several times by the Muslim invaders.

To protect the deities, the idols were transferred to several faraway places during different periods. Towards end of 17th century,

Jagannath temple, Puri was attacked several times by Taqi Khan, when Ramachandra Deva was the Gajapati king.

As per legend and hearsay, the deities were hidden in the surrounding areas of Chilika lake, like – Marada, Khurda Garh, Chikiti, Tikabali, Bankuda Kuda, Athgarh Patna, NAIRI and Kankana Sikhri etc. (Details are covered under Lord Jagannath of Puri, in a separate book "Golden Triangle of Odisha" of the Author).

Chilika was the second home of the Lord and it acted as the safest place for shelter of Lord Jagannath for many times in the history.

As per some researchers the deities were taken from the Dobandha Ghat of Bhargavi river to Kankana Kuda (ie. known as Kankana Sikhari), an Island of Chilika. The water of Chilika are sanctified for providing shelter to Lord Jagannath, Balabhadra and Subhadra.

The deities were kept hidden and moved from place to place like – Mainisa, Gurubai, Gabapadar, NAIRI and Kankana Sikhari etc. They were kept mainly at – NAIRI, Kankana Sikhari, Gurubai and Chakanashi.

Gurubai has already been described under Parikuda Island, in the earlier paragraphs.

The details of NAIRI, Kankana Sikhari and Chakanashi are described in the following paragraphs.

Nairi Village

This village is on the bank of Chilika lake having mythological link and is a heritage village.

As stated earlier, when Moghul Nawab Taqi khan attacked Puri, the servitors fled with deities to Dobandha chapa, near present day Kanasa of Puri and then to Niari, covering a distance of around 45-kms by boat. They were kept in the Harihara Deva temple for around one year (ie. in the later part of 17th century). As per some hearsay, Lord Jagannath and his siblings had spent 7-months and 27-days at Harihareshwar temple.

This beautiful Harihareshwar temple was built by Jagannath Mansingh, the then king of Parikuda.

The idols were installed in 3-circular stones which are known as "Bije Chaka".

Both Lord Shiv and Vishnu were worshipped at this place and is the meeting point of two cults (ie. Shivaism and Vaishnavism).

There are 3-pindis (pedestals) where the three deities used to sit during exile.

The three Chaka Asthanas (ie. pedestals) are preserved and worshipped in the Jagmohan of this temple to commemorate the stay of Lord Jagannath at this place. Lord was kept here 2-times for protection, as understood.

Here, one will find 2-pits, ie. round shaped pit represents Lord Shiv and oval shaped pit represents Lord Vishnu.

Jay -Vijay and Nandi -Bhurungi are considered as gate keepers of the temple. There is another temple of Laxmi -Nrushingh in the temple complex.

There is a Gundicha temple at the end of the village and a well known as Gundicha well. It is also a pilgrimage center.

The Radha Mohan Temple in front of the palace of Bada NAIRI is also beautiful.

Ratha Yatra was observed during their stay at this place (ie. in 1732 AD). The Paikas and the guards of Parikuda king were taking care of the Lord.

Gundicha kupa, Badadanda and Gundicha banyan tree are the remnants still found here.

Thereafter, they were shifted Marada temple in Ganjam, where the deities were worshipped for 2-years and 4-moths. (Details of Marda -Jagannath temple has been described by the Author in the book- Incredible South and Central Odisha).

Recently a throne was installed at Hari-Hara temple by the Administration of Jagannath Mandir.

Hari-Hara Dev Temple is around 85-kms from Bhubaneswar and from Nachuni Chowk, one has to take left turn and has to move around 5-kms to reach the spot.

From here, one can reach Kankana-Sikhari Island by boat.

KANKANA SIKHARI

This hill stands tall inside the lake and is at a small distance from PENTHAGRAM NAGRI.

The hill is filled with KANKANA herbs/ Kankada herbs (spine gourd) and hence the name. In the past it was full of trees and animals.

As per researchers/ folk lore, Lord Jagannath, Balabhadra and Mata Subhadra were worshipped here for about 4-months, when the deities were hidden and shifted from place to place in Chilika for their protection, from the attack of Jagannath Temple during the period of Taqi khan towards end of 17th century / early part of 18th century.

HISTORY

TAKI KHAN, an anti Hindu, was the Subedar of Odisha in 1727 AD. He imprisined the king of KHORDHA, ie. Ramchandra Deb – II in -1732 AD.

When he was attempting to attack the Jagannath temple, the priests of the temple came to know about this and they shifted the images of the Lord initially, to NAIRI -HARISHWAR TEMPLE in -1733AD.

When they felt that, the place is not safe, they shifted the images to the KANKANA SIKHARI temple inside Chilika.

This was the 12th day of the month of Bhadra(August-September). They brought fresh water from Jamuna Nirjhar / Jamuna stream and used the same to worship Lord, as Chilika water is salty. They had also offered the kankada vegetables(ie. spine gourd) to the Lord for the first time due to scarcity of appropriate food items.

Hence, one will find this item(ie. kankada, ie. spine gourd) in the offering of the Lord Jagannath till date in his 56 items of food (ie. CHHAPAN BHOG).

The name of the place (Kankana Sikhari) might have been originated from the vegetable "Kankada".

The local people and the Jagannath Mandir Administration had planted saplings around this Island during 9th Feb, 2015AD. A sandalwood grinding stone was found at the time of planting.

Jagannath temple, puri had also donated a wheel of Nandhighosh Rath on 21st March -2015 AD. A priest was appointed and a well was dug for the Lord at the temple.

The boat ride is also free for the devotees who want to visit the Island from Nairi from 8-am to 5-pm.

Ganga and Yamuna streams, Kankana hills and Harihareshwar temple are mute spectators narrating the tales of lord's exile.

One can learn lot about Jagannath cult at this place along with scenic beauty of the Island.

This spiritual Island which is surrounded by the blue water of Chilika, with boating activities as an addition, would charm the visitor.

One can reach Kankana Sikhari from Nachuni. One has to move 2-kms from Nachuni to reach Gangadharpur railway station and from there one has to move 3-kms to reach NAIRI village. From NAIRI, one can take a boat to cross Chilika to reach Kankana Sikhari.

One can also reach the destination by boat after covering Sorana, Kalupada, Baradi, Balugaon and Satapada along with some nearby villages.

CHAKANASI / MAHISANASHI

This is another holy place. As per Madalapanji, to save the idols of Lord Jaggannath, Balabhadra and Subhadra, from the attacks of Kalyan Mall, they were taken to MAHISHA NASI. The Lord was migrated to Mahisanasi through Satapada and Berhempura. It is believed that, the name Berhempur of Satapada, had come from the Darubrahma of the Lord. Mahishanashi is 3-kms north, from Berhempura.

The idols of Lord Jagannath/Trinity were kept here, during the period-june -1611 AD to May -1612 AD, for around one year.

Lord had escaped through this Berhempura route by the Sevayats.

With passage of time, Mahisanasi has been changed to CHAKANASI, because the wheel of the Lord is present here.

As per the historian, Radha Raman panda, there are three wheels of Black stone and in the middle wheel, the Nine planets (Navagraha) are engraved.

There is a thatched structure and inside it, the people of two villages ie. Berhempura and Mahisha offer puja to the Lord.

As per local people, three round shaped stones on which the images of deities had been placed were found near the bush.

It would take around 45-minutes through a country boat/ 25-minutes through motor boat to reach the place.

OTHERS

Chilika lake has many other Islands like Phulbari, Berhampura and Noapara etc, which are scenic spots between water and greeneries.

These Islands are good for boating, fishing, picnic, camping and enjoying the vacation.

In all the Islands one will find large number of birds like sea-eagles, gulls, and many migratory birds between September and March.

During a study in 2000AD about the lake, it was observed that the lake contributes substantially to the economy of the state in the areas like – Fishery, Tourism, inland navigation, foreign exchange earnings and thereby making it an important asset of the state. The lake requires further restoration to preserve it's bio-diversity.

Chilika lake which is unique, is also included in the tentative list as a world heritage center under UNESCO. While submitting the proposal by the state, the points like -this is one of the largest lagoons in the world, brackish in nature with estuarine character, largest water ground of migratory birds in the sub-continent, home to Irrawaddy dolphins(ie. only two lagoons in the world to support this dolphin) which are threatened, amazing bio-diversity and rich cultural heritage with highly productive fishery resources and sustaining more than 2-lac fishermen etc. were elaborated for consideration.

Chilika lake which is economically important for the state and a part of local culture, is a beautiful spot for the visitors of all age groups. The lake is so vast that one should try to spend some more time/ days to enjoy and explore the beauty of the lake and it's surrounding.

As observed by some visitors, visit to the lake is a bliss and is the most unforgettable time of their lives.

This is the place where the dolphins play, birds fly around your boat as you sail, a perfect place to observe many of the birds of India/ world, the flamingos, tranquil beach and one of it's kind rare ecosystem which is home to a lot of endangered species.

CHAPTER 5

Pipili

PIPILI –THE APPLIQUÉ CAPITAL

It is a small town and the place is famous for the appliqué work.This is the craft hub of Odisha.This is the place, where the age old appliqué art originated in the country, although one will find such crafts in Bihar and Rajasthan also. This centre is known globally as the 'center of Indian appliqué'.

When one will visit the area, a series of shops with decorated and bright appliqué work will greet the customer. One will find lamp-shades, decorated wall cloths, table covers, sofa covers, canopy, tent, and various cloths designed by skilled crafts men.

Here, many artisans continue to practice the technique and create both traditional and contemporary items. Embroidery work is done mostly by women and cutting work by men. Earlier, the design was mostly of nature, deity and mythological figures.

Throughout the state, everyone knows about PIPILI CHANDUA (ie. local name of the handicrafts). With passage of time many new items like-purses, blouses, dress materials, modern umbrellas, mythical figures, celestial bodies and motifs of Flora and fauna have been introduced. Sometimes schematic motifs are made which, represent society, nature and deities.One will find many patterns and designs of these items.

In lamp shade, alone, one will find thousand designs and patterns. Hence, these items will not be out of trend for a long time. There is heavy demand of these items from the foreign tourists.

The traditional coloured materials also hold symbolic significance depending upon the colour chosen. (ie. -Red -sign of prosperity, yellow-spirituality and enlightenment, green-hope and new beginnings, black-to ward of evil, white – peace and purity). Now other colours are also used. For many, it has become an integral part of life.

Appliqué, a French word means -to apply/ to put on. In textiles, it is superimposing of embellishments, such as small fabrics and mirrors on a large base fabric. Here different type of fabrics and ornaments including small mirrors, are sewn on top of another to create elaborate motifs in the overall design. A lot of needle work is also involved in designing the material. There are two techniques.

In one technique, a fabric shape is stitched over a base layer. Another is reverse technique, where layers of fabrics are laid down and a shape is cut out from the upper layer. It is having the GI mark by Govt of india.

The 54-meters long pipili -appliqué work depicting the freedom struggle of the country, has also entered in the Limca Book of records, as the world's largest thematic appliqué work.

ORIGIN

This art form ascribes it's origin to Jagannath Cult. The use of all these products are associated with various religious ceremonies of Lord. The canvas cloth which is used to cover the chariots of the Lord at Puri, are designed by these artisans.The appliqué work looks most beautiful when the cloth cover of three chariots move during Ratha Yatra. The colour combination, of the cloth coverings of the chariots--- -taladhawaja (ie. chariot of Lord Balabhadra) is bright green and red, Darpadalan (ie. chariot of Goddess Subhadra) is bright red and black and Nandighosha (ie. chariot of Lord Jagannath) is bright red and yellow. The basic design of these clothes are narrow and wide strips and there are mythical motifs of Rahu, Chandra and motifs from nature like, flowers etc, from which the devotees identify the chariots from a long distance. Seats and pillows in appliqué are made for ceremonial use during bathing festival(ie. Snana Yatra).

The items are also used in various procession of the deities, where an umbrella shaped canopy can be seen. The pipili appliqué items are now a household commodity in almost every religious work. These items look simple and stylish.

As per some researchers, the Kings of Puri had engaged craftsmen for the services of the Lord Jagannath. They had set -up this village for their living. This art which originated as a temple art, has now turned in to a thriving business and an item of the common man. A lot of effort goes in making these items. Each and every family of the village is engaged mostly on this craft and to earn their day to day living.

Now with rising inflation, the craftsmen are finding it difficult to continue this family tradition. Both public and Government should take more initiative to help this art to survive.

Religious Tourism

There are many places near by Pipili, which attracts large number of visitors. The Jaigopal Temple of Pipili is a famous religious place of the area. The nearby religious tourist places of Pipili are as under:

Gopinath Temple-Kakudia

This is 7-kms from Pipili on the left side of Pipili-Jatni Road. It is on the right banks of Daya River.The attractive images of Lord Krishna and Radha made of stone are liked by the visitors.

DANDA MUKUNDPUR is famous for great Devotee-SALBEG, a Muslim follower who was in love with Lord Jagannath.

There are many festivals like - NRUSHINGHNATH FESTIVAL, held every year in Baisakh Chaturdashi (April), THE JAI GOPAL FESTIVAL, in Champak Dwadashi(June) and Devotee DASIA BAURI PITHA'S anniversary (ie. Odiya-Janmatithi) in Kartik month (October-November) etc. which attracts large number of visitors.

This craft and culture capital is a must visit destination. The journey to this place through coconut and palm trees and passing through green rice fields is enchanting.It is a nice place to enjoy rural tourism. One and all should visit this place to have a glimpse of these colourful items enriched with history and heredity and to encourage the Craftsmen for it's beauty, by purchasing some items like coloured canopies, blooming garden lamps, bags and bright beach umbrella etc., as a memory.

Historical Importance Of Pipili

Pipili is important in the history of Odisha due to it's strategic location. Pipili was occupied by prince Khurram (ie. later emperor Sahajahan) in 1621 AD, when he advanced from Deccan to Cuttack and then to capture Bengal (ie. when he was in revolt against his father). The Marathas were defeated here from the Britishers in 1803 AD in a pitched battle.

During Paika Rebellion, the first war of independence, the place was occupied by the Paika warriors in 1817AD. Some Muslim monuments reminiscent of the era are found here.

There are 5-pira Stanas nearby where both Hindus and Muslims worship.

As per Odisha Gazetteer, a mosque has been constructed in village Narasinghapur in place of an old dilapidated mosque, believed to be constructed during the period of Aurangzeb, contained an inscription which is now with the local Muslims. There is a Muktab near the mosque.

Similarly, the Baptist Church of Pipili is said to be more than hundred yearsold.

Pipili is around 20 -kms from Bhubaneswar on Bhubaneswar-Puri Road and this destination forms an integral part of Golden Triangle circuit.

There are also many other places around Pipli, famous for religious tourists and scenic beauty.

CHAPTER 6

Raghurajpur

This small but scenic village of RAGHURAJPUR filled with coconut, palm, mango and jackfruit trees, is famous mostly for PATTACHITRA PAINTINGS.

It is the first heritage and craft village of the state. It has an interpretation centre and a rest house.

Many domestic and international tourists visit this village. The place is also famous, as the birth place of renowned Odissi exponent Guru Kelu Charan Mahapatra. One will find many Padma Bhushan and Padma Shri awardees in the fields of craft, in this village.

Every house of the village is artistic. During visit, people from every house request the tourists to visit their house to purchase PATTACHITRA PAINTINGS, umbrellas, lamp-shades and other items etc.

Now Pattachitras are made and available on dried coconut shells and bottles also. One will feel as if, every member of the house is an artist and their house is their studio. One will find how the walls of the houses are decorated with colourful murals of various Gods / Goddesses, many episodes from the epics, flowers and forests etc.

One can also experience, how PATTACHITRA paintings are made over a peace of cloth or a dried palm leaf, which are painted with chalk and gum and intricate pictures of various Gods, Goddess and mythological scene with ornamentation of flowers and trees etc. are drawn on it.

The price depends upon the intricacies of the paintings.

This art form is very old. It is believed that during rein of emperor Ashok, some artisans were chosen to create paintings and handiwork to decorate Gods / Goddesses and places of worship. These artisans were given land at RAGHURAJPUR to practice and to continue this art. This art form, is their legacy.

Art Of Raghurajpur

To gain the right to work for God /to work at the Jagannath temple, the chitrkaras (ie. Artists /Artisans) of this village also undergo Upanayan ceremony, like Brahmins.

Out of 120 families, 18 of them are believed to come from the lineage of such Chitrakars at RAGHURAJPUR. Their families are only permitted to paint at Lord Jagannath temple. Their learning is passed on, generations after generations through their family members or through the family school.

Their names are mostly Mohapatra or Moharana etc. They create one of the finest art, through their fingers and imagination. They work along with the priests in the temple and are busy during Rath Yatra and when the deities become sick after ritualistic bath.

They create ANASAR PATTI PAINTINGS, to worship God during the period of sickness. This is one of the speciality of this place.

Besides Pattachitra, this village is also famous for traditional masks, stone items, sculptures, wooden toys, Tusser paintings, painting with cow dung, Palm leave engravings etc.

The paintings on Tusser sarees, especially Sambalpuri Sarees depicting Rasa Leela of Lord Krishna, Ayodhya Vijay, Mathura vijay of Krishna are mostly originated from this village.

Due to the efforts of late Jagannath Mohapatra and others this art form has become popular in the country and abroad.

PATTA used under the throne of Lord Jagannath and on the three chariots during Ratha Yatra is supplied from this place.

The village is also famous for GOTIPUA DANCE, which was the precursor to Odissi dance.

The village is having more than hundred houses and the main village is having two streets.

During February-March, tourism department celebrates annual Vasantha Ustav (ie. spring festival), when large number of tourists visit the place.

This is a must visit destination for any visitor to know the creative inhabitants of the village who are carrying on their profession, ancestors after ancestors for more than two thousand years.

Discarded bottles, coconut shells, paper waste and clothes etc. are used by several artists to create recycled art like -paper -mache masks, animals, toys, colourful bottles and door hangers using coconut shells etc.

There are temples of Bhuasuni (village Goddess), Radha Mohan, Gopinath, Dasabhuja, Raghunath, Laxminarayan and Gouranga etc.

One should visit the village to know this popular craft, dances like Odissi and Gotipua etc. and it's history.

This village is a role model for rural tourism in Odisha.

One has to travel on the Bhubaneswar-Puri Road up to Chandanpur. From Chandanpur Bazar, it is 1-km. It is on the southern bank of river Bhargavi.